TRIAL PRACTICE:
EXERCISES IN WITNESS
EXAMINATION AND THE
RULES OF EVIDENCE

By

Paul S. Milich

Professor of Law,
Georgia State University College of Law

THOMSON
WEST

Mat #40397707

© 2005 Thomson/West
     610 Opperman Drive
     P.O. Box 64526
     St. Paul, MN 55164–0526
     1–800–328–9352

Printed in the United States of America

ISBN 0–314–16305–0

TEXT IS PRINTED ON 10% POST CONSUMER RECYCLED PAPER

Preface

The idea for a course like this one first hit me while I was preparing for my first jury trial 25 years ago. I had earned "A"s in Evidence and a general Trial Advocacy course at a fine law school. Why then was I spending so much of my trial preparation looking up dozens of basic evidence rules and trying to figure out how to lay the simplest foundations for evidence at trial? I vowed then that if I ever taught law I would design a course that would give third year students an intensive training in the practical application of the rules of evidence and the arts of direct and cross-examination. Twenty years ago I designed such a course and I have been tweaking and polishing the materials ever since. The 35 courtroom simulation exercises in this book are the fruits of those efforts.

I decided early on to focus the students' training on recognizing and arguing evidentiary issues and on the preparation and presentation of direct and cross-examinations. Too many trial advocacy courses attempt to cover too many skills with the result that none are covered in suffcent depth. This course gives the students intensive training in the core skills so that by the end of the semester they have developed the habit of careful preparation and the competence and confidence to handle themselves and witnesses in the courtroom.

I designed these materials and the Teacher's Manual with the adjunct professor in mind. This is a great course for a trial attorney or judge to teach. There are two advantages here for the adjunct professor. First, the professor will have no lectures to prepare. The course is 100% trial simulations. The instructor's job mainly is to react to what happens during the exercises and lead the class critique of the performances. Second, the very detailed Teacher's Manual covers every evidentiary issue clearly and succinctly.

It has been a joy teaching this course and watching the students progress from tentative, bumbling novices to more confident and skilled student litigators who begin to discover their personal courtroom strengths and styles. Any comments or suggestions for improving these materials are most welcome.

PAUL S. MILICH

pmilich@gsu.edu

Atlanta, Georgia

*

TABLE OF CONTENTS

*

TRIAL PRACTICE:

EXERCISES IN WITNESS EXAMINATION AND THE RULES OF EVIDENCE

INTRODUCTION

The primary purpose of this course is to develop the students' courtroom skills, particularly the use of the rules of evidence. Each class consists of trial simulations in which students play the roles of lawyers, judges, witnesses and jurors.

Here is how it works. The class will be divided into two groups: "A"s and "B"s. Each Exercise has an "A" and "B" version. We will do three Exercises each week. Each side tries to get in its own evidence and challenge the opponent's evidence. Oral motions *in limine* are expected (though no written motions will be accepted). The Federal Rules of Evidence apply to all Exercises.

The roles of witnesses and judges are assigned a week in advance. Those assigned as witnesses should divvy up the parts for the following week's Exercises. Those assigned as Judges should prepare to preside at any one of the following week's Exercises.

For the first 9 weeks, assignments of counsel for each Exercise will not be made until the evening for which that Exercise is scheduled. Thus everyone who is not assigned as a witness or a judge must be prepared the following week to do any of the three Exercises assigned for that week. For the final four weeks, counsel will be pre-assigned specific Exercises.

PREPARATION TIPS

As a Witness—Witnesses who know their parts well and stay in character throughout the Exercise are essential to the simulation. Witnesses should not materially stray from the facts, though facts can be added if they are *reasonably* inferable from those given. Stick to your part. Even though you know that other witnesses or documents will contradict what you have been given to say, don't alter your testimony to fit theirs.

Some exhibits are provided in the Exercises but other times the Exercises merely refer to a document or thing. Witnesses should prepare in advance a simple facsimile of any documents or physical evidence counsel likely would want to use in examining them. Again, you should not make up exhibits or evidence that are not expressly referred to in the Exercise.

As a Judge—You will be called upon to handle one of the Exercises. The more prepared you are on the evidence issues, the more you will get out of your time on the bench. Like a real judge, part of your job is to keep things moving.

As Counsel—In the beginning, the amount of time required to properly prepare for these Exercises is quite considerable. Indeed, part of the purpose of this course is to get you through this initial stage and make you more efficient at preparing witness examinations and evidentiary argument. It takes considerable practice. This is why for the first nine weeks you are required to prepare all three Exercises for the week you are up as counsel.

There should be three major parts in your preparation.

(1) *Mastering the facts.* This is more than just learning them—it is thinking about them, picturing them, getting an angle on them—seeing what is important—seeing your case—(or at least the fragment presented)—and any and all weaknesses in the opponent's case. When you read each Exercise you should see more than just cold facts. You should see part of the story that you want to tell the jury and the competing story that your opponent will try to tell. Your goal is to squeeze everything you can out of the facts.

(2) *Evidence*—Go over how you will prove every fact and look for objections your opponent is likely to make. Outline clear, succinct arguments to handle any objections. Go over any foundational requirements for your evidence. Prepare a checklist for any documents or other exhibits you intend to offer. Outline any problems you imagine your opponent will have with his or her evidence. Outline any motions *in limine* you should bring.

(3) *Witness Notes*—prepare a simple list of the facts you want to get from each witness, including the foundation you'll need. Play with the order—think about what you want to start with, end with—where will you peak? Now start doing the direct examination out loud to yourself. Play with different kinds of questions, experiment with different tones and cadence. Prepare a final checklist of the key facts you must get from the witness, a checklist you can easily refer to before you turn the witness over for cross. Do the same for the witnesses you will cross-examine. One of the most common preventable errors of inexperienced litigators is to "forget" to cover certain facts or issues.

When you have more than one witness, think about the order in which you should present them. You don't have to call a witness if you believe that's the better tactic, (and in a few Exercises, it is), though you should be prepared to defend your decision.

You will be given a few minutes before each Exercise begins to meet with your witnesses. (You may meet with them at any other time if you like). Of course counsel may not encourage the witness to lie or embellish the facts in counsel's preferred way.

Some Basic Rules:

Some of the Exercises have an "ADDENDUM." This is information given to one side only and is designed to add some element of surprise, particularly in criminal cases. Do not allow anyone on the opposing side to learn the contents of your Addendum or even the fact that there is one for a particular Exercise. For this reason, you may work on Exercises only with students who are on the same side ("A" or "B") as you. Do not assume that information provided in an Addendum is admissible evidence.

A student should disclose an Addendum to opposing counsel at the time a witness is asked about the facts in the Addendum, at the latest. If the facts in the Addendum are of questionable admissibility, counsel may wish to disclose the Addendum to the court and opposing counsel outside the presence of the jury and get a ruling before charging ahead.

When the Federal Rules call for advanced written notice of something, giving the opponent a brief handwritten statement at any time before the Exercise begins is sufficient. Although FRE 404(b) requires notice of the prosecution's intent to present evidence of independent crimes or acts only when the defense requests it, in this class notice is **not** required to offer any evidence against a criminal defendant under 404(b).

In a few Exercises, a plaintiff or prosecutor is given evidence that should be admissible only in rebuttal. Counsel is expected to ask permission to present that evidence in rebuttal at the close of defendant's case. In most instances, however, the Judge will not allow rebuttal evidence on matters that could have been offered earlier.

Most of the Exercises do not refer to specific years but rather say "5 years ago" or "last year." Witnesses and counsel should translate these into specific years when presenting testimony.

The Exercises will run in "real time" without stopping. Counsel, witnesses and judges must remain in character until the end of the Exercise. Once a witness takes the stand, you are to assume a jury is present and act accordingly. Ask to approach the bench before discussing any sensitive matters that the jury should not hear. In order for the whole class to hear the discussion, however, you will merely take one step forward when the bench tells you that you may approach. Likewise, you should ask for limiting instructions at appropriate times, though the bench will not actually instruct the "jury."

You should preserve any errors in rulings for appellate review. Obviously, motions for mistrial will not be granted but counsel should move for mistrial when necessary to preserve error for review.

All of the Exercises present only pieces of a larger case. The following presumptions apply unless otherwise stated in the Exercise:

— in criminal cases, the only prior convictions or bad acts of the accused are those stated in the Exercise;

— no motions to suppress evidence in criminal cases based on constitutional grounds;

— no dispositive motions;

— when the prosecution offers a statement as a co-conspirator admission, assume that the prosecution has sufficient evidence that a conspiracy existed and that the declarant belonged to the conspiracy; all other foundation must be satisfied;

— when a student is playing the part of an expert witness, he or she may know nothing of the expert subject area other than what is supplied in the Exercise. When opposing counsel happens to know more about the expert area than the student/witness, an Exercise can quickly unravel. Thus opposing counsel may not cross-examine an expert on matters beyond the scope of direct and may not impeach the "expert" by demonstrating his or her unfamiliarity with the area of expertise.

A change to Federal Rule 803(6)—the business record exception—in the year 2000 allows the use of a certified affidavit, in lieu of live testimony, to lay foundation for the document. (See 902(11),(12) for specifics regarding the certification). In this course, you will not use such a certification but will lay foundation, the old fashioned way, with a live witness. (*See,* "Some Sample Evidentiary Foundations" in the back of this book).

Note that in the back of this book are some comments on witness examination, some sample evidentiary foundations and some common objections to the form of the question. These materials should be useful to you in the first weeks of your training.

Exercise #1—Version A

Your client, Sam Donalds, has been charged with robbing the Brown Hat Liquor Store at 11:00 p.m., June 5, with a revolver. Your client's alibi is that he was with his girlfriend, Mary, at 11:00 p.m. on June 5 at a bar across town called "The Shadow."

Your witness is <u>Charlie Jones</u>, a life long friend of Sam.

Charlie says that at about 11:15 p.m., June 5, Sam called him at home from "The Shadow" and asked him to come down and join Mary and him for a nightcap. Charlie says he could hear Mary talking and laughing in the background.

Charlie has known Sam all his life and says Sam is an honest and peaceful person and very opposed to handguns. He says Sam does not own a handgun.

You also want the court to take judicial notice that the scene of the liquor store robbery is 15 miles by road from "The Shadow" and that it would take at least 25 minutes to drive from one to the other. (You personally drove from one to the other and it took 26 minutes in light traffic).

Exercise #1—Version B

You are the prosecutor. Sam Donalds, the defendant, has been charged with robbing the Brown Hat Liquor Store at 11:00 p.m. on June 5 with a revolver. Sam's alibi is that he was with his girlfriend, Mary, at 11:00 p.m. on June 5 at a bar called "The Shadow" across town.

One of your witnesses is Pat Johnson, the clerk at the liquor store at the time of the robbery. Pat identified Sam in a lineup on June 7. On June 18, Pat was in a car accident and was just released from the hospital a few days ago. She sustained a head injury but the prognosis is good. An unfortunate side effect is that she can only vaguely remember the robbery and could not recognize the robber today. However, she does clearly recall the lineup and being able to identify the robber at that time.

Your other witness is Detective Dennis Dunn who arrested Sam at his home on June 8. After reading Sam the *Miranda* warnings, Dunn said to Sam's mother, "I guess your boy really messed up this time. He knocked over a liquor store." Sam's mother then turned to Sam and said "Did you do that?" Sam just looked at the floor, ashamed, and did not answer. Later, as Detective Dunn was taking Sam to his car, Sam turned to his mother and said "I'm sorry."

(Detective Dunn did not attend the lineup where Pat identified the defendant).

Exercise #2—Version A

You are plaintiff's counsel in a personal injury case. Your client, Mary Dewey, was walking in a crosswalk in an uncontrolled intersection when the defendant, Larry Truman, hit her with his 1966 Mustang. The accident occurred at 9:30 p.m. on June 9.

Your witness is <u>Police Officer Alice Barkley</u>. Officer Barkley arrived at the scene about 10 minutes after the accident. She says Mary had a broken right arm (the bone was partially protruding through her skin), and severe lacerations and contusions on her right leg. Officer Barkley cited the driver of the defendant's vehicle, Larry, for excessive speed (35 in a 25) based on the statement of Fred, a witness to the accident.

Fred told Officer Barkley that Larry passed him about one-half block before the accident "going about 35."

Larry told Officer Barkley that he was sorry about the accident. Larry said Mary stepped out right in front of him as he approached the intersection.

Larry also told Officer Barkley he was going to have his brakes checked the next day.

A state statute says the driver of an automobile must yield to a pedestrian in a crosswalk.

Exercise #2—Version B

Your client, Larry Truman, is defendant in a personal injury case. Mary Dewey, the plaintiff was walking in a crosswalk on June 9, at 9:30 p.m., when Larry struck her with his 1966 Mustang. Your client claims he was driving the speed limit when Mary jumped out into the crosswalk.

Your witness is Fred Thompson, an unemployed dental assistant who saw the accident. The accident occurred at the uncontrolled intersection of Dyer and 14th Street. Fred and Larry were traveling in the same direction, north on Dyer, a four lane road. Larry was traveling in the far right lane and Fred, the witness, was a car length behind him in the center right lane. There were cars parked along the curb of Dyer all the way up to 14th Street.

Fred did not see Mary in the crosswalk as he was approaching the intersection. He heard Larry's brakes and he saw the right front fender of Larry's car strike Mary. Mary was no more than 6 ft. from the curb.

Fred heard Mary say while lying on the ground right after the accident, "I'm dying, somebody get me a bartender." Fred says Mary appeared to be drunk.

Fred told the investigating police officer, Officer Barkley, that Larry passed him right before the accident going 35 mph. (This is a 25 mph zone). Fred now says he mis-spoke and that Larry was not going 35 but only 25. Fred testified to this effect at traffic court where Larry was charged with excessive speed. Larry won his case in traffic court.

Immediately after the accident, Fred heard someone whom he never identified yell "That lady jumped right in front of that car."

Fred will admit that he and Larry have been dating since they met at the accident.

Exercise #3—Version A

Your client is Linda Jones, a former salesperson in Big X Corporation where she worked for three years. Linda is suing Big X Corp. and her supervisor, Tom Smyth, for defamation. She alleges that Tom, acting on what he claims was an anonymous tip, fired her for using illegal drugs while on the job. Linda denies ever using illegal drugs. Linda's contract of employment with Big X allows her to be terminated at will and she does not challenge her firing. She alleges that Big X told other employees that she was a drug user, thus harming her reputation and that Tom Smyth told prospective employers that she was a drug user, thus hurting her efforts to find a new job. Your witness is <u>Linda</u>

Linda heard from Mary Rice, a former co-worker at Big X, that a week after Linda was fired, there was a big meeting of employees and management to talk about drugs on the job. The speaker, a drug abuse consultant to Big X, said "As you may know, this company had to let a saleswoman go last week who was into drugs." Linda was the only woman on the sales staff at that time. A few weeks after telling Linda about the meeting, Mary quit her job and ran off to Tahiti with a banker. She is unavailable for trial.

Linda was out of a job for 3 months. She interviewed for a job with Jack Simmons. A few days later, Jack told her that he would not hire her because her former boss, Tom, told him "Linda is a drug case—she probably just works to get her next fix." Jack is the only employer who told her that Tom killed her chances by calling her a drug user. However, Linda suspects that two other employers did not hire her for the same reason. She believes this because they were very friendly to her and eager to hire her in the interviews and then had their secretaries call a few days later to tell her she was no longer being considered. Jack has moved to Europe and is unavailable for trial.

Linda made $11,000 the last 3 months at Big X Corporation and $11,200 the first three months of her new job.

Exercise #3—Version B

You represent Big X Corp. Big X is being sued, along with its sales supervisor, Tom Smyth, for defamation. The plaintiff, Linda Jones, was a salesperson at Big X Corp. She alleges that Tom Smyth, acting on what he claims was an anonymous tip, fired her for using illegal drugs while on the job. She also claims that Tom told other persons who were thinking about hiring Linda that she was a drug user. (Linda's contract with Big X allows her to be terminated at will. Thus Linda does not contest her firing. Her only claim is for defamation).

Your witness is <u>Tom Smyth</u>. He admits that he got an anonymous phone call to the effect that Linda was using cocaine regularly on the job but when he confronted Linda with it, she flew off the handle, called him foul names, and so he fired her. He says he did not fire her for drug use but because of her poor attitude and that he had been planning to fire her for some time.

Tom says that since he fired Linda, a number of her former co-workers have told him that Linda was using drugs.

Tom claims he never said anything to anyone about Linda using drugs. However, he has told employers who have called about her that she was fired for a poor work attitude. Tom has a copy of a job performance review on Linda he filled out three weeks before he fired her. (See next page) The review states nothing regarding drug use.

Tom never heard anyone at Big X say anything about Linda being fired for drug use.

BIG X CORPORATION

"If We Don't Have It, You Don't Need It."

Quarterly Job Review – Sales Department

Employee   Linda Jones

Length of Service   3 years

Job Title   Sales Associate

Supervisor   Tom Smyth

Date   May 10, (last year)

Scale: 1 (excellent) 2 (good) 3 (average) 4 (poor) 5 (unacceptable)

Productivity   4

Communication Skills   3

Appearance   2

Attitude   4

Comments:

Linda needs to get that chip off her shoulder and work harder.

Tom Smyth

Exercise #4—Version A

You represent Brenda Bower, the defendant in a dog bite case. On May 19, the plaintiff, Bud Macy, was walking down Fir Street when Checkers, a large collie, ran onto the sidewalk and bit him on the back of the left leg. Your client claims that Checkers only bit Bud after Bud maced him. Bud maintains that he did not mace Checkers until after the dog bit him.

Your witnesses:

Brenda—Brenda says she heard Checkers barking and looked out the window to see what was happening. She saw Checkers a few feet behind Bud. Bud turned and maced Checkers and Checkers then lunged at Bud but missed. Bud turned to run away and Checkers bit him in the left leg.

She says she always ties Checkers up but that he slipped his collar on the day in question—something he had never done before. She says she has had Checkers for four years, since he was a puppy, and he has never bit anyone.

Brenda says Bud is the neighborhood weirdo. Once, when she was walking Checkers on a leash and Checkers had stopped to pay his respects to one of Bud's azaleas, Bud came rushing out of the house, mace can in hand, and threatened to "fumigate that little beast" if he ever caught him on his property again.

Exercise #4—Version B

You represent Bud Macy, plaintiff in a dog bite case. On May 19, Bud was walking down Fir Street when Checkers, a large collie, ran onto the sidewalk and bit him on the back of the left leg. Bud claims that after Checkers bit him, he maced the animal. Checkers belongs to the defendant, Brenda Bower. Brenda claims Checkers bit Bud only after Bud maced him.

Your witness is <u>Bud</u>. Bud is a landscaper but has not been employed for the last 18 months. He was fired from his last job for attacking a co-worker with a shovel. Bud says he walks by Brenda's house two or three times a week as it is on route between his house and the bus stop. Checkers is usually tied up and never fails to bark and growl at Bud. Bud bought the mace because he was afraid Checkers would one day break the rope holding him back.

On the day of the incident, Bud noticed Checkers on the porch but assumed that he was tied up as usual. The next thing he knew, Checkers was growling and snapping at the back of his legs. As he felt the dog's fangs drive into his left leg, he turned and let Checkers have it with the mace. Checkers let out a bloodcurdling yelp and Brenda came out of the house screaming "What did you do to my dog?" Bud replied "Your dog just bit me." To which Brenda answered "You probably deserved it!" Checkers then ran over to Brenda whimpering and rubbing his face on the ground. Brenda shook her finger at him and said "Bad boy— you should never do that."

Bud says that a few minutes later, Brenda offered him $100 to sign a release and not report the incident to County Animal Control but he refused. Bud also will testify that ever since the incident, he has had recurring nightmares in which packs of wild collies chew him slowly to death. He also feels the stress of the incident aggravated his asthma condition which he has had since childhood.

Exercise #5—Version A

You are the prosecutor in an armed robbery case. It is alleged that the defendant, Ronald James, wearing a nylon stocking over his head, held up a Speedy Mart convenience store at noon on August 9 of last year by brandishing a pistol at the store clerk and forcing the clerk to empty the cash register. The robber escaped with about $300.

Your witness is <u>Detective Don Caruso</u>. He says the store clerk told him after the robbery that he could not identify the robber but he could identify the pistol if he saw it again since it was a very unusual piece—a long barreled .32 with an orange grip. Caruso says that when he arrested Ronald at his house, on August 20, on a warrant for another offense (also an armed robbery) he saw a long barreled .32 with an orange grip on the top of Ronald's bedside table. Caruso has been a policeman for 16 years and has never seen such a gun. When he asked Ronald where he got the pistol, Ronald said his father gave it to him years ago.

Caruso says he showed the pistol to the store clerk in the subject robbery and the clerk immediately recognized it as the weapon used by the robber. (Assume that the clerk will testify to this effect later in the trial). He returned the pistol to the evidence room at police headquarters but the pistol somehow became lost. Caruso has determined that the unusual pistol in question was one of only several hundred produced in the 1950s by a small company in Ohio. (Caruso is not a gun expert and obtained his information about this particular gun from a Web page sponsored by the National Association of Gun Dealers). He has obtained another pistol of the same type from a local gun collector and will testify that it is substantially the same in appearance as the pistol he found in the accused's possession and which was identified by the store clerk.

Caruso also found an unopened pack of nylon stockings on the top of the bedroom dresser (in plain sight) at Ronald's house. Ronald lives alone.

Caruso will testify that he read Ronald the *Miranda* warnings and that Ronald replied that he wished to speak to Caruso and "clear all this up." Ronald's motion to suppress all his statements to Caruso as a violation of *Miranda* was denied.

Exercise #5—Version B

Your client, Ronald James, has been charged with armed robbery. The prosecution alleges that Ronald, wearing a nylon stocking over his head, held up a Speedy Mart convenience store at noon on August 9 of last year by brandishing a pistol at the store clerk and forcing the clerk to empty the cash register. The robber escaped with about $300. The pistol used in the robbery was quite unusual: a long-barreled .32 with an orange grip.

Ronald was arrested and charged with committing another, unrelated, armed robbery, but those charges have since been dropped because of insufficient evidence. It was while the police were arresting Ronald on this other charge, on August 20, that they saw an unusual pistol, of the type described above, on Ronald's bedside table.

Your witness is <u>Ronald</u>. Ronald is a carpenter but has not worked in over a year. He denies committing the robbery. In regard to the pistol, he says he found it in a vacant lot just a few days before the police seized it from his home (and insists that this is what he told Det. Caruso at his house—not that his father had given him the gun).

Ronald admits he lives alone but is engaged to be married to Grace Williams (who left a package of nylon stockings on his bedroom dresser).

Ronald says he has never been convicted of a serious crime.

Exercise #6—Version A

You defend Arrow Food Processors, Inc., in a products liability case. (There is no claim for negligence). The plaintiff, Jerome Grant, a carpenter, lost his thumb on May 5, two years ago, when he removed the lid and stuck his hand into the cutting bowl of the food processor to dislodge a carrot. Most food processors have a safety feature that automatically stops the food processor when the lid is removed. Arrow's did not. Arrow changed its design to include one, however, a few months after this accident. Jerome is suing for medical expenses, lost wages, pain and suffering, and lost of future earnings due to the disability.

Your witness is <u>Dr. Bill Brown</u>. The parties have stipulated that Dr. Brown is a qualified expert witness in medicine. Dr. Brown treated Jerome when he lost his thumb. Dr. Brown is prepared to testify to the following.

(1) When Jerome's wife brought him into the emergency room at the hospital, she told Dr. Brown "If I told him once I told him a thousand times that it was dangerous to stick his hand down there but he never listens."

(2) During an appointment about a month after the accident, Jerome told Dr. Brown that he hoped to make enough money off the lawsuit against Arrow Food Processors to buy a house on the beach and never work again.

(3) Jerome's physical therapist told Dr. Brown that Jerome was missing appointments and showing a negative attitude towards therapy.

Exercise #6—Version B

You are plaintiff's counsel in a products liability case. Your client, Jerome Grant, a 38 year old carpenter, had his right thumb amputated by an Arrow food processor on May 5, two years ago, when he removed the lid and stuck his hand in the cutting bowl to dislodge some carrots that had become stuck in the blades. Jerome is suing for medical expenses, lost wages, pain and suffering, and lost of future earnings due to the disability.

Your witness is <u>Lynn Jones</u>, a product safety expert. The parties have stipulated that Lynn Jones is a qualified expert on "idiot proof" safety designs for home appliances. In Lynn's opinion, any food processor without an auto-stop feature is a danger to consumers.

<u>Lynn</u> is prepared to testify to the following.

(1) Lynn has a copy of a report by the Consumer Product Safety Commission five years ago which warned that food processors that do not automatically stop when the lid is removed are dangerous to consumers.

(2) Arrow changed its design to add an automatic stop feature a few months after Jerome lost his thumb.

(3) Lynn has spoken with numerous participants in the consumer goods design and manufacturing industry and Arrow has a poor reputation for product safety, particularly for its food processors.

(4) It is not obvious to most consumers that it is dangerous to manually free the blades when they become lodged in food. In one study, (published five years ago by the University of Toronto Journal of Home Safety), participants were shown a food processor and how it works and then asked whether they thought that if food got caught in the bowl and stopped the blades, they could use a hand to dislodge the food and quickly remove the hand before the blades could hurt it. For most participants, the eye was quicker than the hand—they thought they could do it. Lynn does not have a copy of the published study with her.

Exercise #7—Version A

You are defense counsel in a criminal case. Your client, Doris Daye, has been charged with selling cocaine to Don Jahn, an undercover officer, on May 6. Doris denies selling any cocaine to Don and Don is the only witness to the alleged sale.

Your witness is <u>Doris</u>. Doris frequents a bar called "The Shadow" where Don was working undercover as a bartender. She claims Don was always making passes at her but she thought he was a creep and tried to ignore him. On May 6, Don asked her to locate some cocaine for him to buy. When she refused, he got angry and said she'd be sorry for the way she had treated him. An hour later, Don returned with several uniformed police officers and arrested Doris. He held up a small packet of white powder he claimed Doris had sold him. Don then searched Doris' purse and produced a $100 bill with a serial number that matched a number on a list of serial numbers that Don says he prepared earlier that week to record the bills he was using in the drug buys at the Shadow. Doris says she had never seen the $100 bill. Doris tells you she does not use and has never sold cocaine.

Doris says she got a phone call from Don a few days after she was released on bail. He said he'd see that the charges were dropped if she would grant him certain sexual favors. She refused. Doris admits that she did not report the call to the police.

You also have reliable evidence that two years ago, Don was accused of taking bribes from a drug dealer. An internal police investigation cleared him of the bribery charges but suspended him for 30 days for making misleading statements to the review board.

Exercise #7—Version B

You are prosecutor in a criminal case. The defendant, Doris Daye, is charged with selling cocaine to Don Jahn, an undercover officer, on May 6. Doris denies selling any cocaine to Don and Don is the only witness to the alleged sale.

Your witness is <u>Officer Don Jahn</u>. Don was working undercover as a bartender at The Shadow. Doris went to the bar rather frequently and Don heard around the bar that Doris sold drugs. Doris was always very friendly to Don.

On the evening of May 6, at the bar, Don asked Doris if she knew where he could get some coke. Doris said yes and asked for and received $100 from Don. A few minutes later, Doris returned to the bar and handed him a small packet of white powder. (Assume the court already has admitted the packet and the testimony of a crime lab technician indicating that the packet contains cocaine).

Later that evening, Don returned to the bar and arrested Doris and two other suspects. Don searched Doris' purse and found a $100 bill with a serial number that matches a number on a list of serial numbers that Don says he prepared earlier that week to record the bills he was using in the drug buys at the Shadow.

Exercise #8—Version A

You represent Z Corporation, defendant in a breach of contract suit. On April 5, Z Corp. entered into a contract with B & T Enterprises (a partnership of Bob and Tina Ross). The contract stated that B & T would *"use its best efforts to locate 50,000 sq. ft. of suitable office space for Z Corp. to purchase."* It also provided that Z Corp. would pay for this service *"2% of the purchase price of any purchase of described office space."* The contract included a merger clause.

B & T worked on the project for 4 months, bringing four different locations to Z Corp. Z Corp. turned them all down. On August 15, Z Corp. purchased 50,000 sq. ft. of office space for $3.0 million. B & T is claiming 2% or $60,000 but Z Corp. refuses to pay on the grounds that the property they purchased was not found by B & T but by a member of Z Corp.'s own staff.

Your witness is <u>Zeb McDonald</u>, the president of Z Corporation. He can testify to any of the above facts. Zeb will say he had a conversation with Tina Ross of B & T a few days before the contract was signed in which he told Tina that he understood their deal to mean that if Z Corp. found a place without B & T's help, Z Corp. would owe no fee to B & T. Tina concurred.

Zeb told Bob Ross that the four places they suggested were all too far from the city to fit Z Corp.'s needs.

On August 1, Zeb received a letter from Bob. (See letter following this Exercise) Zeb understood the August 1 letter to mean that B & T wasn't going to keep looking.

Exercise #8—Version B

You represent B & T Enterprises, a partnership of Bob and Tina Ross, which is suing Z Corp. for $60,000 under a service contract. The contract, entered into on April 5, stated that B & T would *"use its best efforts to locate 50,000 sq. ft. of suitable office space for Z Corp. to purchase."* It also provided that Z Corp. would pay for the service *"2% of the purchase price of any purchase of described office space."* The contract included a merger clause.

B & T worked on the project for four months, bringing four different locations to Z Corp. Z Corp. turned them all down. On August 15, Z Corp. purchased 50,000 sq. ft. of office space for $3.0 million. B & T claimed 2% or $60,000 but Z Corp. refused to pay on the grounds that the property they purchased was not found by B & T but by a member of Z Corp.'s own staff.

Your witness is <u>Bob Ross</u>. Bob says it was his understanding of the contract that B & T would get paid as long as they used best efforts and Z Corp. bought some property.

Bob says Zeb, the president of Z Corp., told him in July that B & T had until the end of August to find something suitable. This was agreeable to Bob and he wrote a letter to Zeb on August 1 simply to clarify that B & T was not guaranteeing that it could find space for Zeb in time. (See letter following this Exercise)

Bob says that a few days before the lawsuit was filed, Zeb told him "Look, we might owe you something for your trouble," and offered Bob $25,000. Bob refused the offer.

Bob has been brokering commercial real estate for 7 years. He says that it is common in the commercial brokerage field for the broker to get paid for using "best efforts" to find a client space, even if the client fails to find space or finds space through some other means.

Bob has a summary of the hours that he and Tina spent on the Z. Corporation contract. (See Summary following this Exercise). This kind of summary is prepared for every project when the project is finished and is used to evaluate B & T's efficiency. The underlying time sheets are not in court.

B & T ENTERPRISES L.L.P.

1002 Second Ave. Bolinga

Zeb McDonald
President,
Z Corporation
408 Bolinga Dr.
Suite 900
Bolinga

August 1, (this year)

Re: April 5 Office Space Contract

Dear Zeb:

We have been using our best efforts to locate suitable office space for your company pursuant to our contract of April 5 of this year. Due to your failure to accept any of the four locations we have presented to you, we do not accept responsibility for your company's failure to find a new location.

Have a nice day.

Sincerely,

Bob Ross

Robert R. Ross
Partner,
B & T Enterprises

B & T ENTERPRISES L.L.P.

1002 Second Ave. Bolinga

Post Project Report

Project: Z Corp. April 5 Office Space Contract

Date Began: April 5, this year

Date Completed: August 15, this year

Investment

Hours (Bob Ross)	230
Hours (Tina Ross)	240
Hours (other staff)	40
Expenses	$ 1, 800

Gross Income From Project to Date: 0

Deena Shafer
Accounting

Exercise #9—Version A

You represent Bob Mason who has been sued by Adam Smith for $100,000 for assault, trespass, and intentional infliction of emotional distress. Adam alleges that Bob came over into his yard and shot and killed his dog, Leo. Bob lives directly across the street from Adam.

Your witnesses:

<u>Bob</u>—denies shooting Adam's dog. He says everyone in the neighborhood hated the dog because it wailed all night long and growled and snarled at anything that moved. Bob says he called and complained to the police and the City dozens of times and knows Adam was cited at least twice for violations of City noise ordinances.

Bob admits he owns a shotgun which he keeps in the house for personal protection. He says he does not own any other guns.

<u>Dr. Carl Rogers</u>—has been a licensed veterinarian for nearly a year. Adam took the fatally wounded Leo to Dr. Rogers to see if there was anything the good doctor could do. Rogers will testify that although he is not an expert on firearms or gunshot wounds, there were only two obvious wounds on Leo (though there was a lot of blood and that could have misled Adam as to the extent of the wounds)—a small pencil sized wound on the right, front neck and a larger, outward tear wound above the left shoulder—probably the exit wound. He didn't see any bullets or shotgun pellets.

Dr. Rogers had treated Leo several times and will testify that Leo was a very neurotic, aggressive doggie who would have great difficulty making friends in the neighborhood.

Exercise #9—Version B

You represent Adam Smith who is suing Bob Mason for $100,000 for assault, trespass, and intentional infliction of emotional distress. Adam alleges that Bob came over into his yard and shot and killed his dog, Leo. Bob lives directly across the street from Adam.

Your witness:

<u>Adam</u>—will testify that he came home from work to discover that his dog, Leo had been shot in the backyard. He rushed Leo to the vet but to no avail. When he first looked at Leo in the backyard, he observed several pellets that he believes were from a shotgun, on and near his dog. He also noticed that Leo was bleeding from many small wounds, from his neck to his legs. (Unfortunately, Adam did not save any of the pellets). Adam does not own any guns and is only generally familiar with the difference between a shotgun and a rifle.

Adam admits that Leo sometimes disturbed the neighbors with his barking and admits he was cited twice for violations of City noise ordinances because of Leo's barking. Bob complained to Adam on several occasions about the barking and once told Adam that he (Adam) should put Leo to sleep.

A few days before Leo was executed, someone phoned Adam and said his dog had been sentenced to death. Adam can't be sure, but he thinks the caller was Bob—though the caller clearly was trying to disguise his voice. The caller only identified himself as the "Prince of Darkness." The next day, Adam asked Bob if he knew who the Prince of Darkness was. Bob just grinned and walked away.

Adam has a color photo of a bloody Leo, lying still among the backyard weeds. The photo gives no indication as to the size, location or nature of the wounds.

24

Exercise #10—Version A

You are the prosecutor. The defendants, Chrissy Madison and Mark Tyler, have been arrested for burglary and assault with a deadly weapon for an incident at the Acme Drug Co., at 1:00 a.m., on November 3, in which cocaine was stolen and a security guard was struck unconscious with a crowbar. Mark Tyler also has been charged in the incident and will be tried along with Chrissy but with separate counsel. Mark asserts his 5th Amendment privilege not to testify. Your witnesses:

Al Capp is the wounded security guard. He will testify that he saw a woman and a man enter through the back window of the store. It was quite dark in the store and Al admits that he did not get a real good look at either perpetrator before someone hit him on the back of the head and he fell unconscious. He cannot positively identify Chrissy as the woman he saw in the store but he believes it probably is her. He thinks it was the male who hit him with the crowbar—but he can't be sure. "It all happened so fast." He says that as he was slipping into unconsciousness, he heard someone say "Not that way Chrissy—lets get out the back."

Detective William Wright will testify that he interrogated Mark at the police station after Mark had been read his rights and signed a waiver form indicating his desire to make a voluntary statement without his lawyer present. Mark told Det. Wright that he and Chrissy "did the Acme Drug job" but that "Chrissy hit the guard." Det. Wright will admit that he tried to induce Mark's confession by telling him that Chrissy had confessed (this was false) and that the law would go easier on him if he confessed.

As prosecutor, you need to offer evidence admissible against Chrissy and/or Mark (even though no one is representing Mark in this Exercise).

Exercise #10—Version B

Your client, Chrissy Madison, has been arrested for burglary and assault with a deadly weapon arising out of an incident at the Acme Drug Co., at 1:00 a.m., on November 3, in which cocaine was stolen and a security guard, Al Capp, was struck unconscious with a crowbar. Mark Tyler also has been charged in the incident and will be tried along with Chrissy but with separate counsel. Mark asserts his 5th Amendment privilege not to testify.

Sherry Williams will testify that at about 11:30 on the night of November 2, she talked on the phone with Mark, a friend of Chrissy's, who told her that he and Chrissy "were high on acid and wouldn't be going out all night." She says Chrissy called her about an hour later and sounded "very high." Chrissy said Mark had gone out to buy more drugs but that she was going to take some Valium and try to sleep.

Sherry will testify that she has taken LSD with Mark and Chrissy on at least a dozen occasions and, in her opinion, Chrissy couldn't leave the house yet alone pull off a robbery while in that condition. Mark, on the other hand, usually functions pretty well while on the drug.

Sherry also will testify that she has been friends with Chrissy for over four years and has never known Chrissy to steal or assault anyone. She feels Chrissy is a peaceful person.

Exercise #11—Version A

You are plaintiff's counsel in a medical malpractice case. Your client, Roger Smithe, claims he went to Dr. Tad, the defendant, after a knee injury suffered in a tag football game. Dr. Tad physically examined his knee, took x-rays, and then diagnosed the injury as just a bruise. Dr. Tad prescribed aspirin, told Roger to keep the leg immobilized, and to call him if the swelling got worse. Twenty-four hours later, his knee swollen to the size of a cantaloupe, Roger went to the emergency room at a local hospital where new x-rays showed a large broken fragment in his knee that had torn muscle and cartilage. The knee was operated on and Roger was in the hospital for four days.

Your witnesses:

Roger—Roger says he went to Dr. Tad because one of the players in the tag football game said Dr. Tad was a knee specialist. While Dr. Tad was examining him, Roger said "I hear you're some sort of knee specialist." The doctor didn't say anything but just looked at Roger. Roger took the expression on the doctor's face to say "Of course I am you idiot."

Sally Sauer—Sally was Dr. Tad's nurse at the time in question. She has since left Dr. Tad's employ. Sal will say Dr. Tad is the most incompetent physician with whom she has ever worked. She says Tad prescribed aspirin and rest for everything.

Sally says that after Dr. Tad examined Roger, he told Sally to call Dr. Barney, a local knee specialist with whom Dr. Tad often consulted. Sally tried to reach Dr. Barney but was unsuccessful. Dr. Tad did not ask her to call any other doctor. In the six months Sal worked with Dr. Tad, she saw five serious knee injuries come in, including Roger's, and the other four were all referred by Dr. Tad to Dr. Barney.

Exercise #11—Version B

You represent Dr. Thomas Tad who is being sued for medical malpractice. The plaintiff, Roger Smith, claims he went to Dr. Tad after a knee injury suffered in a tag football game. Dr. Tad physically examined the knee, had x-rays taken, and diagnosed the injury as just a bruise. He prescribed aspirin and told Roger to keep the leg immobilized. Twenty-four hours later, his knee swollen to the size of a cantaloupe, Roger went to the emergency room at a local hospital where new x-rays were taken that showed a large bone fragment in his knee which had tore muscles and cartilage. Your witness is Dr. Paladin.

Dr. Al Paladin—Both parties have stipulated that Dr. Paladin is qualified as an expert in orthopaedics. He has been hired as an expert 83 times and has testified in court 11 times, all for the defense. He has reviewed the medical records, talked to Dr. Tad, and heard the testimony of all the plaintiff's witnesses.

Dr. Paladin's opinion is that Dr. Tad's diagnosis and prescribed treatment was reasonable and professionally competent under the circumstances. He says the bone fragment did not appear on Dr. Tad's x-rays because the equipment Dr. Tad was using, though standard for an office practice, was not sophisticated enough to pick it up. It is most efficient in cases like this one to send the patient home with instructions to call if there is any increase in swelling or pain. If there is a worsening of the condition, referral to a hospital is indicated to take a closer look at the knee.

Dr. Paladin went over Dr. Tad's x-rays in this case with Dr. Doe, a colleague who is a radiologist. Dr. Paladin says Dr. Doe agrees it is very hard to pick up such fragments with the equipment Dr. Tad was using.

Exercise #12—Version A

You are prosecutor in a criminal fraud case. The indictment alleges that the defendant, Terry Harrison, knowingly misrepresented to numerous residents at the Sunny Days Rest Home that he owned certain tracts of land in Bolinga County that were about to be developed into a shopping center. It is alleged that at the time he made these representations, Terry knew that he did not own such tracts but merely had options to buy them and that he had no factual basis to claim the area was about to be developed.

Terry sold some of the tracts to residents at Sunny Days Rest Home but was unable to exercise his options and actually buy the property because his partner, Philip Jones, took all the money and skipped town. Philip hasn't been seen since. Terry's defense is that Philip made the misrepresentations and Terry was unaware of them.

Your witness is <u>Todd Miller</u>, one of the victims of the fraud. Todd says Philip gave the sales pitch at Sunny Days and assured everyone that he had the deeds to the property. Todd invested $40,000–nearly all of his life savings. He says he only spoke with Terry once when he called Terry on the phone a few days after purchasing his land. At that time, Terry told him that he had the deeds to the properties in his office safe and after the lawyers went over them the deeds would be sent to the investors.

A few weeks later, Todd called again and spoke with Philip who in response to Todd's demand for his deed, said: "Look, Terry is handling that end. I only do and say what he tells me."

You have a certified record of a conviction against Terry Harrison 12 years ago in California where he was tried and convicted of criminal fraud. On that occasion, Terry sold gold he didn't own to retirees. He served 16 months of a 3 year prison sentence.

Exercise #12—Version B

You are defense counsel in a criminal fraud case. The indictment alleges that your client, Terry Harrison, knowingly misrepresented to numerous people at the Sunny Days Rest Home that he owned certain tracts of land in Bolinga County that were about to be developed into a shopping center. The indictment alleges that when he made these statements, Terry knew that he did not own such tracts but merely had options to buy them and that he had no factual basis to claim the area was about to be developed.

Terry sold some of the tracts to residents at Sunny Days but was unable to exercise his options and actually buy the property because his partner, Philip Jones, took the money and skipped town. Terry's defense is that it was Philip who made the misrepresentations and Terry was unaware of them.

Terry will testify that he was mainly involved behind the scenes, finding the land, securing the options, paying the bills, and so forth, while Philip did the actual sales work. Terry was unaware Philip was lying to the clients.

Terry says he cannot recall ever speaking with Todd Miller on the phone or in person.

Terry will testify that Philip telephoned him the night before he disappeared and confessed that he had "stretched the truth" in his sales pitch to the folks at Sunny Days by telling them they had the deeds in hand and that the area was scheduled for commercial development. Terry blew up at Philip and at the end of their conversation, Philip said "I'm sorry I didn't tell you earlier." The next morning, Terry discovered that the partnership bank account had been emptied and Philip hasn't been seen since.

Terry says that he is a member of the Kiwanis Club and a Little League coach. He feels he is an honest person but sometimes too gullible as he too was taken in by Philip and "lost everything."

Exercise #13—Version A

Your client, Tess Tyler, is suing the Bolinga County School District and the members of its Board in federal court for violating her constitutional rights to free speech and assembly. On Saturday, March 25, Tess attended a protest demonstration at a local nuclear weapons facility. She joined in a sit-in at the entrance to the facility and was arrested, along with 50 others, for criminal trespass. A few hours after the arrest, the charges were dropped and she and the others were released.

That evening, the local newscast showed footage of Tess being dragged to a police van. A few minutes after the newscast, Tess received a call from the School Board Chair, Herb Stanton, demanding to know why she was arrested. According to Tess, when she explained she was there to protest nuclear weapons and had participated in the sit-in, Herb replied, "You'd better have a better story than that when the school board meets Monday night or we'll have your job."

Tess attended the school board meeting on Monday evening. There was no discussion of her at the open meeting and she was not asked any questions. During a closed session following the meeting, the Board considered "personnel issues." Tess was informed on Tuesday morning that she had been terminated effective June 15 for "professional incompetence."

Tess had been teaching English at Bolinga High School for three years and her evaluations by her principal were not good but they are better than some teachers who have been retained in the past.

Your witness is <u>Tess</u>. In addition to the facts above, Tess says that one of the Board members, Greg Jones (who is a defendant in this case) told her that at the closed meeting, Herb said Tess was "a leftist radical; what we used to call a commie." Greg told her that the Board fired her because of her political views, not her teaching.

The School Board rules prohibit any member of the Board from revealing any statements made by other members during closed deliberations of the Board.

[Note: This is not a breach of contract case.]

Exercise #13—Version B

You represent the Bolinga County School District and the seven members of its Board who are being sued in federal court for violating the constitutional rights of one of its teachers. On Saturday, March 25, Tess Tyler, an English teacher at Bolinga High School, attended a protest demonstration at a local nuclear weapons facility. She joined a sit-in at the facility and was arrested along with 50 others for criminal trespass. A few hours after the arrest, all charges were dropped and she and the others were released.

That evening, the local newscast showed footage of Tess being dragged to a police van. The following Monday night, the School Board held an open meeting attended by Tess. In its closed deliberations following the meeting, the Board decided to terminate Tess at the end of the school year for "professional incompetence."

Your witness is Herb Stanton, Chair of the School Board. Herb admits he saw the newscast showing Tess being arrested but says it did not really bother him. Herb admits he called Tess that same evening and asked her to attend the upcoming meeting of the Bolinga County School Board but that he did so only because he knew that Tess's teaching competence had been questioned and he wanted her there in case any of the Board members wanted to ask her some questions.

Herb insists that Tess was fired for incompetence, not her political activities, though he admits that some members were upset with Tess's arrest. Herb denies that he called Tess a "commie." Herb notes that two other teachers were fired for incompetence at the same meeting.

Herb has copies of Tess's annual teaching reviews by her principal for the past three years. In each, she was rated overall as "poor."

Exercise #14—Version A

Your client, Tom Jones, bought a 2001 Ford Escort for $6,000 from Joe's Used Cars. The odometer showed 55,000 miles. Two months later the car broke down and Tom was forced to sell it for junk. It has been stipulated by both parties that the odometer on the Escort had been rolled back 40,000 miles. Tom is suing Joe for the tort of fraud and is asking for compensatory and punitive damages. Joe denies any fraud and claims that he had no idea the odometer had been rolled back.

Your witness is Al Smith, a former salesman at Joe's Used Cars. He will testify that after Tom left the lot in the Escort, Joe started laughing and said, "There goes another one." Al says Joe meant by that: "There goes another sucker."

Al says Joe once told him it was "easy" to roll odometers back and though Al never saw Joe do it, he believes Joe did it all the time.

Al says Joe never instructed him to warn customers that odometer readings on used cars were unreliable. Instead, Joe told him to tell any customer asking about the odometer reading that the odometer reading was "certified." Al admits that Joe required anyone who sold him a car or traded one in to sign a written form that the odometer reading was correct and had not been altered.

Al says he finally quit working for Joe "because I got sick and tired of cheating people." He says Joe often "oversold" cars; i.e. made them sound much better than they really were. Al says that last year, Joe told him he had inherited over $500,000 from his grandmother.

Exercise #14—Version B

Tom Jones bought a 2001 Ford Escort with 55,000 miles on it for $6,000 from Joe's Used Cars, your client. Two months later the car broke down and Tom was forced to sell it for junk. Both parties have stipulated that the odometer on the Escort had been rolled back 40,000 miles. Tom is suing Joe for fraud and is asking for compensatory and punitive damages.

Joe Taylor, owner of Joe's Used Cars, says he did not roll the odometer back on the Escort and does not know who did. (He will admit that he knows how to do it). He took the Escort as a trade-in a few weeks before he resold it to Tom. He says it is his standard procedure to require that anyone selling him a car or trading one in sign a form stating that the odometer reading is correct. He says the guy who traded in the Escort signed such a form but he has searched for, but not found, that form.

Joe says he routinely warns customers that "these days, one can hardly vouch for the odometer reading on any used car."

Joe says he fired Al a few months ago for drinking alcohol on the job.

Nine years ago (when he was 19) Joe was working as a mechanic at his uncle's car lot in Tennessee. Both were convicted for selling stolen cars. The uncle got 3—5 years. Joe got 15 months probation and has no criminal record since.

Joe will admit that his grandmother left him over $500,000 when she passed away last year.

Exercise #15—Version A

You are the prosecutor in a homicide case. The defendant, Jesse Johnson, is a 35 year-old accountant. The State claims Jesse killed his wife, Brenda, by kicking her out of a rowboat in the middle of Bolinga Lake. Brenda didn't know how to swim and was not wearing a life preserver. Jesse claims it was an accident. He claims the boat capsized when Brenda, very drunk, stood up in the rowboat and began dancing wildly. Your witnesses are Harry and Margaret.

<u>Harry Morgan</u>—Harry rented Jesse the rowboat. He says Jesse and Brenda did not seem drunk at that time but he noticed they had a full bottle of wine.

As Jesse and Brenda were rowing away from shore, Harry heard Brenda ask Jesse what the "orange things" (shoulder strap life preservers) were for. He heard Jesse tell her they were seat cushions. Harry says the boat was "about 50 yards" from the dock when he heard this, though he says he is not very good at judging distances. Harry admits that he gave Jesse and Brenda no safety instructions.

<u>Margaret Mitchell</u>—Margaret and Brenda were friends for many years. In a conversation with Jesse and Brenda at a dinner party the night before the drowning, Margaret heard Brenda say "Jesse is going to kill me one of these days, aren't you Jesse?" Jesse, who was very drunk at the time, slurred "Maybe sooner than you think, Pumpkin."

Margaret said she knew Brenda for 10 years and Brenda never drank very much and she never saw her drunk.

Margaret says that about a year ago Brenda came over to her house one night bruised and cut. Brenda told Margaret that Jesse had beaten her. The police were not called and a few days later, Brenda and Jesse made up and Brenda went home.

Exercise #15—Version B

You are defense attorney in a homicide case. Your client is Jesse Johnson, a 35 year-old accountant. The State claims Jesse killed his wife, Brenda, by kicking her out of a rowboat in the middle of Bolinga Lake. Brenda didn't know how to swim and was not wearing a life preserver. Jesse claims it was an accident. They took the rowboat out and drank a bottle of wine. The boat capsized when Brenda, very drunk, got up in the rowboat and began to dance wildly.

Your witness is <u>Joan Carson</u>. Joan was a close friend of Brenda's and has known Margaret (a key prosecution witness) for 10 years.

Joan says Margaret hated Jesse and she once heard Margaret tell Brenda that she saw Jesse kissing another woman. Margaret later told Joan that she had made that story up in order to get Jesse in trouble with Brenda. Joan thinks Margaret is a compulsive liar.

Joan says Brenda never said anything to her about Jesse beating her or mistreating her in any way. Joan never saw Brenda with cuts or bruises. She says Jesse and Brenda's marriage was above average in terms of stability and mutual affection.

Joan says Brenda didn't drink often but didn't need much to get drunk. She had seen Brenda very drunk a few times in the past ten years.

Exercise #16—Version A

You are defense counsel. On Sunday, May 17 of last year, the State Patrol stopped a rented van, northbound on I–85, near Peachtree City. The driver of the van was Ray Marx. The van contained 150 pounds of marijuana. The rental papers indicate the van was rented out to Chad Brown of Atlanta, your client. Ray Marx escaped from jail a few days after his arrest and his current whereabouts are unknown.

Chad will testify in his own behalf. He is a city bus driver. He says he was in Atlanta on May 16, his day off, and he did not rent or authorize the rental of any van. He has met Ray Marx a few times but they are not really friends.

Chad says he lost his wallet in late April of last year but it turned up a few days later in his car with nothing missing. He didn't think anything of it until now. At your suggestion, Chad used a color copier and a dime store lamination kit to reproduce a copy of his driver's license with a picture of Jay Leno superimposed over his own picture. Chad says he has had no special training or experience with printing or document reproduction. You want the court to allow you to show Chad's altered ID to the jury (it looks pretty authentic).

Chad was convicted 14 years ago for selling controlled substances and served 2 years on a 5 year sentence.

It is over 300 miles from Panama City, Florida to Atlanta, Georgia.

Exercise #16—Version B

You are the prosecutor. On Sunday, May 17 of last year, the State Patrol stopped a rented van, northbound on I–85, near Peachtree City. The driver of the van was Ray Marx. The van contained 150 pounds of marijuana. The rental papers indicate the van was rented out to Chad Brown of Atlanta, the defendant in this action. Ray Marx escaped from jail a few days after his arrest and his current whereabouts are unknown.

Your witness:

Stewart Little is the regional records manager for Atlas Rent-a-Van.

You have the Rental Agreement found in the van when Ray Marx was placed under arrest. It says that Chevy Van license number PTN 173 (the number of the van seized on May 17) was rented in Panama City, Florida on May 16, at 1:05 p.m. to Chad Brown, 414 Gold St., Atlanta, Ga. (this is Chad's address), to be returned in Atlanta on May 18 before 6:00 p.m. The renter's signature is just a short squiggly line. The Agreement indicates the renter paid cash. (This agency does not require a credit card). Stewart says the clerks always examine the renter's driver's license to confirm the name and address on the rental agreement. None of the Atlas clerks in Panama City could identify either Ray or Chad in a lineup. (Panama City is over 300 miles from Atlanta).

Exercise #17—Version A

You represent Earl Miles, who has been charged with armed robbery. The prosecution alleges that on November 3, at 8:00 p.m., Earl, acting alone, entered a Savemore drug store in Midtown wearing a ski mask and brandishing a pistol. He fired several rounds into the ceiling, ordered everyone on the floor, and stole over $2,500 worth of Schedule II and III controlled substances.

Your witness:

Willy Wilson is a friend and neighbor of Earl's. He will testify that he and Earl were fishing near Lake Murray on November 3 and they did not get home until 11:00 p.m. (Lake Murray is 100 miles from Willy's home).

Willy has known Earl for 5 years and believes he is an honest person. Willy is a bricklayer, though he has been out of work for the last 9 months.

Six years ago, when he was 16, Willy was charged as a juvenile with possession of cocaine and was adjudicated guilty.

Exercise #17—Version B

You are the prosecutor. The prosecution alleges that on November 3, Earl Miles, acting alone, entered a Savemore drug store in Midtown wearing a ski mask and brandishing a pistol. He fired several rounds into the ceiling, ordered everyone on the floor, and stole over $2,500 worth of Schedule II and III controlled substances.

Your witnesses:

Mildred Stowe was outside the store, waiting for a bus, when she saw a young man standing near the door to Savemore. He pulled a ski mask from his pocket and pulled it over his face and walked into the store. Mildred saw him rush out of the store about 5 minutes later and run around the corner. She was standing about 40 feet from the door and believes the robber didn't see her because she was standing behind a tree.

Mildred identified Earl in a line up on November 18. Earl had been arrested the day before for aggravated assault in an unrelated case. (Case still pending). Mildred is very nervous. Ever since the line up, when Earl accidentally saw her face to face, she has been worried that he will try to harm her. She has told her neighbor, Harriet, of her fears.

Captain Bill Miller is chief investigator, narcotics division, Bolinga City Police Department. On November 28, he received a note from Earl, who was in jail, that Earl had some information for him regarding local drug dealers. Miller visited Earl on November 30. Miller says he read Earl his rights. Earl wanted to trade information for leniency on the robbery charge. Miller told him he could not make a deal but he could make recommendations to the prosecutor. Miller told Earl that he and the prosecutor were old friends.

Miller asked Earl what he did with the drugs he stole from Savemore. Earl replied "That's old news. That stuff's long gone." Miller and Earl were not able to agree and reach a deal. Miller was not convinced Earl had any valuable info. The defense's motion to suppress this evidence on constitutional and *Miranda* grounds was denied.

Earl has been in continuous police custody since November 17.

Exercise #18—Version A

You represent Lee Jones, who is suing Leyla Barnes for breach of contract. Lee is a general contractor who entered into an agreement with Leyla to build her a house for $550,000. Leyla has paid Lee a total of $500,000. Under their contract, the final payment of $50,000 became due when a Certificate of Occupancy was issued by the county building department. That certificate was issued 14 months ago but Leyla refuses to pay the remaining $50,000. Leyla claims the house was built on insufficient foundation and is already beginning to crack.

Your witness is <u>Lee</u>. Lee has been building large expensive homes for 8 years. He does not have a college degree. He worked as a carpenter for 5 years before starting his own construction company.

Lee has several reports from his soil engineer and his structural engineer which were completed during and after construction of the foundation. Each report includes the signature of the engineer and a seal indicating that the engineer is licensed in this State. All reports indicate normal soil conditions and satisfactory construction of the foundation.

Lee says superficial cracking of the concrete is due to shrinkage and is normal. He says his engineers have found no structural problems with Leyla's house.

Lee says that at a settlement conference he and Leyla attended a month ago at the offices of her attorney, he was in the restroom and overheard two people—one man and one woman—talking in the hallway outside the door. The woman said "Do you think a jury will buy this nonsense about the foundation?" He heard the man reply "The expert we hired could convince a jury that the earth was flat." Lee opened the restroom door and there stood Leyla and her attorney. He didn't say anything and walked past them. Leyla let out a short gasp and said nothing. As he was walking away, he heard the attorney say to her "I don't think he heard us." (Leyla says that such a "hallway conference" with her attorney never took place and is the product of Lee's imagination.)

The contract between Lee and Leyla provides: *"All work shall meet or exceed County Building Code standards."* County Building Code § 51 requires that foundations for residences be "safe and serviceable." Lee understands this to mean that the foundation must be structurally sound and usable. Building Code § 108 provides that a Certificate of Occupancy shall not be issued unless a building meets the requirements of section 51.

(Just to make things difficult for you, assume that Lee's engineers will not be testifying at trial).

Exercise #18—Version B

You represent Leyla Barnes, who is being sued by Lee Jones for breach of contract. Lee is a general contractor and Leyla entered into a contract with him to build her home for $550,000. She has paid $500,000. The last $50,000 was due when a Certificate of Occupancy was issued by the county building department. The certificate was issued 14 months ago but Leyla refuses to pay any more money.

Leyla claims the house was built on insufficient foundation and is already beginning to crack. Their contract provides: "*All work shall meet or exceed County Building Code requirements.*"

County Building Code § 51 requires that all foundations for residences be "safe and serviceable."

County Building Code § 108 provides that a Certificate of Occupancy shall not be issued unless the building meets the requirements of § 51.

Your witness is Zeek Thompson, a licensed structural engineer for over 21 years. He has a B.S. in engineering from M.I.T. He has extensive experience with soils engineering, concrete foundations, and foundation support. Zeek has been hired as an expert for litigation 146 times and has testified at trial 19 times.

Zeek has examined Leyla's new home and believes it is structurally unsound due to insufficient compaction of the soil and poor techniques in pouring the concrete for the foundation. He says added pilings must be driven into the soil at various points in the foundation to keep the house from deteriorating further. He has a written estimate which he prepared of the cost of repairing the house at $49,000. He says that without these repairs, the cracks in the concrete will grow and lead to uneven floors and misaligned walls and doors.

Zeek admits that the structural problems do not create safety concerns but he believes that they make the house less than serviceable (usable). Zeek says that the County Building Code provisions are minimums which might be acceptable in a cheap house but not a $550,000 home.

Exercise #19—Version A

You are the prosecutor in a bribery case. The indictment alleges that the defendant, Sheriff Chuck Cole of Bolinga County, accepted $5,000 to allow a drug dealer to land a plane loaded with cocaine on a landing strip in the county and to see that no one interfered with the plane and its passengers and cargo. As it turned out, the "drug dealer" was Agent Bill Hill of the Federal Bureau of Investigation. Cole's defense is that he was laying a trap for what he thought were cocaine dealers and that he was going to arrest them when they landed with the drugs.

Your witnesses:

Agent Hill—Agent Howard "Bill" Hill has been with the FBI for fifteen years. He received a tip from a reliable informer that Sheriff Cole is willing to do business with drug dealers if the price is right. Hill went undercover posing as a drug runner looking for a safe landing strip. He will testify that he approached Cole on February 23, about making some money on the side. Cole seemed interested. Hill told Cole that it involved landing some drugs in the county. Cole replied that for $5,000 they could land whatever they wanted in his county.

A meeting was arranged for February 26, at 11 p.m. in Hill's room at the Bolinga Holiday Inn. What transpired was videotaped by hidden cameras. [If your Instructor has a video for this Exercise, you will be told how to obtain it so that it may be previewed before class and presented during the Exercise. If there is no video, you are to pretend there is one and use the transcript on the following page for the contents of the video.]

Hill says that when the audio cuts out (he knows not why) he and Cole were talking about restaurants in Bolinga and nothing else.

Hill also will testify that he has never heard of a sheriff in a small county like Bolinga not informing the FBI, DEA, or at least the state police when the sheriff tried to set up a major drug bust. In his opinion, Sheriff Cole's small office lacked anything near the resources required to set up this size of bust without outside help.

Deputy Daniel Dowd—Dowd is one of Cole's two full-time deputies. He will testify that Cole never mentioned anything to him about laying a trap for some drug dealers. He also will testify that Cole often complained he was underpaid (Cole's salary is $39,000 per year) and was very bitter when the county commission refused his request for a raise this year.

Transcript of Videotape of Agent Bill Hill and Sheriff Chuck Cole

[Video begins with Agent Hill, seated alone, at a table in a hotel room.]

Hill: I am Special Agent Bill Hill of the Federal Bureau of Investigation. It is February 26, 10:56 p.m., and I am at the Holiday Inn in Bolinga County, Room 222. I received a tip from a reliable informer two weeks ago that Sheriff Cole had taken bribes from area drug dealers. In response, the Bureau set up this sting operation. I approached Sheriff Cole three days ago, posing as drug dealer who wanted to land a plane load of cocaine on a small private airstrip here in Bolinga County. I offered the sheriff $5,000 for his cooperation. Sheriff Cole was enthusiastic in his support and even offered to help unload the plane for me.

Sheriff Cole and I agreed to meet here at my hotel tonight at 11:00 p.m. where he can collect his $5,000. Once he pockets the money and attempts to leave, we will place him under arrest. [Pause] It appears Sheriff Cole has arrived.

[Hill gets up, walks off camera to the hotel door and admits Sheriff Cole. The two walk into camera view and sit down at the table].

Hill: I'm glad you made it. You have a nice little town here. Any good places to eat around here?

Cole: The restaurant here at the Holiday Inn is pretty good. There's also Bud's Café at the crossroads but ... [here the sound on the video goes out for some reason—the two men keep talking but there is no sound for about 10 seconds when the audio suddenly comes on again] ...

Hill: Yeh, I love good barbeque too. Well, let's get down to business. The plane carrying my cocaine will fly in here three nights from now, around 10:30. I'll have a truck to drive it out Highway 16 and up to the Interstate. Any problems there?

Cole: Nope. Are you sure you don't need any help unloading the stuff?

Hill: Nah. I'll have several of my guys with me. [Hill removes an envelope from his pocket and hands it to Cole]. There should be 50 Franklins in there. You can count 'em.

Cole: I don't have to count them. You're not that stupid. [Cole peeks in the envelope and then stuffs it into his pocket].

Hill: I hear you got a Deputy, Deputy Dowd, who is supposed to be some kind of Boy Scout. How you gonna handle him?

Cole: I'll handle Dowd, don't worry.

Hill: If this goes well, we might like to come through here on a regular basis; maybe once a month. That could mean a lot of easy money for a certain sheriff.

Cole: Yeh, we'll see.

Hill: Okay then. Its good doing business with you, Sheriff Cole.

[Hill and Cole shake hands and Cole gets up and starts heading for the door. As he walks toward the camera, another FBI agent is heard coming into the room and seen walking up to Cole].

Voice: FBI! Sheriff Cole. You are under arrest . . .

Cole: No, you are under arrest . . . you are under arrest.

[The tape suddenly ends].

Exercise #19—Version B

You represent Sheriff Chuck Cole of Bolinga County in his defense against a charge of bribery. The indictment alleges that Sheriff Cole accepted $5,000 to allow a drug dealer to land a plane loaded with cocaine on a landing strip in his county. It turns out the drug dealer was an FBI agent acting undercover. Your client's defense is that he was laying a trap for what he thought were cocaine dealers and that he was going to arrest them when they landed with the drugs.

Your witnesses:

Cole—Cole has been sheriff of this rural county for 10 years. He will testify that Bolinga County is a quiet county with no major crime. He saw his chance to make the biggest bust of his life—a planeload of cocaine—so he led this guy along with the idea of busting him and his co-perpetrators when they landed. The only person he told about his plan was Deputy Davis, one of his two full-time deputies. (Davis died in a car accident two days after Cole was arrested.)

Cole didn't tell his other deputy, Deputy Dowd, about the plan. Cole says he caught Dowd accepting a small bribe from a traffic offender a year ago and didn't trust him.

Marvin Miller—Marvin is a lifelong friend of Cole's. He says he saw Deputy Davis just a few minutes after the feds announced Sheriff Cole's arrest. Davis said he was on his way to visit Cole in jail. Davis told Marvin the arrest was all a foul up and that Cole would be released when the FBI realized that Cole was only leading the drug dealers on so he could make a big bust.

Marvin says Cole has always been a law-abiding person who hates drug dealers.

Exercise #20—Version A

Your client, Big Moon Supermarkets, is the defendant in a slip and fall case. The plaintiff, Lois Murphy, 18, claims she slipped on spilt milk in the dairy section. She injured her hip and claims damages for medical costs, pain and suffering, and permanent partial disability.

Your witnesses:

Fred Smith was the dairy stocker at the Big Moon in question on the day of the accident. He has worked at that job for 8 years. He says spilt material has never remained on the floor of his section for more than 60 seconds. He says that he and his co-employees constantly scan the floor and the dairy case.

He recalls that on the day in question, he was working in the dairy case when he heard a noise like a carton of milk splattering and someone cry "Oh, no." He immediately stopped what he was doing and walked out front. By the time he got there (10 seconds at the most), Lois was on the floor, acting like she was in pain. There was a broken carton of milk beside her, its contents spilt all around her. He bent down to talk to her and he smelled alcohol on her breath. The fall occurred around 11:00 a.m.

Charley Angel is a private investigator. He was hired by you to keep an eye on Lois. About a month ago, he followed her for seven days. He says Lois is a big boozer and drug abuser. She seems fully recovered from her hip injury. Angel saw her playing badminton and dancing at a bar. He also saw her snorting cocaine in the same bar.

Angel will admit that 90% of his work is for insurance companies. Last year, he sent a promotional flyer to the city's insurance defense firms. A copy follows this Exercise.

Exercise #20—Version B

Your client, Lois Murphy, 18, slipped on spilt milk at a Big Moon Supermarket and injured her hip. She seeks damages for medical costs, pain and suffering, and permanent, partial disability. The store claims the milk had been there for only 10 seconds.

Your witnesses:

Clive Jones is an unemployed, former cashier at the Big Moon in question. He was fired 9 months ago for "insubordination" but was working at the store on the day of the accident. He heard a scream from the dairy section and went over to investigate. He saw Lois on the floor, crying over the spilt milk and in obvious pain. Fred, the dairy stocker, was very upset and kept muttering that Bob (a trainee) was supposed to mop this mess up 30 minutes ago.

Clive says the dairy section was usually clean but he has seen spills that were not cleaned for 30 or 40 minutes.

Madge Long, 23, is a friend of Lois' who was with her at the store on the day of the accident. They had stopped to pick up a carton of eggs and had not noticed the floor was wet. Lois was wearing hard heeled shoes and lost her balance. Madge did not see a broken milk container on the floor. She thinks the milk Lois slipped on was skim milk because it was very light and almost invisible against the light colored floor of the dairy section.

She says her and Lois had been together all morning and Lois had not been drinking.

Right after Lois fell, a woman standing nearby said: "That spill has been there over an hour." Madge didn't get the person's name.

Madge was convicted of shoplifting in Texas 3 years ago (a misdemeanor). She was given a suspended sentence.

CHARLEY ANGEL

"Who's looking over your shoulder?"

To My Friends in the Insurance Business:

Are you sick and tired of lowlife fakers cheating you out of millions of dollars in fraudulent claims ???

Charley Angel is on the case.

Angel gets the goods on would be plaintiffs - I guarantee it, or your money back!

or your money back!

or your money back!

Exercise #21—Version A

Your client, Jack Swanson, has been charged with armed robbery and assault with a deadly weapon. The prosecution alleges that Jack entered the Shadow Bar at about 11:30 p.m., June 6, robbed the bartender at gun point and then shot the bartender in the foot. The robbery netted $250.

Your only witness is Jack Swanson. Jack is 33 and works as a roofer though he hasn't had a steady job in the last year. He is married to Rene (a part time nurse's aide) and is the father of two boys, 7 and 5.

Jack has two prior convictions. The first was 12 years ago when he was convicted in Murray County Superior Court of aggravated assault for beating a cable television repairman with a fireplace poker when the repairman failed to fix his cable connection properly. He was sentenced to 2 years and served 14 months. Five years ago, he was convicted in the same court of selling a half ounce of cocaine to an 8th grader. He was sentenced to 3 years and released after 2 years.

Jack says that he was downtown the evening of June 6 for an evening out with his wife. They had gone to a few bars and were headed home when Jack realized he was out of cigarettes so he stopped and ran into a convenience store to buy a pack while his wife waited in the truck.

When he got back to the truck and started to drive away, his wife (who was very drunk) started yelling at him about work and smoking and all kinds of complaints and he did not notice that there was a police car behind him. He admits he may have been speeding a bit because his wife was distracting him and getting him angry. Finally, he swerved into a fire hydrant and only then did he notice that the police were behind him. Jack admits he had been drinking more than he should.

Jack denies that he heard his wife say anything to Sgt. Cramer. He also denies that he said anything to her or that he threatened her in any way.

Exercise #21—Version B

Your are the prosecutor. The accused, Jack Swanson, has been charged with armed robbery and assault with a deadly weapon. The prosecution alleges that Jack entered the Shadow Bar at about 11:30 p.m., June 6, robbed the bartender at gun point and then shot the bartender in the foot. The robbery netted $250.

Your witness:

Sergeant Russ Cramer has been in law enforcement with the Bolinga Police Department for 21 years. He will testify that he received a radio call from dispatch at 11:35 p.m., June 6, telling him that there had been an armed robbery at The Shadow Bar and to be on the lookout for a white male in his late twenties, about 6 feet tall and 200 pounds, wearing a red short sleeve shirt with a large picture of Homer Simpson on the front.

As he drove toward the Shadow, he saw the defendant, (a white male, about 6 feet tall and 200 pounds), getting into an old pickup truck parked on Broadway, about three blocks from the Shadow Bar. The defendant was wearing a red short sleeve shirt with a large picture of Homer Simpson on the front. There was a female passenger in the truck.

As the truck pulled away from the curb, Sgt. Cramer drove up behind it and turned on his emergency lights. The truck sped up and it appeared to Cramer that the truck was trying to evade him. After about 30 seconds of the truck speeding through traffic, the truck attempted a sharp right turn and collided with a fire hydrant before coming to a stop. No one in the truck was hurt.

Sgt. Cramer determined that the female passenger was the defendant's spouse, Rene Swanson. Rene was quite intoxicated. When Sgt. Cramer asked her what her husband had been up to that evening, Rene slurred: "Robbing folks, as usual." Sgt. Cramer believes Jack heard her statement and a few minutes later he heard Jack whisper to Rene: "You say another word to the police or try to go to court against me and I'll kill you this time for sure." Rene has refused to speak to the police since that evening and she has asserted her marital privilege and refused to testify in this case.

You also have a transcript (next page) of a "911" call from the Shadow Bar at 11:33 p.m. on June 6. The parties have stipulated that this is a fair and accurate transcript of the "911" call but the defense has reserved all objections other than authentication and best evidence. The caller, Jim Jones, has moved out of state and cannot be located for trial.

TRANSCRIPT OF 911 CALL—JUNE 6—2333 hours—Operator 33

Operator:	"911. What is your emergency?"
Caller:	"We've just been robbed and my boss was shot!"
Operator:	"What is your location?"
Caller:	"This is Jim Jones and I'm calling from the Shadow Bar, downtown Bolinga. A crazy guy just shot my boss and robbed us. He was wearing a Homer Simpson shirt."
Operator:	"Homer Simpson? You were robbed by Homer Simpson?"
Caller:	"No. The robber was wearing a shirt with Homer Simpson's picture on it."
Operator:	"Homer Simpson the cartoon character?"
Caller:	"Yes. Send an ambulance. My boss was shot in the foot."
Operator:	"An ambulance has been dispatched to your location. That's the Shadow Bar on First St.?"
Caller:	"That's right."
Operator:	"And your name again?"
Caller:	"Jim Jones, I'm the cook."
Operator:	"Did you see the person who shot your boss?"
Caller:	"Uh huh."
Operator:	"Could you describe him?"
Caller:	"He was a white guy, really kind of ugly. About 6 foot and maybe 200."
Operator:	"Did he leave in a vehicle? Did you see if . . . "
Caller:	"No. He just ran out the door and down the street—toward Broadway."
Operator:	"The police have been dispatched and will be at your location in just a few minutes."

Exercise #22—Version A

You represent the plaintiff, Ted Mays, who is suing his former employer, Howie Products, under the Age Discrimination in Employment Act (ADEA). Ted, who is now 58, claims that Howie fired him 2 years ago last December, because of his age. Howie claims it fired him because of poor job performance. Your witnesses:

<u>Ted</u> worked for Howie Products in sales for nearly 25 years. He was promoted to assistant district sales manager 20 years ago and to district sales manager 15 years ago. Sales in his district have grown nearly every year since then. His base salary for the last three years of his employment: 5 years ago ($63,000); 4 years ago ($66,000); 3 years ago, his last year, ($70,000). His commissions for the same years: ($32,000); ($39,000); ($33,000). Howie Products recognized him as national "Salesperson of the Year" five years ago. He is currently unemployed.

Ted says no one at Howie ever told him his performance was slipping or that he needed to improve. His boss, Gus Bond, simply came into his office in December two years ago and told him that the company needed "new blood" and was giving him 30 days notice. Ted admits that sales slowed his last year but points out that the advertising budget had been cut 35%. Ted denies he has a drinking problem, though he admits he likes to drink.

<u>Loraine Murphy</u> used to work in the personnel department at Howie. She says 2 years ago last October she overheard Gus telling her boss that it doesn't make sense to carry an old-timer at 70 grand when these young kids will do the same job for half that. She did not hear any names mentioned. Gus will claim he never said anything like that. Loraine was fired from Howie in January of last year when she was caught drinking vodka on the job.

Loraine has a copy of an intra office memo, dated October 8, 2 years ago. (Copy at end of this Exercise). She says she made a copy of the memo and kept it when Ted was fired.

[Note: Your legal research suggests that it is a violation of the ADEA to fire an older worker and replace him or her with a younger person in order to save on the salary differential. Older workers, by virtue of their experience and seniority, naturally occupy the higher end of salary scales. To allow an employer to fire older workers because their salaries are higher than younger workers would undermine the protection intended by the ADEA.]

Exercise #22—Version B

You represent the defendant, Howie Products (1,100 employees nationwide; sales last year = $330 million). Howie is being sued by Ted Mays, a former employee, under the Age Discrimination in Employment Act (ADEA). Ted, who is 58, claims that Howie fired him 2 years ago last December because of his age. Howie claims it fired him because of poor job performance. Your witness:

<u>Gus Bond</u>, 53, is regional sales manager at Howie and had been Ted's immediate superior for 5 years. He says that Ted was once a great salesman but had lost his edge. He says Ted drank too much and that caused him to sometimes miss appointments or become belligerent with buyers. One buyer, Sam Adams, told Gus that Ted had called him on the phone last August and when he told Ted that he didn't wish to place any orders at that time, Ted called Sam a "scumbag." (Ted denies this ever happened). The buyer was so offended that he took his $500,000 worth of annual business elsewhere. (Ted would admit that Sam Adams took his half million account to another company).

Gus filled Ted's position with a 30 year old, Skip, whose starting salary was $35,000. Skip's sales the last two years have been about 95% of what Ted's were in his last two years at Howie Products. Gus will admit that another district sales manager, Russ, 63, was fired 2 years ago last November and replaced with a 35 year old, Dana, at 60% of Russ' base salary. Dana's sales are about the same as Russ' for the same period.

Gus cannot recall the October 8 memo, has no evidence of it in his file, and thinks Lorraine just made it up.

An excerpt from Gus's deposition: [p. 17]

<u>Gus</u> -	"Our sales were good that year, not great, but solid. But the company had borrowed a lot of money in some buy-out and was desperate to cut costs."
<u>Counsel</u> -	"Is that why you fired Ted, to cut costs?"
<u>Gus</u> -	"You're asking me, you're asking me a hypothetical. I mean would I have let Ted go if there was no need to cut, no budget problems? I dunno, Ted's my friend, and you know, you like to work something out."
<u>Counsel</u> -	"Yes. But is the reason, then, that you fired Ted was to cut costs? [Pause] Let the record reflect counsel is whispering to the witness."
<u>Gus</u> -	"I had to let Ted go. He was hurting, not helping us. His drinking was just too much. It had nothing to do with his age or his salary or whatever—Ted earned his money. But you just can't have your sales people insulting customers and stuff."

HOWIE PRODUCTS

"Where people matter more than money."

~~~ INTEROFFICE MEMORANDUM ~~~

TO: Personnel Dept.

FROM: Gus Bond, Regional Sales Manager

DATE: October 8, (two years ago)

Please forward to me as soon as possible a complete list of all employees in the Sales Department who are over the age of 55 with complete information on each employee's current salary and commission rates.

Exercise #23—Version A

You are the prosecutor. The defendant, Fred Green, was arrested on May 3, for shoplifting. Fred was apprehended by a security guard, Joe Marshall, just outside of the Jock Shop, a local sporting goods store. Fred was carrying a new Atlanta Hawks team jacket with the price tag still attached. Fred claims that he paid cash for the item, but he has no receipt or sales slip as evidence of the purchase.

Your witnesses:

Milo Bender—Milo has worked as a cashier at his uncle's store, the Jock Shop, for 9 months and was cashier on the day in question. He will testify that Fred never paid him for the item and that store policy is to produce three copies of the sales slip with each purchase. One goes to the purchaser and two are kept by the store for internal accounting purposes. No copies of the sales slip can be found.

Milo also reviewed the cash register tape for the morning in question and it showed no entry for $82.00, the price of the jacket. (Though Milo says the tape has since been lost). Milo also will testify that it is store policy to pull the price tag off of an item when it is rung up.

Joe Marshall—Joe is a plain clothes security guard at the Jock Shop. He will testify that he stopped Jack outside the store because he was carrying a new jacket with the price tag still attached and did not have a store bag. He will testify that when he confronted Fred and asked him if he had paid for the coat, Fred offered him $20 "to forget the whole thing." When Joe refused, Fred took a swing at him.

Exercise #23—Version B

Your client, Fred Green, was arrested on May 3, for shoplifting. He was apprehended by a security guard just outside of the Jock Shop, a local sporting goods store. Fred was carrying an Atlanta Hawks team jacket with the price tag still attached. Fred claims that he paid cash for the item but he has no receipt or sales slip as evidence of the purchase.

Your witness:

Fred—He will testify that when he paid cash for the jacket, the cashier, Milo, rang up something on the cash register but didn't put the money in the register but placed it off to one side and said "This one's for me." Fred says he declined when Milo offered him a bag for his purchase.

Fred says that when Joe (the security guard) approached him outside the store, he thought he was a mugger and that's why he took a swing at him. He denies offering Joe $20.

Fred also has a receipt from an automated teller machine that shows a withdrawal of $100 cash at 9:12 a.m. May 3. Fred was arrested at 11:30 a.m. that same morning.

You also have a photostatic copy of an "Inmate Personal Inventory" card with a statement that it is "a true and accurate copy of the original in my custody," signed by the county jailer. The card shows that when he was booked, Fred had $13.58 cash in his possession. (The jacket would have been $86.92, including tax). Fred signed the "Inmate Personal Inventory" card when he was booked into custody on May 3.

Exercise #24—Version A

Your client, Lulu & the Country Boys, contracted with Minnie's Restaurant and Lounge to play during the peak holiday season. (The contract was $38,000 for 4 weeks, 6 nights a week, from December 11, through January 8). Clause 45 of their contract provided that Minnie's could cancel the contract upon 24 hours notice if the *"performers engage in conduct that is illegal or deleterious to the Owner."*

On the morning of December 15, Mr. Tim Tip, general manager of Minnie's, told Lulu Smith that they were canceling their contract effective immediately pursuant to Clause 45. Tip claims that on December 14, Lulu removed her shirt in a provocative manner during the band's final set. Lulu & the Country Boys are suing Minnie's Restaurant and Lounge for breach of contract.

Your witness:

Lulu Levitt—The band plays basic country music suitable for dancing and Lulu & the Country Boys attracted full house crowds every night before they were fired. Lulu says that Minnie's is a pretty rowdy bar and there were at least two or three fights every night. Lulu admits she took her shirt off during the performance but says she had a bikini top on underneath and only took her shirt off because it was very hot in the Lounge.

Lulu will testify that on December 22, Jack Strong, the Lounge Manager at Minnie's, told her Mr. Tip only fired her because he wanted to book his nephew's band, "The Four Aces," into the Lounge. Jack was responsible for hiring Lulu's band in the first place. Lulu says "the Four Aces" did in fact take over after her band left. Jack himself was fired from Minnie's on December 25th and died in an auto accident on January 12, before his deposition could be taken.

Lulu denies that Jack ever told her that the Lounge was under pressure from the City and that she had to be particularly careful about stirring up the customers.

Exercise #24—Version B

Your client, Minnie's Restaurant & Lounge, contracted with the plaintiffs, Lulu & the Country Boys, to play during the peak holiday season. (The contract was $38,000 for 4 weeks, 6 nights a week, from December 11, through January 8). Clause 45 of their contract provided that Minnie's could cancel the contract upon 24 hours notice if the *"performers engage in conduct that is illegal or deleterious to the Owner."*

On the morning of December 15, Mr. Tim Tip, general manager of Minnie's, told Lulu that they were canceling their contract effective immediately pursuant to Clause 45. He claims that on December 14, Lulu removed her shirt in a provocative manner during the band's final set.

Your witness is <u>Mr. Tip</u>, the general manager of Minnie's. He will testify that on the morning of December 15, he received several calls from customers (he can't recall their names) complaining that Lulu had been indecent on stage the night before and had acted like a stripper. Mr. Tip was not at Minnie's on the night in question. One of the callers threatened to call the police. Mr. Tip says that, in the past, Minnie's has had a rather wild reputation but says he has tried to change that image over the past year since he took over as General Manager. He says the Lounge has been under pressure from the City to clean up its acts or face revocation of its liquor license.

On December 16, Mr. Tip replaced Lulu & the Country Boys with another group, "The Four Aces," in which Tip's nephew, Fred, is the lead singer.

Jack Strong, the Lounge manager and Tip's subordinate, hired Lulu's band in the first place. Jack was fired on December 25, and died in a car accident a few weeks later. Mr. Tip has a memo from Jack, addressed to him, dated November 3 (copy follows this Exercise).

You have a certified copy of applicable Municipal Ordinance § 45–7 which states, in part, that it shall be a misdemeanor for a tavern, without a permit, "to employ performers who undress in a lascivious manner." Your client has no such permit.

Minnie's Restaurant & Lounge

TO: Tim Tip, General Manager

FROM: Jack Strong, Lounge Manager

DATE: November 3, (last year)

RE: Band booked for Christmas Holidays

I went ahead and booked Lulu & the Country Boys for the holidays. We had them here a couple years ago and they packed the place. They don't do Jingle Bells but they do good country and our customers will love them.

I signed them to our standard contract. The terms are $38,000 for 4 weeks, 6 nights a week, from December 11, through January 8.

Pursuant to our discussion, I sat down with Lulu and explained to her that the City was breathing down our necks about some fights and other problems we've had at the Lounge in the past and that it was real important that she and her boys not stir the crowd up too much. I particularly warned her against any profanity and any sexual stuff. Keep it squeaky clean is what I told her. She told me she understands.

Exercise #25—Version A

You represent Gary Torr in an action brought against him by the estate of Donald Lendar to recover from him as guarantor on a promissory note for $100,000. (See the Note at the end of this Exercise). The note was payable in full in 12 months and is now overdue. The note was signed by Arthur Diamond, as maker, two years ago but Mr. Diamond has passed away and his estate is broke. The note indicates that Gary Torr signed as guarantor of the note. Gary denies any connection with the note.

Your witnesses:

<u>Gary Torr</u>—is sole owner of a plastics plant. He admits that he personally signed three notes as guarantor for Arthur Diamond over the past 12 years—but not this one. He and Arthur were old friends and he was happy to help Arthur out on his "projects," many of which were quite successful (though Arthur could never hold on to money). Five years ago, however, Gary and Arthur had a falling out. Gary believed that Arthur had stolen Gary's idea for a new plastics impeller, received a patent on it, and sold it to a competitor of Gary's. The two didn't speak for several years and never socialized or did business with one another again.

Gary says neither Donald Lendar nor anyone else ever contacted him about this note. He says he never has and never would authorize anyone to sign his name on an important legal document. He thinks it is preposterous that the law would even allow such a thing. Gary would admit that his business is in terrible financial condition but he feels this is only a temporary downturn.

<u>Hugh Morgan</u>—is a banker. He will testify that he knew Arthur Diamond for over 30 years and they were friends. He says he had a conversation with Arthur about two years ago (he can't recall exactly when), in which Arthur said Donald Lendar was so senile that he didn't even check out the guarantor on a $100,000 promissory note. Hugh has no idea whether Arthur was referring to a specific note of his own or someone else's.

Hugh will testify that in his opinion, Arthur was not a truthful person when it came to raising money for his "projects." Hugh says that other members of the local banking community share his opinion.

Hugh would admit that his bank holds about $6 million dollars in notes from Gary's plastics company.

Exercise #25—Version B

You represent the estate of Donald Lendar in an action to recover from a guarantor on a promissory note for $100,000. The note was payable in full in 12 months and is now overdue. The note was signed by Arthur Diamond, as maker, two years ago but Mr. Diamond has passed away and his estate is broke. The note indicates that Gary Torr signed as guarantor of the note and he is the defendant. Gary denies any connection with the note.

Your witnesses:

Lilly Langtree—was Arthur Diamond's assistant for the last 20 years. She will testify that Donald Lendar lent Arthur the $100,000 two years ago to develop and promote a new kind of stereo speaker Arthur had invented. Lendar must have been aware that Arthur had few assets and demanded an approved guarantor on the note. Lilly was in Arthur's office when she saw him sign both his own name, as maker, and Gary Torr's, as guarantor. When Lilly asked him what he was doing, Arthur explained that Gary had agreed to guarantee the note and had authorized him to sign the note on his behalf. (UCC 3–403 says that if Gary did authorize Arthur to sign for him, Gary is bound).

Lilly has copies from Arthur's files (which she maintained for him) of three other promissory notes, all paid, from over the past 12 years, for a total of $185,000. Gary Torr personally signed as the guarantor on each of them. The most recent note is 5½ years old.

Earl Dukes—was Donald Lendar's secretary for the last 9 years. He will testify that Donald was a very wealthy man who liked to help out inventors and entrepreneurs like Arthur but he was always hard nosed about the terms of loans and having adequate security. When Arthur proposed Gary as a guarantor, Donald asked Earl to check Gary's credit while he personally contacted Gary to verify the guarantee. This was Donald's standard procedure before he would accept a large note. Several days after Earl sent Donald a favorable report on Gary's credit, Donald gave him the fully executed promissory note to place in the safe and asked him to draw a check for $94,000 payable to Arthur. (The borrower nets $94,000 for his promise to pay back $100,000 in 12 months).

Earl was responsible for keeping all of Donald's business account records. He has reviewed those records and can testify based both on those records and his own personal knowledge, that nothing has been paid on the subject note.

PROMISSORY NOTE

On this date of August 27, (two years ago), in return for valuable consideration received, the undersigned borrower promises to pay to Donald Lendar or bearer the sum of $100,000 Dollars on or before August 27, (one year ago).

Late Fees: In the event that a payment due under this Note is not made within ten (10) days of the time set forth herein, the Borrower shall pay an additional late fee in the amount of $ 500 plus interest at the rate of $18.00 per day.

Default - In the event of default, the borrower agrees to pay all costs and expenses incurred by the Lender or bearer, including all reasonable attorney fees (including both hourly and contingent attorney fees as permitted by law) for the collection of this Note upon default, and including reasonable collection charges (including, where consistent with industry practices, a collection charge set as a percentage of the outstanding balance of this Note) should collection be referred to a collection agency.

Transfer of the Note - The borrower hereby waives any notice of the transfer of this Note by the Lender or by any subsequent holder of this Note, and agrees to remain bound by the terms of this Note subsequent to any transfer, and agree that the terms of this Note may be fully enforced by any subsequent holder of this Note.

Arthur Diamond, as maker.

Gary Torr, as guarantor.

Exercise #26—Version A

You represent Marvin Jones, charged with attempting to smuggle 30 ounces of cocaine into the U.S. last January 15. The cocaine was in a teddy bear the defendant was carrying when he went through customs after a flight from Caracas, Venezuela to Atlanta. Marvin claims he had no knowledge that the teddy bear contained contraband and that an elderly woman at the airport in Caracas gave him the teddy bear to give to her granddaughter in Atlanta. Marvin did not recall the name of the granddaughter but the old woman said her daughter worked at the airport in Atlanta and would meet him at the baggage claim to pick up the teddy bear.

Your witness:

Kyle Brown is Marvin's business partner. They own a small communications business. Kyle will testify that Marvin went to Caracas to meet with a client, a hotel developer who had purchased equipment and consulting services from Marvin and Kyle's company in the past.

Kyle says he spoke with the Caracas client the day after Marvin was arrested. He didn't tell the client about Marvin's misfortune but the client did mention that he had driven Marvin to the airport because they were afraid Marvin might miss his flight. Kyle later offered to fly the Caracas client up to the U.S. to testify at Marvin's trial but the client refused.

Kyle says he has known Marvin for 12 years and believes he is a very law-abiding, conservative, and very religious person who is opposed to drug use. Marvin has been married to the same person for 20 years and has 5 children. Marvin earns about $250,000 per year from their business. He has never been charged with a crime; not even a traffic ticket. He says Marvin was a Green Beret in the 1970's and an Eagle Scout before that. Marvin and Kyle both have "Top Secret" clearances from the Defense Department because of their work with government agencies.

Exercise #26—Version B

You are the prosecutor. The defendant, Marvin Jones, is charged with attempting to smuggle 30 ounces of cocaine into the U.S. on January 15. The cocaine was in a teddy bear the defendant was carrying when he went through customs after a flight from Caracas, Venezuela to Atlanta. The defendant claims he had no knowledge that the teddy bear contained contraband and that an elderly woman at the airport in Caracas gave him the teddy bear to give to her granddaughter in Atlanta. Marvin did not recall the name of the granddaughter but the old woman said her daughter worked at the airport in Atlanta and would meet him at the baggage claim to pick up the teddy bear.

Your witnesses:

Agent Sara Stone is a U.S. Customs officer. She will testify that she had a tip from an anonymous informer that someone was using stuffed animals to smuggle cocaine into the U.S. from Caracas. When she saw Marvin carrying a teddy bear, she asked him a few innocuous questions about how long he'd been gone and the purpose of his visit. She noticed that Marvin was nervous and, after 11 years with Customs, she has developed a fine sense of when someone is hiding something from her. When she asked Marvin where he got the teddy bear, Marvin replied that he picked it up in Caracas as a gift for his nephew. She believed he was lying. When she asked to inspect the teddy bear, Marvin became very nervous and agitated. When she discovered the cocaine hidden in the teddy bear, Marvin exclaimed: "I've been set up!"

Douglas Banks was a passenger on the same flight from Caracas to Atlanta. He will testify that he saw Marvin emerge from a cab at the Caracas airport carrying a teddy bear in his arms. He remembers because he thought it odd to see a grown man clutching a teddy bear and he recognized Marvin later when he boarded the plane to Atlanta. When he saw Marvin being arrested in Atlanta, he spoke to the Customs agents and they asked Douglas to stick around. A half hour later, a Customs agent (not Agent Stone) asked him to confirm that Marvin was the person he saw get out of a taxi at the Caracas airport with a teddy bear in his hands. He looked into the office, saw Marvin sitting in a chair, and confirmed that he was indeed the same person he saw exit the taxi in Caracas.

Douglas is a struggling actor in his late 30s. Douglas sought some publicity after the arrest, offering himself for interviews. One local TV station ran an interview of him the day after the arrest in which Douglas said he was suspicious when he saw Marvin get out of the taxi in front of the airport carrying that teddy bear.

Exercise #27—Version A

You represent Bob Dibble who was seriously injured in an automobile collision on June 8 of last year. Dibble was a passenger in a car struck by a truck driven by Bill Ford and owned by defendant Ace Trucking Co. Bill Ford died in the accident.

Your witness is <u>Howard Hill</u>, Vice President of Ace Trucking, Bill Ford's employer. You have a photocopy of a Mechanical Inspection Report (MIR) dated June 7 of last year. (See copy at the end of this Exercise).

Howard will admit that the subject truck was assigned the company number "18." (The company runs about 25 trucks). He says the MIRs are filled out by the mechanics and filed each evening for each truck scheduled to leave the garage the following morning.

He admits ACE had a mechanic in June of last year named Joe Oz who left the company the following July for parts unknown. He says he does not know Joe's handwriting or signature. He can recall no other ACE mechanics with the initials "J.O."

Howard says that although this MIR looks like the ones used by his company, he had never seen a copy of this particular MIR until it was shown to him at his deposition two months ago. His office has looked for but found no trace of the original or any copies of this MIR in its files. Nor has he been able to locate any MIR for truck 18 dated June 7 of last year.

You have copies of six other MIRs written and initialed by "J.O." These came from a stack of 1,250 MIRs provided by ACE in response to plaintiff's request to produce copies of all MIRs from May through June of last year.

Two months ago, plaintiff sent a Request for Admission to Ace Trucking that stated: "The brake drums on the truck in question were not repaired or replaced on June 7 or June 8." Ace did not reply to this Request for Admission.

Exercise #27—Version B

You represent Ace Trucking which is being sued by Bob Dibble, a passenger in a car which was struck by a truck driven by Bill Ford, ACE's driver, on June 8 of last year. Bill Ford died in the accident.

Your witness is <u>Dave Edwards</u>, a mechanic for the past 36 years at ACE. He says Joe Oz was with the company for a couple of months and was a good mechanic. He says that under normal procedures, a mechanic will write "Do Not Drive" on the Mechanical Inspection Report (MIR) when a truck fails inspection. A driver is not given a truck without a clean MIR. He says that in his 36 years, ACE has never overruled a mechanic's decision to pull a truck off the road. He says that although they operate over 25 trucks, this is ACE's first serious accident in five years.

Your opponent will call Howard Hill, your vice-president. Howard says he fired an office clerk, Jodie England, in July of last year, when he caught Jodie rifling through the MIR files (where she had no business). Howard says he wished he had searched Jodie at the time because he now suspects that Jodie removed the real MIR for truck #18, dated June 7, and stole a blank MIR form for Dibble to forge plaintiff's exhibit. (Plaintiff's counsel says he received the copy of the MIR for #18 in the mail with no return address and only a note that said: "A friend . . .").

ACE TRUCKING

"Safety is our business."

MECHANICAL INSPECTION REPORT

DATE: *June 7, (last year)*

TRUCK # *18*

Inspected By: *J O*

Comments:

Brake drums in bad shape. <u>Do not drive</u> until drums are replaced.

Exercise #28—Version A

You represent Wilda Stone who is being sued by Nina Wise for assault and battery arising out of an incident at the Shadow Bar on March 15. Nina claims that Wilda came up behind her while she was sitting on a bar stool, pulled her down to the floor by her ponytail and began kicking her repeatedly. Wilda claims she was provoked and acted in self defense.

Your witnesses:

Deeter Downs—Deeter is a motorcycle mechanic who was accompanying Wilda on the evening in question. When they arrived, Nina was sitting at the bar with George Jones, Wilda's ex-boyfriend and the father of Wilda's daughter, Moonbeam. Deeter says Nina made an obscene gesture with her middle finger when he and Wilda came into the bar. A few minutes later, Wilda went up to the bar to order herself a drink and Deeter saw Nina put out her leg as if to try to trip Wilda. Wilda avoided the trip but lost her balance in the process, began to fall, and knocked Nina off her stool to the floor. Nina and Wilda pushed and shoved each other a bit on the floor and that was pretty much the end of it.

Deeter has lived near Nina for 7 years and says she has a reputation in the neighborhood for violent conduct. He says Wilda told him a week before the incident in question that she "was afraid Nina was looking for a fight with her."

Wilda—At the time of the incident, Wilda was wearing a black leather jumpsuit with stiletto heels and her hair was dyed bright red and purple. You have cleaned her up for trial and her hair is now short and its original mousey brown. She basically tells the same story as Deeter. She says she is not the violent type, goes to church (Episcopalian) regularly, and harbors no ill will toward Nina. Wilda currently is suing George for unpaid child support pursuant to a court order in which George admitted paternity of Wilda's daughter, Moonbeam.

Wilda says someone called her twice very late at night during the week prior to the incident. The caller was a woman but did not identify herself. She warned Wilda that if she didn't stop "hassling" George she'd soon be "dead meat." Wilda is not familiar with Nina's voice but believes it was Nina who made the calls because Nina is dating George.

Exercise #28—Version B

You represent Nina Wise who is suing Wilda Stone for assault and battery arising out of an incident at the Shadow Bar on March 15. Nina claims that Wilda came up behind her while she was sitting on a bar stool, pulled her down to the floor by her ponytail and began kicking her repeatedly. Wilda claims she was provoked and acted in self defense.

Your witnesses:

George Jones—George is Wilda's former and Nina's current boyfriend. George was with Nina on the night in question and will tell Nina's side of the story. He will say that Wilda has a very violent temper and beat up another woman, Sue, a year ago because she thought Sue was flirting with him.

George will admit that Wilda currently is suing him for unpaid child support pursuant to a court order in which George admitted paternity of Wilda's daughter, Moonbeam.

George says Nina is a very peaceful person. He took her to a boxing match once and she asked to leave in the middle because she couldn't stand the violence.

Zax Taylor—Zax is the bartender at the Shadow. He was on the other side of the bar when the fight broke out. He says he heard someone yell "Stop kicking her!" and ran over to see Nina on the floor and Wilda kicking her in the head. As one of the patrons was pulling Wilda away, Zax heard a bystander say "The blond never saw her coming." Nina is blond, Wilda's hair was red with purple streaks (though at trial her hair is brown). When Zax asked Wilda to leave after the fight, she threw a beer bottle and smashed it against the wall on her way out.

Exercise #29—Version A

You are the prosecutor. The defendant, Bill Turner, is charged with the illegal possession of two cases of U.S. Army issue grenades.

Agent Chris Curry—is with the U.S. Bureau of Alcohol, Tobacco, and Firearms. (ATF) On May 10, he received a tip from a reliable informer that Bill was offering to sell a case of grenades to a local gang. Bill was placed under surveillance immediately. In three days of surveillance, Curry saw Bill visiting known haunts of members of a local gang called "White Fight"—a "skinhead" group that avows racist philosophy and idolizes Hitler. The members of the gang seemed very friendly to Bill and bought him beers. ATF intelligence files indicate that Bill was a leader of "White Fight" about 6 years ago.

On May 15, the fourth day of surveillance, Bill was seen removing a large, heavy box from the trunk of his car and entering an apartment occupied by the current leader of the gang. Fearing that the box might contain grenades and that they were about to be given to the gang, ATF agents rushed in. The box contained 48 copies of Hitler's book, MEIN KAMPF. The surveillance blown, the ATF went to Bill's apartment at 1232 First Ave. and, executing a search warrant, discovered two cases of grenades in a closet under the stairway.

After he was under arrest and had been advised of his rights, Bill told Agent Curry that he shared the apartment with another man, Todd Jones, and that the grenades must have belonged to Todd. Curry says Bill's living room walls were covered with Nazi and KKK posters and the living room bookshelves contained dozens of Nazi and skinhead type books and pamphlets. There were no such posters or books found in Bill's bedroom.

Bill was convicted 9 years ago for inciting a riot (of skinheads) (served one year), and 6 years ago for conspiracy (served 18 months). The conspiracy charge grew out of the failed effort of Bill and a few friends from "White Fight" to steal machine guns from a local National Guard armory. Agent Curry was the agent in charge of the investigation of the latter crime.

Exercise #29—Version B

Your client, Bill Turner, has been charged with illegal possession of two cases of U.S. Army issue grenades. Agents of the Bureau of Alcohol, Tobacco, and Firearms (ATF) responded to a tip that Bill intended to sell grenades to his buddies in "White Fight," a local, militant "skinhead" group that avows racist philosophy and idolizes Hitler.

Bill was under surveillance for several days when, on May 15, agents of the ATF seized a box he was carrying into the gang's headquarters. (The box contained four dozen copies of MEIN KAMPF). Their surveillance blown, the ATF immediately executed a search warrant at Bill's apartment at 1232 First Ave. and found the grenades stashed in a closet beneath the stairs. Your client's defense is that the grenades must have belonged to his roommate, Todd Jones, and he never knew they were there.

Your witnesses:

Stella Kowalski—Stella has been Bill's girlfriend for 2 years. She says Todd was Bill's roommate until a few weeks before the arrest. Bill was living alone at the time of his arrest. Todd was a real "Rambo." He wore army fatigues everywhere and talked endlessly about war and weapons. Bill told her that Todd had been kicked out of the Marines because he was too violent. Todd once told Stella when he was drunk that he had stolen two cases of grenades and was saving them for a good cause. She thought he was just making it up.

Stella says Todd moved out because he was broke and couldn't afford the rent. Todd left some of his books and some other things when he left because he said he was moving into a real small place with two other guys. She thinks Todd kept his apartment key. She says Todd disappeared the day after Bill was arrested. Neither she nor any of her or Todd's friends have seen him.

Stella would testify that Bill has worked steady as a carpenter for the last two years. Although he still hangs around with some of his old friends from the gang, he is no longer a member of White Fight and not really interested in their politics. Stella calls herself apolitical and encourages the same in Bill. She admits there are a couple of Nazi and KKK posters on the walls of Bill's apartment but says those were put up by Todd. When she visited Bill at jail the day after his arrest, he told her that he didn't even know there was a closet under the stairs.

Your other witness is Mildred Smyth. She is regional ticketing manager for Eirie (pronounced "eye-rie") Airlines. She has a copy of a passenger manifest for Eirie Flight 602 to Jamaica on May 16. (Copy at end of this Exercise).

EIRIE AIRLINES

"No Problems ... Usually"

Passenger Manifest

Flight #   **602**

From: Bolinga Airport   (BOL)

To: Montego Bay, Jamaica   (MBJ)

Date: May 16, (last year)

Time Departure: 1205 hours

Time Arrival: 1635 hours

Boarded Passengers	Ticket Status *
Bob Andy	RT -R
Carl McDonald	RT -R
Todd Jones	O -NR
Rob Symeonn	RT -R
Bailey Alassie	RT -O
Robert Z. Marley	RT -R
Peter Tosh	RT -R
Chris Potter	RT -O
Nancy Drew	RT -O
Mikey Jarrett	RT -R
Sheya Mission	RT -R
George Gobel	RT -O
Tony Rankin	RT -R
Nadia Samie	RT -R
Fredrick Sasser	RT -O

*   RT -R — round trip return flight
     RT -O — round trip outbound flight
     O -NR – one way, no return booked

Exercise #30—Version A

You are the prosecutor in a murder case. The prosecution claims that the accused, Miles Mulder, shot and killed his business partner, Davis Fox, after the two had quarreled over the declining fortunes of their business.

Your witness:

<u>Molly Fox</u> was Davis' wife for ten years. She will testify that at about 9 p.m. on the night of the murder, she drove to her husband's office because they had planned a late dinner together. She had made reservations at a restaurant near the office for 9:30. As she entered the building, she heard two people arguing upstairs near her husband's office, though she could not make out what they were saying. As she walked up the stairs, she recognized her husband's voice and then Miles' voice. Halfway up the stairs, she heard a shot. She heard someone leaving by the fire exit in the rear of the office but she did not see who it was. Her husband was sprawled across his desk, dead.

When Molly first was questioned by police, she told them she recognized one of the voices she heard as that of her husband, Davis, but she did not recognize the other voice. A week later, she went to a psychiatrist to treat her emotional trauma. The psychiatrist used hypnotherapy to relieve some of Molly's anxiety. It was in hypnosis that Molly recognized the "other voice" as that of Miles. Her current conviction to that effect is unshakable.

Molly will testify that Davis' and Miles' business (a small chain of video arcades) was losing money and going under. Miles blamed everything on Davis and the two argued constantly. The night before he was shot, her husband told her "I'm afraid to be around Miles anymore, I'm afraid he'll do something desperate. He carries a pistol around with him now."

Molly's marriage with Davis was anything but blissful. Davis was not always a faithful husband. Molly is the sole beneficiary of Davis' estate—valued at about $350,000.

Exercise #30—Version B

You are the defense attorney in a murder case. The state claims that the accused, Miles Mulder, shot and killed his business partner, Davis Fox, after the two had quarreled over the declining fortunes of their business.

Your witnesses:

Sidney Marks was the accountant and long-time friend to both Miles and Davis. He said their business was managed well but video arcades are going out of fashion and Miles' and Davis' business was just about finished.

Miles and Davis were close friends for over 20 years and although they argued from time to time, they never got violent and always made up quickly.

Sidney says Molly, Davis' wife of ten years, disliked Miles and wasn't overly fond of her husband either. She often spoke of "dumping him." As far as Sidney knows, neither Miles nor Davis ever owned a gun. Sidney says Davis tended to be a womanizer and a month before the murder, he heard Molly scream at Davis in his office, "The next time I catch you with another woman you're dead!"

Sally Thompson was Miles' and Davis' secretary for the last nine years. She says Davis called her at home at about 8:30 on the night of the murder to ask about some papers she'd left on his desk. At that time, Davis said: "Miles has gone home and I'm left with this mess." She says she asked if he wanted her to bring him by some dinner and he declined, saying he would just grab a cheeseburger at the corner.

Sally says Davis was afraid of his wife, Molly. Sometimes he came into work with bruises visible on his arms and face. Once he came in with a black eye.

Sally will admit that she hates Molly very much. She had a brief affair with Davis six years ago (Molly never discovered it) but since then the relationship has been platonic and a bit maternalistic on Sally's part. Sally thinks Miles is a wonderful, peaceful guy who wouldn't hurt a fly and who loved Davis very much. She thinks Molly killed her husband.

Exercise #31—Version A

You are the prosecutor. The defendant, Sylvia Black, is accused of hit-and-run and vehicular homicide. The accident occurred July 1 of last year, at 7:30 p.m., at the intersection of 10th and Juniper St., in Bolinga. Sylvia, a 32 year old woman, allegedly smashed her car into the rear of a car driven by a 70 year old woman, Nancy Jones, who was stopped at the intersection in the center lane, waiting to turn left onto 10th. Mrs. Jones died an hour after the accident from severe head injuries. Sylvia's car tag number is LKE 319, and her car is a blue Honda. Sylvia has platinum blonde hair.

Your witnesses:

Mack Miller—an ambulance driver who was called to the scene of the accident. Mack says that when he first arrived, Nancy Jones kept crying out, "She was going too fast, I knew she was going to hit me. I knew I was a goner."

Mack will admit that Mrs. Jones was in very bad shape and much of what she said was indecipherable or gibberish. But he did gather from what she said that she was hit by a small blue car with a woman driver who had hair so blonde it was almost white. She slipped into unconsciousness on the trip to the hospital and died a few minutes after arriving at the hospital.

Jill Jackson—was standing on the corner of the intersection just before the accident. She saw Mrs. Jones stopped at the intersection when suddenly a speeding car "came out of nowhere" and slammed into the back of Mrs. Jones' car, backed up, and drove away. She says the car was bluish.

Jill says the driver had platinum hair and obviously was "drunk or stoned or something like that." Jill says she was standing about 20 feet from the accident and wearing her glasses.

Jill says that 5 minutes after the accident, she wrote down the license number of the blue Honda on a slip of paper. "LKE 319" She brought that slip of paper with her to trial.

Exercise #31—Version B

You are defending Sylvia Black against criminal charges of hit-and-run and vehicular homicide. The accident occurred July 1 of last year, at 7:30 p.m., at the intersection of 10th and Juniper St., Bolinga. Sylvia, a 32 year old woman, allegedly smashed her car into the rear of a car driven by a 70 year old woman, Nancy Jones, who was stopped at an intersection in the center lane, waiting to turn left onto 10th. Mrs. Jones died an hour after the accident from severe head injuries. Sylvia's car tag number is LKE 319, and her car is a blue Honda.

Your witnesses:

Jack Jackson—Jack is Jill's former husband. They were married for 5 years but divorced in September of last year. He will testify that Jill can't see 5 feet in front of her without her glasses. He says he doubts she was wearing glasses on the day of the accident because "back then she was real vain about wearing glasses in public."

Jack also says Jill is an incurable liar who will tell tales to seek attention and feel needed. (Jack is a professor of psychology at a local college). He says that when Jill came home the night of the accident she was all excited about being an eyewitness.

Sylvia—Sylvia has platinum blonde hair. Sylvia will deny she ran into Mrs. Jones or anyone else. She says she drove alone to Loganville, (100 miles east of Bolinga), on the afternoon of July 1 to meet a friend but he didn't show up. Bored, she went to a movie around 8:30. When the film was over, at about 10:30 pm, she returned to the parking lot to discover her car had been stolen. She reported this immediately to the Loganville Police but the car has not been found to this day.

Sylvia still has a half ticket stub that says "7/1 Bijou Theater." You have the Loganville Yellow Pages which lists a Bijou Theater in Loganville. You also have a copy of the Bolinga Yellow Pages which show no listing for a "Bijou Theater" in Bolinga.

Exercise #32—Version A

Your client, Sally North, is suing Bill's Mexican Restaurant and Pizzeria for negligence and strict liability, claiming she was poisoned when she dined there on the evening of October 3 of last year.

Your witnesses:

Sally—Sally is an accountant at AT & T where she has worked for 5 years. She worked at IBM for 5 years before that. On October 3, Sally and her friend and co-worker, Alice Adams, went to Bill's at about 5:30 p.m. Sally's only lunch was a slice of cheesecake that Alice brought to work. Alice ate it too. Alice never got sick.

At dinner, Sally had the enchiladas del diablo ("the devil's enchiladas") and Alice had two pieces of pepperoni pizza. Sally says she had nothing more to eat before going to bed at 11:30 p.m. At about 4:00 a.m., Sally woke up feeling very, very sick. Skipping the unpleasant details . . . she went to the Emergency Room at County Hospital at 5:00 a.m. where she was admitted and remained until the next day.

On October 5, Sally called Bill's and asked to speak to the owner or manager. The voice at the other end told her they were out but he could take a message. When she said she thought she was poisoned at Bill's on the 3rd, the voice said: "Not another one."

A few hours later, someone identifying himself as Bill called and told her he didn't want her spreading "false accusations" about his restaurant. When Sally mentioned she might sue, Bill replied, "Why do you want to get a bunch of crooked lawyers involved?" Sally replied, "Because you won't even admit that you poisoned me!" Bill then said, "Look, I'll admit it was probably us, satisfied? Now take $500 and let's drop the whole thing." Sally declined.

Dr. Gary Golf—Dr. Golf was the ER physician who admitted Sally. He will testify that she came in very sick—nausea, vomiting, diarrhea, severe abdominal pains, etc. She told him she had eaten some bad Mexican food. Golf's diagnosis was gastroenteritis probably caused by food borne salmonella. He ordered no tests to confirm that diagnosis. He bases his diagnosis on her physical symptoms and on the fact that salmonella poisoning takes about 10–24 hours to develop before symptoms appear so if Sally last ate at 5:30 p.m., then her getting sick 10 hours later pointed to salmonella.

The far more common form of food poisoning, staphylococcal, has a shorter, roughly 3 hour, incubation period. Dr. Golf says salmonella can be in any dish, regardless of its ingredients, though it is most common in meat and dairy products. He treated Sally for dehydration and released her from the hospital after 12 hours.

Exercise #32—Version B

Your client, Bill's Mexican Restaurant and Pizzeria, is being sued for negligence and strict liability. The plaintiff, Sally North, claims she was poisoned when she dined at Bill's on the evening of October 3 of last year.

Your witnesses:

Bill O'Neal—Bill owns and manages the restaurant. The restaurant has been open for 8 years and Bill says he has never poisoned a single customer. He says no one else who ate at his place on Oct. 3 complained about the food or ever suggested it was poisoned.

He says all the ingredients in the enchilada del diablo ("devil's enchilada") are fresh: tomato, cheese, onion, red chile, chorizo (Mexican sausage), and corn tortillas made fresh on the premises daily. Bill says the enchilada del diablo is very spicy and customers not accustomed to spicy food sometimes experience mild gastrointestinal disturbance after consuming it. He says all his waiters normally warn customers of this fact.

Bill denies that any of his employees talked to Sally on the phone though he admits the conversation in which he offered to settle the case.

Brad Brown—Brad is Sally's ex-boyfriend and an unemployed bartender. He lived with Sally for 4 years, including the period in question. He says that nearly every night, at about 11:00 p.m., Sally would eat a tablespoon of mayonnaise, straight from the jar, before she went to bed. She thought it was good for her complexion. He said Sally often left the mayonnaise jar open and outside of the refrigerator overnight. Sally was not very neat.

Brad was out of town on October 3, but Sally called him the next day and said she "hadn't felt right all day" before going to dinner at Bill's and "got real sick around 2:00 a.m." Brad also says that Sally lies a lot and he would not believe her on her oath. Sally broke off her relationship with Brad in January of this year and the two have not been on amicable terms ever since.

Exercise #33—Version A

You are plaintiff's counsel in a personal injury case. The plaintiff, George Hoover, is a 60 year old tax lawyer, married, with no children. The defendant is EPS, a national parcel delivery company. Two years ago, George was struck and run over by defendant's truck while he was walking across the street. George's right leg required amputation 8 inches above the knee.

The trial was bifurcated into liability and damages and the plaintiff won a liability verdict against the defendant. This is the damages phase of the trial. (Punitive damages are not at issue).

Your witnesses:

Adam Lang—Dr. Lang earned a Ph.D. in psychology from Auburn University nine years ago. He is a licensed psychologist in this state and maintains a private practice. He has testified "dozens of times" in personal injury and workers compensation cases (all for plaintiffs or claimants). He says he specializes in working with people who are having difficulty coping with life after a very serious injury or disease. He estimates that he has worked with over a hundred patients who fall into this category. He admits that many of his referrals come from lawyers who are concerned about their clients. George was referred to Dr. Lang in this case by George's lawyer.

Dr. Lang has had five sessions with George. He says that George is suffering severe depression and that this depression is proximately caused by the accident and the resulting amputation of his leg. He says that George reports that he has no appetite, has difficulty sleeping and concentrating and has had suicidal thoughts. George and his wife, Carla, reported that he had none of these problems before the accident and was in good mental health. Dr. Lang says George has not made the mental adjustment to his physical change and probably never will given his age.

Dr. Lang will admit he is being paid $500 per hour to testify in this case.

Carla Hoover—is George's wife. Carla is 59, a moderately successful writer of children books and a multi-millionaire heiress. She says that George has been severely depressed ever since the accident. He is miserable all the time, complains of pain in his phantom limb, and has no passion for anything. She says George used to be a very positive and energetic person but now he is always morose and tired. She says George has admitted to her that he has contemplated suicide several times.

Exercise #33—Version B

You are defense counsel in a personal injury case. The plaintiff, George Hoover, is a 60 year old tax lawyer, married, with no children. The defendant is EPS, a national parcel delivery company. Two years ago, George was struck and run over by defendant's truck while he was walking across the street. George's right leg required amputation 8 inches above the knee.

The trial was bifurcated into liability and damages and the plaintiff won a liability verdict against the defendant. This is the damages phase of the trial.

Your witnesses:

Chris Cross—is a physical rehabilitation therapist who worked with George for nearly 2 years. (He recently gave up his therapist job and entered the Police Academy). He will testify that George was a good patient who worked hard at his therapy. His attitude was great and he showed a wonderful sense of humor. Chris does not believe that George is suffering depression. He says that George did have initial difficulty adjusting to a prosthesis for his leg but that he is getting used to it and doing much better.

Chris has a copy of an e-mail that George sent him 3 months ago. (See copy at the end of this Exercise). When Chris thanked him for the e-mail at their next session, George just smiled.

Ashley Fairchild—is a fellow partner at George's law firm who specializes in mergers and acquisitions. He will testify that George "was a little down" for a few months after the accident but for the last year he has returned to his old, agreeable self and "seems very well adjusted" to his prosthesis and even makes jokes about it. At a firm social function last month, he saw George driving around in his Porsche, piloting his new speedboat on the lake, golfing, swimming, and being the life of the party.

Ashley has spoken to other partners in the firm (there are 9 partners in all) and they all agree that George is as good a tax lawyer as ever and as hard working as ever. Ashley would admit that he and George are not the best of friends but they have been law partners for 25 years.

FROM: George Hoover

DATE: February 10, (this year)

TO: Chris Cross

RE: Thank You

I just want to thank you for all your efforts on my behalf and wish you luck at the Police Academy. You are a very caring human being and deserve all the best.

I feel my life has turned a new corner and that I am more open than ever to what life has to offer. Maybe this accident, in the end, was a good thing for me since it woke me up.

Thanks again.

George H.

Exercise #34—Version A

You represent Herman and Phyllis Gray who are defendants in a declaratory judgment action brought by SOMESTATES INSURANCE Co. which insured a house at 129 Fairview Rd., Bolinga, owned by the Grays. On October 11 of last year, the house was destroyed by fire. SOMESTATES claims it is not obligated to pay the Grays $85,000 under their policy because the Grays intentionally had their nephew set the fire. Your witness is Herman.

Herman is 74 and Phyllis is 72. They have been married 53 years. Herman is a retired plumber. Phyllis is a retired nurse. Their combined annual retirement income is about $12,000 a year. They own the house they live in outright. Their only significant debt is $25,000 principal on the mortgage for the rental house at 129 Fairview. (Monthly mortg/tax/ins pymt = $375). They have about $300 in the bank and no savings.

Tenants moved out of the Fairview house in June of last year and it had not been re-rented at the time of the fire. It had rented for $500 per month. Herman says the house needed a little work before he tried to rent it again but he had not been well and kept putting it off. He says he called his nephew, Paul, who lives nearby, several times in early October because he wanted him to help clean up the house on Fairview. He says his nephew, Paul, is "a bum" and he rarely sees him. Herman and Phyllis had no children of their own but had provided a temporary foster home for children for over 20 years. Two years ago they had to quit the foster care program because of their advanced age. They had earned roughly $9,000 a year from the State for taking care of foster children.

Herman has a copy of a letter from Morgan Bank, dated October 9 of last year. (See copy at end of Exercise).

You also have a certified copy of an acquittal by jury verdict of Paul Gray, dated February 15 of this year, on the charge of arson in connection with the fire at 129 Fairview Rd. Paul left the state shortly after that trial for parts unknown. Paul is 28 years old and has red hair and brown eyes.

From Paul Gray's direct examination testimony at his criminal trial:

"I went by the Fairview house on the night of October 11th to look at it because my uncle wanted me to help fix it. When I got there, there were these three bums who must have broken in, sitting in the living room. The power was off and they had a little fire, sterno I guess. I could see them from the window. I yelled at them but they began to come after me and one was carrying a gun. I ran back to my car and left. A few minutes later, I saw this pickup chasing me and I thought it was the bums or whoever, coming after me. I didn't call the police because I was scared so I just kept driving all around that night. The next morning my uncle called and told me the house had burned down. It must have been the bums."

Exercise #34—Version B

You represent SOMESTATES INSURANCE Co. which has brought a declaratory judgment action against Herman and Phyllis Gray, insureds on a homeowner's policy issued by SOMESTATES to cover a two bedroom house at 129 Fairview Rd., Bolinga. The house was destroyed by fire on October 11 of last year, at approximately 11:00 p.m. The insurance company claims it is not obligated to pay the Grays $85,000 under their policy because the Grays intentionally had their nephew set the fire. Your witnesses:

Alex Young lives at 126 Fairview Rd. He will testify he stepped outside to get some air at around 11:00 p.m. and saw flames flickering in the living room of the empty house at 129. He saw someone pulling away from the curb about 70 feet down the road in a Honda Civic. It pulled away like someone was in a hurry. Alex jumped into his pickup truck and gave chase. The driver of the Civic (a male in his late twenties, red hair and brown eyes) spotted him and tried to shake him off. Alex had to give up the chase when his fuel light started blinking. He did get the license number, "BTI 991". (You have a properly certified copy of State records which shows a 1998 Civic, license number BTI 991, issued to Paul Gray of Bolinga).

Fred Wilson is Chief Arson Investigator for the County Fire Marshall. He has a copy of the County Fire Marshall's report on this fire. The report says the fire started in an old mattress in the living room and was accelerated by gasoline liberally applied to the wooden floors of the living room. The report concludes the fire was the result of arson. The author of the report was Jack Jones, but Jones left the Office last year and has been unavailable for deposition or trial. Fred has reviewed this report and thinks it is valid.

You have a certified copy of the conviction of Herman Gray 25 years ago, for arson in a fire that destroyed a rental house he owned. He was given a 3 year suspended sentence and placed on probation. Another rental home owned by Mr. Gray burned to the ground 15 years ago, but no claim of arson was made and the insurance company paid the Grays $55,000. The Grays owned one other rental property for a few years about 20 years ago but never made a fire claim on it.

You also have a certified copy of a NOTICE OF VIOLATION issued by the County Building Dept., dated July 1 of last year. (See copy at the end of this Exercise).

You also have a copy of a written estimate by Sparky Electric Co., addressed to Herman Gray. (See copy at end of Exercise). (In his deposition, Herman admitted he received this estimate in late September of last year).

MORGAN BANK

"Where We Treat Your Money Like Its Ours."

Herman and Phyllis Gray
714 Windsor Dr.
Bolinga

October 9, (last year)

Dear Mr. and Mrs. Gray:

Thank you for your application for a home improvement loan on your rental property at 129 Fairview, Bolinga. We are happy to approve your application for a loan of $15,000 to be secured by a first mortgage on your residence at 714 Windsor Dr., Bolinga. This will be a 5 year loan with monthly payments of $350.

Please call me at your earliest convenience to discuss the next step in the process.

Thank you for thinking of MORGAN BANK.

Sincerely,

Jay Peevey

Jay Peevey
Loan Officer
Morgan Bank, Bolinga

CITY OF BOLINGA

"The City of Yesterday Today!"

NOTICE OF CODE VIOLATION

129 Fairview Road
Bolinga

The house at 129 Fairview Rd. was inspected on June 30, and was found to be in violation of the following sections of the Bolinga Electric Code: 452, 453, 467, 482, 512, 515, 516, 518, 528, 532, 535, 536, 537, 538, 544, 548, 555, 556, 557, 559, 566, 577, 588, 592, 593, 606, 608, 611, 612, 614, 616, 617, 668, 693, 702 and 814.

ORDERED: The house at 129 Fairview Rd. **MAY NOT BE OCCUPIED** until these violations are corrected and approved by the Bolinga Building Inspection Department.

Have a Nice Day.

July 1, (last year)

Inspector: *Lynda Houser*

Lynda A. Houser

I, Lynda Houser, affirm that I personally served a copy of this Notice of Code Violation on Herman Gray on July 2, (last year) at 2:30 p.m., at his home at 714 Windsor Dr., Bolinga.

Lynda Houser

SPARKY ELECTRIC

"We'll Keep You Turned On."

Herman and Phyllis Gray
714 Windsor Dr.
Bolinga

September 25, (last year)

Dear Mr. and Mrs. Gray:

I have reviewed the Notice of Violation of Electrical Code and done an inspection of your house at 129 Fairview, Bolinga. We can bring the house entirely up to Code for $14,000. The job would take about one week.

Please let me know if you wish to go forward on this project and we can get you on our schedule.

Sincerely,

Bob

Bob Barker
Sparky Electric

Exercise #35—Version A

You are the prosecutor. The defendant, Gene L. Toon, has been indicted for the murder of Stella Herz, 23, a part-time actress and telephone receptionist at Massive Enterprises. Gene, 49, is vice-president of Massive Enterprises and married to the Dooddle Cookie heiress, Gloria Toon. The prosecution alleges that Gene had been carrying on an affair with Stella for a few months. Gene caught wind of a plan by Stella and her friend, Ross, to extort money from him so he strangled her in her bed on the evening of May 8 of last year.

Your witnesses:

Detective Kirk Menace will testify he made a thorough search of the murder scene. One item that he recovered from the bedroom of Stella's apartment is a monogrammed handkerchief with the initials "GLT". He also found the victim's address book which includes the entry: "Gene T. 857–4111." Menace dialed that number and a person answered: "Mr. Toon's office." He was connected to Mr. Toon and arranged a meeting at the defendant's home. When he questioned the defendant at his home the next day, the defendant seemed very nervous and hesitant and said he had never heard of Stella. He then refused to say anything more without his lawyer present.

Menace also will testify that a few days after the murder he received a phone call from someone who identified himself as Ross Smith who told him he had been Stella's agent and friend. Ross said he had helped Stella squeeze money out of this rich guy she was dating named Gene Toon. Stella had given Ross some of Gene's more kinky letters and on May 2, Ross sent Gene a copy of the letters and a demand for $25,000 for the originals. Ross and Det. Menace arranged to meet that evening but Ross did not show and has not been seen or heard from since.

Rhonda Jones was Stella's best friend. She says Stella talked about this rich guy she was seeing though Rhonda never actually did get to meet him. Stella said the guy was married to some heiress so they had to be very discreet. Rhonda says Stella seemed to have a lot more money the last few months and had lots of new clothes. Stella hadn't had a paying acting part in over a year.

The night of the murder, at about 8:00 pm., Stella and Rhonda were talking on the phone when Stella suddenly said, "I've got to go. My rich boy is here. He'll probably want to stay in all night as usual." That's the last Rhonda ever heard from Stella.

Exercise #35—Version B

Your client Gene L. Toon, has been indicted for the murder of Stella Herz, 23, a part-time actress and telephone receptionist at Massive Enterprises. Gene, 49, is vice-president of Massive Enterprises and married to the Dooddle Cookie heiress, Gloria Toon. The prosecution alleges that Gene had been carrying on with Stella for a few months when Gene caught wind of a plan by Stella and her friend, Ross, to extort money from him so he strangled Stella in her bed on the evening of May 8 of last year.

Your witnesses:

Gene—Gene says he only knew Stella as one of many telephone receptionists at Massive Enterprises. Massive has over 300 employees at corporate headquarters where Gene and Stella worked.

Gene says he might have talked to her briefly a few times "around the water cooler" but has never dated her or been to her apartment. Gene says he has been faithful to his wife for the entire 28 years of their marriage. They have six children. He says he doesn't own any monographed handkerchiefs. Gene says he doesn't know anyone named Ross and never received an extortion demand from Ross or anyone else. He says that on the evening of the murder, he worked late at the office (no witnesses) and went home at about 11:00 pm.

Maggie Stewart—Maggie was Stella's friend and next door neighbor the past 6 years. She says she never heard Stella mention Gene by name or saw him around Stella's place. She says Stella often "made up rich or famous boyfriends" to impress others.

Maggie knows Ross and thinks he is the one who probably murdered Stella. She says Ross is known in the neighborhood as a small time bookmaker and scam artist and she would not trust Ross. Stella was friendly to Ross only because he sold her cocaine at a discount. Based on her observations of Ross, Maggie believes Ross had a crush on Stella but she wasn't interested in him romantically and that often upset him. About a week before she was murdered, Maggie saw Ross slap Stella while they were having an argument.

RULES OF EVIDENCE FOR UNITED STATES COURTS AND MAGISTRATES

Pub.L. 93–595, § 1, January 2, 1975, 88 Stat. 1926
Amendments received to November 1, 2004

ARTICLE I.   GENERAL PROVISIONS

ARTICLE II.   JUDICIAL NOTICE

ARTICLE III.   PRESUMPTIONS IN CIVIL ACTIONS AND PROCEEDINGS

ARTICLE IV.   RELEVANCY AND ITS LIMITS

ARTICLE V.   PRIVILEGES

ARTICLE VI.   WITNESSES

ARTICLE I. GENERAL PROVISIONS

HISTORICAL NOTES

Rule 101. Scope

These rules govern proceedings in the courts of the United States and before the United States bankruptcy judges and United States magistrate judges, to the extent and with the exceptions stated in rule 1101.

Rule 102. Purpose and Construction

These rules shall be construed to secure fairness in administration, elimination of unjustifiable expense and delay, and promotion of growth and development of the law of evidence to the end that the truth may be ascertained and proceedings justly determined.

Rule 103. Rulings on Evidence

(a) **Effect of Erroneous Ruling.**—Error may not be predicated upon a ruling which admits or excludes evidence unless a substantial right of the party is affected, and

(1) **Objection.**—In case the ruling is one admitting evidence, a timely objection or motion to strike appears of record, stating the specific ground of objection, if the specific ground was not apparent from the context; or

(2) **Offer of Proof.**—In case the ruling is one excluding evidence, the substance of the evidence was made known to the court by offer or was apparent from the context within which questions were asked.

Once the court makes a definitive ruling on the record admitting or excluding evidence, either at or before trial, a party need not renew an objection or offer of proof to preserve a claim of error for appeal.

(b) **Record of Offer and Ruling.**—The court may add any other or further statement which shows the character of the evidence, the form in which it was offered, the objection made, and the ruling thereon. It may direct the making of an offer in question and answer form.

(c) **Hearing of Jury.**—In jury cases, proceedings shall be conducted, to the extent practicable, so as to prevent inadmissible evidence from being suggested to the jury by any means, such as making statements or offers of proof or asking questions in the hearing of the jury.

(d) **Plain Error.**—Nothing in this rule precludes taking notice of plain errors affecting substantial rights although they were not brought to the attention of the court.

ADVISORY COMMITTEE NOTES

1972 Proposed Rules

Note to Subdivision (a). Subdivision (a) states the law as generally accepted today. Rulings on evidence cannot be assigned as error unless (1) a substantial right is affected, and (2) the nature of the error was called to the attention of the judge, so as to alert him to the proper course of action and enable opposing counsel to take proper corrective measures. The objection and the offer of proof are the techniques for accomplishing these objectives. For similar provisions see Uniform Rules 4 and 5; California Evidence Code §§ 353 and 354; Kansas Code of Civil Procedure §§ 60–404 and 60–405. The rule does not purport to change the law with respect to harmless error. See 28 USC § 2111, F.R.Civ.P. 61, F.R.Crim.P. 52, and decisions construing them. The status of constitutional error as harmless or not is treated in Chapman v. California, 386 U.S. 18, 87 S.Ct. 824, 17 L.Ed.2d 705 (1967), reh. denied id. 987, 87 S.Ct. 1283, 18 L.Ed.2d 241.

Note to Subdivision (b). The first sentence is the third sentence of Rule 43(c) of the Federal Rules of Civil Procedure virtually verbatim. Its purpose is to reproduce for an appellate court, insofar as possible, a true reflection of what occurred in the trial court. The second sentence is in part derived from the final sentence of Rule 43(c). It is designed to resolve doubts as to what testimony the witness would have in fact given, and, in nonjury cases, to provide the appellate court with material for a possible final disposition of the case in the event of reversal of a ruling which excluded evidence. See 5 Moore's Federal Practice § 43.11 (2d ed. 1968). Application is made discretionary in view of the practical impossibility of formulating a satisfactory rule in mandatory terms.

Note to Subdivision (c). This subdivision proceeds on the supposition that a ruling which excludes evidence in a jury case is likely to be a pointless procedure if the excluded evidence nevertheless comes to the attention of the jury. *Bruton v. United States*, 389 U.S. 818, 88 S.Ct. 126, 19 L.Ed.2d 70 (1968). Rule 43(c) of the Federal Rules of Civil Procedure provides: "The court may require the offer to be made out of the hearing of the jury." *In re McConnell*, 370 U.S. 230, 82 S.Ct. 1288, 8 L.Ed.2d 434 (1962), left some doubt whether questions on which an offer is based must first be asked in the presence of the jury. The subdivision answers in the negative. The judge can foreclose a particular line of testimony and counsel can protect his record without a series of questions before the jury, designed at best to waste time and at worst "to waft into the jury box" the very matter sought to be excluded.

Note to Subdivision (d). This wording of the plain error principle is from Rule 52(b) of the Federal Rules of Criminal Procedure. While judicial unwillingness to be constructed by mechanical breakdowns of the adversary system has been more pronounced in criminal cases, there is no scarcity of decisions to the same effect in civil cases. In general, see Campbell, Extent to Which Courts of Review Will Consider Questions Not Properly Raised and Preserved, 7 Wis.L.Rev. 91, 160 (1932); Vestal, Sua Sponte Consideration in Appellate Review, 27 Fordham L.Rev. 477 (1958–59); 64 Harv.L.Rev. 652 (1951). In the nature of things the application of the plain error rule will be more likely with respect to the admission of evidence than to exclusion, since failure to comply with normal requirements of offers of proof is likely to produce a record which simply does not disclose the error.

2000 Amendment

The amendment applies to all rulings on evidence whether they occur at or before trial, including so-called "*in limine*" rulings. One of the most difficult questions arising from *in limine* and other evidentiary rulings is whether a losing party must renew an objection or offer of proof when the evidence is or would be offered at trial, in order to preserve a claim of error on appeal. Courts have taken differing approaches to this question. Some courts have held that a renewal at the time the evidence is to be offered at trial is always required. *See, e.g., Collins v. Wayne Corp.*, 621 F.2d 777 (5th Cir. 1980). Some courts have taken a more flexible approach, holding that renewal is not required if the issue decided is one that (1) was fairly presented to the trial court for an initial ruling, (2) may be decided as a final matter before the evidence is actually offered, and (3) was ruled on definitively by the trial judge, *See, e.g., Rosenfeld v. Basquiat*, 78 F.3d 84 (2d Cir. 1996) (admissibility of former testimony under the Dead Man's Statute; renewal not required). Other courts have distinguished between objections to evidence, which must be renewed when evidence is offered, and offers of proof, which need not be renewed after a definitive determination is made that the evidence is inadmissible. *See, e.g., Fusco v. General Motors Corp.*, 11 F.3d 259 (1st Cir. 1993). Another court, aware of this Committee's proposed amendment, has adopted its approach. *Wilson v. Williams*, 182 F. 3d 562 (7th Cir.1999) (en banc). Differing views on this question create uncertainty for litigants and unnecessary work for the appellate courts.

The amendment provides that a claim of error with respect to a definitive ruling is preserved for review when the party has otherwise satisfied the objection or offer of proof requirements of Rule 103(a). When the ruling is definitive, a renewed objection or offer of proof at the time the evidence is to be offered is more a formalism than a necessity. *See* Fed.R.Civ.P. 46 (formal exceptions unnecessary); Fed.R.Cr.P. 51 (same); *United States v. Mejia–Alarcon*, 995 F.2d 982, 986 (10th Cir. 1993) ("Requiring a party to renew an objection when the district court has issued a definitive ruling on a matter that can be fairly decided before trial would be in the nature of a formal exception and therefore unnecessary."). On the other hand, when the trial court appears to have reserved its ruling or to have indicated that the ruling is provisional, it makes sense to require the party to bring the issue to the court's attention subsequently. *See, e.g., United States v. Vest*, 116 F.3d 1179, 1188 (7th Cir. 1997) (where the trial court ruled *in limine* that testimony from defense witnesses could not be admitted, but allowed the defendant to seek leave at trial to call the witnesses should their testimony turn out to be relevant, the defendant's failure to seek such leave at trial meant that it was "too late to reopen the issue now on appeal"); *United States v. Valenti*, 60 F.3d 941 (2d Cir. 1995) (failure to proffer evidence at trial waives any claim of error where the trial judge had stated that he would reserve judgment on the *in limine* motion until he had heard the trial evidence).

The amendment imposes the obligation on counsel to clarify whether an *in limine* or other evidentiary ruling is definitive when there is doubt on that point. *See, e.g., Walden v. Georgia–Pacific Corp.*, 126 F.3d 506, 520 (3d Cir. 1997) (although "the district court told plaintiffs' counsel not to reargue every ruling, it did not countermand its clear opening statement that all of its rulings were tentative, and counsel never requested clarification, as he might have done.").

Even where the court's ruling is definitive, nothing in the amendment prohibits the court from revisiting its decision when the evidence is to be offered. If the court changes its initial ruling, or if the opposing party violates the terms of the initial ruling, objection must be made when the evidence is offered to preserve the claim of error for appeal. The error, if any, in such a situation occurs only when the evidence is offered and admitted. *United States Aviation Underwriters, Inc. v. Olympia Wings, Inc.*, 896 F.2d 949, 956 (5th Cir. 1990) ("objection is required to preserve error when an opponent, or the court itself, violates a motion *in limine* that was granted"); *United States v. Roenigk*, 810 F.2d 809 (8th Cir. 1987) (claim of error was not preserved where the defendant failed to object at trial to secure the benefit of a favorable advance ruling).

A definitive advance ruling is reviewed in light of the facts and circumstances before the trial court at the time of the ruling. If the relevant facts and circumstances change materially after the advance ruling has been made, those facts and circumstances cannot be relied upon on appeal unless they have been brought to the attention of the trial court by way of a renewed, and timely, objection, offer of proof, or motion to strike. *See Old Chief v. United States*, 519 U.S. 172, 182, n.6 (1997) ("It is important that a reviewing court evaluate the trial court's decision from its perspective when it had to rule and not indulge in review by hindsight."). Similarly, if the court decides in an advance ruling that proffered evidence is admissible subject to the eventual introduction by the proponent of a foundation for the evidence, and that foundation is never provided, the opponent cannot claim error based on the failure to establish the foundation unless the opponent calls that failure to the court's attention by a timely motion to strike or other suitable motion. *See Huddleston v. United States*, 485 U.S. 681, 690, n.7 (1988) ("It is, of course, not the responsibility of the judge *sua sponte* to ensure that the foundation evidence is offered; the objector must move to strike the evidence if at the close of the trial the offeror has failed to satisfy the condition.").

Nothing in the amendment is intended to affect the provisions of Fed.R.Civ.P. 72(a) or 28 U.S.C. § 636(b)(1) pertaining to nondispositive pretrial rulings by magistrate judges in proceedings that are not before a magistrate judge by consent of the parties. Fed.R.Civ.P. 72(a) provides that a party who fails to file a written objection to a magistrate judge's nondispositive order within ten days of receiving a copy "may not thereafter assign as error a defect" in the order. 28 U.S.C. § 636(b)(1) provides that any party "may serve and file written objections to such proposed findings and recommendations as provided by rules of court" within ten days of receiving a copy of the order. Several courts have held that a party must comply with this statutory provision in order to preserve a claim of error. *See, e.g., Wells v. Shriners Hospital*, 109 F.3d 198, 200 (4th Cir. 1997)("[i]n this circuit, as in others, a party 'may' file objections within ten days or he may not, as he chooses, but he 'shall' do so if he wishes further consideration."). When Fed.R.Civ.P. 72(a) or 28 U.S.C. § 636(b)(1) is operative, its requirement must be satisfied in order for a party to preserve a claim of error on appeal, even where Evidence Rule 103(a) would not require a subsequent objection or offer of proof.

Nothing in the amendment is intended to affect the rule set forth in *Luce v. United States*, 469 U.S. 38 (1984), and its progeny. The amendment provides that an objection or offer of proof need not be renewed to preserve a claim of error with respect to a definitive pretrial ruling. *Luce* answers affirmatively a separate question: whether a criminal defendant must testify at trial in order to preserve a claim of error predicated upon a trial court's decision to admit the defendant's prior convictions for impeachment. The *Luce* principle has been extended by many lower courts to other situations. *See United States v. DiMatteo*, 759 F.2d 831 (11th Cir. 1985) (applying *Luce* where the defendant's witness would be impeached with evidence offered under Rule 608). *See also United States v. Goldman*, 41 F.3d 785, 788 (1st Cir. 1994) ("Although *Luce* involved impeachment by conviction under Rule 609, the reasons given by the Supreme Court for requiring the defendant to testify apply with full force to the kind of Rule 403 and 404 objections that are advanced by Goldman in this case."); *Palmieri v. DeFaria*, 88 F.3d 136 (2d Cir. 1996) (where the plaintiff decided to take an adverse judgment rather than challenge an advance ruling by putting on evidence at trial, the *in limine* ruling would not be reviewed on appeal); *United States v. Ortiz*, 857 F.2d 900 (2d Cir. 1988) (where uncharged misconduct is ruled admissible if the defendant pursues a certain defense, the defendant must actually pursue that defense at trial in order to preserve a claim of error on appeal); *United States v. Bond*, 87 F.3d 695 (5th Cir. 1996) (where the trial court rules *in limine* that the defendant would waive his fifth amendment privilege were he to testify, the defendant must take the stand and testify in order to challenge that ruling on appeal).

The amendment does not purport to answer whether a party who objects to evidence that the court finds admissible in a definitive ruling, and who then offers the evidence to "remove the sting" of its anticipated prejudicial effect, thereby waives the right to appeal the trial court's ruling. *See, e.g., United States v. Fisher*, 106 F.3d 622 (5th Cir. 1997) (where the trial judge ruled *in limine* that the government could use a prior conviction to impeach the defendant if he testified, the defendant did not waive his right to appeal by introducing the conviction on direct examination); *Judd v. Rodman*, 105 F.3d 1339 (11th Cir. 1997) (an objection made *in limine* is sufficient to preserve a claim of error when the movant, as a matter of trial strategy, presents the objectionable evidence herself on direct examination to minimize its prejudicial effect); *Gill v. Thomas*, 83 F.3d 537, 540 (1st Cir. 1996) ("by offering the misdemeanor evidence himself, Gill waived his opportunity to object and thus did not preserve the issue for appeal"); *United States v. Williams*, 939 F.2d 721 (9th Cir. 1991) (objection to impeachment evidence was waived where the defendant was impeached on direct examination).

Rule 104. Preliminary Questions

(a) Questions of admissibility generally. Preliminary questions concerning the qualification of a person to be a witness, the existence of a privilege, or the admissibility of evidence shall be determined by the court, subject to the provisions of subdivision (b). In making its determination it is not bound by the rules of evidence except those with respect to privileges.

(b) Relevancy conditioned on fact. When the relevancy of evidence depends upon the fulfillment of a condition of fact, the court shall admit it upon, or subject to, the introduction of evidence sufficient to support a finding of the fulfillment of the condition.

(c) Hearing of jury. Hearings on the admissibility of confessions shall in all cases be conducted out of the hearing of the jury. Hearings on other preliminary matters shall be so conducted when the interests of justice require, or when an accused is a witness and so requests.

(d) Testimony by accused. The accused does not, by testifying upon a preliminary matter, become subject to cross-examination as to other issues in the case.

(e) Weight and credibility. This rule does not limit the right of a party to introduce before the jury evidence relevant to weight or credibility.

ADVISORY COMMITTEE NOTES
1972 Proposed Rule

Note to Subdivision (a). The applicability of a particular rule of evidence often depends upon the existence of a condition. Is the alleged expert a qualified physician? Is a witness whose former testimony is offered unavailable? Was a stranger present during a conversation between attorney and client? In each instance the admissibility of evidence will turn upon the answer to the question of the existence of the condition. Accepted practice, incorporated in the rule, places on the judge the responsibility for these determinations. McCormick § 53; Morgan, Basic Problems of Evidence 45–50 (1962).

To the extent that these inquiries are factual, the judge acts as a trier of fact. Often, however, rulings on evidence call for an evaluation in terms of a legally set standard. Thus when a hearsay statement is offered as a declaration against interest, a decision must be made whether it possesses the required against-interest characteristics. These decisions, too, are made by the judge.

In view of these considerations, this subdivision refers to preliminary requirements generally by the broad term "questions," without attempt at specification.

This subdivision is of general application. It must, however, be read as subject to the special provisions for "conditional relevancy" in subdivision (b) and those for confessions in subdivision (d).

If the question is factual in nature, the judge will of necessity receive evidence pro and con on the issue. The rule provides that the rules of evidence in general do not apply to this process. McCormick § 53, p. 123, n. 8, points out that the authorities are "scattered and inconclusive," and observes:

"Should the exclusionary law of evidence, 'the child of the jury system' in Thayer's phrase, be applied to this hearing before the judge? Sound sense backs the view that it should not, and that the judge should be empowered to hear any relevant evidence, such as affidavits or other reliable hearsay."

This view is reinforced by practical necessity in certain situations. An item, offered and objected to, may itself be considered in ruling on admissibility, though not yet admitted in evidence. Thus, the content of an asserted declaration against interest must be considered in ruling whether it is against interest. Again, common practice calls for considering the testimony of a witness, particularly a child, in determining competency. Another example is the requirement of Rule 602 dealing with personal knowledge. In the case of hearsay, it is enough, if the declarant "so far as appears [has] had an opportunity to observe the fact declared." McCormick, § 10, p. 19.

If concern is felt over the use of affidavits by the judge in preliminary hearings on admissibility, attention is directed to the many important judicial determinations made on the basis of affidavits. Rule 47 of the Federal Rules of Criminal Procedure provides:

"An application to the court for an order shall be by motion. * * * It may be supported by affidavit."

The Rules of Civil Procedure are more detailed. Rule 43(e), dealing with motions generally, provides:

"When a motion is based on facts not appearing of record the court may hear the matter on affidavits presented by the respective parties, but the court may direct that the matter be heard wholly or partly on oral testimony or depositions." Rule 4(g) provides for proof of service by affidavit. Rule 56 provides in detail for the entry of summary judgment based on affidavits. Affidavits may supply the foundation for temporary restraining orders under Rule 65(b).

The study made for the California Law Revision Commission recommended an amendment to Uniform Rule 2 as follows:

"In the determination of the issue aforesaid [preliminary determination], exclusionary rules shall not apply, subject, however, to Rule 45 and any valid claim of privilege." Tentative Recommendation and a Study Relating to the Uniform Rules of Evidence (Article VIII, Hearsay), Cal.Law Revision Comm'n, Rep., Rec. & Studies, 470 (1962). The proposal was not adopted in the California Evidence Code. The Uniform Rules are likewise silent on the subject. However, New Jersey Evidence Rule 8(1), dealing with preliminary inquiry by the judge, provides:

"In his determination the rules of evidence shall not apply except for Rule 4 [exclusion on grounds of confusion, etc.] or a valid claim of privilege."

Note to Subdivision (b). In some situations, the relevancy of an item of evidence, in the large sense, depends upon the existence of a particular preliminary fact. Thus when a spoken statement is relied upon to prove notice to X, it is without probative value unless X heard it. Or if a letter purporting to be from Y is relied upon to establish an admission by him, it has no probative value unless Y wrote or authorized it. Relevance in this sense has been labelled "conditional relevancy." Morgan, Basic Problems of Evidence 45–46 (1962). Problems arising in connection with it are to be distinguished from problems of logical relevancy, e.g., evidence in a murder case that accused on the day before purchased a weapon of the kind used in the killing, treated in Rule 401.

If preliminary questions of conditional relevancy were determined solely by the judge, as provided in subdivision (a), the functioning of the jury as a trier of fact would be greatly restricted and in some cases virtually destroyed. These are appropriate questions for juries. Accepted treatment, as provided in the rule, is consistent with that given fact questions generally. The judge makes a preliminary determination whether the foundation evidence is sufficient to support a finding of fulfillment of the condition. If so, the item is admitted. If after all the evidence on the issue is in, pro and con, the jury could reasonably conclude that fulfillment of the condition is not established, the issue is for them. If the evidence is not such as to allow a finding, the judge withdraws the matter from their consideration. Morgan, *supra;* California Evidence Code § 403; New Jersey Rule 8(2). See also Uniform Rules 19 and 67.

The order of proof here, as generally, is subject to the control of the judge.

Note to Subdivision (c). Preliminary hearings on the admissibility of confessions must be conducted outside the hearing of the jury. See *Jackson v. Denno*, 378 U.S. 368, 84 S.Ct. 1774, 12 L.Ed.2d 908 (1964). Otherwise, detailed treatment of when preliminary matters should be heard outside the hearing of the jury is not feasible. The procedure is time consuming. Not infrequently the same evidence which is relevant to the issue of establishment of fulfillment of a condition precedent to admissibility is also relevant to weight or credibility, and time is saved by taking foundation proof in the presence of the jury. Much evidence on preliminary questions, though not relevant to jury issues, may be heard by the jury with no adverse effect. A great deal must be left to the discretion of the judge who will act as the interests of justice require.

Note to Subdivision (d). The limitation upon cross-examination is designed to encourage participation by the accused in the determination of preliminary matters. He may testify concerning them without exposing himself to cross-examination generally. The provision is necessary because of the breadth of cross-examination under Rule 611(b).

The rule does not address itself to questions of the subsequent use of testimony given by an accused at a hearing on a preliminary matter. See *Walder v. United States*, 347 U.S. 62 (1954); *Simmons v. United States*, 390 U.S. 377 (1968); *Harris v. New York*, 401 U.S. 222 (1971).

Note to Subdivision (e). For similar provisions see Uniform Rule 8; California Evidence Code § 406; Kansas Code of Civil Procedure § 60–408; New Jersey Evidence Rule 8(1).

1974 Enactment

Rule 104(c) as submitted to the Congress provided that hearings on the admissibility of confessions shall be conducted outside the presence of the jury and hearings on all other preliminary matters should be so conducted when the interests of justice require. The Committee amended the Rule to provide that where an accused is a witness as to a preliminary matter, he has the right, upon his request, to be heard outside the jury's presence. Although recognizing that in some cases duplication of evidence would occur and that the procedure could be subject to abuse, the Committee believed that a proper regard for the right of an accused not to testify generally in the case dictates that he be given an option to testify out of the presence of the jury on preliminary matters.

The Committee construes the second sentence of subdivision (c) as applying to civil actions and proceedings as well as to criminal cases, and on this assumption has left the sentence unamended. House Report No. 93–650.

Under rule 104(c) the hearing on a preliminary matter may at times be conducted in front of the jury. Should an accused testify in such a hearing, waiving his privilege against self-incrimination as to the preliminary issue, rule 104(d) provides that he will not generally be subject to cross-examination as to any other issue. This rule is not, however, intended to immunize the accused from cross-examination where, in testifying about a preliminary issue, he injects other issues into the hearing. If he could not be cross-examined about any issues gratuitously raised by him beyond the scope of the preliminary matters, injustice might result. Accordingly, in order to prevent any such unjust result, the committee intends the rule to be construed to provide that the accused may subject himself to cross-examination as to issues raised by his own testimony upon a preliminary matter before a jury. Senate Report No. 93–1277.

Rule 105.   Limited Admissibility

When evidence which is admissible as to one party or for one purpose but not admissible as to another party or for another purpose is admitted, the court, upon request, shall restrict the evidence to its proper scope and instruct the jury accordingly.

ADVISORY COMMITTEE NOTES

1972 Proposed Rules

A close relationship exists between this rule and Rule 403 which requires exclusion when "probative value is substantially outweighed by the danger of unfair prejudice, confusion of the issues, or misleading the jury." The present rule recognizes the practice of admitting evidence for a limited purpose and instructing the jury accordingly. The availability and effectiveness of this practice must be taken into consideration in reaching a decision whether to exclude for unfair prejudice under Rule 403. In *Bruton v. United States*, 389 U.S. 818, 88 S.Ct. 126, 19 L.Ed.2d 70 (1968), the Court ruled that a limiting instruction did not effectively protect the accused against the prejudicial effect of admitting in evidence the confession of a codefendant which implicated him. The decision does not, however, bar the use of limited admissibility with an instruction where the risk of prejudice is less serious.

Similar provisions are found in Uniform Rule 6; California Evidence Code § 355; Kansas Code of Civil Procedure § 60–406; New Jersey Evidence Rule 6. The wording of the present rule differs, however, in repelling any implication that limiting or curative instructions are sufficient in all situations.

1974 Enactment

Rule 106 as submitted by the Supreme Court (now Rule 105 in the bill) dealt with the subject of evidence which is admissible as to one party or for one purpose but is not admissible against another party or for another purpose. The Committee adopted this Rule without change on the understanding that it does not affect the authority of a court to order a severance in a multi-defendant case. House Report No. 93–650.

Rule 106.   Remainder of or Related Writings or Recorded Statements

When a writing or recorded statement or part thereof is introduced by a party, an adverse party may require the introduction at that time of any other part or any other writing or recorded statement which ought in fairness to be considered contemporaneously with it.

ADVISORY COMMITTEE NOTES

1972 Proposed Rules

The rule is an expression of the rule of completeness. McCormick § 56. It is manifested as to depositions in Rule 32(a)(4) of the Federal Rules of Civil Procedure, of which the proposed rule is substantially a restatement.

The rule is based on two considerations. The first is the misleading impression created by taking matters out of context. The second is the inadequacy of repair work when delayed to a point later in the trial. See McCormick § 56; California Evidence Code § 356. The rule does not in any way circumscribe the right of the adversary to develop the matter on cross-examination or as part of his own case.

For practical reasons, the rule is limited to writings and recorded statements and does not apply to conversations.

ARTICLE II. JUDICIAL NOTICE

Rule 201. Judicial Notice of Adjudicative Facts

(a) Scope of rule. This rule governs only judicial notice of adjudicative facts.

(b) Kinds of facts. A judicially noticed fact must be one not subject to reasonable dispute in that it is either (1) generally known within the territorial jurisdiction of the trial court or (2) capable of accurate and ready determination by resort to sources whose accuracy cannot reasonably be questioned.

(c) When discretionary. A court may take judicial notice, whether requested or not.

(d) When mandatory. A court shall take judicial notice if requested by a party and supplied with the necessary information.

(e) Opportunity to be heard. A party is entitled upon timely request to an opportunity to be heard as to the propriety of taking judicial notice and the tenor of the matter noticed. In the absence of prior notification, the request may be made after judicial notice has been taken.

(f) Time of taking notice. Judicial notice may be taken at any stage of the proceeding.

(g) Instructing jury. In a civil action or proceeding, the court shall instruct the jury to accept as conclusive any fact judicially noticed. In a criminal case, the court shall instruct the jury that it may, but is not required to, accept as conclusive any fact judicially noticed.

ADVISORY COMMITTEE NOTES

1972 Proposed Rules

Note to Subdivision (a). This is the only evidence rule on the subject of judicial notice. It deals only with judicial notice of "adjudicative" facts. No rule deals with judicial notice of "legislative" facts. Judicial notice of matters of foreign law is treated in Rule 44.1 of the Federal Rules of Civil Procedure and Rule 26.1 of the Federal Rules of Criminal Procedure.

The omission of any treatment of legislative facts results from fundamental differences between adjudicative facts and legislative facts. Adjudicative facts are simply the facts of the particular case. Legislative facts, on the other hand, are those which have relevance to legal reasoning and the lawmaking process, whether in the formulation of a legal principle or ruling by a judge or court or in the enactment of a legislative body. The terminology was coined by Professor Kenneth Davis in his article An Approach to Problems of Evidence in the Administrative Process, 55 Harv.L.Rev. 364, 404–407 (1942). The following discussion draws extensively upon his writings. In addition, see the same author's Judicial Notice, 55 Colum.L.Rev. 945 (1955); Administrative Law Treatise, ch. 15 (1958); A System of Judicial Notice Based on Fairness and Convenience, in Perspectives of Law 69 (1964).

The usual method of establishing adjudicative facts is through the introduction of evidence, ordinarily consisting of the testimony of witnesses. If particular facts are outside the area of reasonable controversy, this process is dispensed with as unnecessary. A high degree of indisputability is the essential prerequisite.

Legislative facts are quite different. As Professor Davis says:

"My opinion is that judge-made law would stop growing if judges, in thinking about questions of law and policy, were forbidden to take into account the facts they believe, as distinguished from facts which are 'clearly * * * within the domain of the indisputable.' Facts most needed in thinking about difficult problems of law and policy have a way of being outside the domain of the clearly indisputable." A System of Judicial Notice Based on Fairness and Convenience, *supra*, at 82.

An illustration is *Hawkins v. United States*, 358 U.S. 74, 79 S.Ct. 136, 3 L.Ed.2d 125 (1958), in which the Court refused to discard the common law rule that one spouse could not testify against the other, saying, "Adverse testimony given in criminal proceedings would, we think, be likely to destroy almost any marriage." This conclusion has a large intermixture of fact, but the factual aspect is scarcely "indisputable." See Hutchins and Slesinger, Some Observations on the Law of Evidence—Family Relations, 13 Minn.L.Rev. 675 (1929). If the destructive effect of the giving of adverse testimony by a spouse is not indisputable, should the Court have refrained from considering it in the absence of supporting evidence?

"If the Model Code or the Uniform Rules had been applicable, the Court would have been barred from thinking about the essential factual ingredient of the problems before it, and such a result would be obviously intolerable. What the law needs at its growing points is more, not less, judicial thinking about the factual ingredients of problems of what the law ought to be, and the needed facts are seldom 'clearly' indisputable." Davis, *supra*, at 83.

Professor Morgan gave the following description of the methodology of determining domestic law:

"In determining the content or applicability of a rule of domestic law, the judge is unrestricted in his investigation and conclusion. He may reject the propositions of either party or of both parties. He may consult the sources of pertinent data to which they refer, or he may refuse to do so. He may make an independent search for persuasive data or rest content with what he has or what the parties present. * * * [T]he parties do no more than to assist; they control no part of the process." Morgan, Judicial Notice, 57 Harv.L.Rev. 269, 270–271 (1944). This is the view which should govern judicial access to legislative facts. It renders inappropriate any limitation in the form of indisputability, any formal requirements of notice other than those already inherent in affording opportunity to hear and be heard and exchanging briefs, and any requirement of formal findings at any level. It should, however leave open the possibility of introducing evidence through regular channels in appropriate situations. See *Borden's Farm Products Co. v. Baldwin*, 293 U.S. 194, 55 S.Ct. 187, 79 L.Ed. 281 (1934), where the cause was remanded for the taking of evidence as to the economic conditions and trade practices underlying the New York Milk Control Law.

Similar considerations govern the judicial use of non-adjudicative facts in ways other than formulating laws and rules. Thayer described them as a part of the judicial reasoning process.

"In conducting a process of judicial reasoning, as of other reasoning, not a step can be taken without assuming something which has not been proved; and the capacity to do this with competent judgment and efficiency, is imputed to judges and juries as part of their necessary mental outfit." Thayer, Preliminary Treatise on Evidence 279–280 (1898).

As Professor Davis points out, A System of Judicial Notice Based on Fairness and Convenience, in Perspectives of Law 69, 73 (1964), every case involves the use of hundreds or thousands of non-evidence facts. When a witness in an automobile accident case says "car," everyone, judge and jury included, furnishes, from non-evidence sources within himself, the supplementing information that the "car" is an automobile, not a railroad car, that it is self-propelled, probably by an internal combustion engine, that it may be assumed to have four wheels with pneumatic rubber tires, and so on. The judicial process cannot construct every case from scratch, like Descartes creating a world based on the postulate *Cogito, ergo sum*. These items could not possibly be introduced into evidence, and no one suggests that they be. Nor are they appropriate subjects for any formalized treatment of judicial notice of facts. See Levin and Levy, Persuading the Jury with Facts Not in Evidence: The Fiction–Science Spectrum, 105 U.Pa.L.Rev. 139 (1956).

Another aspect of what Thayer had in mind is the use of non-evidence facts to appraise or assess the adjudicative facts of the case. Pairs of cases from two jurisdictions illustrate this use and also the difference between non-evidence facts thus used and adjudicative facts. In People v. Strook, 347 Ill. 460, 179 N.E. 821 (1932), venue in Cook County had been held not established by testimony that the crime was committed at 7956 South Chicago Avenue, since judicial notice would not be taken that the address was in Chicago. However, the same court subsequently ruled that venue in Cook County was established by testimony that a crime occurred at 8900 South Anthony Avenue, since notice would be taken of the common practice of omitting the name of the city when speaking of local addresses, and the witness was testifying in Chicago. *People v. Pride*, 16 Ill.2d 82, 156 N.E.2d 551 (1951). And in *Hughes v. Vestal*, 264 N.C. 500, 142 S.E.2d 361 (1965), the Supreme Court of North Carolina disapproved the trial judge's admission in evidence of a state-published table of automobile stopping distances on the basis of judicial notice, though the court itself had referred to the same table in an earlier case in a "rhetorical and illustrative" way in determining that the defendant could not have stopped her car in time to avoid striking a child who suddenly appeared in the highway and that a nonsuit was properly granted. *Ennis v. Dupree*, 262 N.C. 224, 136 S.E.2d 702 (1964). See also *Brown v. Hale*, 263 N.C. 176, 139 S.E.2d 210 (1964); *Clayton v. Rimmer*, 262 N.C. 302, 136 S.E.2d 562 (1964). It is apparent that this use of non-evidence facts in evaluating the adjudicative facts of the case is not an appropriate subject for a formalized judicial notice treatment.

In view of these considerations, the regulation of judicial notice of facts by the present rule extends only to adjudicative facts.

What, then, are "adjudicative" facts? Davis refers to them as those "which relate to the parties," or more fully:

"When a court or an agency finds facts concerning the immediate parties—who did what, where, when, how, and with what motive or intent—the court or agency is performing an adjudicative function, and the facts are conveniently called adjudicative facts. * * *

"Stated in other terms, the adjudicative facts are those to which the law is applied in the process of adjudication. They are the facts that normally go to the jury in a jury case. They relate to the parties, their activities, their properties, their businesses." 2 Administrative Law Treatise 353.

Note to Subdivision (b). With respect to judicial notice of adjudicative facts, the tradition has been one of caution in requiring that the matter be beyond reasonable controversy. This tradition of circumspection appears to be soundly based, and no reason to depart from it is apparent. As Professor Davis says:

"The reason we use trial-type procedure, I think, is that we make the practical judgment, on the basis of experience, that taking evidence, subject to cross-examination and rebuttal, is the best way to resolve controversies involving disputes of adjudicative facts, that is, facts pertaining to the parties. The reason we require a determination on the record is that we think fair procedure in resolving disputes of adjudicative facts calls for giving each party a chance to meet in the appropriate fashion the facts that come to the tribunal's attention, and the appropriate fashion for meeting disputed adjudicative facts includes rebuttal evidence, cross-examination, usually confrontation, and argument (either written or oral or both). The key to a fair trial is opportunity to use the appropriate weapons (rebuttal evidence, cross-examination, and argument) to meet adverse materials that come to the tribunal's attention." A System of Judicial Notice Based on Fairness and Convenience, in Perspectives of Law 69, 93 (1964).

The rule proceeds upon the theory that these considerations call for dispensing with traditional methods of proof only in clear cases. Compare Professor Davis' conclusion that judicial notice should be a matter of convenience, subject to requirements of procedural fairness. *Id.,* 94.

This rule is consistent with Uniform Rule 9(1) and (2) which limit judicial notice of facts to those "so universally known that they cannot reasonably be the subject of dispute," those "so generally known or of such common notoriety within the territorial jurisdiction of the court that they cannot reasonably be the subject of dispute," and those "capable of immediate and accurate determination by resort to easily accessible sources of indisputable accuracy." The traditional textbook treatment has included these general categories (matters of common knowledge, facts capable of verification), McCormick §§ 324, 325, and then has passed on into detailed treatment of such specific topics as facts relating to the personnel and records of the court, *Id.* § 327, and other governmental facts, *Id.* § 328. The California draftsmen, with a background of detailed statutory regulation of judicial notice, followed a somewhat similar pattern. California Evidence Code §§ 451, 452. The Uniform Rules, however, were drafted on the theory that these particular matters are included within the general categories and need no specific mention. This approach is followed in the present rule.

The phrase "propositions of generalized knowledge," found in Uniform Rule 9(1) and (2) is not included in the present rule. It was, it is believed, originally included in Model Code Rules 801 and 802 primarily in order to afford some minimum recognition to the right of the judge in his "legislative" capacity (not acting as the trier of fact) to take judicial notice of very limited categories of generalized knowledge. The limitations thus imposed have been discarded herein as undesirable, unworkable, and contrary to existing practice. What is left, then, to be considered, is the status of a "proposition of generalized knowledge" as an "adjudicative" fact to be noticed judicially and communicated by the judge to the jury. Thus viewed, it is considered to be lacking practical significance. While judges use judicial notice of "propositions of generalized knowledge" in a variety of situations: determining the validity and meaning of statutes, formulating common law rules, deciding whether evidence should be admitted, assessing the sufficiency and effect of evidence, all are essentially nonadjudicative in nature. When judicial notice is seen as a significant vehicle for progress in the law, these are the areas involved, particularly in developing fields of scientific knowledge. See McCormick 712. It is not believed that judges now instruct juries as to "propositions of generalized knowledge" derived from encyclopedias or other sources, or that they are likely to do so, or, indeed, that it is desirable that they do so. There is a vast difference between ruling on the basis of judicial notice that radar evidence of speed is admissible and explaining to the jury its principles and degree of accuracy, or between using a table of stopping distances of automobiles at various speeds in a judicial evaluation of testimony and telling the jury its precise application in the case. For cases raising doubt as to the propriety of the use of medical texts by lay triers of fact in passing on disability claims in administrative proceedings, see *Sayers v. Gardner*, 380 F.2d 940 (6th Cir.1967); *Ross v. Gardner*, 365 F.2d 554 (6th Cir.1966); *Sosna v. Celebrezze*, 234 F.Supp. 289 (E.D.Pa.1964); *Glendenning v. Ribicoff*, 213 F.Supp. 301 (W.D.Mo.1962).

Notes to Subdivisions (c) and (d). Under subdivision (c) the judge has a discretionary authority to take judicial notice, regardless of whether he is so requested by a party. The taking of judicial notice is mandatory, under subdivision (d), only when a party requests it and the necessary information is supplied. This scheme is believed to reflect existing practice. It is simple and workable. It avoids troublesome distinctions in the many situations in which the process of taking judicial notice is not recognized as such.

Compare Uniform Rule 9 making judicial notice of facts universally known mandatory without request, and making judicial notice of facts generally known in the jurisdiction or capable of determination by resort to accurate sources discretionary in the absence of request but mandatory if request is made and the information furnished. But see Uniform Rule 10(3), which directs the judge to decline to take judicial notice if available information fails to convince him that the matter falls clearly within Uniform Rule 9 or is insufficient to enable him to notice it judicially. Substantially the same approach is found in California Evidence Code §§ 451–453 and in New Jersey Evidence Rule 9. In contrast, the present rule treats alike all adjudicative facts which are subject to judicial notice.

Note to Subdivision (e). Basic considerations of procedural fairness demand an opportunity to be heard on the propriety of taking judicial notice and the tenor of the matter noticed. The rule requires the granting of that opportunity upon request. No formal scheme of giving notice is provided. An adversely affected party may learn in advance that judicial notice is in contemplation, either by virtue of being served with a copy of a request by another party under subdivision (d) that judicial notice be taken, or through an advance indication by the judge. Or he may have no advance notice at all. The likelihood of the latter is enhanced by the frequent failure to recognize judicial notice as such. And in the absence of advance notice, a request made after the fact could not in fairness be considered untimely. See the provision for hearing on timely request in the Administrative Procedure Act, 5 U.S.C. § 556(e). See also Revised Model State Administrative Procedure Act (1961), 9C U.L.A. § 10(4) (Supp. 1967).

Note to Subdivision (f). In accord with the usual view, judicial notice may be taken at any stage of the proceedings, whether in the trial court or on appeal. Uniform Rule 12; California Evidence Code § 459; Kansas Rules of Evidence § 60–412; New Jersey Evidence Rule 12; McCormick § 330, p. 712.

Note to Subdivision (g). Much of the controversy about judicial notice has centered upon the question whether evidence should be admitted in disproof of facts of which judicial notice is taken.

The writers have been divided. Favoring admissibility are Thayer, Preliminary Treatise on Evidence 308 (1898); 9 Wigmore § 2567; Davis, A System of Judicial Notice Based on Fairness and Convenience, in Perspectives of Law, 69, 76–77 (1964). Opposing admissibility are Keeffe, Landis and Shaad, Sense and Nonsense about Judicial Notice, 2 Stan.L.Rev. 664, 668 (1950); McNaughton, Judicial Notice—Excerpts Relating to the Morgan–Whitmore Controversy, 14 Vand.L.Rev. 779 (1961); Morgan, Judicial Notice, 57 Harv.L.Rev. 269, 279 (1944); McCormick 710–711. The Model Code and the Uniform Rules are predicated upon indisputability of judicially noticed facts.

The proponents of admitting evidence in disproof have concentrated largely upon legislative facts. Since the present rule deals only with judicial notice of adjudicative facts, arguments directed to legislative facts lose their relevancy.

Within its relatively narrow area of adjudicative facts, the rule contemplates there is to be no evidence before the jury in disproof. The judge instructs the jury to take judicially noticed facts as established. This position is justified by the undesirable effects of the opposite rule in limiting the rebutting party, though not his opponent, to admissible evidence, in defeating the reasons for judicial notice, and in affecting the substantive law to an extent and in ways largely unforeseeable. Ample protection and flexibility are afforded by the broad provision for opportunity to be heard on request, set forth in subdivision (e).

Authority upon the propriety of taking judicial notice against an accused in a criminal case with respect to matters other than venue is relatively meager. Proceeding upon the theory that the right of jury trial does not extend to matters which are beyond reasonable dispute, the rule does not distinguish between criminal and civil cases. *People v. Mayes,* 113 Cal. 618, 45 P. 860 (1896); *Ross v. United States,* 374 F.2d 97 (8th Cir.1967). Cf. *State v. Main,* 94 R.I. 338, 180 A.2d 814 (1962); *State v. Lawrence,* 120 Utah 323, 234 P.2d 600 (1951).

Note on Judicial Notice of Law. By rules effective July 1, 1966, the method of invoking the law of a foreign country is covered elsewhere. Rule 44.1 of the Federal Rules of Civil Procedure; Rule 26.1 of the Federal Rules of Criminal Procedure. These two new admirably designed rules are founded upon the assumption that the manner in which law is fed into the judicial process is never a proper concern of the rules of evidence but rather of the rules of procedure. The Advisory Committee on Evidence, believing that this assumption is entirely correct, proposes no evidence rule with respect to judicial notice of law, and suggests that those matters of law which, in addition to foreign-country law, have traditionally been treated as requiring pleading and proof and more recently as the subject of judicial notice be left to the Rules of Civil and Criminal Procedure.

1974 Enactment

Rule 201(g) as received from the Supreme Court provided that when judicial notice of a fact is taken, the court shall instruct the jury to accept that fact as established. Being of the view that mandatory instruction to a jury in a criminal case to accept as conclusive any fact judicially noticed is inappropriate because contrary to the spirit of the Sixth Amendment right to a jury trial, the Committee adopted the 1969 Advisory Committee draft of this subsection, allowing a mandatory instruction in civil actions and proceedings and a discretionary instruction in criminal cases. House Report No. 93–650.

ARTICLE III. PRESUMPTIONS IN CIVIL ACTIONS AND PROCEEDINGS

Rule 301. Presumptions in General in Civil Actions and Proceedings

In all civil actions and proceedings not otherwise provided for by Act of Congress or by these rules, a presumption imposes on the party against whom it is directed the burden of going forward with evidence to rebut or meet the presumption, but does not shift to such party the burden of proof in the sense of the risk of nonpersuasion, which remains throughout the trial upon the party on whom it was originally cast.

ADVISORY COMMITTEE NOTES

1972 Proposed Rules

This rule governs presumptions generally. See Rule 302 for presumptions controlled by state law and Rule 303 [deleted] for those against an accused in a criminal case.

Presumptions governed by this rule are given the effect of placing upon the opposing party the burden of establishing the nonexistence of the presumed fact, once the party invoking the presumption establishes the basic facts giving rise to it. The same considerations of fairness, policy, and probability which

dictate the allocation of the burden of the various elements of a case as between the prima facie case of a plaintiff and affirmative defenses also underlie the creation of presumptions. These considerations are not satisfied by giving a lesser effect to presumptions. Morgan and Maguire, Looking Backward and Forward at Evidence, 50 Harv.L.Rev. 909, 913 (1937); Morgan, Instructing the Jury upon Presumptions and Burden of Proof, 47 Harv.L.Rev. 59, 82 (1933); Cleary, Presuming and Pleading: An Essay on Juristic Immaturity, 12 Stan.L.Rev. 5 (1959).

The so-called "bursting bubble" theory, under which a presumption vanishes upon the introduction of evidence which would support a finding of the nonexistence of the presumed fact, even though not believed, is rejected as according presumptions too "slight and evanescent" an effect. Morgan and Maguire, *supra,* at p. 913.

In the opinion of the Advisory Committee, no constitutional infirmity attends this view of presumptions. In *Mobile, J. & K. C. R. Co. v. Turnipseed,* 219 U.S. 35, 31 S.Ct. 136, 55 L.Ed. 78 (1910), the Court upheld a Mississippi statute which provided that in actions against railroads proof of injury inflicted by the running of trains should be prima facie evidence of negligence by the railroad. The injury in the case had resulted from a derailment. The opinion made the points (1) that the only effect of the statute was to impose on the railroad the duty of producing some evidence to the contrary, (2) that an inference may be supplied by law if there is a rational connection between the fact proved and the fact presumed, as long as the opposite party is not precluded from presenting his evidence to the contrary, and (3) that considerations of public policy arising from the character of the business justified the application in question. Nineteen years later, in *Western & Atlantic R. Co. v. Henderson*, 279 U.S. 639, 49 S.Ct. 445, 73 L.Ed. 884 (1929), the Court overturned a Georgia statute making railroads liable for damages done by trains, unless the railroad made it appear that reasonable care had been used, the presumption being against the railroad. The declaration alleged the death of plaintiff's husband from a grade crossing collision, due to specified acts of negligence by defendant. The jury were instructed that proof of the injury raised a presumption of negligence; the burden shifted to the railroad to prove ordinary care; and unless it did so, they should find for plaintiff. The instruction was held erroneous in an opinion stating (1) that there was no rational connection between the mere fact of collision and negligence on the part of anyone, and (2) that the statute was different from that in *Turnipseed* in imposing a burden upon the railroad. The reader is left in a state of some confusion. Is the difference between a derailment and a grade crossing collision of no significance? Would the *Turnipseed* presumption have been bad if it had imposed a burden of persuasion on defendant, although that would in nowise have impaired its "rational connection"? If *Henderson* forbids imposing a burden of persuasion on defendants, what happens to affirmative defenses?

Two factors serve to explain *Henderson.* The first was that it was common ground that negligence was indispensable to liability. Plaintiff thought so, drafted her complaint accordingly, and relied upon the presumption. But how in logic could the same presumption establish her alternative grounds of negligence that the engineer was so blind he could not see decedent's truck and that he failed to stop after he saw it? Second, take away the basic assumption of no liability without fault, as *Turnipseed* intimated might be done ("considerations of public policy arising out of the character of the business"), and the structure of the decision in *Henderson* fails. No question of logic would have arisen if the statute had simply said: a prima facie case of liability is made by proof of injury by a train; lack of negligence is an affirmative defense, to be pleaded and proved as other affirmative defenses. The problem would be one of economic due process only. While it seems likely that the Supreme Court of 1929 would have voted that due process was denied, that result today would be unlikely. See, for example, the shift in the direction of absolute liability in the consumer cases. Prosser, The Assault upon the Citadel (Strict Liability to the Consumer), 69 Yale L.J. 1099 (1960).

Any doubt as to the constitutional permissibility of a presumption imposing a burden of persuasion of the nonexistence of the presumed fact in civil cases is laid at rest by *Dick v. New York Life Ins. Co.*, 359 U.S. 437, 79 S.Ct. 921, 3 L.Ed.2d 935 (1959). The Court unhesitatingly applied the North Dakota rule that the presumption against suicide imposed on defendant the burden of proving that the death of insured, under an accidental death clause, was due to suicide.

"Proof of coverage and of death by gunshot wound shifts the burden to the insurer to establish that the death of the insured was due to his suicide." 359 U.S. at 443, 79 S.Ct. at 925.

"In a case like this one, North Dakota presumes that death was accidental and places on the insurer the burden of proving that death resulted from suicide." *Id.* at 446, 79 S.Ct. at 927.

The rational connection requirement survives in criminal cases, *Tot v. United States*, 319 U.S. 463, 63 S.Ct. 1241, 87 L.Ed. 1519 (1943), because the Court has been unwilling to extend into that area the greater-includes-the-lesser theory of *Ferry v. Ramsey*, 277 U.S. 88, 48 S.Ct. 443, 72 L.Ed. 796 (1928). In that case the Court sustained a Kansas statute under which bank directors were personally liable for deposits made with their assent and with knowledge of insolvency, and the fact of insolvency was prima facie evidence of assent and knowledge of insolvency. Mr. Justice Holmes pointed out that the state

legislature could have made the directors personally liable to depositors in every case. Since the statute imposed a less stringent liability, "the thing to be considered is the result reached, not the possibly inartificial or clumsy way of reaching it." *Id.* at 94, 48 S.Ct. at 444. Mr. Justice Sutherland dissented: though the state could have created an absolute liability, it did not purport to do so; a rational connection was necessary, but lacking, between the liability created and the prima facie evidence of it; the result might be different if the basis of the presumption were being open for business.

The Sutherland view has prevailed in criminal cases by virtue of the higher standard of notice there required. The fiction that everyone is presumed to know the law is applied to the substantive law of crimes as an alternative to complete unenforceability. But the need does not extend to criminal evidence and procedure, and the fiction does not encompass them. "Rational connection" is not fictional or artificial, and so it is reasonable to suppose that Gainey should have known that his presence at the site of an illicit still could convict him of being connected with (carrying on) the business, *United States v. Gainey*, 380 U.S. 63, 85 S.Ct. 754, 13 L.Ed.2d 658 (1965), but not that Romano should have known that his presence at a still could convict him of possessing it, *United States v. Romano*, 382 U.S. 136, 86 S.Ct. 279, 15 L.Ed.2d 210 (1965).

In his dissent in Gainey, Mr. Justice Black put it more artistically:

"It might be argued, although the Court does not so argue or hold, that Congress if it wished could make presence at a still a crime in itself, and so Congress should be free to create crimes which are called 'possession' and 'carrying on an illegal distillery business' but which are defined in such a way that unexplained presence is sufficient and indisputable evidence in all cases to support conviction for those offenses. See *Ferry v. Ramsey*, 277 U.S. 88, 48 S.Ct. 443, 72 L.Ed. 796. Assuming for the sake of argument that Congress could make unexplained presence a criminal act, and ignoring also the refusal of this Court in other cases to uphold a statutory presumption on such a theory, see *Heiner v. Donnan*, 285 U.S. 312, 52 S.Ct. 358, 76 L.Ed. 772, there is no indication here that Congress intended to adopt such a misleading method of draftsmanship, nor in my judgment could the statutory provisions if so construed escape condemnation for vagueness, under the principles applied in *Lanzetta v. New Jersey*, 306 U.S. 451, 59 S.Ct. 618, 83 L.Ed. 888, and many other cases." 380 U.S. at 84, n. 12, 85 S.Ct. at 766.

And the majority opinion in *Romano* agreed with him:

"It may be, of course, that Congress has the power to make presence at an illegal still a punishable crime, but we find no clear indication that it intended to so exercise this power. The crime remains possession, not presence, and with all due deference to the judgment of Congress, the former may not constitutionally be inferred from the latter." 382 U.S. at 144, 86 S.Ct. at 284.

The rule does not spell out the procedural aspects of its application. Questions as to when the evidence warrants submission of a presumption and what instructions are proper under varying states of fact are believed to present no particular difficulties.

1974 Enactment

Rule 301 as submitted by the Supreme Court provided that in all cases a presumption imposes on the party against whom it is directed the burden of proving that the nonexistence of the presumed fact is more probable than its existence. The Committee limited the scope of Rule 301 to "civil actions and proceedings" to effectuate its decision not to deal with the question of presumptions in criminal cases. (See note on [proposed] Rule 303 in discussion of Rules deleted). With respect to the weight to be given a presumption in a civil case, the Committee agreed with the judgment implicit in the Court's version that the so-called "bursting bubble" theory of presumptions, whereby a presumption vanishes upon the appearance of any contradicting evidence by the other party, gives to presumptions too slight an effect. On the other hand, the Committee believed that the Rule proposed by the Court, whereby a presumption permanently alters the burden of persuasion, no matter how much contradicting evidence is introduced—a view shared by only a few courts—lends too great a force to presumptions. Accordingly, the Committee amended the Rule to adopt an intermediate position under which a presumption does not vanish upon the introduction of contradicting evidence, and does not change the burden of persuasion; instead it is merely deemed sufficient evidence of the fact presumed, to be considered by the jury or other finder of fact. House Report No. 93–650.

The rule governs presumptions in civil cases generally. Rule 302 provides for presumptions in cases controlled by State law.

As submitted by the Supreme Court, presumptions governed by this rule were given the effect of placing upon the opposing party the burden of establishing the nonexistence of the presumed fact, once the party invoking the presumption established the basic facts giving rise to it.

Instead of imposing a burden of persuasion on the party against whom the presumption is directed, the House adopted a provision which shifted the burden of going forward with the evidence. They further provided that "even though met with contradicting evidence, a presumption is sufficient evidence of the fact presumed, to be considered by the trier of fact." The effect of the amendment is that presumptions are to be treated as evidence.

The committee feels the House amendment is ill-advised. As the joint committees (the Standing Committee on Practice and Procedure of the Judicial Conference and the Advisory Committee on the Rules of Evidence) stated: "Presumptions are not evidence, but ways of dealing with evidence." This treatment requires juries to perform the task of considering "as evidence" facts upon which they have no direct evidence and which may confuse them in performance of their duties. California had a rule much like that contained in the House amendment. It was sharply criticized by Justice Traynor in *Speck v. Sarver* [20 Cal.2d 585, 128 P.2d 16, 21 (1942)] and was repealed after 93 troublesome years [Cal.Ev.Code 1965 § 600].

Professor McCormick gives a concise and compelling critique of the presumption as evidence rule:

"Another solution, formerly more popular than now, is to instruct the jury that the presumption is 'evidence', to be weighed and considered with the testimony in the case. This avoids the danger that the jury may infer that the presumption is conclusive, but it probably means little to the jury, and certainly runs counter to accepted theories of the nature of evidence." [McCormick, Evidence, 669 (1954); *Id.* 825 (2d ed. 1972)].

For these reasons the committee has deleted that provision of the House-passed rule that treats presumptions as evidence. The effect of the rule as adopted by the committee is to make clear that while evidence of facts giving rise to a presumption shifts the burden of coming forward with evidence to rebut or meet the presumption, it does not shift the burden of persuasion on the existence of the presumed facts. The burden of persuasion remains on the party to whom it is allocated under the rules governing the allocation in the first instance.

The court may instruct the jury that they may infer the existence of the presumed fact from proof of the basic facts giving rise to the presumption. However, it would be inappropriate under this rule to instruct the jury that the inference they are to draw is conclusive. Senate Report 93–1277.

The House bill provides that a presumption in civil actions and proceedings shifts to the party against whom it is directed the burden of going forward with evidence to meet or rebut it.

Even though evidence contradicting the presumption is offered, a presumption is considered sufficient evidence of the presumed fact to be considered by the jury. The Senate amendment provides that a presumption shifts to the party against whom it is directed the burden of going forward with evidence to meet or rebut the presumption, but it does not shift to that party the burden of persuasion on the existence of the presumed fact.

Under the Senate amendment, a presumption is sufficient to get a party past an adverse party's motion to dismiss made at the end of his case-in-chief. If the adverse party offers no evidence contradicting the presumed fact, the court will instruct the jury that if it finds the basic facts, it may presume the existence of the presumed fact. If the adverse party does offer evidence contradicting the presumed fact, the court cannot instruct the jury that it may *presume* the existence of the presumed fact from proof of the basic facts. The court may, however, instruct the jury that it may infer the existence of the presumed fact from proof of the basic facts.

The conference adopts the Senate amendment. House Conference Report No. 93–1597.

Rule 302. Applicability of State Law in Civil Actions and Proceedings

In civil actions and proceedings, the effect of a presumption respecting a fact which is an element of a claim or defense as to which State law supplies the rule of decision is determined in accordance with State law. (Pub.L. 93–595, § 1, Jan. 2, 1975, 88 Stat. 1931.)

ADVISORY COMMITTEE NOTES
1972 Proposed Rules

A series of Supreme Court decisions in diversity cases leaves no doubt of the relevance of *Erie Railroad Co. v. Tompkins*, 304 U.S. 64, 58 S.Ct. 817, 82 L.Ed. 1188 (1938), to questions of burden of proof. These decisions are *Cities Service Oil Co. v. Dunlap*, 308 U.S. 208, 60 S.Ct. 201, 84 L.Ed. 196 (1939), *Palmer v. Hoffman*, 318 U.S. 109, 63 S.Ct. 477, 87 L.Ed. 645 (1943), and *Dick v. New York Life Ins. Co.*, 359 U.S. 437, 79 S.Ct. 921, 3 L.Ed.2d 935 (1959). They involved burden of proof, respectively, as to status as bona fide purchaser, contributory negligence, and nonaccidental death (suicide) of an insured. In each instance the state rule was held to be applicable. It does not follow, however, that all presumptions in diversity cases are governed by state law. In each case cited, the burden of proof question had to do with a substantive element of the claim or defense. Application of the state law is called for only when the presumption operates upon such an element. Accordingly the rule does not apply state law when the presumption operates upon a lesser aspect of the case, i.e. "tactical" presumptions.

The situations in which the state law is applied have been tagged for convenience in the preceding discussion as "diversity cases." The designation is not a completely accurate one since *Erie* applies to any claim or issue having its source in state law, regardless of the basis of federal jurisdiction, and does not apply to a federal claim or issue, even though jurisdiction is based on diversity. *Vestal, Erie R.R. v. Tompkins:* A Projection, 48 Iowa L.Rev. 248, 257 (1963); Hart and Wechsler, The Federal Courts and the Federal System, 697 (1953); 1A Moore, Federal Practice ¶ 0.305[3] (2d ed. 1965); Wright, Federal Courts, 217–218 (1963). Hence the rule employs, as appropriately descriptive, the phrase "as to which state law supplies the rule of decision." See A.L.I. Study of the Division of Jurisdiction Between State and Federal Courts, § 2344(c), p. 40, P.F.D. No. 1 (1965).

ARTICLE IV. RELEVANCY AND ITS LIMITS

Rule 401. Definition of "Relevant Evidence"

"Relevant evidence" means evidence having any tendency to make the existence of any fact that is of consequence to the determination of the action more probable or less probable than it would be without the evidence.

ADVISORY COMMITTEE NOTES
1972 Proposed Rules

Problems of relevancy call for an answer to the question whether an item of evidence, when tested by the processes of legal reasoning, possesses sufficient probative value to justify receiving it in evidence. Thus, assessment of the probative value of evidence that a person purchased a revolver shortly prior to a fatal shooting with which he is charged is a matter of analysis and reasoning.

The variety of relevancy problems is coextensive with the ingenuity of counsel in using circumstantial evidence as a means of proof. An enormous number of cases fall in no set pattern, and this rule is designed as a guide for handling them. On the other hand, some situations recur with sufficient frequency to create patterns susceptible of treatment by specific rules. Rule 404 and those following it are of that variety; they also serve as illustrations of the application of the present rule as limited by the exclusionary principles of Rule 403.

Passing mention should be made of so-called "conditional" relevancy. Morgan, Basic Problems of Evidence 45–46 (1962). In this situation, probative value depends not only upon satisfying the basic requirement of relevancy as described above but also upon the existence of some matter of fact. For example, if evidence of a spoken statement is relied upon to prove notice, probative value is lacking unless the person sought to be charged heard the statement. The problem is one of fact, and the only rules needed are for the purpose of determining the respective functions of judge and jury. See Rules 104(b) and 901. The discussion which follows in the present note is concerned with relevancy generally, not with any particular problem of conditional relevancy.

Relevancy is not an inherent characteristic of any item of evidence but exists only as a relation between an item of evidence and a matter properly provable in the case. Does the item of evidence tend to prove the matter sought to be proved? Whether the relationship exists depends upon principles evolved by experience or science, applied logically to the situation at hand. James, Relevancy, Probability and the Law, 29 Calif.L.Rev. 689, 696, n. 15 (1941), in Selected Writings on Evidence and Trial 610, 615, n. 15 (Fryer ed. 1957). The rule summarizes this relationship as a "tendency to make the existence" of the fact to be proved "more probable or less probable." Compare Uniform Rule 1(2) which states the crux of relevancy as a "tendency in reason," thus perhaps emphasizing unduly the logical process and ignoring the need to draw upon experience or science to validate the general principle upon which relevancy in a particular situation depends.

The standard of probability under the rule is "more * * * probable than it would be without the evidence." Any more stringent requirement is unworkable and unrealistic. As McCormick § 152, p. 317, says, "A brick is not a wall," or, as Falknor, Extrinsic Policies Affecting Admissibility, 10 Rutgers L.Rev. 574, 576 (1956), quotes Professor McBaine, " * * * [I]t is not to be supposed that every witness can make a home run." Dealing with probability in the language of the rule has the added virtue of avoiding confusion between questions of admissibility and questions of the sufficiency of the evidence.

The rule uses the phrase "fact that is of consequence to the determination of the action" to describe the kind of fact to which proof may properly be directed. The language is that of California Evidence Code § 210; it has the advantage of avoiding the loosely used and ambiguous word "material." Tentative Recommendation and a Study Relating to the Uniform Rules of Evidence (Art. I. General Provisions), Cal.Law Revision Comm'n, Rep., Rec. & Studies, 10–11 (1964). The fact to be proved may be ultimate, intermediate, or evidentiary; it matters not, so long as it is of consequence in the determination of the action. Cf. Uniform Rule 1(2) which requires that the evidence relate to a "material" fact.

The fact to which the evidence is directed need not be in dispute. While situations will arise which call for the exclusion of evidence offered to prove a point conceded by the opponent, the ruling should be made on the basis of such considerations as waste of time and undue prejudice (see Rule 403), rather than under any general requirement that evidence is admissible only if directed to matters in dispute. Evidence which is essentially background in nature can scarcely be said to involve disputed matter, yet it is universally offered and admitted as an aid to understanding. Charts, photographs, views of real estate, murder weapons, and many other items of evidence fall in this category. A rule limiting admissibility to evidence directed to a controversial point would invite the exclusion of this helpful evidence, or at least the raising of endless questions over its admission. Cf. California Evidence Code § 210, defining relevant evidence in terms of tendency to prove a disputed fact.

Rule 402. Relevant Evidence Generally Admissible; Irrelevant Evidence Inadmissible

All relevant evidence is admissible, except as otherwise provided by the Constitution of the United States, by Act of Congress, by these rules, or by other rules prescribed by the Supreme Court pursuant to statutory authority. Evidence which is not relevant is not admissible.

ADVISORY COMMITTEE NOTES
1972 Proposed Rules

The provisions that all relevant evidence is admissible, with certain exceptions, and that evidence which is not relevant is not admissible are "a presupposition involved in the very conception of a rational system of evidence." Thayer, Preliminary Treatise on Evidence 264 (1898). They constitute the foundation upon which the structure of admission and exclusion rests. For similar provisions see California Evidence Code §§ 350, 351. Provisions that all relevant evidence is admissible are found in Uniform Rule 7(f); Kansas Code of Civil Procedure § 60–407(f); and New Jersey Evidence Rule 7(f); but the exclusion of evidence which is not relevant is left to implication.

Not all relevant evidence is admissible. The exclusion of relevant evidence occurs in a variety of situations and may be called for by these rules, by the Rules of Civil and Criminal Procedure, by Bankruptcy Rules, by Act of Congress, or by constitutional considerations.

Succeeding rules in the present article, in response to the demands of particular policies, require the exclusion of evidence despite its relevancy. In addition, Article V recognizes a number of privileges; Article VI imposes limitations upon witnesses and the manner of dealing with them; Article VII specifies requirements with respect to opinions and expert testimony; Article VIII excludes hearsay not falling within an exception; Article IX spells out the handling of authentication and identification; and Article X restricts the manner of proving the contents of writings and recordings.

The Rules of Civil and Criminal Procedure in some instances require the exclusion of relevant evidence. For example, Rules 30(b) and 32(a)(3) of the Rules of Civil Procedure, by imposing requirements of notice and unavailability of the deponent, place limits on the use of relevant depositions. Similarly, Rule 15 of the Rules of Criminal Procedure restricts the use of depositions in criminal cases, even though relevant. And the effective enforcement of the command, originally statutory and now found in Rule 5(a) of the Rules of Criminal Procedure, that an arrested person be taken without unnecessary delay before a commissioner or other similar officer is held to require the exclusion of statements elicited during detention in violation thereof. *Mallory v. United States*, 354 U.S. 449, 77 S.Ct. 1356, 1 L.Ed.2d 1479 (1957); 18 U.S.C. § 3501(c).

While congressional enactments in the field of evidence have generally tended to expand admissibility beyond the scope of the common law rules, in some particular situations they have restricted the admissibility of relevant evidence. Most of this legislation has consisted of the formulation of a privilege or of a prohibition against disclosure. 8 U.S.C. § 1202(f), records of refusal of visas or permits to enter United States confidential, subject to discretion of Secretary of State to make available to court upon certification of need; 10 U.S.C. § 3693, replacement certificate of honorable discharge from Army not admissible in evidence; 10 U.S.C. § 8693, same as to Air Force; 11 U.S.C. § 25(a)(10), testimony given by bankrupt on his examination not admissible in criminal proceedings against him, except that given in hearing upon objection to discharge; 11 U.S.C. § 205(a), railroad reorganization petition, if dismissed, not admissible in evidence; 11 U.S.C. § 403(a), list of creditors filed with municipal composition plan not an admission; 13 U.S.C. § 9(a), census information confidential, retained copies of reports privileged; 47 U.S.C. § 605, interception and divulgence of wire or radio communications prohibited unless authorized by sender. These statutory provisions would remain undisturbed by the rules.

The rule recognizes but makes no attempt to spell out the constitutional considerations which impose basic limitations upon the admissibility of relevant evidence. Examples are evidence obtained by unlawful search and seizure. *Weeks v. United States*, 232 U.S. 383, 34 S.Ct. 341, 58 L.Ed. 652 (1914); *Katz v. United States*, 389 U.S. 347, 88 S.Ct. 507, 19 L.Ed.2d 576 (1967); incriminating statement elicited from an accused in violation of right to counsel. *Massiah v. United States*, 377 U.S. 201, 84 S.Ct. 1199, 12 L.Ed.2d 246 (1964).

1974 Enactment

Rule 402 as submitted to the Congress contained the phrase "or by other rules adopted by the Supreme Court". To accommodate the view that the Congress should not appear to acquiesce in the Court's judgment that it has authority under the existing Rules Enabling Acts to promulgate Rules of Evidence, the Committee amended the above phrase to read "or by other rules prescribed by the Supreme Court pursuant to statutory authority" in this and other Rules where the reference appears. House Report No. 93–650.

Rule 403. Exclusion of Relevant Evidence on Grounds of Prejudice, Confusion, or Waste of Time

Although relevant, evidence may be excluded if its probative value is substantially outweighed by the danger of unfair prejudice, confusion of the issues, or misleading the jury, or by considerations of undue delay, waste of time, or needless presentation of cumulative evidence.

ADVISORY COMMITTEE NOTES

1972 Proposed Rules

The case law recognizes that certain circumstances call for the exclusion of evidence which is of unquestioned relevance. These circumstances entail risks which range all the way from inducing decision on a purely emotional basis, at one extreme, to nothing more harmful than merely wasting time, at the other extreme. Situations in this area call for balancing the probative value of and need for the evidence against the harm likely to result from its admission. Slough, Relevancy Unraveled, 5 Kan.L.Rev. 1, 12–15 (1956); Trautman, Logical or Legal Relevancy—A Conflict in Theory, 5 Van.L.Rev. 385, 392 (1952); McCormick § 152, pp. 319–321. The rules which follow in this Article are concrete applications evolved for particular situations. However, they reflect the policies underlying the present rule, which is designed as a guide for the handling of situations for which no specific rules have been formulated.

Exclusion for risk of unfair prejudice, confusion of issues, misleading the jury, or waste of time, all find ample support in the authorities. "Unfair prejudice" within its context means an undue tendency to suggest decision on an improper basis, commonly, though not necessarily, an emotional one.

The rule does not enumerate surprise as a ground for exclusion, in this respect following Wigmore's view of the common law. 6 Wigmore § 1849. Cf. McCormick § 152, p. 320, n. 29, listing unfair surprise as a ground for exclusion but stating that it is usually "coupled with the danger of prejudice and confusion of issues." While Uniform Rule 45 incorporates surprise as a ground and is followed in Kansas Code of Civil Procedure § 60–445, surprise is not included in California Evidence Code § 352 or New Jersey Rule 4, though both the latter otherwise substantially embody Uniform Rule 45. While it can scarcely be doubted that claims of unfair surprise may still be justified despite procedural requirements of notice and instrumentalities of discovery, the granting of a continuance is a more appropriate remedy than exclusion of the evidence. Tentative Recommendation and a Study Relating to the Uniform Rules of Evidence (Art. VI. Extrinsic Policies Affecting Admissibility), Cal.Law Revision Comm'n, Rep., Rec. & Studies, 612 (1964). Moreover, the impact of a rule excluding evidence on the ground of surprise would be difficult to estimate.

In reaching a decision whether to exclude on grounds of unfair prejudice, consideration should be given to the probable effectiveness or lack of effectiveness of a limiting instruction. See Rule 106 [now 105] and Advisory Committee's Note thereunder. The availability of other means of proof may also be an appropriate factor.

Rule 404. Character Evidence Not Admissible To Prove Conduct; Exceptions; Other Crimes

(a) Character Evidence Generally.—Evidence of a person's character or a trait of character is not admissible for the purpose of proving action in conformity therewith on a particular occasion, except:

(1) Character of Accused.—Evidence of a pertinent trait of character offered by an accused, or by the prosecution to rebut the same, or if evidence of a trait of character of the alleged victim of the crime is offered by an accused and admitted under Rule 404(a)(2), evidence of the same trait of character of the accused offered by the prosecution;

(2) Character of Alleged Victim.—Evidence of a pertinent trait of character of the alleged victim of the crime offered by an accused, or by the prosecution to rebut the same, or evidence of a character trait of peacefulness of the alleged victim offered by the prosecution in a homicide case to rebut evidence that the alleged victim was the first aggressor;

(3) Character of Witness.—Evidence of the character of a witness, as provided in rules 607, 608, and 609.

(b) Other Crimes, Wrongs, or Acts.—Evidence of other crimes, wrongs, or acts is not admissible to prove the character of a person in order to show action in conformity therewith. It may, however, be admissible for other purposes, such as proof of motive, opportunity, intent, preparation, plan, knowledge, identity, or absence of mistake or accident, provided that upon request by the accused, the prosecution in a criminal case shall provide reasonable notice in advance of trial, or during trial if the court excuses pretrial notice on good cause shown, of the general nature of any such evidence it intends to introduce at trial.

ADVISORY COMMITTEE NOTES

1972 Proposed Rules

Note to Subdivision (a). This subdivision deals with the basic question whether character evidence should be admitted. Once the admissibility of character evidence in some form is established under this rule, reference must then be made to

Rule 405, which follows, in order to determine the appropriate method of proof. If the character is that of a witness, see Rules 608 and 610 for methods of proof.

Character questions arise in two fundamentally different ways. (1) Character may itself be an element of a crime, claim, or defense. A situation of this kind is commonly referred to as "character in issue." Illustrations are: the chastity of the victim under a statute specifying her chastity as an element of the crime of seduction, or the competency of the driver in an action for negligently entrusting a motor vehicle to an incompetent driver. No problem of the general relevancy of character evidence is involved, and the present rule therefore has no provision on the subject. The only question relates to allowable methods of proof, as to which see Rule 405, immediately following. (2) Character evidence is susceptible of being used for the purpose of suggesting an inference that the person acted on the occasion in question consistently with his character. This use of character is often described as "circumstantial." Illustrations are: evidence of a violent disposition to prove that the person was the aggressor in an affray, or evidence of honesty in disproof of a charge of theft. This circumstantial use of character evidence raises questions of relevancy as well as questions of allowable methods of proof.

In most jurisdictions today, the circumstantial use of character is rejected but with important exceptions: (1) an accused may introduce pertinent evidence of good character (often misleadingly described as "putting his character in issue"), in which event the prosecution may rebut with evidence of bad character; (2) an accused may introduce pertinent evidence of the character of the victim, as in support of a claim of self-defense to a charge of homicide or consent in a case of rape, and the prosecution may introduce similar evidence in rebuttal of the character evidence, or, in a homicide case, to rebut a claim that deceased was the first aggressor, however proved; and (3) the character of a witness may be gone into as bearing on his credibility. McCormick §§ 155–161. This pattern is incorporated in the rule. While its basis lies more in history and experience than in logic an underlying justification can fairly be found in terms of the relative presence and absence of prejudice in the various situations. Falknor, Extrinsic Policies Affecting Admissibility, 10 Rutgers L.Rev. 574, 584 (1956); McCormick § 157. In any event, the criminal rule is so deeply imbedded in our jurisprudence as to assume almost constitutional proportions and to override doubts of the basic relevancy of the evidence.

The limitation to pertinent traits of character, rather than character generally, in paragraphs (1) and (2) is in accordance with the prevailing view. McCormick § 158, p. 334. A similar provision in Rule 608, to which reference is made in paragraph (3), limits character evidence respecting witnesses to the trait of truthfulness or untruthfulness.

The argument is made that circumstantial use of character ought to be allowed in civil cases to the same extent as in criminal cases, i.e. evidence of good (nonprejudicial) character would be admissible in the first instance, subject to rebuttal by evidence of bad character. Falknor, Extrinsic Policies Affecting Admissibility, 10 Rutgers L.Rev. 574, 581–583 (1956); Tentative Recommendation and a Study Relating to the Uniform Rules of Evidence (Art. VI. Extrinsic Policies Affecting Admissibility), Cal.Law Revision Comm'n, Rep., Rec. & Studies, 657–658 (1964). Uniform Rule 47 goes farther, in that it assumes that character evidence in general satisfies the conditions of relevancy, except as provided in Uniform Rule 48. The difficulty with expanding the use of character evidence in civil cases is set forth by the California Law Revision Commission in its ultimate rejection of Uniform Rule 47, *id.*, 615:

"Character evidence is of slight probative value and may be very prejudicial. It tends to distract the trier of fact from the main question of what actually happened on the particular occasion. It subtly permits the trier of fact to reward the good man and to punish the bad man because of their respective characters despite what the evidence in the case shows actually happened."

Much of the force of the position of those favoring greater use of character evidence in civil cases is dissipated by their support of Uniform Rule 48 which excludes the evidence in negligence cases, where it could be expected to achieve its maximum usefulness. Moreover, expanding concepts of "character," which seem of necessity to extend into such areas as psychiatric evaluation and psychological testing, coupled with expanded admissibility, would open up such vistas of mental examinations as caused the Court concern in *Schlagenhauf v. Holder*, 379 U.S. 104, 85 S.Ct. 234, 13 L.Ed.2d 152 (1964). It is believed that those espousing change have not met the burden of persuasion.

Note to Subdivision (b). Subdivision (b) deals with a specialized but important application of the general rule excluding circumstantial use of character evidence. Consistently with that rule, evidence of other crimes, wrongs, or acts is not admissible to prove character as a basis for suggesting the inference that conduct on a particular occasion was in conformity with it. However, the evidence may be offered for another purpose, such as proof of motive, opportunity, and so on, which does not fall within the prohibition. In this situation the rule does not require that the evidence be excluded. No mechanical solution is offered. The determination must be made whether the danger of undue prejudice outweighs the probative value of the evidence in view of the availability of other means of proof and other facts appropriate for making decision of this kind under Rule 403. Slough and Knightly, Other Vices, Other Crimes, 41 Iowa L.Rev. 325 (1956).

1974 Enactment

Note to Subdivision (b). The second sentence of Rule 404(b) as submitted to the Congress began with the words "This subdivision does not exclude the evidence when offered". The Committee amended this language to read "It may, however, be admissible", the words used in the 1971 Advisory Committee draft, on the ground that this formulation properly placed greater emphasis on admissibility than did the final Court version. House Report No. 93–650.

Note to Subdivision (b). This rule provides that evidence of other crimes, wrongs, or acts is not admissible to prove character but may be admissible for other specified purposes such as proof of motive.

Although your committee sees no necessity in amending the rule itself, it anticipates that the use of the discretionary word "may" with respect to the admissibility of evidence of crimes, wrongs, or acts is not intended to confer any arbitrary discretion on the trial judge. Rather, it is anticipated that with respect to permissible uses for such evidence, the trial judge may exclude it only on the basis of those considerations set forth in Rule 403, i.e., prejudice, confusion or waste of time. Senate Report No. 93–1277.

1991 Amendments

Rule 404(b) has emerged as one of the most cited Rules in the Rules of Evidence. And in many criminal cases evidence of an accused's extrinsic acts is viewed as an important asset in the prosecution's case against an accused. Although there are a few reported decisions on use of such evidence by the defense, *see, e.g., United States v. McClure*, 546 F.2d 670 (5th Cir.1990) (acts of informant offered in entrapment defense), the overwhelming number of cases involve introduction of that evidence by the prosecution.

The amendment to Rule 404(b) adds a pretrial notice requirement in criminal cases and is intended to reduce surprise and promote early resolution on the issue of admissibility. The notice requirement thus places Rule 404(b) in the mainstream with notice and disclosure provisions in other rules of evidence. *See, e.g.,* Rule 412 (written motion of intent to offer evidence under rule), Rule 609 (written notice of intent to offer conviction older than 10 years), Rule 803(24) and 804(b)(5) (notice of intent to use residual hearsay exceptions).

The Rule expects that counsel for both the defense and the prosecution will submit the necessary request and information in a reasonable and timely fashion. Other than requiring pretrial notice, no specific time limits are stated in recognition that what constitutes a reasonable request or disclosure will depend largely on the circumstances of each case. *Compare* Fla.Stat.Ann. § 90.404(2)(b) (notice must be given at least 10 days before trial) *with* Tex.R.Evid. 404(b) (no time limit).

Likewise, no specific form of notice is required. The Committee considered and rejected a requirement that the notice satisfy the particularity requirements normally required of language used in a charging instrument. *Cf.* Fla.Stat.Ann. § 90.404(2)(b) (written disclosure must describe uncharged misconduct with particularity required of an indictment or information). Instead, the Committee opted for a generalized notice provision which requires the prosecution to apprise the defense of the general nature of the evidence of extrinsic acts. The Committee does not intend that the amendment will supercede other rules of admissibility or disclosure, such as the Jencks Act, 18 U.S.C. § 3500, et. seq. nor require the prosecution to disclose directly or indirectly the names and addresses of its witnesses, something it is currently not required to do under Federal Rule of Criminal Procedure 16.

The amendment requires the prosecution to provide notice, regardless of how it intends to use the extrinsic act evidence at trial, i.e., during its case-in-chief, for impeachment, or for possible rebuttal. The court in its discretion may, under the facts, decide that the particular request or notice was not reasonable, either because of the lack of timeliness or completeness. Because the notice requirement serves as condition precedent to admissibility of 404(b) evidence, the offered evidence is inadmissible if the court decides that the notice requirement has not been met.

Nothing in the amendment precludes the court from requiring the government to provide it with an opportunity to rule *in limine* on 404(b) evidence before it is offered or even mentioned during trial. When ruling *in limine*, the court may require the government to disclose to it the specifics of such evidence which the court must consider in determining admissibility.

The amendment does not extend to evidence of acts which are "intrinsic" to the charged offense, *see United States v. Williams*, 900 F.2d 823 (5th Cir.1990) (noting distinction between 404(b) evidence and intrinsic offense evidence). Nor is the amendment intended to redefine what evidence would otherwise be admissible under Rule 404(b). Finally, the Committee does not intend through the amendment to affect the role of the court and the jury in considering such evidence. *See United States v. Huddleston*, 485 U.S. 681, 108 S.Ct. 1496 (1988).

2000 Amendments

Rule 404(a)(1) has been amended to provide that when the accused attacks the character of an alleged victim under subdivision (a)(2) of this Rule, the door is opened to an attack on the same character trait of the accused. Current law does not allow the government to introduce negative character evidence as to the accused unless the accused introduces evidence of good character. *See, e.g., United States v. Fountain*, 768 F.2d 790 (7th Cir. 1985) (when the accused offers proof of self-defense, this permits proof of the alleged victim's character trait for peacefulness, but it does not permit proof of the accused's character trait for violence).

The amendment makes clear that the accused cannot attack the alleged victim's character and yet remain shielded from the disclosure of equally relevant evidence concerning the same character trait of the accused. For example, in a murder case with a claim of self-defense, the accused, to bolster this defense, might offer evidence of the alleged victim's violent disposition. If the government has evidence that the accused has a violent character, but is not allowed to offer this evidence as part of its rebuttal, the jury has only part of the information it needs for an informed assessment of the probabilities as to who was the initial aggressor. This may be the case even if evidence of the accused's prior violent acts is admitted under Rule 404(b), because such evidence can be admitted only for limited purposes and not to show action in conformity with the accused's charac-

ter on a specific occasion. Thus, the amendment is designed to permit a more balanced presentation of character evidence when an accused chooses to attack the character of the alleged victim.

The amendment does not affect the admissibility of evidence of specific acts of uncharged misconduct offered for a purpose other than proving character under Rule 404(b). Nor does it affect the standards for proof of character by evidence of other sexual behavior or sexual offenses under Rules 412–415. By its placement in Rule 404(a)(1), the amendment covers only proof of character by way of reputation or opinion.

The amendment does not permit proof of the accused's character if the accused merely uses character evidence for a purpose other than to prove the alleged victim's propensity to act in a certain way. *See United States v. Burks*, 470 F.2d 432, 434–5 (D.C.Cir. 1972) (evidence of the alleged victim's violent character, when known by the accused, was admissible "on the issue of whether or not the defendant reasonably feared he was in danger of imminent great bodily harm"). Finally, the amendment does not permit proof of the accused's character when the accused attacks the alleged victim's character as a witness under Rule 608 or 609.

The term "alleged" is inserted before each reference to "victim" in the Rule, in order to provide consistency with Evidence Rule 412.

Rule 405. Methods of Proving Character

(a) Reputation or opinion. In all cases in which evidence of character or a trait of character of a person is admissible, proof may be made by testimony as to reputation or by testimony in the form of an opinion. On cross-examination, inquiry is allowable into relevant specific instances of conduct.

(b) Specific instances of conduct. In cases in which character or a trait of character of a person is an essential element of a charge, claim, or defense, proof may also be made of specific instances of that person's conduct.

ADVISORY COMMITTEE NOTES
1972 Proposed Rules

The rule deals only with allowable methods of proving character, not with the admissibility of character evidence, which is covered in Rule 404.

Of the three methods of proving character provided by the rule, evidence of specific instances of conduct is the most convincing. At the same time it possesses the greatest capacity to arouse prejudice, to confuse, to surprise, and to consume time. Consequently the rule confines the use of evidence of this kind to cases in which character is, in the strict sense, in issue and hence deserving of a searching inquiry. When character is used circumstantially and hence occupies a lesser status in the case, proof may be only by reputation and opinion. These latter methods are also available when character is in issue. This treatment is, with respect to specific instances of conduct and reputation, conventional contemporary common law doctrine. McCormick § 153.

In recognizing opinion as a means of proving character, the rule departs from usual contemporary practice in favor of that of an earlier day. See 7 Wigmore § 1986, pointing out that the earlier practice permitted opinion and arguing strongly for evidence based on personal knowledge and belief as contrasted with "the secondhand, irresponsible product of multiplied guesses and gossip which we term 'reputation'." It seems likely that the persistence of reputation evidence is due to its largely being opinion in disguise. Traditionally character has been regarded primarily in moral overtones of good and bad: chaste, peaceable, truthful, honest. Nevertheless, on occasion nonmoral considerations crop up, as in the case of the incompetent driver, and this seems bound to happen increasingly. If character is defined as the kind of person one is, then account must be taken of varying ways of arriving at the estimate. These may range from the opinion of the employer who has found the man honest to the opinion of the psychiatrist based upon examination and testing. No effective dividing line exists between character and mental capacity, and the latter traditionally has been provable by opinion.

According to the great majority of cases, on cross-examination inquiry is allowable as to whether the reputation witness has heard of particular instances of conduct pertinent to the trait in question. *Michelson v. United States,* 335 U.S. 469, 69 S.Ct. 213, 93 L.Ed. 168 (1948); Annot., 47 A.L.R.2d 1258. The theory is that, since the reputation witness relates what he has heard, the inquiry tends to shed light on the accuracy of his hearing and reporting. Accordingly, the opinion witness would be asked whether he knew, as well as whether he had heard. The fact is, of course, that these distinctions are of slight if any practical significance, and the second sentence of subdivision (a) eliminates them as a factor in formulating questions. This recognition of the propriety of inquiring into specific instances of conduct does not circumscribe inquiry otherwise into the bases of opinion and reputation testimony.

The express allowance of inquiry into specific instances of conduct on cross-examination in subdivision (a) and the express allowance of it as part of a case in chief when character is actually in issue in subdivision (b) contemplate that testimony of specific instances is not generally permissible on the direct examination of an ordinary opinion witness to character. Similarly as to witnesses to the character of witnesses under Rule 608(b). Opinion testimony on direct in these situations ought in general to correspond to reputation testimony as now given, *i.e.,* be confined to the nature and extent of observation and acquaintance upon which the opinion is based. See Rule 701.

1974 Enactment

Note to Subdivision (a). Rule 405(a) as submitted proposed to change existing law by allowing evidence of character in the form of opinion as well as reputation testimony. Fearing, among other reasons, that wholesale allowance of opinion testimony might tend to turn a trial into a swearing contest between conflicting character witnesses, the Committee decided to delete from this Rule, as well as from Rule 608(a) which involves a related problem, reference to opinion testimony. House Report No. 93–650.

The Senate makes two language changes in the nature of conforming amendments. The Conference adopts the Senate amendments. House Report No. 93–1597.

Rule 406. Habit; Routine Practice

Evidence of the habit of a person or of the routine practice of an organization, whether corroborated or not and regardless of the presence of eyewitnesses, is relevant to prove that the conduct of the person or organization on a particular occasion was in conformity with the habit or routine practice.

ADVISORY COMMITTEE NOTES

1972 Proposed Rules

An oft-quoted paragraph, McCormick, § 162, p. 340, describes habit in terms effectively contrasting it with character:

"Character and habit are close akin. Character is a generalized description of one's disposition, or of one's disposition in respect to a general trait, such as honesty, temperance, or peacefulness. 'Habit,' in modern usage, both lay and psychological, is more specific. It describes one's regular response to a repeated specific situation. If we speak of character for care, we think of the person's tendency to act prudently in all the varying situations of life, in business, family life, in handling automobiles and in walking across the street. A habit, on the other hand, is the person's regular practice of meeting a particular kind of situation with a specific type of conduct, such as the habit of going down a particular stairway two stairs at a time, or of giving the hand-signal for a left turn, or of alighting from

railway cars while they are moving. The doing of the habitual acts may become semi-automatic."

Equivalent behavior on the part of a group is designated "routine practice of an organization" in the rule.

Agreement is general that habit evidence is highly persuasive as proof of conduct on a particular occasion. Again quoting McCormick § 162, p. 341:

"Character may be thought of as the sum of one's habits though doubtless it is more than this. But unquestionably the uniformity of one's response to habit is far greater than the consistency with which one's conduct conforms to character or disposition. Even though character comes in only exceptionally as evidence of an act, surely any sensible man in investigating whether X did a particular act would be greatly helped in his inquiry by evidence as to whether he was in the habit of doing it."

When disagreement has appeared, its focus has been upon the question what constitutes habit, and the reason for this is readily apparent. The extent to which instances must be multiplied and consistency of behavior maintained in order to rise to the status of habit inevitably gives rise to differences of opinion. Lewan, Rationale of Habit Evidence, 16 Syracuse L.Rev. 39, 49 (1964). While adequacy of sampling and uniformity of response are key factors, precise standards for measuring their sufficiency for evidence purposes cannot be formulated.

The rule is consistent with prevailing views. Much evidence is excluded simply because of failure to achieve the status of habit. Thus, evidence of intemperate "habits" is generally excluded when offered as proof of drunkenness in accident cases, Annot., 46 A.L.R.2d 103, and evidence of other assaults is inadmissible to prove the instant one in a civil assault action, Annot., 66 A.L.R.2d 806. In *Levin v. United States,* 119 U.S.App.D.C. 156, 338 F.2d 265 (1964), testimony as to the religious "habits" of the accused, offered as tending to prove that he was at home observing the Sabbath rather than out obtaining money through larceny by trick, was held properly excluded:

"It seems apparent to us that an individual's religious practices would not be the type of activities which would lend themselves to the characterization of 'invariable regularity.' [1 Wigmore 520.] Certainly the very volitional basis of the activity raises serious questions as to its invariable nature, and hence its probative value." *Id.* at 272.

These rulings are not inconsistent with the trend towards admitting evidence of business transactions between one of the parties and a third person as tending to prove that he made the same bargain or proposal in the litigated situation. Slough, Relevancy Unraveled, 6 Kan.L.Rev. 38–41 (1957). Nor are they inconsistent with such cases as *Whittemore v. Lockheed Aircraft Corp.,* 65 Cal.App.2d 737, 151 P.2d 670 (1944), upholding the admission of evidence that plaintiff's intestate had on four other occasions flown planes from defendant's factory for delivery to his employer airline, offered to prove that he was piloting rather than a guest on a plane which crashed and killed all on board while en route for delivery.

A considerable body of authority has required that evidence of the routine practice of an organization be corroborated as a condition precedent to its admission in evidence. Slough, Relevancy Unraveled, 5 Kan.L.Rev. 404, 449 (1957). This requirement is specifically rejected by the rule on the ground that it relates to the sufficiency of the evidence rather than admissibility. A similar position is taken in New Jersey Rule 49. The rule also rejects the requirement of the absence of eyewitnesses, sometimes encountered with respect to admitting habit evidence to prove freedom from contributory negligence in wrongful death cases. For comment critical of the requirements see Frank, J., in *Cereste v. New York,* N.H. & H.R. Co., 231 F.2d 50 (2d Cir.1956), cert. denied 351 U.S. 951, 76 S.Ct. 848, 100 L.Ed. 1475, 10 Vand.L.Rev. 447 (1957); McCormick § 162, p. 342. The omission of the requirement from the California Evidence Code is said to have effected its elimination. Comment, Cal.Ev.Code § 1105.

Rule 407. Subsequent Remedial Measures

When, after an injury or harm allegedly caused by an event, measures are taken that, if taken previously, would have made the injury or harm less likely to occur, evidence of the subsequent measures is not admissible to prove negligence, culpable conduct, a defect in a product, a defect in a product's design, or a need for a warning or instruction. This rule does not require the exclusion of evidence of subsequent measures when offered for another purpose, such as proving ownership, control, or feasibility of precautionary measures, if controverted, or impeachment.

ADVISORY COMMITTEE NOTES

1972 Proposed Rules

The rule incorporates conventional doctrine which excludes evidence of subsequent remedial measures as proof of an admission of fault. The rule rests on two grounds. (1) The conduct is not in fact an admission, since the conduct is equally consistent with injury by mere accident or through contributory negligence. Or, as Baron Bramwell put it, the rule rejects the notion that "because the world gets wiser as it gets older, therefore it was foolish before." *Hart v. Lancashire & Yorkshire Ry. Co.*, 21 L.T.R. N.S. 261, 263 (1869). Under a liberal theory of relevancy this ground alone would not support exclusion as the inference is still a possible one. (2) The other, and more impressive, ground for exclusion rests on a social policy of encouraging people to take, or at least not discouraging them from taking, steps in furtherance of added safety. The courts have applied this principle to exclude evidence of subsequent repairs, installation of safety devices, changes in company rules, and discharge of employees, and the language of the present rule is broad enough to encompass all of them. See Falknor, Extrinsic Policies Affecting Admissibility, 10 Rutgers L.Rev. 574, 590 (1956).

The second sentence of the rule directs attention to the limitations of the rule. Exclusion is called for only when the evidence of subsequent remedial measures is offered as proof of negligence or culpable conduct. In effect it rejects the suggested inference that fault is admitted. Other purposes are, however, allowable, including ownership or control, existence of duty, and feasibility of precautionary measures, if controverted, and impeachment. 2 Wigmore § 283; Annot., 64 A.L.R.2d 1296. Two recent federal cases are illustrative. *Boeing Airplane Co. v. Brown*, 291 F.2d 310 (9th Cir.1961), an action against an airplane manufacturer for using an allegedly defectively designed alternator shaft which caused a plane crash, upheld the admission of evidence of subsequent design modification for the purpose of showing that design changes and safeguards were feasible. And *Powers v. J.B. Michael & Co.*, 329 F.2d 674 (6th Cir.1964), an action against a road contractor for negligent failure to put out warning signs, sustained the admission of evidence that defendant subsequently put out signs to show that the portion of the road in question was under defendant's control. The requirement that the other purpose be controverted calls for automatic exclusion unless a genuine issue be present and allows the opposing party to lay the groundwork for exclusion by making an admission. Otherwise the factors of undue prejudice, confusion of issues, misleading the jury, and waste of time remain for consideration under Rule 403.

For comparable rules, see Uniform Rule 51; California Evidence Code § 1151; Kansas Code of Civil Procedure § 60–451; New Jersey Evidence Rule 51.

1997 Amendments

The amendment to Rule 407 makes two changes in the rule. First, the words "an injury or harm allegedly caused by" were added to clarify that the rule applies only to changes made after the occurrence that produced the damages giving rise to the action. Evidence of measures taken by the defendant prior to the "event" causing "injury or harm" do not fall within the

exclusionary scope of Rule 407 even if they occurred after the manufacture or design of the product. See *Chase v. General Motors Corp.*, 856 F.2d 17, 21–22 (4th Cir. 1988).

Second, Rule 407 has been amended to provide that evidence of subsequent remedial measures may not be used to prove "a defect in a product or its design, or that a warning or instruction should have accompanied a product." This amendment adopts the view of a majority of the circuits that have interpreted Rule 407 to apply to products liability actions. See *Raymond v. Raymond Corp.*, 938 F.2d 1518, 1522 (1st Cir. 1991); *In re Joint Eastern District and Southern District Asbestos Litigation v. Armstrong World industries, Inc.*, 995 F.2d 343 (2d Cir. 1993); *Cann v. Ford Motor Co.*, 658 F.2d 54, 60 (2d Cir. 1981), cert. denied, 456 U.S. 960 (1982); *Kelly v. Crown Equipment Co.*, 970 F.2d 1273, 1275 (3d Cir. 1992); *Werner v. Upjohn, Inc.*, 628 F.2d 848 (4th Cir. 1980); cert. denied, 449 U.S. 1080 (1981); *Grenada Steel Industries, Inc. v. Alabama Oxygen Co., Inc.*, 695 F.2d 883 (5th Cir. 1983); *Bauman v. Volkswagenwerk Aktiengesellschaft*, 621 F.2d 230, 232 (6th Cir. 1980); *Flaminio v. Honda Motor Company, Ltd.*, 733 F.2d 463, 469 (7th Cir. 1984); *Gauthier v. AMF, Inc.*, 788 F.2d 634, 636–37 (9th Cir. 1986).

Although this amendment adopts a uniform federal rule, it should be noted that evidence of subsequent remedial measures may be admissible pursuant to the second sentence of Rule 407. Evidence of subsequent measures that is not barred by Rule 407 may still be subject to exclusion on Rule 403 grounds when the dangers of prejudice or confusion substantially outweigh the probative value of the evidence.

Rule 408. Compromise and Offers to Compromise

Evidence of (1) furnishing or offering or promising to furnish, or (2) accepting or offering or promising to accept, a valuable consideration in compromising or attempting to compromise a claim which was disputed as to either validity or amount, is not admissible to prove liability for or invalidity of the claim or its amount. Evidence of conduct or statements made in compromise negotiations is likewise not admissible. This rule does not require the exclusion of any evidence otherwise discoverable merely because it is presented in the course of compromise negotiations. This rule also does not require exclusion when the evidence is offered for another purpose, such as proving bias or prejudice of a witness, negativing a contention of undue delay, or proving an effort to obstruct a criminal investigation or prosecution.

ADVISORY COMMITTEE NOTES

1972 Proposed Rules

As a matter of general agreement, evidence of an offer to compromise a claim is not receivable in evidence as an admission of, as the case may be, the validity or invalidity of the claim. As with evidence of subsequent remedial measures, dealt with in Rule 407, exclusion may be based on two grounds. (1) The evidence is irrelevant, since the offer may be motivated by a desire for peace rather than from any concession of weakness of position. The validity of this position will vary as the amount of the offer varies in relation to the size of the claim and may also be influenced by other circumstances. (2) A more consistently impressive ground is promotion of the public policy favoring the compromise and settlement of disputes. McCormick §§ 76, 251. While the rule is ordinarily phrased in terms of offers of compromise, it is apparent that a similar attitude must be taken with respect to completed compromises when offered against a party thereto. This latter situation will not, of course, ordinarily occur except when a party to the present litigation has compromised with a third person.

The same policy underlies the provision of Rule 68 of the Federal Rules of Civil Procedure that evidence of an unaccepted offer of judgment is not admissible except in a proceeding to determine costs.

Complete Annotation Materials, see Title 28 U.S.C.A.

The practical value of the common law rule has been greatly diminished by its inapplicability to admissions of fact, even though made in the course of compromise negotiations, unless hypothetical, stated to be "without prejudice," or so connected with the offer as to be inseparable from it. McCormick § 251, pp. 540–541. An inevitable effect is to inhibit freedom of communication with respect to compromise, even among lawyers. Another effect is the generation of controversy over whether a given statement falls within or without the protected area. These considerations account for the expansion of the rule herewith to include evidence of conduct or statements made in compromise negotiations, as well as the offer or completed compromise itself. For similar provisions see California Evidence Code §§ 1152, 1154.

The policy considerations which underlie the rule do not come into play when the effort is to induce a creditor to settle an admittedly due amount for a lesser sum. McCormick § 251, p. 540. Hence the rule requires that the claim be disputed as to either validity or amount.

The final sentence of the rule serves to point out some limitations upon its applicability. Since the rule excludes only when the purpose is proving the validity or invalidity of the claim or its amount, an offer for another purpose is not within the rule. The illustrative situations mentioned in the rule are supported by the authorities. As to proving bias or prejudice of a witness, see Annot., 161 A.L.R. 395, *contra, Fenberg v. Rosenthal*, 348 Ill.App. 510, 109 N.E.2d 402 (1952), and negativing a contention of lack of due diligence in presenting a claim, 4 Wigmore § 1061. An effort to "buy off" the prosecution or a prosecuting witness in a criminal case is not within the policy of the rule of exclusion. McCormick § 251, p. 542.

For other rules of similar import, see Uniform Rules 52 and 53; California Evidence Code §§ 1152, 1154; Kansas Code of Civil Procedure §§ 60–452, 60–453; New Jersey Evidence Rules 52 and 53.

1974 Enactment

Under existing federal law evidence of conduct and statements made in compromise negotiations is admissible in subsequent litigation between the parties. The second sentence of Rule 408 as submitted by the Supreme Court proposed to reverse that doctrine in the interest of further promoting non-judicial settlement of disputes. Some agencies of government expressed the view that the Court formulation was likely to impede rather than assist efforts to achieve settlement of disputes. For one thing, it is not always easy to tell when compromise negotiations begin, and informal dealings end. Also, parties dealing with government agencies would be reluctant to furnish factual information at preliminary meetings; they would wait until "compromise negotiations" began and thus hopefully effect an immunity for themselves with respect to the evidence supplied. In light of these considerations, the Committee recast the Rule so that admissions of liability or opinions given during compromise negotiations continue inadmissible, but evidence of unqualified factual assertions is admissible. The latter aspect of the Rule is drafted, however, so as to preserve other possible objections to the introduction of such evidence. The Committee intends no modification of current law whereby a party may protect himself from future use of his statements by couching them in hypothetical conditional form. House Report No. 93–650.

This rule as reported makes evidence of settlement or attempted settlement of a disputed claim inadmissible when offered as an admission of liability or the amount of liability. The purpose of this rule is to encourage settlements which would be discouraged if such evidence were admissible.

Under present law, in most jurisdictions, statements of fact made during settlement negotiations, however, are excepted from this ban and are admissible. The only escape from admissibility of statements of fact made in a settlement negotiation is if the declarant or his representative expressly states that the statement is hypothetical in nature or is made without prejudice. Rule 408 as submitted by the Court reversed the traditional rule. It would have brought statements of fact within the ban and made them, as well as an offer of settlement, inadmissible.

The House amended the rule and would continue to make evidence of facts disclosed during compromise negotiations admissible. It thus reverted to the traditional rule. The House committee report states that the committee intends to preserve current law under which a party may protect himself by couching his statements in hypothetical form [See House Report No. 93–650 above]. The real impact of this amendment, however, is to deprive the rule of much of its salutary effect. The exception for factual admissions was believed by the Advisory Committee to hamper free communication between parties and thus to constitute an unjustifiable restraint upon efforts to negotiate settlements—the encouragement of which is the purpose of the rule. Further, by protecting hypothetically phrased statements, it constituted a preference for the sophisticated, and a trap for the unwary.

Three States which had adopted rules of evidence patterned after the proposed rules prescribed by the Supreme Court opted for versions of rule 408 identical with the Supreme Court draft with respect to the inadmissibility of conduct or statements made in compromise negotiations [Nev.Rev.Stats. § 48.105; N.Mex.Stats.Anno. (1973 Supp.) § 20–4–408; West's Wis.Stats. Anno. (1973 Supp.) § 904.08].

For these reasons, the committee has deleted the House amendment and restored the rule to the version submitted by the Supreme Court with one additional amendment. This amendment adds a sentence to insure that evidence, such as documents, is not rendered inadmissible merely because it is presented in the course of compromise negotiations if the evidence is otherwise discoverable. A party should not be able to immunize from admissibility documents otherwise discoverable merely by offering them in a compromise negotiation. Senate Report No. 93–1277.

The House bill provides that evidence of admissions of liability or opinions given during compromise negotiations is not admissible, but that evidence of facts disclosed during compromise negotiations is not inadmissible by virtue of having been first disclosed in the compromise negotiations. The Senate amendment provides that evidence of conduct or statements made in compromise negotiations is not admissible. The Senate amendment also provides that the rule does not require the exclusion of any evidence otherwise discoverable merely because it is presented in the course of compromise negotiations.

The House bill was drafted to meet the objection of executive agencies that under the rule as proposed by the Supreme Court, a party could present a fact during compromise negotiations and thereby prevent an opposing party from offering evidence of that fact at trial even though such evidence was obtained from independent sources. The Senate amendment expressly precludes this result.

The Conference adopts the Senate amendment. House Report No. 93–1597.

Rule 409. Payment of Medical and Similar Expenses

Evidence of furnishing or offering or promising to pay medical, hospital, or similar expenses occasioned by an injury is not admissible to prove liability for the injury.

ADVISORY COMMITTEE NOTES

1972 Proposed Rules

The considerations underlying this rule parallel those underlying Rules 407 and 408, which deal respectively with subsequent remedial measures and offers of compromise. As stated in Annot., 20 A.L.R.2d 291, 293:

"[G]enerally, evidence of payment of medical, hospital, or similar expenses of an injured party by the opposing party, is not admissible, the reason often given being that such payment or offer is usually made from humane impulses and not from an admission of liability, and that to hold otherwise would tend to discourage assistance to the injured person."

Contrary to Rule 408, dealing with offers of compromise, the present rule does not extend to conduct or statements not a part of the act of furnishing or offering or promising to pay. This difference in treatment arises from fundamental differences in nature. Communication is essential if compromises are to be effected, and consequently broad protection of statements is needed. This is not so in cases of payments or offers or promises to pay medical expenses, where factual statements may be expected to be incidental in nature.

For rules on the same subject, but phrased in terms of "humanitarian motives," see Uniform Rule 52; California Evidence Code § 1152; Kansas Code of Civil Procedure § 60–452; New Jersey Evidence Rule 52.

Rule 410. Inadmissibility of Pleas, Plea Discussions, and Related Statements

Except as otherwise provided in this rule, evidence of the following is not, in any civil or criminal proceeding, admissible against the defendant who made the plea or was a participant in the plea discussions:

(1) a plea of guilty which was later withdrawn;

(2) a plea of nolo contendere;

(3) any statement made in the course of any proceedings under Rule 11 of the Federal Rules of Criminal Procedure or comparable state procedure regarding either of the foregoing pleas; or

(4) any statement made in the course of plea discussions with an attorney for the prosecuting authority which do not result in a plea of guilty or which result in a plea of guilty later withdrawn.

However, such a statement is admissible (i) in any proceeding wherein another statement made in the course of the same plea or plea discussions has been introduced and the statement ought in fairness be considered contemporaneously with it, or (ii) in a criminal proceeding for perjury or false statement if the statement was made by the defendant under oath, on the record and in the presence of counsel.

ADVISORY COMMITTEE NOTES

1972 Proposed Rules

Withdrawn pleas of guilty were held inadmissible in federal prosecutions in *Kercheval v. United States,* 274 U.S. 220, 47 S.Ct. 582, 71 L.Ed. 1009 (1927). The Court pointed out that to admit the withdrawn plea would effectively set at naught the allowance of withdrawal and place the accused in a dilemma utterly inconsistent with the decision to award him a trial. The New York Court of Appeals, in *People v. Spitaleri,* 9 N.Y.2d 168, 212 N.Y.S.2d 53, 173 N.E.2d 35 (1961), reexamined and overturned its earlier decisions which had allowed admission. In addition to the reasons set forth in Kercheval, which was quoted at length, the court pointed out that the effect of admitting the plea was to compel defendant to take the stand by way of explanation and to open the way for the prosecution to call the lawyer who had represented him at the time of entering the plea. State court decisions for and against admissibility are collected in Annot., 86 A.L.R.2d 326.

Pleas of *nolo contendere* are recognized by Rule 11 of the Rules of Criminal Procedure, although the law of numerous States is to the contrary. The present rule gives effect to the principal traditional characteristic of the *nolo* plea, i.e. avoiding the admission of guilt which is inherent in pleas of guilty. This position is consistent with the construction of Section 5 of the Clayton Act, 15 U.S.C. § 16(a), recognizing the inconclusive and compromise nature of judgments based on *nolo* pleas. *General Electric Co. v. City of San Antonio,* 334 F.2d 480 (5th Cir.1964);

Commonwealth Edison Co. v. Allis–Chalmers Mfg. Co., 323 F.2d 412 (7th Cir.1963), cert. denied 376 U.S. 939, 84 S.Ct. 794, 11 L.Ed.2d 659; *Armco Steel Corp. v. North Dakota,* 376 F.2d 206 (8th Cir.1967); *City of Burbank v. General Electric Co.,* 329 F.2d 825 (9th Cir.1964). See also state court decisions in Annot., 18 A.L.R.2d 1287, 1314.

Exclusion of offers to plead guilty or *nolo* has as its purpose the promotion of disposition of criminal cases by compromise. As pointed out in McCormick § 251, p. 543.

"Effective criminal law administration in many localities would hardly be possible if a large proportion of the charges were not disposed of by such compromises."

See also *People v. Hamilton,* 60 Cal.2d 105, 32 Cal.Rptr. 4, 383 P.2d 412 (1963), discussing legislation designed to achieve this result. As with compromise offers generally, Rule 408, free communication is needed, and security against having an offer of compromise or related statement admitted in evidence effectively encourages it.

Limiting the exclusionary rule to use against the accused is consistent with the purpose of the rule, since the possibility of use for or against other persons will not impair the effectiveness of withdrawing pleas or the freedom of discussion which the rule is designed to foster. See A.B.A. Standards Relating to Pleas of Guilty § 2.2 (1968). See also the narrower provisions of New Jersey Evidence Rule 52(2) and the unlimited exclusion provided in California Evidence Code § 1153.

1974 Enactment

The Committee added the phrase "Except as otherwise provided by Act of Congress" to Rule 410 as submitted by the Court in order to preserve particular congressional policy judgments as to the effect of a plea of guilty or of nolo contendere. See 15 U.S.C. 16(a). The Committee intends that its amendment refers to both present statutes and statutes subsequently enacted. House Report No. 93–650.

As adopted by the House, rule 410 would make inadmissible pleas of guilty or nolo contendere subsequently withdrawn as well as offers to make such pleas. Such a rule is clearly justified as a means of encouraging pleading. However, the House rule would then go on to render inadmissible for any purpose statements made in connection with these pleas or offers as well.

The committee finds this aspect of the House rule unjustified. Of course, in certain circumstances such statements should be excluded. If, for example, a plea is vitiated because of coercion, statements made in connection with the plea may also have been coerced and should be inadmissible on that basis. In other cases, however, voluntary statements of an accused made in court on the record, in connection with a plea, and determined by a court to be reliable should be admissible even though the plea is subsequently withdrawn. This is particularly true in those cases where, if the House rule were in effect, a defendant would be able to contradict his previous statements and thereby lie with impunity [See *Harris v. New York,* 401 U.S. 222 (1971)]. To prevent such an injustice, the rule has been modified to permit the use of such statements for the limited purposes of impeachment and in subsequent perjury or false statement prosecutions. Senate Report No. 93–1277.

The House bill provides that evidence of a guilty or nolo contendere plea, of an offer of either plea, or of statements made in connection with such pleas or offers of such pleas, is inadmissible in any civil or criminal action, case or proceeding against the person making such plea or offer. The Senate amendment makes the rule inapplicable to a voluntary and reliable statement made in court on the record where the statement is offered in a subsequent prosecution of the declarant for perjury or false statement.

The issues raised by Rule 410 are also raised by proposed Rule 11(e)(6) of the Federal Rules of Criminal Procedure presently pending before Congress. This proposed rule, which deals with the admissibility of pleas of guilty or nolo contendere, offers to make such pleas, and statements made in connection with such pleas, was promulgated by the Supreme Court on April 22,

1974, and in the absence of congressional action will become effective on August 1, 1975. The conferees intend to make no change in the presently-existing case law until that date, leaving the courts free to develop rules in this area on a case-by-case basis.

The Conferees further determined that the issues presented by the use of guilty and nolo contendere pleas, offers of such pleas, and statements made in connection with such pleas or offers, can be explored in greater detail during Congressional consideration of Rule 11(e)(6) of the Federal Rules of Criminal Procedure. The Conferees believe, therefore, that it is best to defer its effective date until August 1, 1975. The Conferees intend that Rule 410 would be superseded by any subsequent Federal Rule of Criminal Procedure or act of Congress with which it is inconsistent, if the Federal Rule of Criminal Procedure or Act of Congress takes effect or becomes law after the date of the enactment of the act establishing the rules of evidence.

The conference adopts the Senate amendment with an amendment that expresses the above intentions. House Report No. 93–1597.

1979 Amendments

Present rule 410 conforms to rule 11(e)(6) of the Federal Rules of Criminal Procedure. A proposed amendment to rule 11(e)(6) would clarify the circumstances in which pleas, plea discussions and related statements are inadmissible in evidence: see Advisory Committee Note thereto. The amendment proposed above would make comparable changes in rule 410.

Rule 411.   Liability Insurance

Evidence that a person was or was not insured against liability is not admissible upon the issue whether the person acted negligently or otherwise wrongfully. This rule does not require the exclusion of evidence of insurance against liability when offered for another purpose, such as proof of agency, ownership, or control, or bias or prejudice of a witness.

ADVISORY COMMITTEE NOTES
1972 Proposed Rules

The courts have with substantial unanimity rejected evidence of liability insurance for the purpose of proving fault, and absence of liability insurance as proof of lack of fault. At best the inference of fault from the fact of insurance coverage is a tenuous one, as is its converse. More important, no doubt, has been the feeling that knowledge of the presence or absence of liability insurance would induce juries to decide cases on improper grounds. McCormick § 168; Annot., 4 A.L.R.2d 761. The rule is drafted in broad terms so as to include contributory negligence or other fault of a plaintiff as well as fault of a defendant.

The second sentence points out the limits of the rule, using well established illustrations. *Id.*

For similar rules see Uniform Rule 54; California Evidence Code § 1155; Kansas Code of Civil Procedure § 60–454; New Jersey Evidence Rule 54.

Rule 412.   Sex Offense Cases; Relevance of Alleged Victim's Past Sexual Behavior or Alleged Sexual Predisposition

(a) Evidence generally inadmissible.—The following evidence is not admissible in any civil or criminal proceeding involving alleged sexual misconduct except as provided in subdivisions (b) and (c):

(1) Evidence offered to prove that any alleged victim engaged in other sexual behavior.

(2) Evidence offered to prove any alleged victim's sexual predisposition.

(b) Exceptions.—

(1) In a criminal case, the following evidence is admissible, if otherwise admissible under these rules:

(A) evidence of specific instances of sexual behavior by the alleged victim offered to prove that a person other than the accused was the source of semen, injury or other physical evidence;

(B) evidence of specific instances of sexual behavior by the alleged victim with respect to the person accused of the sexual misconduct offered by the accused to prove consent or by the prosecution; and

(C) evidence the exclusion of which would violate the constitutional rights of the defendant.

(2) In a civil case, evidence offered to prove the sexual behavior or sexual predisposition of any alleged victim is admissible if it is otherwise admissible under these rules and its probative value substantially outweighs the danger of harm to any victim and of unfair prejudice to any party. Evidence of an alleged victim's reputation is admissible only if it has been placed in controversy by the alleged victim.

(c) Procedure to determine admissibility.—

(1) A party intending to offer evidence under subdivision (b) must—

(A) file a written motion at least 14 days before trial specifically describing the evidence and stating the purpose for which it is offered unless the court, for good cause requires a different time for filing or permits filing during trial; and

(B) serve the motion on all parties and notify the alleged victim or, when appropriate, the alleged victim's guardian or representative.

(2) Before admitting evidence under this rule the court must conduct a hearing in camera and afford the victim and parties a right to attend and be heard. The motion, related papers, and the record of the hearing must be sealed and remain under seal unless the court orders otherwise.

ADVISORY COMMITTEE NOTES
1994 Amendments

Rule 412 has been revised to diminish some of the confusion engendered by the original rule and to expand the protection afforded alleged victims of sexual misconduct. Rule 412 applies to both civil and criminal proceedings. The rule aims to safeguard the alleged victim against the invasion of privacy, potential embarrassment and sexual stereotyping that is associated with public disclosure of intimate sexual details and the infusion of sexual innuendo into the factfinding process. By affording victims protection in most instances, the rule also encourages victims of sexual misconduct to institute and to participate in legal proceedings against alleged offenders

Rule 412 seeks to achieve these objectives by barring evidence relating to the alleged victim's sexual behavior or alleged sexual predisposition, whether offered as substantive evidence of for impeachment, except in designated circumstances in which the probative value of the evidence significantly outweighs possible harm to the victim.

The revised rule applies in all cases involving sexual misconduct without regard to whether the alleged victim or person accused is a party to the litigation. Rule 412 extends to "pattern" witnesses in both criminal and civil cases whose testimony about other instances of sexual misconduct by the person accused is otherwise admissible. When the case does not involve alleged sexual misconduct, evidence relating to a third-party witness' alleged sexual activities is not within the ambit of Rule 412. The witness will, however, be protected by other rules such as Rules 404 and 608, as well as Rule 403.

The terminology "alleged victim" is used because there will frequently be a factual dispute as to whether sexual misconduct occurred. It does not connote any requirement that the misconduct be alleged in the pleadings. Rule 412 does not, however, apply unless the person against whom the evidence is offered can reasonably be characterized as a "victim of alleged sexual misconduct." When this is not the case, as for instance in a defamation action involving statements concerning sexual misconduct in which the evidence is offered to show that the alleged defamatory statements were true or did not damage the plaintiff's reputation, neither Rule 404 nor this rule will operate to bar the evidence; Rule 401 and 403 will continue to control. Rule 412 will, however, apply in a Title VII action in which the plaintiff has alleged sexual harassment.

The reference to a person "accused" is also used in a non-technical sense. There is no requirement that there be a criminal charge pending against the person or even that the misconduct would constitute a criminal offense. Evidence offered to prove allegedly false prior claims by the victim is not barred by Rule 412. However, the evidence is subject to the requirements of Rule 404.

Subdivision (a). As amended, Rule 412 bars evidence offered to prove the victim's sexual behavior and alleged sexual predisposition. Evidence, which might otherwise be admissible under Rules 402, 404(b), 405, 607, 608, 609 of some other evidence rule, must be excluded if Rule 412 so requires. The word "other" is used to suggest some flexibility in admitting evidence "intrinsic" to the alleged sexual misconduct. *Cf.* Committee Note to 1991 amendment to Rule 404(b)

Past sexual behavior connotes all activities that involve actual physical conduct, i.e. sexual intercourse or sexual contact. *See, e.g., United States v. Galloway,* 937 F.2d 542 (10th Cir. 1991), *cert. denied,* 113 S.Ct. 418 (1992) (use of contraceptives inadmissible since use implies sexual activity); *United States v. One Feather,* 702 F.2d 736 (8th Cir. 1983) (birth of an illegitimate child inadmissible); *State v. Carmichael,* 727 P.2d 918, 925 (Kan. 1986) (evidence of venereal disease inadmissible). In addition, the word "behavior" should be construed to include activities of the mind, such as fantasies of dreams. *See* 23 C. Wright and K. Graham, Jr., *Federal Practice and Procedure,* § 5384 at p. 548 (1980) ("While there may be some doubt under statutes that require 'conduct,' it would seem that the language of Rule 412 is broad enough to encompass the behavior of the mind.").

The rule has been amended to also exclude all other evidence relating to an alleged victim of sexual misconduct that is offered to prove a sexual predisposition. This amendment is designed to exclude evidence that does not directly refer to sexual activities or thoughts but that the proponent believes may have a sexual connotation for the factfinder. Admission of such evidence would contravene Rule 412's objectives of shielding the alleged victim from potential embarrassment and safeguarding the victim against stereotypical thinking. Consequently, unless the (b)(2) exception is satisfied, evidence such as that relating to the alleged victim's mode of dress, speech, or life-style will not be admissible.

The introductory phrase in subdivision (a) was deleted because it lacked clarity and contained no explicit reference to the other provisions of the law that were intended to be overridden. The conditional clause, "except as provided in subdivisions (b) and (c)" is intended to make clear that evidence of the types described in subdivision (a) is admissible only under the strictures of those sections.

The reason for extending the rule to all criminal cases is obvious. The strong social policy of protecting a victim's privacy and encouraging victims to come forward to report criminal acts is not confined to cases that involve a charge of sexual assault. The need to protect the victim is equally great when a defendant is charged with kidnapping, and evidence is offered, either to prove motive or as background, that the defendant sexually assaulted the victim.

The reason for extending Rule 412 to civil cases is equally obvious. The need to protect alleged victims against invasions of privacy, potential embarrassment, and unwarranted sexual stereotyping, and the wish to encourage victims to come forward when they have been sexually molested do not disappear because the context has shifted from a criminal prosecution to a claim for damages or injunctive relief. There is a strong social policy in not only punishing those who engage in sexual misconduct, but in also providing relief to the victim. Thus, Rule 412 applies in any civil case in which a person claims to be the victim of sexual misconduct, such as actions for sexual battery or sexual harassment.

Subdivision (b). Subdivision (b) spells out the specific circumstances in which some evidence may be admissible that would otherwise be barred by the general rule expressed in subdivision (a). As amended, Rule 412 will be virtually unchanged in criminal cases, but will provide protection to any person alleged to be a victim of sexual misconduct regardless of the charge actually brought against an accused. A new exception has been added for civil cases.

In a criminal case, evidence may be admitted under subdivision (b)(1) pursuant to three possible exceptions, provided the evidence also satisfies other requirements for admissibility specified in the Federal Rules of Evidence, including Rule 403. Subdivisions (b)(1)(A) and (b)(1)(B) require proof in the form of specific instances of sexual behavior in recognition of the limited probative value and dubious reliability of evidence of reputation or evidence in the form of an opinion.

Under subdivision (b)(1)(A), evidence of specific instances of sexual behavior with persons other than the person whose sexual misconduct is alleged may be admissible if it is offered to prove that another person was the source of semen, injury or other physical evidence. Where the prosecution has directly or indirectly asserted that the physical evidence originated with the accused, the defendant must be afforded an opportunity to prove that another person was responsible. See *United States v. Begay,* 937 F.2d 515, 523 n. 10 (10th Cir. 1991). Evidence offered for the specific purpose identified in this subdivision may still be excluded if it does not satisfy Rules 401 or 403. *See, e.g., United States v. Azure,* 845 F.2d 1503, 1505-06 (8th Cir. 1988) (10 year old victim's injuries indicated recent use of force; court excluded evidence of consensual sexual activities with witness who testified at in camera hearing that he had never hurt victim and failed to establish recent activities).

Under the exception in subdivision (b)(1)(B), evidence of specific instances of sexual behavior with respect to the person whose sexual misconduct is alleged is admissible if offered to prove consent, or offered by the prosecution. Admissible pursuant to this exception might be evidence of prior instances of sexual activities between the alleged victim and the accused, as well as statements in which the alleged victim expresses an intent to engage in sexual intercourse with the accused, or voiced sexual fantasies involving that specific accused. In a prosecution for child sexual abuse, for example, evidence of uncharged sexual activity between the accused and the alleged victim offered by the prosecution may be admissible pursuant to Rule 404(b) to show a pattern of behavior. Evidence relating to the victim's alleged sexual predisposition is not admissible pursuant to this exception.

Under subdivision (b)(1)(C), evidence of specific instances of conduct may not be excluded if the result would be to deny a criminal defendant the protections afforded by the Constitution. For example, statements in which the victim has expressed an intent to have sex with the first person encountered on a particular occasion might not be excluded without violating the due process right of a rape defendant seeking to prove consent. Recognition of this basic principle was expressed on subdivision (b)(1) of the original rule. The United States Supreme Court has recognized that in various circumstances a defendant may have a right to introduce evidence otherwise precluded by an evidence rule under the Confrontation Clause. *See, e.g., Olden v. Kentucky,* 488 U.S. 227 (1988) (defendant in rape cases had right to inquire into alleged victim's cohabitation with another man to show bias).

Subdivision (b)(2) governs the admissibility of otherwise proscribed evidence in civil cases. It employs a balancing test rather than the specific exceptions stated in subdivision (b)(1) in recognition of the difficulty of foreseeing future developments in the law. Greater flexibility is needed to accommodate evolving causes of action such as claims for sexual harassment.

The balancing test requires the proponent of the evidence, whether plaintiff or defendant, to convince the court that the probative value of the proffered evidence "substantially outweighs the danger of harm to any victim and of unfair prejudice of any party." This test for admitting evidence offered to prove sexual behavior or sexual propensity in civil cases differs in three respects from the general rule governing admissibility set forth in Rule 403. First, it Reverses that usual procedure spelled out in Rule 403 by shifting the burden to the proponent to demonstrate admissibility rather than making the opponent justify exclusion of the evidence. Second, the standard expressed in subdivision (b)(2) is more stringent than in the original rule; it raises the threshold for admission by requiring that the probative value of the evidence *substantially* outweigh the specified dangers. Finally, the Rule 412 test puts "harm to the victim" on the scale in addition to prejudice to the parties.

Evidence of reputation may be received in a civil case only if the alleged victim has put his or her reputation into controversy. The victim may do so without making a specific allegation in a pleading. *Cf.* Fed.R.Civ.P. 35(a).

Subdivision (c). Amended subdivision (c) is more concise and understandable than the subdivision it replaces. The requirement of a motion before trial is continued in the amended rule, as is the provision that a late motion may be permitted for good cause shown. In deciding whether to permit late filing, the court may take into account the conditions previously included in the rule: namely whether the evidence is newly discovered and could not have been obtained earlier through the existence of due diligence, and whether the issue to which such evidence relates has newly arisen in the case. The rule recognizes that in some instances the circumstances that justify an application to introduce evidence otherwise barred by Rule 412 will not become apparent until trial.

The amended rule provides that before admitting evidence that falls within that prohibition of Rule 412(a), the court must hold a hearing in camera at which the alleged victim and any party must be afforded the right to be present and an opportunity to be heard. All papers connected with the motion must be kept and remain under seal during the course of trial and appellate proceedings unless otherwise ordered. This is to assure that the privacy of the alleged victim is preserved in all cases in which the court rules that proffered evidence is not admissible, and in which the hearing refers to matters that are not received, or are received in another form.

The procedures set forth in subdivision (c) do not apply to discovery of a victim's past sexual conduct or predisposition in civil cases, which will be continued to be governed by Fed. R. Civ. P. 26. In order not to undermine the rationale of Rule 412, however, courts should enter appropriate orders pursuant to Fed. R. Civ. P. 26 (c) to protect the victim against unwarranted inquiries and to ensure confidentiality. Courts should presumptively issue protective orders barring discovery unless the party seeking discovery makes a showing that the evidence sought to be discovered would be relevant under the facts and theories of the particular case, and cannot be obtained except through discovery. In an action for sexual harassment, for instance, while some evidence of the alleged victim's sexual behavior and/or predisposition in the workplace may perhaps be relevant, non-work place conduct will usually be irrelevant. *Cf. Burns v. McGregor Electronic Industries, Inc.*, 989 F.2d 959, 962-63 (8th Cir. 1993) (posing for a nude magazine outside work hours is irrelevant to issue of unwelcomeness of sexual advances at work). Confidentiality orders should be presumptively granted as well.

One substantive change made in subdivision (c) is the elimination of the following sentence: "Notwithstanding subdivision (b) of Rule 104, if the relevancy of the evidence which the accused seeks to offer in trial depends upon the fulfillment of a condition of fact, the court, at the hearing in chambers or at a subsequent hearing in chambers scheduled for such purpose, shall accept evidence on the issue of whether such condition of fact is fulfilled and shall determine such issue." On its face, this language would appear to authorize a trial judge to exclude evidence of past sexual conduct between alleged victim and an accused or a defendant in a civil case based upon the judge's belief that such past acts did not occur. Such an authorization raises questions of invasion of the right to a jury trial under the Sixth and Seventh Amendments. *See* 1 S. Saltzburg & M. Martin, *Federal Rules of Evidence Manual*, 396-97 (5th ed. 1990).

The Advisory Committee concluded that the amended rule provided adequate protection for all persons claiming to be the victims of sexual misconduct, and that it was inadvisable to continue to include a provision in the rule that has been confusing and that raises substantial constitutional issues.

[Advisory Committee Note adopted by Congressional Conference Report accompanying Pub.L. 103–322. See H.R. Conf. Rep. No. 103–711, 103rd Cong., 2nd Sess., 383 (1994).]

Rule 413. Evidence of Similar Crimes in Sexual Assault Cases

(a) In a criminal case in which the defendant is accused of an offense of sexual assault, evidence of the defendant's commission of another offense or offenses of sexual assault is admissible, and may be considered for its bearing on any matter to which it is relevant.

(b) In a case in which the Government intends to offer evidence under this rule, the attorney for the Government shall disclose the evidence to the defendant, including statements of witnesses or a summary of the substance of any testimony that is expected to be offered, at least fifteen days before the scheduled date of trial or at such later time as the court may allow for good cause.

(c) This rule shall not be construed to limit the admission or consideration of evidence under any other rule.

(d) For purposes of this rule and Rule 415, "offense of sexual assault" means a crime under Federal law or the law of a State (as defined in section 513 of title 18, United States Code) that involved—

(1) any conduct proscribed by chapter 109A of title 18, United States Code;

(2) contact, without consent, between any part of the defendant's body or an object and the genitals or anus of another person;

(3) contact, without consent, between the genitals or anus of the defendant and any part of another person's body;

(4) deriving sexual pleasure or gratification from the infliction of death, bodily injury, or physical pain on another person; or

(5) an attempt or conspiracy to engage in conduct described in paragraphs (1)–(4).

Rule 414. Evidence of Similar Crimes in Child Molestation Cases

(a) In a criminal case in which the defendant is accused of an offense of child molestation, evidence of the defendant's commission of another offense or offenses of child molestation is admissible, and may be considered for its bearing on any matter to which it is relevant.

(b) In a case in which the Government intends to offer evidence under this rule, the attorney for the Government shall disclose the evidence to the defendant, including statements of witnesses or a summary of the substance of any testimony that is expected to be offered, at least fifteen days before the scheduled date of trial or at such later time as the court may allow for good cause.

(c) This rule shall not be construed to limit the admission or consideration of evidence under any other rule.

(d) For purposes of this rule and Rule 415, "child" means a person below the age of fourteen, and "offense of child molestation" means a crime under Federal law or the law of a State (as defined in section 513 of title 18, United States Code) that involved—

(1) any conduct proscribed by chapter 109A of title 18, United States Code, that was committed in relation to a child;

(2) any conduct proscribed by chapter 110 of title 18, United States Code;

(3) contact between any part of the defendant's body or an object and the genitals or anus of a child;

(4) contact between the genitals or anus of the defendant and any part of the body of a child;

(5) deriving sexual pleasure or gratification from the infliction of death, bodily injury, or physical pain on a child; or

(6) an attempt or conspiracy to engage in conduct described in paragraphs (1)–(5).

Rule 415. Evidence of Similar Acts in Civil Cases Concerning Sexual Assault or Child Molestation

(a) In a civil case in which a claim for damages or other relief is predicated on a party's alleged commission of conduct constituting an offense of sexual assault or child molestation, evidence of that party's commission of another offense or offenses of sexual assault or child molestation is admissible and may be considered as provided in Rule 413 and Rule 414 of these rules.

(b) A party who intends to offer evidence under this Rule shall disclose the evidence to the party against whom it will be offered, including statements of witnesses or a summary of the substance of any testimony that is expected to be offered, at least fifteen days before the scheduled date of trial or at such later time as the court may allow for good cause.

(c) This rule shall not be construed to limit the admission or consideration of evidence under any other rule.

ARTICLE V.　PRIVILEGES

Rule 501. General Rule

Except as otherwise required by the Constitution of the United States or provided by Act of Congress or in rules prescribed by the Supreme Court pursuant to statutory authority, the privilege of a witness, person, government, State, or political subdivision thereof shall be governed by the principles of the common law as they may be interpreted by the courts of the United States in the light of reason and experience. However, in civil actions and proceedings, with respect to an element of a claim or defense as to which State law supplies the rule of decision, the privilege of a witness, person, government, State, or political subdivision thereof shall be determined in accordance with State law.

ARTICLE VI.　WITNESSES

Rule 601. General Rule of Competency

Every person is competent to be a witness except as otherwise provided in these rules. However, in civil actions and proceedings, with respect to an element of a claim or defense as to which State law supplies the rule of decision, the competency of a witness shall be determined in accordance with State law.

ADVISORY COMMITTEE NOTES
1972 Proposed Rules

This general ground-clearing eliminates all grounds of incompetency not specifically recognized in the succeeding rules of this Article. Included among the grounds thus abolished are religious belief, conviction of crime, and connection with the litigation as a party or interested person or spouse of a party or interested person. With the exception of the so-called Dead Man's Acts, American jurisdictions generally have ceased to recognize these grounds.

The Dead Man's Acts are surviving traces of the common law disqualification of parties and interested persons. They exist in variety too great to convey conviction of their wisdom and effectiveness. These rules contain no provision of this kind. For the reasoning underlying the decision not to give effect to state statutes in diversity cases, see the Advisory Committee's Note to Rule 501.

No mental or moral qualifications for testifying as a witness are specified. Standards of mental capacity have proved elusive in actual application. A leading commentator observes that few witnesses are disqualified on that ground. Weihofen, Testimonial Competence and Credibility, 34 Geo.Wash.L.Rev. 53 (1965).

Discretion is regularly exercised in favor of allowing the testimony. A witness wholly without capacity is difficult to imagine. The question is one particularly suited to the jury as one of weight and credibility, subject to judicial authority to review the sufficiency of the evidence. 2 Wigmore §§ 501, 509. Standards of moral qualification in practice consist essentially of evaluating a person's truthfulness in terms of his own answers about it. Their principal utility is in affording an opportunity on voir dire examination to impress upon the witness his moral duty. This result may, however, be accomplished more directly, and without haggling in terms of legal standards, by the manner of administering the oath or affirmation under Rule 603.

Admissibility of religious belief as a ground of impeachment is treated in Rule 610. Conviction of crime as a ground of impeachment is the subject of Rule 609. Marital relationship is the basis for privilege under Rule 505. Interest in the outcome of litigation and mental capacity are, of course, highly relevant to credibility and require no special treatment to render them admissible along with other matters bearing upon the perception, memory, and narration of witnesses.

1974 Enactment

Rule 601 as submitted to the Congress provided that "Every person is competent to be a witness except as otherwise provided in these rules." One effect of the Rule as proposed would have been to abolish age, mental capacity, and other grounds recognized in some State jurisdictions as making a person incompetent as a witness. The greatest controversy centered around the Rule's rendering inapplicable in the federal courts the so-called Dead Man's Statutes which exist in some States. Acknowledging that there is substantial disagreement as to the merit of Dead Man's Statutes, the Committee nevertheless believed that where such statutes have been enacted they represent State policy which should not be overturned in the absence of a compelling federal interest. The Committee therefore amended the Rule to make competency in civil actions determinable in accordance with State law with respect to elements of claims or defenses as to which State law supplies the rule of decision. Cf. *Courtland v. Walston & Co., Inc.*, 340 F.Supp. 1076, 1087–1092 (S.D.N.Y.1972). House Report No. 93–650.

The amendment to rule 601 parallels the treatment accorded Rule 501 discussed immediately above. Senate Report No. 93–1277.

Rule 601 deals with competency of witnesses. Both the House and Senate bills provide that federal competency law applies in criminal cases. In civil actions and proceedings, the House bill provides that state competency law applies "to an element of a claim or defense as to which State law supplies the rule of decision." The Senate bill provides that "in civil actions and proceedings arising under 28 U.S.C. § 1332 or 28 U.S.C. § 1335, or between citizens of different States and removed under 28 U.S.C. § 1441(b) the competency of a witness, person, government, State or political subdivision thereof is determined in accordance with State law, unless with respect to the particular claim or defense, Federal law supplies the rule of decision."

The wording of the House and Senate bills differs in the treatment of civil actions and proceedings. The rule in the House bill applies to evidence that relates to "an element of a claim or defense." If an item of proof tends to support or defeat a claim or defense, or an element of a claim or defense, and if state law supplies the rule of decision for that claim or defense, then state competency law applies to that item of proof.

For reasons similar to those underlying its action on Rule 501, the Conference adopts the House provision. House Report No. 93–1597.

Rule 602.   Lack of Personal Knowledge

A witness may not testify to a matter unless evidence is introduced sufficient to support a finding that the witness has personal knowledge of the matter. Evidence to prove personal knowledge may, but need not, consist of the witness' own testimony. This rule is subject to the provisions of rule 703, relating to opinion testimony by expert witnesses.

ADVISORY COMMITTEE NOTES

1972 Proposed Rules

" * * * [T]he rule requiring that a witness who testifies to a fact which can be perceived by the senses must have had an opportunity to observe, and must have actually observed the fact" is a "most pervasive manifestation" of the common law insistence upon "the most reliable sources of information." McCormick § 10, p. 19. These foundation requirements may, of course, be furnished by the testimony of the witness himself; hence personal knowledge is not an absolute but may consist of what the witness thinks he knows from personal perception. 2 Wigmore § 650. It will be observed that the rule is in fact a specialized application of the provisions of Rule 104(b) on conditional relevancy.

This rule does not govern the situation of a witness who testifies to a hearsay statement as such, if he has personal knowledge of the making of the statement. Rules 801 and 805 would be applicable. This rule would, however, prevent him from testifying to the subject matter of the hearsay statement, as he has no personal knowledge of it.

The reference to Rule 703 is designed to avoid any question of conflict between the present rule and the provisions of that rule allowing an expert to express opinions based on facts of which he does not have personal knowledge.

Rule 603.   Oath or Affirmation

Before testifying, every witness shall be required to declare that the witness will testify truthfully, by oath or affirmation administered in a form calculated to awaken the witness' conscience and impress the witness' mind with the duty to do so.

ADVISORY COMMITTEE NOTES

1972 Proposed Rules

The rule is designed to afford the flexibility required in dealing with religious adults, atheists, conscientious objectors, mental defectives, and children. Affirmation is simply a solemn undertaking to tell the truth; no special verbal formula is required. As is true generally, affirmation is recognized by federal law. "Oath" includes affirmation, 1 U.S.C. § 1; judges and clerks may administer oaths and affirmations, 28 U.S.C. §§ 459, 953; and affirmations are acceptable in lieu of oaths under Rule 43(d) of the Federal Rules of Civil Procedure. Perjury by a witness is a crime, 18 U.S.C. § 1621.

Rule 604.   Interpreters

An interpreter is subject to the provisions of these rules relating to qualification as an expert and the administration of an oath or affirmation to make a true translation.

ADVISORY COMMITTEE NOTES

1972 Proposed Rules

The rule implements Rule 43(f) of the Federal Rules of Civil Procedure and Rule 28(b) of the Federal Rules of Criminal Procedure, both of which contain provisions for the appointment and compensation of interpreters.

Rule 605.   Competency of Judge as Witness

The judge presiding at the trial may not testify in that trial as a witness. No objection need be made in order to preserve the point.

ADVISORY COMMITTEE NOTES

1972 Proposed Rules

In view of the mandate of 28 U.S.C. § 455 that a judge disqualify himself in "any case in which he * * * is or has been a material witness," the likelihood that the presiding judge in a federal court might be called to testify in the trial over which he is presiding is slight. Nevertheless the possibility is not totally eliminated.

The solution here presented is a broad rule of incompetency, rather than such alternatives as incompetency only as to material matters, leaving the matter to the discretion of the judge, or recognizing no incompetency. The choice is the result of inability to evolve satisfactory answers to questions which arise when the judge abandons the bench for the witness stand. Who rules on objections? Who compels him to answer? Can he rule impartially on the weight and admissibility of his own testimony? Can he be impeached or cross-examined effectively? Can he, in a jury trial, avoid conferring his seal of approval on one side in the eyes of the jury? Can he, in a bench trial, avoid an involvement destructive of impartiality? The rule of general incompetency has substantial support. See Report of the Special Committee on the Propriety of Judges Appearing as Witnesses, 36 A.B.A.J. 630 (1950); cases collected in Annot. 157 A.L.R. 311; McCormick § 68, p. 147; Uniform Rule 42; California Evidence Code § 703; Kansas Code of Civil Procedure § 60–442; New Jersey Evidence Rule 42. Cf. 6 Wigmore § 1909, which advocates leaving the matter to the discretion of the judge, and statutes to that effect collected in Annot. 157 A.L.R. 311.

The rule provides an "automatic" objection. To require an actual objection would confront the opponent with a choice between not objecting, with the result of allowing the testimony, and objecting, with the probable result of excluding the testimony but at the price of continuing the trial before a judge likely to feel that his integrity had been attacked by the objector.

Rule 606. Competency of Juror as Witness

(a) At the trial. A member of the jury may not testify as a witness before that jury in the trial of the case in which the juror is sitting. If the juror is called so to testify, the opposing party shall be afforded an opportunity to object out of the presence of the jury.

(b) Inquiry into validity of verdict or indictment. Upon an inquiry into the validity of a verdict or indictment, a juror may not testify as to any matter or statement occurring during the course of the jury's deliberations or to the effect of anything upon that or any other juror's mind or emotions as influencing the juror to assent to or dissent from the verdict or indictment or concerning the juror's mental processes in connection therewith, except that a juror may testify on the question whether extraneous prejudicial information was improperly brought to the jury's attention or whether any outside influence was improperly brought to bear upon any juror. Nor may a juror's affidavit or evidence of any statement by the juror concerning a matter about which the juror would be precluded from testifying be received for these purposes.

ADVISORY COMMITTEE NOTES
1972 Proposed Rules

Note to Subdivision (a). The considerations which bear upon the permissibility of testimony by a juror in the trial in which he is sitting as juror bear an obvious similarity to those evoked when the judge is called as a witness. See Advisory Committee's Note to Rule 605. The judge is not, however in this instance so involved as to call for departure from usual principles requiring objection to be made; hence the only provision on objection is that opportunity be afforded for its making out of the presence of the jury. Compare Rule 605.

Note to Subdivision (b). Whether testimony, affidavits, or statements of jurors should be received for the purpose of invalidating or supporting a verdict or indictment, and if so, under what circumstances, has given rise to substantial differences of opinion. The familiar rubric that a juror may not impeach his own verdict, dating from Lord Mansfield's time, is a gross oversimplification. The values sought to be promoted by excluding the evidence include freedom of deliberation, stability and finality of verdicts, and protection of jurors against annoyance and embarrassment. *McDonald v. Pless*, 238 U.S. 264, 35 S.Ct. 783, 59 L.Ed. 1300 (1915). On the other hand, simply putting verdicts beyond effective reach can only promote irregularity and injustice. The rule offers an accommodation between these competing considerations.

The mental operations and emotional reactions of jurors in arriving at a given result would, if allowed as a subject of inquiry, place every verdict at the mercy of jurors and invite tampering and harassment. See *Grenz v. Werre*, 129 N.W.2d 681 (N.D.1964). The authorities are in virtually complete accord in excluding the evidence. Fryer, Note on Disqualification of Witnesses, Selected Writings on Evidence and Trial 345, 347 (Fryer ed. 1957); Maguire, Weinstein, et al., Cases on Evidence 887 (5th ed. 1965); 8 Wigmore § 2349 (McNaughton Rev.1961). As to matters other than mental operations and emotional reactions of jurors, substantial authority refuses to allow a juror to disclose irregularities which occur in the jury room, but allows his testimony as to irregularities occurring outside and allows outsiders to testify as to occurrences both inside and out. 8 Wigmore § 2354 (McNaughton Rev.1961). However, the door of the jury room is not necessarily a satisfactory dividing point, and the Supreme Court has refused to accept it for every situation.

Mattox v. United States, 146 U.S. 140, 13 S.Ct. 50, 36 L.Ed. 917 (1892).

Under the federal decisions the central focus has been upon insulation of the manner in which the jury reached its verdict, and this protection extends to each of the components of deliberation, including arguments, statements, discussions, mental and emotional reactions, votes, and any other feature of the process. Thus testimony or affidavits of jurors have been held incompetent to show a compromise verdict. *Hyde v. United States*, 225 U.S. 347, 382 (1912); a quotient verdict, *McDonald v. Pless*, 238 U.S. 264 (1915); speculation as to insurance coverage. *Holden v. Porter*, 405 F.2d 878 (10th Cir.1969); *Farmers Coop. Elev. Ass'n v. Strand*, 382 F.2d 224, 230 (8th Cir.1967), cert. denied 389 U.S. 1014; misinterpretation of instructions, *Farmers Coop. Elev. Ass'n v. Strand*, supra; mistake in returning verdict, *United States v. Chereton*, 309 F.2d 197 (6th Cir.1962); interpretation of guilty plea by one defendant as implicating others, *United States v. Crosby*, 294 F.2d 928, 949 (2d Cir.1961). The policy does not, however, foreclose testimony by jurors as to prejudicial extraneous information or influences injected into or brought to bear upon the deliberative process. Thus a juror is recognized as competent to testify to statements by the bailiff or the introduction of a prejudicial newspaper account into the jury room, *Mattox v. United States*, 146 U.S. 140 (1892). See also *Parker v. Gladden*, 385 U.S. 363 (1966).

This rule does not purport to specify the substantive grounds for setting aside verdicts for irregularity; it deals only with the competency of jurors to testify concerning those grounds. Allowing them to testify as to matters other than their own inner reactions involves no particular hazard to the values sought to be protected. The rule is based upon this conclusion. It makes no attempt to specify the substantive grounds for setting aside verdicts for irregularity.

See also Rule 6(e) of the Federal Rules of Criminal Procedure and 18 U.S.C. § 3500, governing the secrecy of grand jury proceedings. The present rule does not relate to secrecy and disclosure but to the competency of certain witnesses and evidence.

1974 Enactment

Note to Subdivision (b). As proposed by the Court, Rule 606(b) limited testimony by a juror in the course of an inquiry into the validity of a verdict or indictment. He could testify as to the influence of extraneous prejudicial information brought to the jury's attention (e.g. a radio newscast or a newspaper account) or an outside influence which improperly had been brought to bear upon a juror (e.g. a threat to the safety of a member of his family), but he could not testify as to other irregularities which occurred in the jury room. Under this formulation a quotient verdict could not be attacked through the testimony of a juror, nor could a juror testify to the drunken condition of a fellow juror which so disabled him that he could not participate in the jury's deliberations.

The 1969 and 1971 Advisory Committee drafts would have permitted a member of the jury to testify concerning these kinds of irregularities in the jury room. The Advisory Committee note in the 1971 draft stated that " * * * the door of the jury room is not a satisfactory dividing point, and the Supreme Court has refused to accept it." The Advisory Committee further commented that—

The trend has been to draw the dividing line between testimony as to mental processes, on the one hand, and as to the existence of conditions or occurrences of events calculated improperly to influence the verdict on the other hand, without regard to whether the happening is within or without the jury room. * * * The jurors are the persons who know what really happened. Allowing them to testify as to matters other than their own reactions involves no particular hazard to the values sought to be protected. The rule is based upon this conclusion. It makes no attempt to specify the substantive grounds for setting aside verdicts for irregularity.

Objective jury misconduct may be testified to in California, Florida, Iowa, Kansas, Nebraska, New Jersey, North Dakota, Ohio, Oregon, Tennessee, Texas, and Washington.

Persuaded that the better practice is that provided for in the earlier drafts, the Committee amended subdivision (b) to read in the text of those drafts. House Report No. 93–650.

Note to Subdivision (b). As adopted by the House, this rule would permit the impeachment of verdicts by inquiry into, not the mental processes of the jurors, but what happened in terms of conduct in the jury room. This extension of the ability to impeach a verdict is felt to be unwarranted and ill-advised.

The rule passed by the House embodies a suggestion by the Advisory Committee of the Judicial Conference that is considerably broader than the final version adopted by the Supreme Court, which embodied long-accepted Federal law. Although forbidding the impeachment of verdicts by inquiry into the jurors' mental processes, it deletes from the Supreme Court version the proscription against testimony "as to any matter or statement occurring during the course of the jury's deliberations." This deletion would have the effect of opening verdicts up to challenge on the basis of what happened during the jury's internal deliberations, for example, where a juror alleged that the jury refused to follow the trial judge's instructions or that some of the jurors did not take part in deliberations.

Permitting an individual to attack a jury verdict based upon the jury's internal deliberations has long been recognized as unwise by the Supreme Court. In *McDonald v. Pless*, the Court stated:

$$*\quad*\quad*\quad*\quad*\quad*\quad*$$

[L]et it once be established that verdicts solemnly made and publicly returned into court can be attacked and set aside on the testimony of those who took part in their publication and all verdicts could be, and many would be, followed by an inquiry in the hope of discovering something which might invalidate the finding. Jurors would be harassed and beset by the defeated party in an effort to secure from them evidence of facts which might establish misconduct sufficient to set aside a verdict. If evidence thus secured could be thus used, the result would be to make what was intended to be a private deliberation, the constant subject of public investigation—to the destruction of all frankness and freedom of discussion and conference [238 U.S. 264, at 267 (1914)].

$$*\quad*\quad*\quad*\quad*\quad*\quad*$$

As it stands then, the rule would permit the harassment of former jurors by losing parties as well as the possible exploitation of disgruntled or otherwise badly-motivated ex-jurors.

Public policy requires a finality to litigation. And common fairness requires that absolute privacy be preserved for jurors to engage in the full and free debate necessary to the attainment of just verdicts. Jurors will not be able to function effectively if their deliberations are to be scrutinized in post-trial litigation. In the interest of protecting the jury system and the citizens who make it work, rule 606 should not permit any inquiry into the internal deliberations of the jurors. Senate Report No. 93–1277.

Note to Subdivision (b). Rule 606(b) deals with juror testimony in an inquiry into the validity of a verdict or indictment. The House bill provides that a juror cannot testify about his mental processes or about the effect of anything upon his or another juror's mind as influencing him to assent to or dissent from a verdict or indictment. Thus, the House bill allows a juror to testify about objective matters occurring during the jury's deliberation, such as the misconduct of another juror or the reaching of a quotient verdict. The Senate bill does not permit juror testimony about any matter or statement occurring during the course of the jury's deliberations. The Senate bill does provide, however, that a juror may testify on the question whether extraneous prejudicial information was improperly brought to the jury's attention and on the question whether any outside influence was improperly brought to bear on any juror.

The Conference adopts the Senate amendment. The Conferees believe that jurors should be encouraged to be conscientious in promptly reporting to the court misconduct that occurs during jury deliberations. House Report No. 93–1597.

Rule 607. Who May Impeach

The credibility of a witness may be attacked by any party, including the party calling the witness.

ADVISORY COMMITTEE NOTES

1972 Proposed Rules

The traditional rule against impeaching one's own witness is abandoned as based on false premises. A party does not hold out his witnesses as worthy of belief, since he rarely has a free choice in selecting them. Denial of the right leaves the party at the mercy of the witness and the adversary. If the impeachment is by a prior statement, it is free from hearsay dangers and is excluded from the category of hearsay under Rule 801(d)(1). Ladd, Impeachment of One's Own Witness—New Developments, 4 U.Chi.L.Rev. 69 (1936); McCormick § 38; 3 Wigmore §§ 896–918. The substantial inroads into the old rule made over the years by decisions, rules, and statutes are evidence of doubts as to its basic soundness and workability. Cases are collected in 3 Wigmore § 905. Revised Rule 32(a)(1) of the Federal Rules of Civil Procedure allows any party to impeach a witness by means of his deposition, and Rule 43(b) has allowed the calling and impeachment of an adverse party or person identified with him. Illustrative statutes allowing a party to impeach his own witness under varying circumstances are Ill.Rev.Stats.1967, c. 110, § 60; Mass.Laws Annot. 1959, c. 233, § 23; 20 N.M.Stats.Annot. 1953, § 20–2–4; N.Y. CPLR § 4514 (McKinney 1963); 12 Vt.Stats.Annot.1959, §§ 1641a, 1642. Complete judicial rejection of the old rule is found in *United States v. Freeman*, 302 F.2d 347 (2d Cir.1962). The same result is reached in Uniform Rule 20; California Evidence Code § 785; Kansas Code of Civil Procedure § 60–420. See also New Jersey Evidence Rule 20.

Rule 608. Evidence of Character and Conduct of Witness

(a) Opinion and reputation evidence of character. The credibility of a witness may be attacked or supported by evidence in the form of opinion or reputation, but subject to these limitations: (1) the evidence may refer only to character for truthfulness or untruthfulness, and (2) evidence of truthful character is admissible only after the character of the witness for truthfulness has been attacked by opinion or reputation evidence or otherwise.

(b) Specific instances of conduct. Specific instances of the conduct of a witness, for the purpose of attacking or supporting the witness' character for truthfulness, other than conviction of crime as provided in rule 609, may not be proved by extrinsic evidence. They may, however, in the discretion of the court, if probative of truthfulness or untruthfulness, be inquired into on cross-examination of the witness (1) concerning the witness' character for truthfulness or untruthfulness, or (2) concerning the character for truthfulness or untruthfulness of another witness as to which character the witness being cross-examined has testified.

The giving of testimony, whether by an accused or by any other witness, does not operate as a waiver of the accused's or the witness' privilege against self-incrimination when examined with respect to matters that relate only to character for truthfulness.

ADVISORY COMMITTEE NOTES
1972 Proposed Rules

Note to Subdivision (a). In Rule 404(a) the general position is taken that character evidence is not admissible for the purpose of proving that the person acted in conformity therewith, subject, however, to several exceptions, one of which is character evidence of a witness as bearing upon his credibility. The present rule develops that exception.

In accordance with the bulk of judicial authority, the inquiry is strictly limited to character for veracity, rather than allowing evidence as to character generally. The result is to sharpen relevancy, to reduce surprise, waste of time, and confusion, and to make the lot of the witness somewhat less unattractive. McCormick § 44.

The use of opinion and reputation evidence as means of proving the character of witnesses is consistent with Rule 405(a). While the modern practice has purported to exclude opinion, witnesses who testify to reputation seem in fact often to be giving their opinions, disguised somewhat misleadingly as reputation. See McCormick § 44. And even under the modern practice, a common relaxation has allowed inquiry as to whether the witnesses would believe the principal witness under oath. *United States v. Walker,* 313 F.2d 236 (6th Cir.1963), and cases cited therein; McCormick § 44, pp. 94–95, n. 3.

Character evidence in support of credibility is admissible under the rule only after the witness' character has first been attacked, as has been the case at common law. Maguire, Weinstein, et al., Cases on Evidence 295 (5th ed. 1965); McCormick § 49, p. 105; 4 Wigmore § 1104. The enormous needless consumption of time which a contrary practice would entail justifies the limitation. Opinion or reputation that the witness is untruthful specifically qualifies as an attack under the rule, and evidence of misconduct, including conviction of crime, and of corruption also fall within this category. Evidence of bias or interest does not. McCormick § 49; 4 Wigmore §§ 1106, 1107. Whether evidence in the form of contradiction is an attack upon the character of the witness must depend upon the circumstances. McCormick § 49. Cf. 4 Wigmore §§ 1108, 1109.

As to the use of specific instances on direct by an opinion witness, see the Advisory Committee's Note to Rule 405, *supra.*

Note to Subdivision (b). In conformity with Rule 405, which forecloses use of evidence of specific incidents as proof in chief of character unless character is an issue in the case, the present rule generally bars evidence of specific instances of conduct of a witness for the purpose of attacking or supporting his credibility. There are, however, two exceptions: (1) specific instances are provable when they have been the subject of criminal conviction, and (2) specific instances may be inquired into on cross-examination of the principal witness or of a witness giving an opinion of his character for truthfulness.

(1) Conviction of crime as a technique of impeachment is treated in detail in Rule 609, and here is merely recognized as an exception to the general rule excluding evidence of specific incidents for impeachment purposes.

(2) Particular instances of conduct, though not the subject of criminal conviction, may be inquired into on cross-examination of the principal witness himself or of a witness who testifies concerning his character for truthfulness. Effective cross-examination demands that some allowance be made for going into matters of this kind, but the possibilities of abuse are substantial. Consequently safeguards are erected in the form of specific requirements that the instances inquired into be probative of truthfulness or its opposite and not remote in time. Also, the overriding protection of Rule 403 requires that probative value not be outweighed by danger of unfair prejudice, confusion of issues, or misleading the jury, and that of Rule 611 bars harassment and undue embarrassment.

The final sentence constitutes a rejection of the doctrine of such cases as *People v. Sorge,* 301 N.Y. 198, 93 N.E.2d 637 (1950), that any past criminal act relevant to credibility may be inquired into on cross-examination, in apparent disregard of the privilege against self-incrimination. While it is clear that an ordinary witness cannot make a partial disclosure of incriminating matter and then invoke the privilege on cross-examination, no tenable contention can be made that merely by testifying he waives his right to foreclose inquiry on cross-examination into criminal activities for the purpose of attacking his credibility. So to hold would reduce the privilege to a nullity. While it is true that an accused, unlike an ordinary witness, has an option whether to testify, if the option can be exercised only at the price of opening up inquiry as to any and all criminal acts committed during his lifetime, the right to testify could scarcely be said to possess much vitality. In *Griffin v. California,* 380 U.S. 609, 85 S.Ct. 1229, 14 L.Ed.2d 106 (1965), the Court held that allowing comment on the election of an accused not to testify exacted a constitutionally impermissible price, and so here. While no specific provision in terms confers constitutional status on the right of an accused to take the stand in his own defense, the existence of the right is so completely recognized that a denial of it or substantial infringement upon it would surely be of due process dimensions. See *Ferguson v. Georgia,* 365 U.S. 570, 81 S.Ct. 756, 5 L.Ed.2d 783 (1961); McCormick § 131; 8 Wigmore § 2276 (McNaughton Rev.1961). In any event, wholly aside from constitutional considerations, the provision represents a sound policy.

1974 Enactment

Note to Subdivision (a). Rule 608(a) as submitted by the Court permitted attack to be made upon the character for truthfulness or untruthfulness of a witness either by reputation or opinion testimony. For the same reason underlying its decision to eliminate the admissibility of opinion testimony in Rule 405(a), the Committee amended Rule 608(a) to delete the reference to opinion testimony.

Note to Subdivision (b). The second sentence of Rule 608(b) as submitted by the Court permitted specific instances of misconduct of a witness to be inquired into on cross-examination for the purpose of attacking his credibility, if probative of truthfulness or untruthfulness, "and not remote in time". Such cross-examination could be of the witness himself or of another witness who testifies as to "his" character for truthfulness or untruthfulness.

The Committee amended the Rule to emphasize the discretionary power of the court in permitting such testimony and deleted the reference to remoteness in time as being unnecessary and confusing (remoteness from time of trial or remoteness from the incident involved?). As recast, the Committee amendment also makes clear the antecedent of "his" in the original Court proposal. House Report No. 93–650.

The Senate amendment adds the words "opinion or" to conform the first sentence of the rule with the remainder of the rule.

The Conference adopts the Senate amendment. House Report No. 93–1597.

2003 Amendments

The Rule has been amended to clarify that the absolute prohibition on extrinsic evidence applies only when the sole reason for proffering that evidence is to attack or support the witness' character for truthfulness. *See United States v. Abel,* 469 U.S. 45 (1984); *United States v. Fusco,* 748 F.2d 996 (5th Cir. 1984) (Rule 608(b) limits the use of evidence "designed to show that the witness has done things, unrelated to the suit being tried, that make him more or less believable per se"); Ohio R.Evid. 608(b). On occasion the Rule's use of the overbroad term "credibility" has been read "to bar extrinsic evidence for bias, competency and contradiction impeachment since they too deal with credibility." American Bar Association Section of Litigation, *Emerging Problems Under the Federal Rules of Evidence* at 161 (3d ed. 1998). The amendment conforms the language of the Rule to its original intent, which was to impose an absolute bar on extrinsic evidence only if the sole purpose for offering the evidence was to prove the witness' character for veracity. *See* Advisory Committee Note to Rule 608(b) (stating that the Rule is "[i]n conformity with Rule 405, which forecloses use of evidence of specific incidents as proof in chief of character unless character is in issue in the case . . . ").

By limiting the application of the Rule to proof of a witness' character for truthfulness, the amendment leaves the admissibility of extrinsic evidence offered for other grounds of impeachment (such as contradiction, prior inconsistent statement, bias and mental capacity) to Rules 402 and 403. *See, e.g., United States v. Winchenbach,* 197 F.3d 548 (1st Cir. 1999) (admissibility of a prior inconsistent statement offered for impeachment is governed by Rules 402 and 403, not Rule 608(b)); *United States v. Tarantino,* 846 F.2d 1384 (D.C. Cir. 1988) (admissibility of extrinsic evidence offered to contradict a witness is governed by Rules 402 and 403); *United States v. Lindemann,* 85 F.3d 1232 (7th Cir. 1996) (admissibility of extrinsic evidence of bias is governed by Rules 402 and 403).

It should be noted that the extrinsic evidence prohibition of Rule 608(b) bars any reference to the consequences that a witness might have suffered as a result of an alleged bad act. For example, Rule 608(b) prohibits counsel from mentioning that a witness was suspended or disciplined for the conduct that is the subject of impeachment, when that conduct is offered only to prove the character of the witness. *See United States v. Davis,* 183 F.3d 231, 257 n.12 (3d Cir. 1999) (emphasizing that in attacking the defendant's character for truthfulness "the government cannot make reference to Davis's forty-four day suspension or that Internal Affairs found that he lied about" an incident because "[s]uch evidence would not only be hearsay to the extent it contains assertion of fact, it would be inadmissible extrinsic evidence under Rule 608(b)"). *See also* Stephen A. Saltzburg, *Impeaching the Witness: Prior Bad Acts and Extrinsic Evidence,* 7 Crim. Just. 28, 31 (Winter 1993) ("counsel should not be permitted to circumvent the no-extrinsic-evidence provision by tucking a third person's opinion about prior acts into a question asked of the witness who has denied the act").

For purposes of consistency the term "credibility" has been replaced by the term "character for truthfulness" in the last sentence of subdivision (b). The term "credibility" is also used in subdivision (a). But the Committee found it unnecessary to substitute "character for truthfulness" for "credibility" in Rule 608(a), because subdivision (a)(1) already serves to limit impeachment to proof of such character.

Rules 609(a) and 610 also use the term "credibility" when the intent of those Rules is to regulate impeachment of a witness' character for truthfulness. No inference should be derived from the fact that the Committee proposed an amendment to Rule 608(b) but not to Rules 609 and 610.

Rule 609.   Impeachment by Evidence of Conviction of Crime

(a) General rule.   For the purpose of attacking the credibility of a witness,

(1) evidence that a witness other than an accused has been convicted of a crime shall be admitted, subject to Rule 403, if the crime was punishable by death or imprisonment in excess of one year under the law under which the witness was convicted, and evidence that an accused has been convicted of such a crime shall be admitted if the court determines that the probative value of admitting this evidence outweighs its prejudicial effect to the accused; and

(2) evidence that any witness has been convicted of a crime shall be admitted if it involved dishonesty or false statement, regardless of the punishment.

(b) Time limit.   Evidence of a conviction under this rule is not admissible if a period of more than ten years has elapsed since the date of the conviction or of the release of the witness from the confinement imposed for that conviction, whichever is the later date, unless the court determines, in the interests of justice, that the probative value of the conviction supported by specific

facts and circumstances substantially outweighs its prejudicial effect.   However, evidence of a conviction more than 10 years old as calculated herein, is not admissible unless the proponent gives to the adverse party sufficient advance written notice of intent to use such evidence to provide the adverse party with a fair opportunity to contest the use of such evidence.

(c) Effect of pardon, annulment, or certificate of rehabilitation.   Evidence of a conviction is not admissible under this rule if (1) the conviction has been the subject of a pardon, annulment, certificate of rehabilitation, or other equivalent procedure based on a finding of the rehabilitation of the person convicted, and that person has not been convicted of a subsequent crime which was punishable by death or imprisonment in excess of one year, or (2) the conviction has been the subject of a pardon, annulment, or other equivalent procedure based on a finding of innocence.

(d) Juvenile adjudications.   Evidence of juvenile adjudications is generally not admissible under this rule. The court may, however, in a criminal case allow evidence of a juvenile adjudication of a witness other than the accused if conviction of the offense would be admissible to attack the credibility of an adult and the court is satisfied that admission in evidence is necessary for a fair determination of the issue of guilt or innocence.

(e) Pendency of appeal.   The pendency of an appeal therefrom does not render evidence of a conviction inadmissible.   Evidence of the pendency of an appeal is admissible.

ADVISORY COMMITTEE NOTES
1972 Proposed Rules

As a means of impeachment, evidence of conviction of crime is significant only because it stands as proof of the commission of the underlying criminal act.   There is little dissent from the general proposition that at least some crimes are relevant to credibility but much disagreement among the cases and commentators about which crimes are usable for this purpose.   See McCormick § 43; 2 Wright, Federal Practice and Procedure: Criminal § 416 (1969).   The weight of traditional authority has been to allow use of felonies generally, without regard to the nature of the particular offense, and of *crimen falsi* without regard to the grade of the offense.   This is the view accepted by Congress in the 1970 amendment of § 14–305 of the District of Columbia Code, P.L. 91–358, 84 Stat. 473.   Uniform Rule 21 and Model Code Rule 106 permit only crimes involving "dishonesty or false statement."   Others have thought that the trial judge should have discretion to exclude convictions if the probative value of the evidence of the crime is substantially outweighed by the danger of unfair prejudice.   *Luck v. United States,* 121 U.S.App.D.C. 151, 348 F.2d 763 (1965); McGowan, Impeachment of Criminal Defendants by Prior Convictions, 1970 Law & Soc.Order 1.   Whatever may be the merits of those views, this rule is drafted to accord with the Congressional policy manifested in the 1970 legislation.

The proposed rule incorporates certain basic safeguards, in terms applicable to all witnesses but of particular significance to an accused who elects to testify.   These protections include the imposition of definite time limitations, giving effect to demonstrated rehabilitation, and generally excluding juvenile adjudications.

Note to Subdivision (a).   For purposes of impeachment, crimes are divided into two categories by the rule: (1) those of what is generally regarded as felony grade, without particular regard to the nature of the offense, and (2) those involving dishonesty or false statement, without regard to the grade of the offense.   Probable convictions are not limited to violations of federal law.   By reason of our constitutional structure, the federal catalog of crimes is far from being a complete one, and resort must be had to the laws of the states for the specification of many crimes. For example, simple theft as compared with theft from interstate commerce. Other instances of borrowing are the Assimilative Crimes Act, making the state law of crimes applicable to the special territorial and maritime jurisdiction of the United States, 18 U.S.C. § 13, and the provision of the Judicial Code disqualifying persons as jurors on the grounds of state as well as federal convictions, 28 U.S.C. § 1865. For evaluation of the crime in terms of seriousness, reference is made to the congressional measurement of felony (subject to imprisonment in excess of one year) rather than adopting state definitions which vary considerably. See 28 U.S.C. § 1865, *supra*, disqualifying jurors for conviction in state or federal court of crime punishable by imprisonment for more than one year.

Note to Subdivision (b). Few statutes recognize a time limit on impeachment by evidence of conviction. However, practical considerations of fairness and relevancy demand that some boundary be recognized. See Ladd, Credibility Tests—Current Trends, 89 U.Pa.L.Rev. 166, 176–177 (1940). This portion of the rule is derived from the proposal advanced in Recommendation Proposing in Evidence Code, § 788(5), p. 142, Cal.Law Rev. Comm'n (1965), though not adopted. See California Evidence Code § 788.

Note to Subdivision (c). A pardon or its equivalent granted solely for the purpose of restoring civil rights lost by virtue of a conviction has no relevance to an inquiry into character. If, however, the pardon or other proceeding is hinged upon a showing of rehabilitation the situation is otherwise. The result under the rule is to render the conviction inadmissible. The alternative of allowing in evidence both the conviction and the rehabilitation has not been adopted for reasons of policy, economy of time, and difficulties of evaluation.

A similar provision is contained in California Evidence Code § 788. Cf. A.L.I. Model Penal Code, Proposed Official Draft § 306.6(3)(e) (1962), and discussion in A.L.I. Proceedings 310 (1961).

Pardons based on innocence have the effect, of course, of nullifying the conviction *ab initio*.

Note to Subdivision (d). The prevailing view has been that a juvenile adjudication is not usable for impeachment. *Thomas v. United States*, 74 App.D.C. 167, 121 F.2d 905 (1941); *Cotton v. United States*, 355 F.2d 480 (10th Cir.1966). This conclusion was based upon a variety of circumstances. By virtue of its informality, frequently diminished quantum of required proof, and other departures from accepted standards for criminal trials under the theory of *parens patriae*, the juvenile adjudication was considered to lack the precision and general probative value of the criminal conviction. While *In re Gault*, 387 U.S. 1, 87 S.Ct. 1428, 18 L.Ed.2d 527 (1967), no doubt eliminates these characteristics insofar as objectionable, other obstacles remain. Practical problems of administration are raised by the common provisions in juvenile legislation that records be kept confidential and that they be destroyed after a short time. While *Gault* was skeptical as to the realities of confidentiality of juvenile records, it also saw no constitutional obstacles to improvement. 387 U.S. at 25, 87 S.Ct. 1428. See also Note, Rights and Rehabilitation in the Juvenile Courts, 67 Colum.L.Rev. 281, 289 (1967). In addition, policy considerations much akin to those which dictate exclusion of adult convictions after rehabilitation has been established strongly suggest a rule of excluding juvenile adjudications. Admittedly, however, the rehabilitative process may in a given case be a demonstrated failure, or the strategic importance of a given witness may be so great as to require the overriding of general policy in the interests of particular justice. See *Giles v. Maryland*, 386 U.S. 66, 87 S.Ct. 793, 17 L.Ed.2d 737 (1967). Wigmore was outspoken in his condemnation of the disallowance of juvenile adjudications to impeach, especially when the witness is the complainant in a case of molesting a minor. 1 Wigmore § 196; 3 *Id.* §§ 924a, 980. The rule recognizes discretion in the judge to effect an accommodation among these various factors by departing from the general principle of exclusion. In deference to the general

pattern and policy of juvenile statutes, however, no discretion is accorded when the witness is the accused in a criminal case.

Note to Subdivision (e). The presumption of correctness which ought to attend judicial proceedings supports the position that pendency of an appeal does not preclude use of a conviction for impeachment. *United States v. Empire Packing Co.*, 174 F.2d 16 (7th Cir.1949), cert. denied 337 U.S. 959, 69 S.Ct. 1534, 93 L.Ed. 1758; *Bloch v. United States*, 226 F.2d 185 (9th Cir.1955), cert. denied 350 U.S. 948, 76 S.Ct. 323, 100 L.Ed. 826 and 353 U.S. 959, 77 S.Ct. 868, 1 L.Ed.2d 910; and see *Newman v. United States*, 331 F.2d 968 (8th Cir.1964). *Contra, Campbell v. United States*, 85 U.S.App.D.C. 133, 176 F.2d 45 (1949). The pendency of an appeal is, however, a qualifying circumstance properly considerable.

1974 Enactment

Note to Subdivision (a). Rule 609(a) as submitted by the Court was modeled after Section 133(a) of Public Law 91–358, 14 D.C.Code 305(b)(1), enacted in 1970. The Rule provided that:

For the purpose of attacking the credibility of a witness, evidence that he has been convicted of a crime is admissible but only if the crime (1) was punishable by death or imprisonment in excess of one year under the law under which he was convicted or (2) involved dishonesty or false statement regardless of the punishment.

As reported to the Committee by the Subcommittee, Rule 609(a) was amended to read as follows:

For the purpose of attacking the credibility of a witness, evidence that he has been convicted of a crime is admissible only if the crime (1) was punishable by death or imprisonment in excess of one year, unless the court determines that the danger of unfair prejudice outweighs the probative value of the evidence of the conviction, or (2) involved dishonesty or false statement.

In full committee, the provision was amended to permit attack upon the credibility of a witness by prior conviction only if the prior crime involved dishonesty or false statement. While recognizing that the prevailing doctrine in the federal courts and in most States allows a witness to be impeached by evidence of prior felony convictions without restriction as to type, the Committee was of the view that, because of the danger of unfair prejudice in such practice and the deterrent effect upon an accused who might wish to testify, and even upon a witness who was not the accused, cross-examination by evidence of prior conviction should be limited to those kinds of convictions bearing directly on credibility, *i.e.*, crimes involving dishonesty or false statement.

Note to Subdivision (b). Rule 609(b) as submitted by the Court was modeled after Section 133(a) of Public Law 91–358, 14 D.C.Code 305(b)(2)(B), enacted in 1970. The Rule provided:

Evidence of a conviction under this rule is not admissible if a period of more than ten years has elapsed since the date of the release of the witness from confinement imposed for his most recent conviction, or the expiration of the period of his parole, probation, or sentence granted or imposed with respect to his most recent conviction, whichever is the later date.

Under this formulation, a witness' entire past record of criminal convictions could be used for impeachment (provided the conviction met the standard of subdivision (a)), if the witness had been most recently released from confinement, or the period of his parole or probation had expired, within ten years of the conviction.

The Committee amended the Rule to read in the text of the 1971 Advisory Committee version to provide that upon the expiration of ten years from the date of a conviction of a witness, or of his release from confinement for that offense, that conviction may no longer be used for impeachment. The Committee was of the view that after ten years following a person's release from confinement (or from the date of his conviction) the probative value of the conviction with respect to that person's credibility diminished to a point where it should no longer be admissible.

Note to Subdivision (c). Rule 609(c) as submitted by the Court provided in part that evidence of a witness' prior conviction is not admissible to attack his credibility if the conviction was the subject of a pardon, annulment, or other equivalent procedure, based on a showing of rehabilitation, and the witness has not been convicted of a subsequent crime. The Committee amended the Rule to provide that the "subsequent crime" must have been "punishable by death or imprisonment in excess of one year", on the ground that a subsequent conviction of an offense not a felony is insufficient to rebut the finding that the witness has been rehabilitated. The Committee also intends that the words "based on a finding of the rehabilitation of the person convicted" apply not only to "certificate of rehabilitation, or other equivalent procedure", but also to "pardon" and "annulment.". House Report No. 93–650.

Note to Subdivision (a). As proposed by the Supreme Court, the rule would allow the use of prior convictions to impeach if the crime was a felony or a misdemeanor if the misdemeanor involved dishonesty or false statement. As modified by the House, the rule would admit prior convictions for impeachment purposes only if the offense, whether felony or misdemeanor, involved dishonesty or false statement.

The committee has adopted a modified version of the House-passed rule. In your committee's view, the danger of unfair prejudice is far greater when the accused, as opposed to other witnesses, testifies, because the jury may be prejudiced not merely on the question of credibility but also on the ultimate question of guilt or innocence. Therefore, with respect to defendants, the committee agreed with the House limitation that only offenses involved false statement or dishonesty may be used. By that phrase, the committee means crimes such as perjury or subornation of perjury, false statement, criminal fraud, embezzlement or false pretense, or any other offense, in the nature of *crimen falsi* the commission of which involves some element of untruthfulness, deceit or falsification bearing on the accused's propensity to testify truthfully.

With respect to other witnesses, in addition to any prior conviction involving false statement or dishonesty, any other felony may be used to impeach if, and only if, the court finds that the probative value of such evidence outweighs its prejudicial effect against the party offering that witness.

Notwithstanding this provision, proof of any prior offense otherwise admissible under Rule 404 could still be offered for the purposes sanctioned by that rule. Furthermore, the committee intends that notwithstanding this rule, a defendant's misrepresentation regarding the existence or nature of prior convictions may be met by rebuttal evidence, including the record of such prior convictions. Similarly, such records may be offered to rebut representations made by the defendant regarding his attitude toward or willingness to commit a general category of offense, although denials or other representations by the defendant regarding the specific conduct which forms the basis of the charge against him shall not make prior convictions admissible to rebut such statement.

In regard to either type of representation, of course, prior convictions may be offered in rebuttal only if the defendant's statement is made in response to defense counsel's questions or is made gratuitously in the course of cross-examination. Prior convictions may not be offered as rebuttal evidence if the prosecution has sought to circumvent the purpose of this rule by asking questions which elicit such representations from the defendant.

One other clarifying amendment has been added to this subsection, that is, to provide that the admissibility of evidence of a prior conviction is permitted only upon cross-examination of a witness. It is not admissible if a person does not testify. It is to be understood, however, that a court record of a prior conviction is admissible to prove that conviction if the witness has forgotten or denies its existence.

Note to Subdivision (b). Although convictions over ten years old generally do not have much probative value, there may be exceptional circumstances under which the conviction substantially bears on the credibility of the witness. Rather than

exclude all convictions over 10 years old, the committee adopted an amendment in the form of a final clause to the section granting the court discretion to admit convictions over 10 years old, but only upon a determination by the court that the probative value of the conviction supported by specific facts and circumstances, substantially outweighs its prejudicial effect.

It is intended that convictions over 10 years old will be admitted very rarely and only in exceptional circumstances. The rules provide that the decision be supported by specific facts and circumstances thus requiring the court to make specific findings on the record as to the particular facts and circumstances it has considered in determining that the probative value of the conviction substantially outweighs its prejudicial impact. It is expected that, in fairness, the court will give the party against whom the conviction is introduced a full and adequate opportunity to contest its admission. Senate Report No. 93–1277.

Rule 609 defines when a party may use evidence of a prior conviction in order to impeach a witness. The Senate amendments make changes in two subsections of Rule 609.

Note to Subdivision (a). The House bill provides that the credibility of a witness can be attacked by proof of prior conviction of a crime only if the crime involves dishonesty or false statement. The Senate amendment provides that a witness' credibility may be attacked if the crime (1) was punishable by death or imprisonment in excess of one year under the law under which he was convicted or (2) involves dishonesty or false statement, regardless of the punishment.

The Conference adopts the Senate amendment with an amendment. The Conference amendment provides that the credibility of a witness, whether a defendant or someone else, may be attacked by proof of a prior conviction but only if the crime: (1) was punishable by death or imprisonment in excess of one year under the law under which he was convicted and the court determines that the probative value of the conviction outweighs its prejudicial effect to the defendant; or (2) involved dishonesty or false statement regardless of the punishment.

By the phrase "dishonesty and false statement" the Conference means crimes such as perjury or subornation of perjury, false statement, criminal fraud, embezzlement, or false pretense, or any other offense in the nature of *crimen falsi*, the commission of which involves some element of deceit, untruthfulness, or falsification bearing on the accused's propensity to testify truthfully.

The admission of prior convictions involving dishonesty and false statement is not within the discretion of the Court. Such convictions are peculiarly probative of credibility and, under this rule, are always to be admitted. Thus, judicial discretion granted with respect to the admissibility of other prior convictions is not applicable to those involving dishonesty or false statement.

With regard to the discretionary standard established by paragraph (1) of Rule 609(a), the Conference determined that the prejudicial effect to be weighed against the probative value of the conviction is specifically the prejudicial effect *to the defendant*. The danger of prejudice to a witness other than the defendant (such as injury to the witness' reputation in his community) was considered and rejected by the Conference as an element to be weighed in determining admissibility. It was the judgment of the Conference that the danger of prejudice to a nondefendant witness is outweighed by the need for the trier of fact to have as much relevant evidence on the issue of credibility as possible. Such evidence should only be excluded where it presents a danger of improperly influencing the outcome of the trial by persuading the trier of fact to convict the defendant on the basis of his prior criminal record.

Note to Subdivision (b). The House bill provides in subsection (b) that evidence of conviction of a crime may not be used for impeachment purposes under subsection (a) if more than ten years have elapsed since the date of the conviction or the date the witness was released from confinement imposed for the conviction, whichever is later. The Senate amendment permits the use of convictions older than ten years, if the court determines, in the interests of justice, that the probative value of the conviction, supported by specific facts and circumstances, substantially outweighs its prejudicial effect.

The Conference adopts the Senate amendment with an amendment requiring notice by a party that he intends to request that the court allow him to use a conviction older than ten years. The Conferees anticipate that a written notice, in order to give the adversary a fair opportunity to contest the use of the evidence, will ordinarily include such information as the date of the conviction, the jurisdiction, and the offense or statute involved. In order to eliminate the possibility that the flexibility of this provision may impair the ability of a party-opponent to prepare for trial, the Conferees intend that the notice provision operate to avoid surprise. House Report No. 93–1597.

1990 Amendments

The amendment to Rule 609(a) makes two changes in the rule. The first change removes from the rule the limitation that the conviction may only be elicited during cross-examination, a limitation that virtually every circuit has found to be inapplicable. It is common for witnesses to reveal on direct examination their convictions to "remove the sting" of the impeachment. *See e.g., United States v. Bad Cob,* 560 F.2d 877 (8th Cir.1977). The amendment does not contemplate that a court will necessarily permit proof of prior convictions through testimony, which might be time-consuming and more prejudicial than proof through a written record. Rules 403 and 611(a) provide sufficient authority for the court to protect against unfair or disruptive methods of proof.

The second change effected by the amendment resolves an ambiguity as to the relationship of Rules 609 and 403 with respect to impeachment of witnesses other than the criminal defendant. *See, Green v. Bock Laundry Machine Co.,* 109 S.Ct. 1981, 490 U.S. 504 (1989). The amendment does not disturb the special balancing test for the criminal defendant who chooses to testify. Thus, the rule recognizes that, in virtually every case in which prior convictions are used to impeach the testifying defendant, the defendant faces a unique risk of prejudice—*i.e.,* the danger that convictions that would be excluded under Fed. R.Evid. 404 will be misused by a jury as propensity evidence despite their introduction solely for impeachment purposes. Although the rule does not forbid all use of convictions to impeach a defendant, it requires that the government show that the probative value of convictions as impeachment evidence outweighs their prejudicial effect.

Prior to the amendment, the rule appeared to give the defendant the benefit of the special balancing test when defense witnesses other than the defendant were called to testify. In practice, however, the concern about unfairness to the defendant is most acute when the defendant's own convictions are offered as evidence. Almost all of the decided cases concern this type of impeachment, and the amendment does not deprive the defendant of any meaningful protection, since Rule 403 now clearly protects against unfair impeachment of any defense witness other than the defendant. There are cases in which a defendant might be prejudiced when a defense witness is impeached. Such cases may arise, for example, when the witness bears a special relationship to the defendant such that the defendant is likely to suffer some spill-over effect from impeachment of the witness.

The amendment also protects other litigants from unfair impeachment of their witnesses. The danger of prejudice from the use of prior convictions is not confined to criminal defendants. Although the danger that prior convictions will be misused as character evidence is particularly acute when the defendant is impeached, the danger exists in other situations as well. The amendment reflects the view that it is desirable to protect all litigants from the unfair use of prior convictions, and that the ordinary balancing test of Rule 403, which provides that evidence shall not be excluded unless its prejudicial effect substantially outweighs its probative value, is appropriate for assessing the admissibility of prior convictions for impeachment of any witness other than a criminal defendant.

The amendment reflects a judgment that decisions interpreting Rule 609(a) as requiring a trial court to admit convictions in

civil cases that have little, if anything, to do with credibility reach undesirable results. *See, e.g., Diggs v. Lyons,* 741 F.2d 577 (3d Cir.1984), *cert. denied,* 105 S.Ct. 2157 (1985). The amendment provides the same protection against unfair prejudice arising from prior convictions used for impeachment purposes as the rules provide for other evidence. The amendment finds support in decided cases. *See, e.g., Petty v. Ideco,* 761 F.2d 1146 (5th Cir.1985); *Czaka v. Hickman,* 703 F.2d 317 (8th Cir.1983).

Fewer decided cases address the question whether Rule 609(a) provides any protection against unduly prejudicial prior convictions used to impeach government witnesses. Some courts have read Rule 609(a) as giving the government no protection for its witnesses. *See, e.g., United States v. Thorne,* 547 F.2d 56 (8th Cir.1976); *United States v. Nevitt,* 563 F.2d 406 (9th Cir.1977), *cert. denied,* 444 U.S. 847 (1979). This approach also is rejected by the amendment. There are cases in which impeachment of government witnesses with prior convictions that have little, if anything, to do with credibility may result in unfair prejudice to the government's interest in a fair trial and unnecessary embarrassment to a witness. Fed.R.Evid. 412 already recognizes this and excluded certain evidence of past sexual behavior in the context of prosecutions for sexual assaults.

The amendment applies the general balancing test of Rule 403 to protect all litigants against unfair impeachment of witnesses. The balancing test protects civil litigants, the government in criminal cases, and the defendant in a criminal case who calls other witnesses. The amendment addresses prior convictions offered under Rule 609, not for other purposes, and does not run afoul, therefore, of *Davis v. Alaska,* 415 U.S. 308 (1974). *Davis* involved the use of a prior juvenile adjudication not to prove a past law violation, but to prove bias. The defendant in a criminal case has the right to demonstrate the bias of a witness and to be assured a fair trial, but not to unduly prejudice a trier of fact. *See generally* Rule 412. In any case in which the trial court believes that confrontation rights require admission of impeachment evidence, obviously the Constitution would take precedence over the rule.

The probability that prior convictions of an ordinary government witness will be unduly prejudicial is low in most criminal cases. Since the behavior of the witness is not the issue in dispute in most cases, there is little chance that the trier of fact will misuse the convictions offered as impeachment evidence as propensity evidence. Thus, trial courts will be skeptical when the government objects to impeachment of its witnesses with prior convictions. Only when the government is able to point to a real danger of prejudice that is sufficient to outweigh substantially the probative value of the conviction for impeachment purposes will the conviction be excluded.

The amendment continues to divide subdivision (a) into subsections (1) and (2) thus facilitating retrieval under current computerized research programs which distinguish the two provisions. The Committee recommended no substantive change in subdivision (a)(2), even though some cases raise a concern about the proper interpretation of the words "dishonesty or false statement." These words were used but not explained in the original Advisory Committee Note accompanying Rule 609. Congress extensively debated the rule, and the Report of the House and Senate Conference Committee states that "[b]y the phrase 'dishonesty and false statement,' the Conference means crimes such as perjury, subornation of perjury, false statement, criminal fraud, embezzlement, or false pretense, or any other offense in the nature of *crimen falsi,* commission of which involves some element of deceit, untruthfulness, or falsification bearing on the accused's propensity to testify truthfully." The Advisory Committee concluded that the Conference Report provides sufficient guidance to trial courts and that no amendment is necessary, notwithstanding some decisions that take an unduly broad view of "dishonesty," admitting convictions such as for bank robbery or bank larceny. Subsection (a)(2) continues to apply to any witness, including a criminal defendant.

Finally, the Committee determined that it was unnecessary to add to the rule language stating that, when a prior conviction is offered under Rule 609, the trial court is to consider the probative value of the prior conviction *for impeachment*, not for other purposes. The Committee concluded that the title of the rule, its first sentence, and its placement among the impeachment rules clearly establish that evidence offered under Rule 609 is offered only for purposes of impeachment.

Rule 610. Religious Beliefs or Opinions

Evidence of the beliefs or opinions of a witness on matters of religion is not admissible for the purpose of showing that by reason of their nature the witness' credibility is impaired or enhanced.

ADVISORY COMMITTEE NOTES
1972 Proposed Rules

While the rule forecloses inquiry into the religious beliefs or opinions of a witness for the purpose of showing that his character for truthfulness is affected by their nature, an inquiry for the purpose of showing interest or bias because of them is not within the prohibition. Thus disclosure of affiliation with a church which is a party to the litigation would be allowable under the rule. Cf. Tucker v. Reil, 51 Ariz. 357, 77 P.2d 203 (1938). To the same effect, though less specifically worded, is California Evidence Code § 789. See 3 Wigmore § 936.

Rule 611. Mode and Order of Interrogation and Presentation

(a) Control by court. The court shall exercise reasonable control over the mode and order of interrogating witnesses and presenting evidence so as to (1) make the interrogation and presentation effective for the ascertainment of the truth, (2) avoid needless consumption of time, and (3) protect witnesses from harassment or undue embarrassment.

(b) Scope of cross-examination. Cross-examination should be limited to the subject matter of the direct examination and matters affecting the credibility of the witness. The court may, in the exercise of discretion, permit inquiry into additional matters as if on direct examination.

(c) Leading questions. Leading questions should not be used on the direct examination of a witness except as may be necessary to develop the witness' testimony. Ordinarily leading questions should be permitted on cross-examination. When a party calls a hostile witness, an adverse party, or a witness identified with an adverse party, interrogation may be by leading questions.

ADVISORY COMMITTEE NOTES
1972 Proposed Rules

Note to Subdivision (a). Spelling out detailed rules to govern the mode and order of interrogating witnesses and presenting evidence is neither desirable nor feasible. The ultimate responsibility for the effective working of the adversary system rests with the judge. The rule sets forth the objectives which he should seek to attain.

Item (1) restates in broad terms the power and obligation of the judge as developed under common law principles. It covers such concerns as whether testimony shall be in the form of a free narrative or responses to specific questions, McCormick § 5, the order of calling witnesses and presenting evidence, 6 Wigmore § 1867, the use of demonstrative evidence, McCormick § 179, and the many other questions arising during the course of a trial which can be solved only by the judge's common sense and fairness in view of the particular circumstances.

Item (2) is addressed to avoidance of needless consumption of time, a matter of daily concern in the disposition of cases. A companion piece is found in the discretion vested in the judge to exclude evidence as a waste of time in Rule 403(b).

Item (3) calls for a judgment under the particular circumstances whether interrogation tactics entail harassment or undue embarrassment. Pertinent circumstances include the importance of the testimony, the nature of the inquiry, its relevance to credibility, waste of time, and confusion. McCormick § 42. In *Alford v. United States*, 282 U.S. 687, 694, 51 S.Ct. 218, 75 L.Ed. 624 (1931), the Court pointed out that, while the trial judge should protect the witness from questions which "go beyond the bounds of proper cross-examination merely to harass, annoy or humiliate," this protection by no means forecloses efforts to discredit the witness. Reference to the transcript of the prosecutor's cross-examination in *Berger v. United States*, 295 U.S. 78, 55 S.Ct. 629, 79 L.Ed. 1314 (1935), serves to lay at rest any doubts as to the need for judicial control in this area.

The inquiry into specific instances of conduct of a witness allowed under Rule 608(b) is, of course, subject to this rule.

Note to Subdivision (b). The tradition in the federal courts and in numerous state courts has been to limit the scope of cross-examination to matters testified to on direct, plus matters bearing upon the credibility of the witness. Various reasons have been advanced to justify the rule of limited cross-examination. (1) A party vouches for his own witness but only to the extent of matters elicited on direct. *Resurrection Gold Mining Co. v. Fortune Gold Mining Co.*, 129 F. 668, 675 (8th Cir.1904), quoted in Maguire, Weinstein, et al., Cases on Evidence 277, n. 38 (5th ed. 1965). But the concept of vouching is discredited, and Rule 607 rejects it. (2) A party cannot ask his own witness leading questions. This is a problem properly solved in terms of what is necessary for a proper development of the testimony rather than by a mechanistic formula similar to the vouching concept. See discussion under subdivision (c). (3) A practice of limited cross-examination promotes orderly presentation of the case. *Finch v. Weiner*, 109 Conn. 616, 145 A. 31 (1929). While this latter reason has merit, the matter is essentially one of the order of presentation and not one in which involvement at the appellate level is likely to prove fruitful. See, for example, *Moyer v. Aetna Life Ins. Co.*, 126 F.2d 141 (3rd Cir.1942); *Butler v. New York Central R. Co.*, 253 F.2d 281 (7th Cir.1958); *United States v. Johnson*, 285 F.2d 35 (9th Cir.1960); *Union Automobile Indemnity Ass'n v. Capitol Indemnity Ins. Co.*, 310 F.2d 318 (7th Cir.1962). In evaluating these considerations, McCormick says:

"The foregoing considerations favoring the wide-open or restrictive rules may well be thought to be fairly evenly balanced. There is another factor, however, which seems to swing the balance overwhelmingly in favor of the wide-open rule. This is the consideration of economy of time and energy. Obviously, the wide-open rule presents little or no opportunity for dispute in its application. The restrictive practice in all its forms, on the other hand, is productive in many court rooms, of continual bickering over the choice of the numerous variations of the 'scope of the direct' criterion, and of their application to particular cross-questions. These controversies are often reventilated on appeal, and reversals for error in their determination are frequent. Observance of these vague and ambiguous restrictions is a matter of constant and hampering concern to the cross-examiner. If these efforts, delays and misprisions were the necessary incidents to the guarding of substantive rights or the fundamentals of fair trial, they might be worth the cost. As the price of the choice of an obviously debatable regulation of the order of evidence, the sacrifice seems misguided. The American Bar Association's Committee for the Improvement of the Law of Evidence for the year 1937–38 said this:

'The rule limiting cross-examination to the precise subject of the direct examination is probably the most frequent rule (except the Opinion rule) leading in the trial practice today to refined and technical quibbles which obstruct the progress of the trial, confuse the jury, and give rise to appeal on technical grounds only. Some of the instances in which Supreme Courts have ordered new trials for the mere transgression of this rule about the order of evidence have been astounding.

'We recommend that the rule allowing questions upon any part of the issue known to the witness * * * be adopted. * * *'" McCormick, § 27, p. 51. See also 5 Moore's Federal Practice ¶ 43.10 (2nd ed. 1964).

The provision of the second sentence, that the judge may in the interests of justice limit inquiry into new matters on cross-examination, is designed for those situations in which the result otherwise would be confusion, complication, or protraction of the case, not as a matter of rule but as demonstrable in the actual development of the particular case.

The rule does not purport to determine the extent to which an accused who elects to testify thereby waives his privilege against self-incrimination. The question is a constitutional one, rather than a mere matter of administering the trial. Under *Simmons v. United States*, 390 U.S. 377, 88 S.Ct. 967, 19 L.Ed.2d 1247 (1968), no general waiver occurs when the accused testifies on such preliminary matters as the validity of a search and seizure or the admissibility of a confession. Rule 104(d), *supra.* When he testifies on the merits, however, can he foreclose inquiry into an aspect or element of the crime by avoiding it on direct? The affirmative answer given in *Tucker v. United States*, 5 F.2d 818 (8th Cir.1925), is inconsistent with the description of the waiver as extending to "all other relevant facts" in *Johnson v. United States*, 318 U.S. 189, 195, 63 S.Ct. 549, 87 L.Ed. 704 (1943). See also *Brown v. United States*, 356 U.S. 148, 78 S.Ct. 622, 2 L.Ed.2d 589 (1958). The situation of an accused who desires to testify on some but not all counts of a multiple-count indictment is one to be approached, in the first instance at least, as a problem of severance under Rule 14 of the Federal Rules of Criminal Procedure. *Cross v. United States*, 118 U.S.App.D.C. 324, 335 F.2d 987 (1964). Cf. *United States v. Baker*, 262 F.Supp. 657, 686 (D.D.C.1966). In all events, the extent of the waiver of the privilege against self-incrimination ought not to be determined as a by-product of a rule on scope of cross-examination.

Note to Subdivision (c). The rule continues the traditional view that the suggestive powers of the leading question are as a general proposition undesirable. Within this tradition, however, numerous exceptions have achieved recognition: The witness who is hostile, unwilling, or biased; the child witness or the adult with communication problems; the witness whose recollection is exhausted; and undisputed preliminary matters. 3 Wigmore §§ 774–778. An almost total unwillingness to reverse for infractions has been manifested by appellate courts. See cases cited in 3 Wigmore § 770. The matter clearly falls within the area of control by the judge over the mode and order of interrogation and presentation and accordingly is phrased in words of suggestion rather than command.

The rule also conforms to tradition in making the use of leading questions on cross-examination a matter of right. The purpose of the qualification "ordinarily" is to furnish a basis for denying the use of leading questions when the cross-examination is cross-examination in form only and not in fact, as for example the "cross-examination" of a party by his own counsel after being called by the opponent (savoring more of re-direct) or of an insured defendant who proves to be friendly to the plaintiff.

The final sentence deals with categories of witnesses automatically regarded and treated as hostile. Rule 43(b) of the Federal Rules of Civil Procedure has included only "an adverse party or an officer, director, or managing agent of a public or private corporation or of a partnership or association which is an adverse party." This limitation virtually to persons whose statements would stand as admissions is believed to be an unduly narrow concept of those who may safely be regarded as hostile without further demonstration. See, for example, *Maryland Casualty Co. v. Kador*, 225 F.2d 120 (5th Cir.1955), and *Degelos v. Fidelity and Casualty Co.*, 313 F.2d 809 (5th Cir.1963), holding despite the language of Rule 43(b) that an insured fell within it, though not a party in an action under the Louisiana direct action statute. The phrase of the rule, "witness identified with" an adverse party, is designed to enlarge the category of persons thus callable.

1974 Enactment

Note to Subdivision (b). As submitted by the Court, Rule 611(b) provided:

A witness may be cross-examined on any matter relevant to any issue in the case, including credibility. In the interests of justice, the judge may limit cross-examination with respect to matters not testified to on direct examination.

The Committee amended this provision to return to the rule which prevails in the federal courts and thirty-nine State jurisdictions. As amended, the Rule is in the text of the 1969 Advisory Committee draft. It limits cross-examination to credibility and to matters testified to on direct examination, unless the judge permits more, in which event the cross-examiner must proceed as if on direct examination. This traditional rule facilitates orderly presentation by each party at trial. Further, in light of existing discovery procedures, there appears to be no need to abandon the traditional rule.

Note to Subdivision (c). The third sentence of Rule 611(c) as submitted by the Court provided that:

In civil cases, a party is entitled to call an adverse party or witness identified with him and interrogate by leading questions.

The Committee amended this Rule to permit leading questions to be used with respect to any hostile witness, not only an adverse party or person identified with such adverse party. The Committee also substituted the word "When" for the phrase "In civil cases" to reflect the possibility that in criminal cases a defendant may be entitled to call witnesses identified with the government, in which event the Committee believed the defendant should be permitted to inquire with leading questions. House Report No. 93–650.

Note to Subdivision (b). Rule 611(b) as submitted by the Supreme Court permitted a broad scope of cross-examination: "cross-examination on any matter relevant to any issue in the case" unless the judge, in the interests of justice, limited the scope of cross-examination.

The House narrowed the Rule to the more traditional practice of limiting cross-examination to the subject matter of direct examination (and credibility), but with discretion in the judge to permit inquiry into additional matters in situations where that would aid in the development of the evidence or otherwise facilitate the conduct of the trial.

The committee agrees with the House amendment. Although there are good arguments in support of broad cross-examination from perspectives of developing all relevant evidence, we believe the factors of insuring an orderly and predictable development of the evidence weigh in favor of the narrower rule, especially when discretion is given to the trial judge to permit inquiry into additional matters. The committee expressly approves this discretion and believes it will permit sufficient flexibility allowing a broader scope of cross-examination whenever appropriate.

The House amendment providing broader discretionary cross-examination permitted inquiry into additional matters only as if on direct examination. As a general rule, we concur with this limitation, however, we would understand that this limitation would not preclude the utilization of leading questions if the conditions of subsection (c) of this rule were met, bearing in mind the judge's discretion in any case to limit the scope of cross-examination [see McCormick on Evidence, §§ 24–26 (especially 24) (2d ed. 1972)].

Further, the committee has received correspondence from Federal judges commenting on the applicability of this rule to section 1407 of title 28. It is the committee's judgment that this rule as reported by the House is flexible enough to provide sufficiently broad cross-examination in appropriate situations in multidistrict litigation.

Note to Subdivision (c). As submitted by the Supreme Court, the rule provided: "In civil cases, a party is entitled to call an adverse party or witness identified with him and interrogate by leading questions."

The final sentence of subsection (c) was amended by the House for the purpose of clarifying the fact that a "hostile witness"—that is a witness who is hostile in fact—could be subject to interrogation by leading questions. The rule as submitted by the Supreme Court declared certain witnesses hostile as a matter of law and thus subject to interrogation by leading questions without any showing of hostility in fact. These were adverse parties or witnesses identified with adverse parties. However, the wording of the first sentence of subsection (c) while generally prohibiting the use of leading questions on direct examination, also provides "except as may be necessary to develop his testimony." Further, the first paragraph of the Advisory Committee note explaining the subsection makes clear that they intended that leading questions could be asked of a hostile witness or a witness who was unwilling or biased and even though that witness was not associated with an adverse party. Thus, we question whether the House amendment was necessary.

However, concluding that it was not intended to affect the meaning of the first sentence of the subsection and was intended solely to clarify the fact that leading questions are permissible in the interrogation of a witness, who is hostile in fact, the committee accepts that House amendment.

The final sentence of this subsection was also amended by the House to cover criminal as well as civil cases. The committee accepts this amendment, but notes that it may be difficult in criminal cases to determine when a witness is "identified with an adverse party," and thus the rule should be applied with caution. Senate Report No. 93–1277.

Rule 612. Writing Used to Refresh Memory

Except as otherwise provided in criminal proceedings by section 3500 of title 18, United States Code, if a witness uses a writing to refresh memory for the purpose of testifying, either—

(1) while testifying, or

(2) before testifying, if the court in its discretion determines it is necessary in the interests of justice,

an adverse party is entitled to have the writing produced at the hearing, to inspect it, to cross-examine the witness thereon, and to introduce in evidence those portions which relate to the testimony of the witness. If it is claimed that the writing contains matters not related to the subject matter of the testimony the court shall examine the writing in camera, excise any portions not so related, and order delivery of the remainder to the party entitled thereto. Any portion withheld over objections shall be preserved and made available to the appellate court in the event of an appeal. If a writing is not produced or delivered pursuant to order under this rule, the court shall make any order justice requires, except that in criminal cases when the prosecution elects not to comply, the order shall be one striking the testimony or, if the court in its discretion determines that the interests of justice so require, declaring a mistrial.

ADVISORY COMMITTEE NOTES
1972 Proposed Rules

The treatment of writings used to refresh recollection while on the stand is in accord with settled doctrine. McCormick § 9, p. 15. The bulk of the case law has, however, denied the existence of any right to access by the opponent when the writing is used prior to taking the stand, though the judge may have discretion in the matter. *Goldman v. United States*, 316 U.S. 129, 62 S.Ct. 993, 86 L.Ed. 1322 (1942); *Needelman v. United States*, 261 F.2d 802 (5th Cir.1958), cert. dismissed 362 U.S. 600, 80 S.Ct. 960, 4 L.Ed.2d 980, rehearing denied 363 U.S. 858, 80 S.Ct. 1606, 4 L.Ed.2d 1739, Annot., 82 A.L.R.2d 473, 562 and 7 A.L.R.3d 181, 247. An increasing group of cases has repudiated the distinction. *People v. Scott*, 29 Ill.2d 97, 193 N.E.2d 814 (1963); *State v. Mucci*, 25 N.J. 423, 136 A.2d 761 (1957); *State v. Hunt*,

25 N.J. 514, 138 A.2d 1 (1958); *State v. Deslovers*, 40 R.I. 89, 100 A. 64 (1917), and this position is believed to be correct. As Wigmore put it, "the risk of imposition and the need of safeguard is just as great" in both situations. 3 Wigmore § 762, p. 111. To the same effect is McCormick, § 9, p. 17.

The purpose of the phrase "for the purpose of testifying" is to safeguard against using the rule as a pretext for wholesale exploration of an opposing party's files and to insure that access is limited only to those writings which may fairly be said in fact to have an impact upon the testimony of the witness.

The purpose of the rule is the same as that of the *Jencks* statute, 18 U.S.C. § 3500: to promote the search of credibility and memory. The same sensitivity to disclosure of government files may be involved; hence the rule is expressly made subject to the statute, subdivision (a) of which provides: "In any criminal prosecution brought by the United States, no statement or report in the possession of the United States which was made by a Government witness or prospective Government witness (other than the defendant) shall be the subject of subpena, discovery, or inspection until said witness has testified on direct examination in the trial of the case." Items falling within the purview of the statute are producible only as provided by its terms, *Palermo v. United States*, 360 U.S. 343, 351 (1959), and disclosure under the rule is limited similarly by the statutory conditions. With this limitation in mind, some differences of application may be noted. The *Jencks* statute applies only to statements of witnesses; the rule is not so limited. The statute applies only to criminal cases; the rule applies to all cases. The statute applies only to government witnesses; the rule applies to all witnesses. The statute contains no requirement that the statement be consulted for purposes of refreshment before or while testifying; the rule so requires. Since many writings would qualify under either statute or rule, a substantial overlap exists, but the identity of procedures makes this of no importance.

The consequences of nonproduction by the government in a criminal case are those of the *Jencks* statute, striking the testimony or in exceptional cases a mistrial. 18 U.S.C. § 3500(d). In other cases these alternatives are unduly limited, and such possibilities as contempt, dismissal, finding issues against the offender, and the like are available. See Rule 16(g) of the Federal Rules of Criminal Procedure and Rule 37(b) of the Federal Rules of Civil Procedure for appropriate sanctions.

1974 Enactment

As submitted to Congress, Rule 612 provided that except as set forth in 18 U.S.C. 3500, if a witness uses a writing to refresh his memory for the purpose of testifying, "either before or while testifying," an adverse party is entitled to have the writing produced at the hearing, to inspect it, to cross-examine the witness on it, and to introduce in evidence those portions relating to the witness' testimony. The Committee amended the Rule so as still to require the production of writings used by a witness while testifying, but to render the production of writings used by a witness to refresh his memory before testifying discretionary with the court in the interests of justice, as is the case under existing federal law. See Goldman v. United States, 316 U.S. 129 (1942). The Committee considered that permitting an adverse party to require the production of writings used before testifying could result in fishing expeditions among a multitude of papers which a witness may have used in preparing for trial.

The Committee intends that nothing in the Rule be construed as barring the assertion of a privilege with respect to writings used by a witness to refresh his memory. House Report No. 93–650.

Rule 613. Prior Statements of Witnesses

(a) **Examining witness concerning prior statement.** In examining a witness concerning a prior statement made by the witness, whether written or not, the statement need not be shown nor its contents disclosed to the witness at that time, but on request the same shall be shown or disclosed to opposing counsel.

(b) Extrinsic evidence of prior inconsistent statement of witness. Extrinsic evidence of a prior inconsistent statement by a witness is not admissible unless the witness is afforded an opportunity to explain or deny the same and the opposite party is afforded an opportunity to interrogate the witness thereon, or the interests of justice otherwise require. This provision does not apply to admissions of a party-opponent as defined in rule 801(d)(2).

ADVISORY COMMITTEE NOTES
1972 Proposed Rules

Note to Subdivision (a). The Queen's Case, 2 Br. & B. 284, 129 Eng.Rep. 976 (1820), laid down the requirement that a cross-examiner, prior to questioning the witness about his own prior statement in writing, must first show it to the witness. Abolished by statute in the country of its origin, the requirement nevertheless gained currency in the United States. The rule abolishes this useless impediment, to cross-examination. Ladd, Some Observations on Credibility: Impeachment of Witnesses, 52 Cornell L.Q. 239, 246–247 (1967); McCormick § 28; 4 Wigmore §§ 1259–1260. Both oral and written statements are included.

The provision for disclosure to counsel is designed to protect against unwarranted insinuations that a statement has been made when the fact is to the contrary.

The rule does not defeat the application of Rule 1002 relating to production of the original when the contents of a writing are sought to be proved. Nor does it defeat the application of Rule 26(b)(3) of the Rules of Civil Procedure, as revised, entitling a person on request to a copy of his own statement, though the operation of the latter may be suspended temporarily.

Note to Subdivision (b). The familiar foundation requirement that an impeaching statement first be shown to the witness before it can be proved by extrinsic evidence is preserved but with some modifications. See Ladd, Some Observations on Credibility: Impeachment of Witnesses, 52 Cornell L.Q. 239, 247 (1967). The traditional insistence that the attendance of the witness be directed to the statement on cross-examination is relaxed in favor of simply providing the witness an opportunity to explain and the opposite party an opportunity to examine on the statement, with no specification of any particular time or sequence. Under this procedure, several collusive witnesses can be examined before disclosure of a joint prior inconsistent statement. See Comment to California Evidence Code § 770. Also, dangers of oversight are reduced. See McCormick § 37, p. 68.

In order to allow for such eventualities as the witness becoming unavailable by the time the statement is discovered, a measure of discretion is conferred upon the judge. Similar provisions are found in California Evidence Code § 770 and New Jersey Evidence Rule 22(b).

Under principles of *expression unius* the rule does not apply to impeachment by evidence of prior inconsistent conduct. The use of inconsistent statements to impeach a hearsay declaration is treated in Rule 806.

Rule 614. Calling and Interrogation of Witnesses by Court

(a) Calling by court. The court may, on its own motion or at the suggestion of a party, call witnesses, and all parties are entitled to cross-examine witnesses thus called.

(b) Interrogation by court. The court may interrogate witnesses, whether called by itself or by a party.

(c) Objections. Objections to the calling of witnesses by the court or to interrogation by it may be made at the

time or at the next available opportunity when the jury is not present.

ADVISORY COMMITTEE NOTES
1972 Proposed Rules

Note to Subdivision (a). While exercised more frequently in criminal than in civil cases, the authority of the judge to call witnesses is well established. McCormick § 8, p. 14; Maguire, Weinstein, et al., Cases on Evidence 303–304 (5th ed. 1965); 9 Wigmore § 2484. One reason for the practice, the old rule against impeaching one's own witness, no longer exists by virtue of Rule 607, *supra.* Other reasons remain, however, to justify the continuation of the practice of calling court's witnesses. The right to cross-examine, with all it implies, is assured. The tendency of juries to associate a witness with the party calling him, regardless of technical aspects of vouching, is avoided. And the judge is not imprisoned within the case as made by the parties.

Note to Subdivision (b). The authority of the judge to question witnesses is also well established. McCormick § 8, pp. 12–13; Maguire, Weinstein, et al., Cases on Evidence 737–739 (5th ed. 1965); 3 Wigmore § 784. The authority is, of course, abused when the judge abandons his proper role and assumes that of advocate, but the manner in which interrogation should be conducted and the proper extent of its exercise are not susceptible of formulation in a rule. The omission in no sense precludes courts of review from continuing to reverse for abuse.

Note to Subdivision (c). The provision relating to objections is designed to relieve counsel of the embarrassment attendant upon objecting to questions by the judge in the presence of the jury, while at the same time assuring that objections are made in apt time to afford the opportunity to take possible corrective measures. Compare the "automatic" objection feature of Rule 605 when the judge is called as a witness.

Rule 615. Exclusion of Witnesses

At the request of a party the court shall order witnesses excluded so that they cannot hear the testimony of other witnesses, and it may make the order of its own motion. This rule does not authorize exclusion of (1) a party who is a natural person, or (2) an officer or employee of a party which is not a natural person designated as its representative by its attorney, or (3) a person whose presence is shown by a party to be essential to the presentation of the party's cause, or (4) a person authorized by statute to be present.

ADVISORY COMMITTEE NOTES
1972 Proposed Rules

The efficacy of excluding or sequestering witnesses has long been recognized as a means of discouraging and exposing fabrication, inaccuracy, and collusion. 6 Wigmore §§ 1837–1838. The authority of the judge is admitted, the only question being whether the matter is committed to his discretion or one of right. The rule takes the latter position. No time is specified for making the request.

Several categories of persons are excepted. (1) Exclusion of persons who are parties would raise serious problems of confrontation and due process. Under accepted practice they are not subject to exclusion. 6 Wigmore § 1841. (2) As the equivalent of the right of a natural-person party to be present, a party which is not a natural person is entitled to have a representative present. Most of the cases have involved allowing a police officer who has been in charge of an investigation to remain in court despite the fact that he will be a witness. United States v. Infanzon, 235 F.2d 318, (2d Cir.1956); *Portomene v. United States,* 221 F.2d 582 (5th Cir.1955); *Powell v. United States,* 208 F.2d 618 (6th Cir.1953); *Jones v. United States,* 252 F.Supp. 781 (W.D.Okl.1966). Designation of the representative by the attorney rather than by the client may at first glance appear to be an inversion of the attorney-client relationship, but it may be assumed that the attorney will follow the wishes of the client, and the solution is simple and workable. See California Evidence Code § 777. (3) The category contemplates such persons as an agent who handled the transaction being litigated or an expert needed to advise counsel in the management of the litigation. See 6 Wigmore § 1841, n. 4.

1974 Enactment

Many district courts permit government counsel to have an investigative agent at counsel table throughout the trial although the agent is or may be a witness. The practice is permitted as an exception to the rule of exclusion and compares with the situation defense counsel finds himself in—he always has the client with him to consult during the trial. The investigative agent's presence may be extremely important to government counsel, especially when the case is complex or involves some specialized subject matter. The agent, too, having lived with the case for a long time, may be able to assist in meeting trial surprises where the best-prepared counsel would otherwise have difficulty. Yet, it would not seem the Government could often meet the burden under rule 615 of showing that the agent's presence is essential. Furthermore, it could be dangerous to use the agent as a witness as early in the case as possible, so that he might then help counsel as a nonwitness, since the agent's testimony could be needed in rebuttal. Using another, nonwitness agent from the same investigative agency would not generally meet government counsel's needs.

This problem is solved if it is clear that investigative agents are within the group specified under the second exception made in the rule, for "an officer or employee of a party which is not a natural person designated as its representative by its attorney." It is our understanding that this was the intention of the House committee. It is certainly this committee's construction of the rule. Senate Report No. 93–1277.

1998 Amendments

The amendment is in response to: (1) the Victim's Rights and Restitution Act of 1990, 42 U.S.C. § 10606, which guarantees, within certain limits, the right of a crime victim to attend the trial; and (2) the Victim Rights Clarification Act of 1997 (18 U.S.C. § 3510).

ARTICLE VII. OPINIONS AND EXPERT TESTIMONY

Rule 701. Opinion Testimony by Lay Witnesses

If the witness is not testifying as an expert, the witness' testimony in the form of opinions or inferences is limited to those opinions or inferences which are (a) rationally based on the perception of the witness, (b) helpful to a clear understanding of the witness' testimony or the determination of a fact in issue, and (c) not based on scientific, technical, or other specialized knowledge within the scope of Rule 702.

ADVISORY COMMITTEE NOTES

1972 Proposed Rules

The rule retains the traditional objective of putting the trier of fact in possession of an accurate reproduction of the event.

Limitation (a) is the familiar requirement of first-hand knowledge or observation.

Limitation (b) is phrased in terms of requiring testimony to be helpful in resolving issues. Witnesses often find difficulty in expressing themselves in language which is not that of an opinion or conclusion. While the courts have made concessions in certain recurring situations, necessity as a standard for permitting opinions and conclusions has proved too elusive and too unadaptable to particular situations for purposes of satisfactory judicial administration. McCormick § 11. Moreover, the practical impossibility of determining by rule what is a "fact," demonstrated by a century of litigation of the question of what is a fact for purposes of pleading under the Field Code, extends into evidence also. 7 Wigmore § 1919. The rule assumes that the natural characteristics of the adversary system will generally lead to an acceptable result, since the detailed account carries more conviction than the broad assertion, and a lawyer can be expected to display his witness to the best advantage. If he fails to do so, cross-examination and argument will point up the weakness. See Ladd, Expert Testimony, 5 Vand.L.Rev. 414, 415–417 (1952). If, despite these considerations, attempts are made to introduce meaningless assertions which amount to little more than choosing up sides, exclusion for lack of helpfulness is called for by the rule.

The language of the rule is substantially that of Uniform Rule 56(1). Similar provisions are California Evidence Code § 800; Kansas Code of Civil Procedure § 60–456(a); New Jersey Evidence Rule 56(1).

2000 Amendments

Rule 701 has been amended to eliminate the risk that the reliability requirements set forth in Rule 702 will be evaded through the simple expedient of proffering an expert in lay witness clothing. Under the amendment, a witness' testimony must be scrutinized under the rules regulating expert opinion to the extent that the witness is providing testimony based on scientific, technical, or other specialized knowledge within the scope of Rule 702. See generally *Asplundh Mfg. Div. v. Benton Harbor Eng'g*, 57 F.3d 1190 (3d Cir. 1995). By channeling testimony that is actually expert testimony to Rule 702, the amendment also ensures that a party will not evade the expert witness disclosure requirements set forth in Fed.R.Civ.P. 26 and Fed.R.Crim.P. 16 by simply calling an expert witness in the guise of a layperson. See Joseph, *Emerging Expert Issues Under the 1993 Disclosure Amendments to the Federal Rules of Civil Procedure*, 164 F.R.D. 97, 108 (1996) (noting that "there is no good reason to allow what is essentially surprise expert testimony." and that "the Court should be vigilant to preclude manipulative conduct designed to thwart the expert disclosure and discovery process") See also *United States v. Figueroa–Lopez*, 125 F.3d 1241, 1246 (9th Cir. 1997) (law enforcement agents testifying that the defendant's conduct was consistent with that of a drug trafficker could not testify as lay witnesses; to permit such testimony under Rule 701 "subverts the requirements of Federal Rule of Criminal Procedure 16(a)(1)(E)").

The amendment does not distinguish between expert and lay *witnesses*, but rather between expert and lay *testimony*. Certainly it is possible for the same witness to provide both lay and expert testimony in a single case. See, e.g, *United States v. Figueroa–Lopez*, 125 F.3d 1241, 1246 (9th Cir. 1997) (law enforcement agents could testify that the defendant was acting suspiciously, without being qualified as experts; however, the rules on experts were applicable where the agents testified on the basis of extensive experience that the defendant was using code words to refer to drug quantities and prices). The amendment makes clear that any part of a witness' testimony that is based upon scientific, technical, or other specialized knowledge within the scope of Rule 702 is governed by the standards of Rule 702 and the corresponding disclosure requirements of the Civil and Criminal Rules.

The amendment is not intended to affect the "prototypical example[s] of the type of evidence contemplated by the adoption of Rule 701 relat[ing] to the appearance of persons or things, identity, the manner of conduct, competency of a person, degrees of light or darkness, sound, size, weight, distance, and an endless number of items that cannot be described factually in words apart from inferences." *Asplundh Mfg. Div. v. Benton Harbor Eng'g,* 57 F.3d 1190, 1196 (3d Cir. 1995).

For example, most courts have permitted the owner or officer of a business to testify to the value or projected profits of the business, without the necessity of qualifying the witness as an accountant, appraiser, or similar expert. *See, e.g., Lightning Lube, Inc. v. Witco Corp.* 4 F.3d 1153 (3d Cir. 1993) (no abuse of discretion in permitting the plaintiff's owner to give lay opinion testimony as to damages, as it was based on his knowledge and participation in the day-to-day affairs of the business). Such opinion testimony is admitted not because of experience, training or specialized knowledge within the realm of an expert, but because of the particularized knowledge that the witness has by virtue of his or her position in the business. The amendment does not purport to change this analysis. Similarly, courts have permitted lay witnesses to testify that a substance appeared to be a narcotic, so long as a foundation of familiarity with the substance is established. *See, e.g., United States v. Westbrook,* 896 F.2d 330 (8th Cir. 1990) (two lay witnesses who were heavy amphetamine users were properly permitted to testify that a substance was amphetamine; but it was error to permit another witness to make such an identification where she had no experience with amphetamines). Such testimony is not based on specialized knowledge within the scope of Rule 702, but rather is based upon a layperson's personal knowledge. If, however, that witness were to describe how a narcotic was manufactured, or to describe the intricate workings of a narcotic distribution network, then the witness would have to qualify as an expert under Rule 702. *United States v. Figueroa–Lopez, supra.*

The amendment incorporates the distinctions set forth in *State v. Brown,* 836 S.W.2d 530, 549 (1992), a case involving former Tennessee Rule of Evidence 701, a rule that precluded lay witness testimony based on "special knowledge." In *Brown,* the court declared that the distinction between lay and expert witness testimony is that lay testimony "results from a process of reasoning familiar in everyday life," while expert testimony "results from a process of reasoning which can be mastered only by specialists in the field." The court in *Brown* noted that a lay witness with experience could testify that a substance appeared to be blood, but that a witness would have to qualify as an expert before he could testify that bruising around the eyes is indicative of skull trauma. That is the kind of distinction made by the amendment to this Rule.

Rule 702.　Testimony by Experts

If scientific, technical, or other specialized knowledge will assist the trier of fact to understand the evidence or to determine a fact in issue, a witness qualified as an expert by knowledge, skill, experience, training, or education, may testify thereto in the form of an opinion or otherwise, if (1) the testimony is based upon sufficient facts or data, (2) the testimony is the product of reliable principles and methods, and (3) the witness has applied the principles and methods reliably to the facts of the case.

ADVISORY COMMITTEE NOTES

1972 Proposed Rules

An intelligent evaluation of facts is often difficult or impossible without the application of some scientific, technical, or other specialized knowledge. The most common source of this knowledge is the expert witness, although there are other techniques for supplying it.

Most of the literature assumes that experts testify only in the form of opinions. The assumption is logically unfounded. The rule accordingly recognizes that an expert on the stand may give a dissertation or exposition of scientific or other principles relevant to the case, leaving the trier of fact to apply them to the facts. Since much of the criticism of expert testimony has centered upon the hypothetical question, it seems wise to recognize that opinions are not indispensable and to encourage the

use of expert testimony in non-opinion form when counsel believes the trier can itself draw the requisite inference. The use of opinions is not abolished by the rule, however. It will continue to be permissible for the experts to take the further step of suggesting the inference which should be drawn from applying the specialized knowledge to the facts. See Rules 703 to 705.

Whether the situation is a proper one for the use of expert testimony is to be determined on the basis of assisting the trier. "There is no more certain test for determining when experts may be used than the common sense inquiry whether the untrained layman would be qualified to determine intelligently and to the best possible degree the particular issue without enlightenment from those having a specialized understanding of the subject involved in the dispute." Ladd, Expert Testimony, 5 Vand.L.Rev. 414, 418 (1952). When opinions are excluded, it is because they are unhelpful and therefore superfluous and a waste of time. 7 Wigmore § 1918.

The rule is broadly phrased. The fields of knowledge which may be drawn upon are not limited merely to the "scientific" and "technical" but extend to all "specialized" knowledge. Similarly, the expert is viewed, not in a narrow sense, but as a person qualified by "knowledge, skill, experience, training or education." Thus within the scope of the rule are not only experts in the strictest sense of the word, e.g., physicians, physicists, and architects, but also the large group sometimes called "skilled" witnesses, such as bankers or landowners testifying to land values.

2000 Amendments

Rule 702 has been amended in response to *Daubert v. Merrell Dow Pharmaceuticals, Inc.,* 509 U.S. 579 (1993), and to the many cases applying *Daubert,* including *Kumho Tire Co. v. Carmichael,* 119 S.Ct. 1167 (1999). In *Daubert* the Court charged trial judges with the responsibility of acting as gatekeepers to exclude unreliable expert testimony, and the Court in *Kumho* clarified that this gatekeeper function applies to all expert testimony, not just testimony based in science. *See also Kumho,* 119 S.Ct. at 1178 (citing the Committee Note to the proposed amendment to Rule 702, which had been released for public comment before the date of the *Kumho* decision). The amendment affirms the trial court's role as gatekeeper and provides some general standards that the trial court must use to assess the reliability and helpfulness of proffered expert testimony. Consistently with *Kumho,* the Rule as amended provides that all types of expert testimony present questions of admissibility for the trial court in deciding whether the evidence is reliable and helpful. Consequently, the admissibility of all expert testimony is governed by the principles of Rule 104(a). Under that Rule, the proponent has the burden of establishing that the pertinent admissibility requirements are met by a preponderance of the evidence. *See Bourjaily v. United States,* 483 U.S. 171 (1987).

Daubert set forth a non-exclusive checklist for trial courts to use in assessing the reliability of scientific expert testimony. The specific factors explicated by the *Daubert* Court are (1) whether the expert's technique or theory can be or has been tested— that is, whether the expert's theory can be challenged in some objective sense, or whether it is instead simply a subjective, conclusory approach that cannot reasonably be assessed for reliability; (2) whether the technique or theory has been subject to peer review and publication; (3) the known or potential rate of error of the technique or theory when applied; (4) the existence and maintenance of standards and controls; and (5) whether the technique or theory has been generally accepted in the scientific community. The Court in *Kumho* held that these factors might also be applicable in assessing the reliability of non-scientific expert testimony, depending upon "the particular circumstances of the particular case at issue." 119 S.Ct. at 1175.

No attempt has been made to "codify" these specific factors. *Daubert* itself emphasized that the factors were neither exclusive nor dispositive. Other cases have recognized that not all of the specific *Daubert* factors can apply to every type of expert testimony. In addition to *Kumho*, 119 S.Ct. at 1175, *see Tyus v. Urban Search Management*, 102 F.3d 256 (7th Cir. 1996) (noting that the factors mentioned by the Court in *Daubert* do not neatly apply to expert testimony from a sociologist). *See also Kannankeril v. Terminix Int'l, Inc.*, 128 F.3d 802, 809 (3d Cir. 1997) (holding that lack of peer review or publication was not dispositive where the expert's opinion was supported by "widely accepted scientific knowledge"). The standards set forth in the amendment are broad enough to require consideration of any or all of the specific *Daubert* factors where appropriate.

Courts both before and after *Daubert* have found other factors relevant in determining whether expert testimony is sufficiently reliable to be considered by the trier of fact. These factors include:

(1) Whether experts are "proposing to testify about matters growing naturally and directly out of research they have conducted independent of the litigation, or whether they have developed their opinions expressly for purposes of testifying." *Daubert v. Merrell Dow Pharmaceuticals, Inc.*, 43 F.3d 1311, 1317 (9th Cir. 1995).

(2) Whether the expert has unjustifiably extrapolated from an accepted premise to an unfounded conclusion. *See General Elec. Co. v. Joiner*, 522 U.S. 136, 146 (1997) (noting that in some cases a trial court "may conclude that there is simply too great an analytical gap between the data and the opinion proffered").

(3) Whether the expert has adequately accounted for obvious alternative explanations. *See Claar v. Burlington N.R.R.*, 29 F.3d 499 (9th Cir. 1994) (testimony excluded where the expert failed to consider other obvious causes for the plaintiff's condition). *Compare Ambrosini v. Labarraque*, 101 F.3d 129 (D.C. Cir. 1996) (the possibility of some uneliminated causes presents a question of weight, so long as the most obvious causes have been considered and reasonably ruled out by the expert).

(4) Whether the expert "is being as careful as he would be in his regular professional work outside his paid litigation consulting." *Sheehan v. Daily Racing Form, Inc.*, 104 F.3d 940, 942 (7th Cir. 1997). *See Kumho Tire Co. v. Carmichael*, 119 S.Ct. 1167, 1176 (1999) (*Daubert* requires the trial court to assure itself that the expert "employs in the courtroom the same level of intellectual rigor that characterizes the practice of an expert in the relevant field").

(5) Whether the field of expertise claimed by the expert is known to reach reliable results for the type of opinion the expert would give. *See Kumho Tire Co. v. Carmichael*, 119 S.Ct.1167, 1175 (1999) (*Daubert's* general acceptance factor does not "help show that an expert's testimony is reliable where the discipline itself lacks reliability, as for example, do theories grounded in any so-called generally accepted principles of astrology or necromancy."), *Moore v. Ashland Chemical, Inc.*, 151 F.3d 269 (5th Cir. 1998) (en banc) (clinical doctor was properly precluded from testifying to the toxicological cause of the plaintiff's respiratory problem, where the opinion was not sufficiently grounded in scientific methodology); *Sterling v. Velsicol Chem. Corp.*, 855 F.2d 1188 (6th Cir. 1988) (rejecting testimony based on "clinical ecology" as unfounded and unreliable).

All of these factors remain relevant to the determination of the reliability of expert testimony under the Rule as amended. Other factors may also be relevant. *See Kumho*, 119 S.Ct. 1167, 1176 ("[W]e conclude that the trial judge must have considerable leeway in deciding in a particular case how to go about determining whether particular expert testimony is reliable."). Yet no single factor is necessarily dispositive of the reliability of a particular expert's testimony. *See, e.g., Heller v. Shaw Industries, Inc.*, 167 F.3d 146, 155 (3d Cir. 1999) ("not only must each stage of the expert's testimony be reliable, but each stage must be evaluated practically and flexibly without bright-line exclusionary (or inclusionary) rules."); *Daubert v. Merrell Dow Pharmaceuticals, Inc.*, 43 F.3d 1311, 1317, n.5 (9th Cir. 1995) (noting that some expert disciplines "have the courtroom as a principal theatre of operations" and as to these disciplines "the fact that

the expert has developed an expertise principally for purposes of litigation will obviously not be a substantial consideration.").

A review of the caselaw after *Daubert* shows that the rejection of expert testimony is the exception rather than the rule. *Daubert* did not work a "seachange over federal evidence law," and "the trial court's role as gatekeeper is not intended to serve as a replacement for the adversary system." *United States v. 14.38 Acres of Land Situated in Leflore County, Mississippi*, 80 F.3d 1074, 1078 (5th Cir. 1996). As the Court in *Daubert* stated: "Vigorous cross-examination, presentation of contrary evidence, and careful instruction on the burden of proof are the traditional and appropriate means of attacking shaky but admissible evidence." 509 U.S. at 595. Likewise, this amendment is not intended to provide an excuse for an automatic challenge to the testimony of every expert. *See Kumho Tire Co. v . Carmichael*, 119 S.Ct.1167, 1176 (1999) (noting that the trial judge has the discretion "both to avoid unnecessary 'reliability' proceedings in ordinary cases where the reliability of an expert's methods is properly taken for granted, and to require appropriate proceedings in the less usual or more complex cases where cause for questioning the expert's reliability arises.").

When a trial court, applying this amendment, rules that an expert's testimony is reliable, this does not necessarily mean that contradictory expert testimony is unreliable. The amendment is broad enough to permit testimony that is the product of competing principles or methods in the same field of expertise. *See, e.g., Heller v. Shaw Industries, Inc.*, 167 F.3d 146, 160 (3d Cir. 1999) (expert testimony cannot be excluded simply because the expert uses one test rather than another, when both tests are accepted in the field and both reach reliable results). As the court stated in *In re Paoli R.R. Yard PCB Litigation*, 35 F.3d 717, 744 (3d Cir. 1994), proponents "do not have to demonstrate to the judge by a preponderance of the evidence that the assessments of their experts are correct, they only have to demonstrate by a preponderance of evidence that their opinions are reliable.... The evidentiary requirement of reliability is lower than the merits standard of correctness." *See also Daubert v. Merrell Dow Pharmaceuticals, Inc.*, 43 F.3d 1311, 1318 (9th Cir. 1995) (scientific experts might be permitted to testify if they could show that the methods they used were also employed by "a recognized minority of scientists in their field."); *Ruiz-Troche v. Pepsi Cola*, 161 F.3d 77, 85 (1st Cir. 1998) ("*Daubert* neither requires nor empowers trial courts to determine which of several competing scientific theories has the best provenance.").

The Court in *Daubert* declared that the "focus, of course, must be solely on principles and methodology, not on the conclusions they generate." 509 U.S. at 595. Yet as the Court later recognized, "conclusions and methodology are not entirely distinct from one another." *General Elec. Co. v. Joiner*, 522 U.S. 136, 146 (1997). Under the amendment, as under *Daubert*, when an expert purports to apply principles and methods in accordance with professional standards, and yet reaches a conclusion that other experts in the field would not reach, the trial court may fairly suspect that the principles and methods have not been faithfully applied. *See Lust v. Merrell Dow Pharmaceuticals, Inc.*, 89 F.3d 594, 598 (9th Cir. 1996). The amendment specifically provides that the trial court must scrutinize not only the principles and methods used by the expert, but also whether those principles and methods have been properly applied to the facts of the case. As the court noted in *In re Paoli R.R. Yard PCB Litig.*, 35 F.3d 717, 745 (3d Cir. 1994), "*any* step that renders the analysis unreliable ... renders the expert's testimony inadmissible. *This is true whether the step completely changes a reliable methodology or merely misapplies that methodology.*"

If the expert purports to apply principles and methods to the facts of the case, it is important that this application be conducted reliably. Yet it might also be important in some cases for an expert to educate the factfinder about general principles, without ever attempting to apply these principles to the specific facts of the case. For example, experts might instruct the factfinder on the principles of thermodynamics, or bloodclotting, or on how financial markets respond to corporate reports, without ever knowing about or trying to tie their testimony into the facts of the case. The amendment does not alter the venerable practice of using expert testimony to educate the factfinder on general principles. For this kind of generalized testimony, Rule 702 simply requires that: (1) the expert be qualified; (2) the testimony address a subject matter on which the factfinder can be assisted by an expert; (3) the testimony be reliable; and (4) the testimony "fit" the facts of the case.

As stated earlier, the amendment does not distinguish between scientific and other forms of expert testimony. The trial court's gatekeeping function applies to testimony by any expert. *See Kumho Tire Co. v. Carmichael*, 119 S.Ct. 1167, 1171 (1999) ("We conclude that *Daubert's* general holding—setting forth the trial judge's general 'gatekeeping' obligation—applies not only to testimony based on 'scientific' knowledge, but also to testimony based on 'technical' and 'other specialized' knowledge."). While the relevant factors for determining reliability will vary from expertise to expertise, the amendment rejects the premise that an expert's testimony should be treated more permissively simply because it is outside the realm of science. An opinion from an expert who is not a scientist should receive the same degree of scrutiny for reliability as an opinion from an expert who purports to be a scientist. *See Watkins v. Telsmith, Inc.*, 121 F.3d 984, 991 (5th Cir. 1997) ("[I]t seems exactly backwards that experts who purport to rely on general engineering principles and practical experience might escape screening by the district court simply by stating that their conclusions were not reached by any particular method or technique."). Some types of expert testimony will be more objectively verifiable, and subject to the expectations of falsifiability, peer review, and publication, than others. Some types of expert testimony will not rely on anything like a scientific method, and so will have to be evaluated by reference to other standard principles attendant to the particular area of expertise. The trial judge in all cases of proffered expert testimony must find that it is properly grounded, well-reasoned, and not speculative before it can be admitted. The expert's testimony must be grounded in an accepted body of learning or experience in the expert's field, and the expert must explain how the conclusion is so grounded. *See, e.g.*, American College of Trial Lawyers, *Standards and Procedures for Determining the Admissibility of Expert Testimony after* Daubert, *157 F.R.D. 571, 579 (1994)* ("[W]hether the testimony concerns economic principles, accounting standards, property valuation or other non-scientific subjects, it should be evaluated by reference to the 'knowledge and experience' of that particular field.").

The amendment requires that the testimony must be the product of reliable principles and methods that are reliably applied to the facts of the case. While the terms "principles" and "methods" may convey a certain impression when applied to scientific knowledge, they remain relevant when applied to testimony based on technical or other specialized knowledge. For example, when a law enforcement agent testifies regarding the use of code words in a drug transaction, the principle used by the agent is that participants in such transactions regularly use code words to conceal the nature of their activities. The method used by the agent is the application of extensive experience to analyze the meaning of the conversations. So long as the principles and methods are reliable and applied reliably to the facts of the case, this type of testimony should be admitted.

Nothing in this amendment is intended to suggest that experience alone—or experience in conjunction with other knowledge, skill, training or education—may not provide a sufficient foundation for expert testimony. To the contrary, the text of Rule 702 expressly contemplates that an expert may be qualified on the basis of experience. In certain fields, experience is the predominant, if not sole, basis for a great deal of reliable expert testimony. *See, e.g., United States v. Jones*, 107 F.3d 1147 (6th Cir. 1997) (no abuse of discretion in admitting the testimony of a handwriting examiner who had years of practical experience and extensive training, and who explained his methodology in detail); *Tassin v. Sears Roebuck*, 946 F.Supp. 1241, 1248 (M.D.La. 1996) (design engineer's testimony can be admissible when the expert's opinions "are based on facts, a reasonable investigation, and traditional technical/mechanical expertise, and he provides a reasonable link between the information and procedures he uses

and the conclusions he reaches"). *See also Kumho Tire Co. v. Carmichael*, 119 S.Ct. 1167, 1178 (1999) (stating that "no one denies that an expert might draw a conclusion from a set of observations based on extensive and specialized experience.").

If the witness is relying solely or primarily on experience, then the witness must explain how that experience leads to the conclusion reached, why that experience is a sufficient basis for the opinion, and how that experience is reliably applied to the facts. The trial court's gatekeeping function requires more than simply "taking the expert's word for it." *See Daubert v. Merrell Dow Pharmaceuticals, Inc.*, 43 F.3d 1311, 1319 (9th Cir. 1995) ("We've been presented with only the experts' qualifications, their conclusions and their assurances of reliability. Under *Daubert*, that's not enough."). The more subjective and controversial the expert's inquiry, the more likely the testimony should be excluded as unreliable. *See O'Conner v. Commonwealth Edison Co.*, 13 F.3d 1090 (7th Cir. 1994) (expert testimony based on a completely subjective methodology held properly excluded). *See also Kumho Tire Co. v. Carmichael*, 119 S.Ct . 1167, 1176 (1999) ("[I]t will at times be useful to ask even of a witness whose expertise is based purely on experience, say, a perfume tester able to distinguish among 140 odors at a sniff, whether his preparation is of a kind that others in the field would recognize as acceptable.").

Subpart (1) of Rule 702 calls for a quantitative rather than qualitative analysis. The amendment requires that expert testimony be based on sufficient underlying "facts or data." The term "data" is intended to encompass the reliable opinions of other experts. See the original Advisory Committee Note to Rule 703. The language "facts or data" is broad enough to allow an expert to rely on hypothetical facts that are supported by the evidence. *Id.*

When facts are in dispute, experts sometimes reach different conclusions based on competing versions of the facts. The emphasis in the amendment on " sufficient facts or data" is not intended to authorize a trial court to exclude an expert's testimony on the ground that the court believes one version of the facts and not the other.

There has been some confusion over the relationship between Rules 702 and 703. The amendment makes clear that the sufficiency of the basis of an expert' s testimony is to be decided under Rule 702. Rule 702 sets forth the overarching requirement of reliability, and an analysis of the sufficiency of the expert's basis cannot be divorced from the ultimate reliability of the expert's opinion. In contrast, the "reasonable reliance" requirement of Rule 703 is a relatively narrow inquiry. When an expert relies on inadmissible information, Rule 703 requires the trial court to determine whether that information is of a type reasonably relied on by other experts in the field. If so, the expert can rely on the information in reaching an opinion. However, the question whether the expert is relying on a *sufficient* basis of information—whether admissible information or not—is governed by the requirements of Rule 702.

The amendment makes no attempt to set forth procedural requirements for exercising the trial court's gatekeeping function over expert testimony. *See* Daniel J. Capra, *The Daubert Puzzle*, 38 Ga.L.Rev. 699, 766 (1998) ("Trial courts should be allowed substantial discretion in dealing with *Daubert* questions; any attempt to codify procedures will likely give rise to unnecessary changes in practice and create difficult questions for appellate review."). Courts have shown considerable ingenuity and flexibility in considering challenges to expert testimony under *Daubert*, and it is contemplated that this will continue under the amended Rule. *See, e.g., Cortes-Irizarry v. Corporacion Insular*, 111 F.3d 184 (1st Cir. 1997) (discussing the application of *Daubert* in ruling on a motion for summary judgment); *In re Paoli R.R. Yard PCB Litig.*, 35 F.3d 717, 736, 739 (3d Cir. 1994) (discussing the use of *in limine* hearings); *Claar v. Burlington N.R.R.*, 29 F.3d 499, 502–05 (9th Cir. 1994) (discussing the trial court's technique of ordering experts to submit serial affidavits explaining the reasoning and methods underlying their conclusions).

The amendment continues the practice of the original Rule in referring to a qualified witness as an "expert." This was done to provide continuity and to minimize change. The use of the term "expert" in the Rule does not, however, mean that a jury should actually be informed that a qualified witness is testifying as an "expert." Indeed, there is much to be said for a practice that prohibits the use of the term "expert" by both the parties and the court at trial. Such a practice "ensures that trial courts do not inadvertently put their stamp of authority" on a witness's opinion, and protects against the jury's being "overwhelmed by the so-called 'experts'." Hon. Charles Richey, *Proposals to Eliminate the Prejudicial Effect of the Use of the Word "Expert" Under the Federal Rules of Evidence in Criminal and Civil Jury Trials*, 154 F.R.D. 537, 559 (1994) (setting forth limiting instructions and a standing order employed to prohibit the use of the term " expert" injury trials).

Rule 703. Bases of Opinion Testimony by Experts

The facts or data in the particular case upon which an expert bases an opinion or inference may be those perceived by or made known to the expert at or before the hearing. If of a type reasonably relied upon by experts in the particular field in forming opinions or inferences upon the subject, the facts or data need not be admissible in evidence in order for the opinion or inference to be admitted. Facts or data that are otherwise inadmissible shall not be disclosed to the jury by the proponent of the opinion or inference unless the court determines that their probative value in assisting the jury to evaluate the expert's opinion substantially outweighs their prejudicial effect.

ADVISORY COMMITTEE NOTES

1972 Proposed Rules

Facts or data upon which expert opinions are based may, under the rule, be derived from three possible sources. The first is the firsthand observation of the witness with opinions based thereon traditionally allowed. A treating physician affords an example. Rheingold, The Basis of Medical Testimony, 15 Vand.L.Rev. 473, 489 (1962). Whether he must first relate his observations is treated in Rule 705. The second source, presentation at the trial, also reflects existing practice. The technique may be the familiar hypothetical question or having the expert attend the trial and hear the testimony establishing the facts. Problems of determining what testimony the expert relied upon, when the latter technique is employed and the testimony is in conflict, may be resolved by resort to Rule 705. The third source contemplated by the rule consists of presentation of data to the expert outside of court and other than by his own perception. In this respect the rule is designed to broaden the basis for expert opinions beyond that current in many jurisdictions and to bring the judicial practice into line with the practice of the experts themselves when not in court. Thus a physician in his own practice bases his diagnosis on information from numerous sources and of considerable variety, including statements by patients and relatives, reports and opinions from nurses, technicians and other doctors, hospital records, and X rays. Most of them are admissible in evidence, but only with the expenditure of substantial time in producing and examining various authenticating witnesses. The physician makes life-and-death decisions in reliance upon them. His validation, expertly performed and subject to cross-examination, ought to suffice for judicial purposes. Rheingold, *supra*, at 531; McCormick § 15. A similar provision is California Evidence Code § 801(b).

The rule also offers a more satisfactory basis for ruling upon the admissibility of public opinion poll evidence. Attention is directed to the validity of the techniques employed rather than to relatively fruitless inquiries whether hearsay is involved. See Judge Feinberg's careful analysis in Zippo Mfg. Co. v. Rogers Imports, Inc., 216 F.Supp. 670 (S.D.N.Y.1963). See also Blum et al., The Art of Opinion Research: A Lawyer's Appraisal of an Emerging Service, 24 U.Chi.L.Rev. 1 (1956); Bonynge Trademark Surveys and Techniques and Their Use in Litigation, 48 A.B.A.J. 329 (1962); Zeisel, The Uniqueness of Survey Evidence, 45 Cornell L.Q. 322 (1960); Annot., 76 A.L.R.2d 919.

If it be feared that enlargement of permissible data may tend to break down the rules of exclusion unduly, notice should be taken that the rule requires that the facts or data "be of a type reasonably relied upon by experts in the particular field." The language would not warrant admitting in evidence the opinion of an "accidentologist" as to the point of impact in an automobile collision based on statements of bystanders since this requirement is not satisfied. See Comment, Cal.Law Rev.Comm'n, Recommendation Proposing an Evidence Code 148–150 (1965).

2000 Amendments

Rule 703 has been amended to emphasize that when an expert reasonably relies on inadmissible information to form an opinion or inference, the underlying information is not admissible simply because the opinion or inference is admitted. Courts have reached different results on how to treat inadmissible information when it is reasonably relied upon by an expert in forming an opinion or drawing an inference. *Compare United States v. Rollins*, 862 F.2d 1282 (7th Cir. 1988) (admitting, as part of the basis of an FBI agent's expert opinion on the meaning of code language, the hearsay statements of an informant), *with United States v. 0.59 Acres of Land*, 109 F.3d 1493 (9th Cir. 1997) (error to admit hearsay offered as the basis of an expert opinion, without a limiting instruction). Commentators have also taken differing views. *See e.g.*, Ronald Carlson, *Policing the Bases of Modern Expert Testimony*, 39 Vand.L.Rev. 577 (1986) (advocating limits on the jury's consideration of otherwise inadmissible evidence used as the basis for an expert opinion); Paul Rice, *Inadmissible Evidence as a Basis for Expert Testimony: A Response to Professor Carlson*, 40 Vand.L.Rev. 583 (1987) (advocating unrestricted use of information reasonably relied upon by an expert).

When information is reasonably relied upon by an expert and yet is admissible only for the purpose of assisting the jury in evaluating an expert's opinion, a trial court applying this Rule must consider the information's probative value in assisting the jury to weigh the expert's opinion on the one hand, and the risk of prejudice resulting from the jury's potential misuse of the information for substantive purposes on the other. The information may be disclosed to the jury, upon objection, only if the trial court finds that the probative value of the information in assisting the jury to evaluate the expert's opinion substantially outweighs its prejudicial effect. If the otherwise inadmissible information is admitted under this balancing test, the trial judge must give a limiting instruction upon request, informing the jury that the underlying information must not be used for substantive purposes. *See* Rule 105. In determining the appropriate course, the trial court should consider the probable effectiveness or lack of effectiveness of a limiting instruction under the particular circumstances.

The amendment governs only the disclosure to the jury of information that is reasonably relied on by an expert, when that information is not admissible for substantive purposes. It is not intended to affect the admissibility of an expert's testimony. Nor does the amendment prevent an expert from relying on information that is inadmissible for substantive purposes.

Nothing in this Rule restricts the presentation of underlying expert facts or data when offered by an adverse party. *See* Rule 705. Of course, an adversary's attack on an expert's basis will often open the door to a proponent's rebuttal with information that was reasonably relied upon by the expert, even if that information would not have been discloseable initially under the balancing test provided by this amendment. Moreover, in some circumstances the proponent might wish to disclose information that is relied upon by the expert in order to "remove the sting" from the opponent's anticipated attack, and thereby prevent the jury from drawing an unfair negative inference. The trial court should take this consideration into account in applying the balancing test provided by this amendment.

This amendment covers facts or data that cannot be admitted for any purpose other than to assist the jury to evaluate the expert's opinion. The balancing test provided in this amendment is not applicable to facts or data that are admissible for any other purpose but have not yet been offered for such a purpose at the time the expert testifies.

The amendment provides a presumption against disclosure to the jury of information used as the basis of an expert's opinion and not admissible for any substantive purpose, when that information is offered by the proponent of the expert. In a multi-party case, where one party proffers an expert whose testimony is also beneficial to other parties, each such party should be deemed a "proponent" within the meaning of the amendment.

Rule 704. Opinion on Ultimate Issue

(a) Except as provided in subdivision (b), testimony in the form of an opinion or inference otherwise admissible is not objectionable because it embraces an ultimate issue to be decided by the trier of fact.

(b) No expert witness testifying with respect to the mental state or condition of a defendant in a criminal case may state an opinion or inference as to whether the defendant did or did not have the mental state or condition constituting an element of the crime charged or of a defense thereto. Such ultimate issues are matters for the trier of fact alone.

ADVISORY COMMITTEE NOTES
1972 Proposed Rules

The basic approach to opinions, lay and expert, in these rules is to admit them when helpful to the trier of fact. In order to render this approach fully effective and to allay any doubt on the subject, the so-called "ultimate issue" rule is specifically abolished by the instant rule.

The older cases often contained strictures against allowing witnesses to express opinions upon ultimate issues, as a particular aspect of the rule against opinions. The rule was unduly restrictive, difficult of application, and generally served only to deprive the trier of fact of useful information. 7 Wigmore §§ 1920, 1921; McCormick § 12. The basis usually assigned for the rule, to prevent the witness from "usurping the province of the jury," is aptly characterized as "empty rhetoric." 7 Wigmore § 1920, p. 17. Efforts to meet the felt needs of particular situations led to odd verbal circumlocutions which were said not to violate the rule. Thus a witness could express his estimate of the criminal responsibility of an accused in terms of sanity or insanity, but not in terms of ability to tell right from wrong or other more modern standard. And in cases of medical causation, witnesses were sometimes required to couch their opinions in cautious phrases of "might or could," rather than "did," though the result was to deprive many opinions of the positiveness to which they were entitled, accompanied by the hazard of a ruling of insufficiency to support a verdict. In other instances the rule was simply disregarded, and, as concessions to need, opinions were allowed upon such matters as intoxication, speed, handwriting, and value, although more precise coincidence with an ultimate issue would scarcely be possible.

Many modern decisions illustrate the trend to abandon the rule completely. People v. Wilson, 25 Cal.2d 341, 153 P.2d 720 (1944), whether abortion necessary to save life of patient; *Clifford–Jacobs Forging Co. v. Industrial Comm.*, 19 Ill.2d 236, 166 N.E.2d 582 (1960), medical causation; *Dowling v. L. H. Shattuck, Inc.*, 91 N.H. 234, 17 A.2d 529 (1941), proper method of shoring ditch; *Schweiger v. Solbeck*, 191 Or. 454, 230 P.2d 195 (1951), cause of landslide. In each instance the opinion was allowed.

The abolition of the ultimate issue rule does not lower the bars so as to admit all opinions. Under Rules 701 and 702, opinions must be helpful to the trier of fact, and Rule 403

provides for exclusion of evidence which wastes time. These provisions afford ample assurances against the admission of opinions which would merely tell the jury what result to reach, somewhat in the manner of the oath-helpers of an earlier day. They also stand ready to exclude opinions phrased in terms of inadequately explored legal criteria. Thus the question, "Did T have capacity to make a will?" would be excluded, while the question, "Did T have sufficient mental capacity to know the nature and extent of his property and the natural objects of his bounty and to formulate a rational scheme of distribution?" would be allowed. McCormick § 12.

For similar provisions see Uniform Rule 56(4); California Evidence Code § 805; Kansas Code of Civil Procedure § 60–456(d); New Jersey Evidence Rule 56(3).

Rule 705. Disclosure of Facts or Data Underlying Expert Opinion

The expert may testify in terms of opinion or inference and give reasons therefor without first testifying to the underlying facts or data, unless the court requires otherwise. The expert may in any event be required to disclose the underlying facts or data on cross-examination.

ADVISORY COMMITTEE NOTES
1972 Proposed Rules

The hypothetical question has been the target of a great deal of criticism as encouraging partisan bias, affording an opportunity for summing up in the middle of the case, and as complex and time consuming. Ladd, Expert Testimony, 5 Vand.L.Rev. 414, 426–427 (1952). While the rule allows counsel to make disclosure of the underlying facts or data as a preliminary to the giving of an expert opinion, if he chooses, the instances in which he is required to do so are reduced. This is true whether the expert bases his opinion on data furnished him at secondhand or observed by him at firsthand.

The elimination of the requirement of preliminary disclosure at the trial of underlying facts or data has a long background of support. In 1937 the Commissioners on Uniform State Laws incorporated a provision to this effect in their Model Expert Testimony Act, which furnished the basis for Uniform Rules 57 and 58. Rule 4515, N.Y. CPLR (McKinney 1963), provides:

"Unless the court orders otherwise, questions calling for the opinion of an expert witness need not be hypothetical in form, and the witness may state his opinion and reasons without first specifying the data upon which it is based. Upon cross-examination, he may be required to specify the data * * *."

See also California Evidence Code § 802; Kansas Code of Civil Procedure §§ 60–456, 60–457; New Jersey Evidence Rules 57, 58.

If the objection is made that leaving it to the cross-examiner to bring out the supporting data is essentially unfair, the answer is that he is under no compulsion to bring out any facts or data except those unfavorable to the opinion. The answer assumes that the cross-examiner has the advance knowledge which is essential for effective cross-examination. This advance knowledge has been afforded, though imperfectly, by the traditional foundation requirement. Rule 26(b)(4) of the Rules of Civil Procedure, as revised, provides for substantial discovery in this area, obviating in large measure the obstacles which have been raised in some instances to discovery of findings, underlying data, and even the identity of the experts. Friedenthal Discovery and Use of an Adverse Party's Expert Information, 14 Stan.L.Rev. 455 (1962).

These safeguards are reinforced by the discretionary power of the judge to require preliminary disclosure in any event.

1993 Amendment

This rule, which relates to the manner of presenting testimony at trial, is revised to avoid an arguable conflict with revised Rules 26(a)(2)(B) and 26(e)(1) of the Federal Rules of Civil

Procedure or with revised Rule 16 of the Federal Rules of Criminal Procedure, which require disclosure in advance of trial of the basis and reasons for an expert's opinions.

If a serious question is raised under Rule 702 or 703 as to the admissibility of expert testimony, disclosure of the underlying facts or data on which opinions are based may, of course, be needed by the court before deciding whether, and to what extent, the person should be allowed to testify. This rule does not preclude such an inquiry.

Rule 706. Court Appointed Experts

(a) Appointment. The court may on its own motion or on the motion of any party enter an order to show cause why expert witnesses should not be appointed, and may request the parties to submit nominations. The court may appoint any expert witnesses agreed upon by the parties, and may appoint expert witnesses of its own selection. An expert witness shall not be appointed by the court unless the witness consents to act. A witness so appointed shall be informed of the witness' duties by the court in writing, a copy of which shall be filed with the clerk, or at a conference in which the parties shall have opportunity to participate. A witness so appointed shall advise the parties of the witness' findings, if any; the witness' deposition may be taken by any party; and the witness may be called to testify by the court or any party. The witness shall be subject to cross-examination by each party, including a party calling the witness.

(b) Compensation. Expert witnesses so appointed are entitled to reasonable compensation in whatever sum the court may allow. The compensation thus fixed is payable from funds which may be provided by law in criminal cases and civil actions and proceedings involving just compensation under the fifth amendment. In other civil actions and proceedings the compensation shall be paid by the parties in such proportion and at such time as the court directs, and thereafter charged in like manner as other costs.

(c) Disclosure of appointment. In the exercise of its discretion, the court may authorize disclosure to the jury of the fact that the court appointed the expert witness.

(d) Parties' experts of own selection. Nothing in this rule limits the parties in calling expert witnesses of their own selection.

ADVISORY COMMITTEE NOTES
1972 Proposed Rules

The practice of shopping for experts, the venality of some experts, and the reluctance of many reputable experts to involve themselves in litigation, have been matters of deep concern. Though the contention is made that court appointed experts acquire an aura of infallibility to which they are not entitled, Levy, Impartial Medical Testimony—Revisited, 34 Temple L.Q. 416 (1961), the trend is increasingly to provide for their use. While experience indicates that actual appointment is a relatively infrequent occurrence, the assumption may be made that the availability of the procedure in itself decreases the need for

resorting to it. The ever-present possibility that the judge may appoint an expert in a given case must inevitably exert a sobering effect on the expert witness of a party and upon the person utilizing his services.

The inherent power of a trial judge to appoint an expert of his own choosing is virtually unquestioned. *Scott v. Spanjer Bros., Inc.,* 298 F.2d 928 (2d Cir.1962); *Danville Tobacco Assn. v. Bryant–Buckner Associates,* Inc., 333 F.2d 202 (4th Cir.1964); Sink, The Unused Power of a Federal Judge to Call His Own Expert Witnesses, 29 S.Cal.L.Rev. 195 (1956); 2 Wigmore § 563, 9 *id.* § 2484; Annot., 95 A.L.R.2d 383. Hence the problem becomes largely one of detail.

The New York plan is well known and is described in Report by Special Committee of the Association of the Bar of the City of New York: Impartial Medical Testimony (1956). On recommendation of the Section of Judicial Administration, local adoption of an impartial medical plan was endorsed by the American Bar Association. 82 A.B.A.Rep. 184–185 (1957). Descriptions and analyses of plans in effect in various parts of the country are found in Van Dusen, A United States District Judge's View of the Impartial Medical Expert System, 32 F.R.D. 498 (1963); Wick and Kightlinger, Impartial Medical Testimony Under the Federal Civil Rules: A Tale of Three Doctors, 34 Ins. Counsel J. 115 (1967); and numerous articles collected in Klein, Judicial Administration and the Legal Profession 393 (1963). Statutes and rules include California Evidence Code §§ 730–733; Illinois Supreme Court Rule 215(d), Ill.Rev.Stat.1969, c. 110A, § 215(d); Burns Indiana Stats.1956, § 9–1702; Wisconsin Stats.Annot.1958, § 957.27.

In the federal practice, a comprehensive scheme for court appointed experts was initiated with the adoption of Rule 28 of the Federal Rules of Criminal Procedure in 1946. The Judicial Conference of the United States in 1953 considered court appointed experts in civil cases, but only with respect to whether they should be compensated from public funds, a proposal which was rejected. Report of the Judicial Conference of the United States 23 (1953). The present rule expands the practice to include civil cases.

Note to Subdivision (a). Subdivision (a) is based on Rule 28 of the Federal Rules of Criminal Procedure, with a few changes, mainly in the interest of clarity. Language has been added to provide specifically for the appointment either on motion of a party or on the judge's own motion. A provision subjecting the court appointed expert to deposition procedures has been incorporated. The rule has been revised to make definite the right of any party, including the party calling him, to cross-examine.

Note to Subdivision (b). Subdivision (b) combines the present provision for compensation in criminal cases with what seems to be a fair and feasible handling of civil cases, originally found in the Model Act and carried from there into Uniform Rule 60. See also California Evidence Code §§ 730–731. The special provision for Fifth Amendment compensation cases is designed to guard against reducing constitutionally guaranteed just compensation by requiring the recipient to pay costs. See Rule 71A(*l*) of the Rules of Civil Procedure.

Note to Subdivision (c). Subdivision (c) seems to be essential if the use of court appointed experts is to be fully effective. Uniform Rule 61 so provides.

Note to Subdivision (d). Subdivision (d) is in essence the last sentence of Rule 28(a) of the Federal Rules of Criminal Procedure.

ARTICLE VIII. HEARSAY

ADVISORY COMMITTEE NOTES
1972 Proposed Rules

Introductory Note; The Hearsay Problem. The factors to be considered in evaluating the testimony of a witness are perception, memory, and narration. Morgan, Hearsay Dangers and the Application of the Hearsay Concept, 62 Harv.L.Rev. 177

(1948), Selected Writings on Evidence and Trial 764, 765 (Fryer ed. 1957); Shientag, Cross–Examination—A Judge's Viewpoint, 3 Record 12 (1948); Strahorn, A Reconsideration of the Hearsay Rule and Admissions, 85 U.Pa.L.Rev. 484, 485 (1937), Selected Writings, *supra*, 756, 757; Weinstein, Probative Force of Hearsay, 46 Iowa L.Rev. 331 (1961). Sometimes a fourth is added, sincerity, but in fact it seems merely to be an aspect of the three already mentioned.

In order to encourage the witness to do his best with respect to each of these factors, and to expose any inaccuracies which may enter in, the Anglo–American tradition has evolved three conditions under which witnesses will ideally be required to testify: (1) under oath, (2) in the personal presence of the trier of fact, (3) subject to cross-examination.

(1) Standard procedure calls for the swearing of witnesses. While the practice is perhaps less effective than in an earlier time, no disposition to relax the requirement is apparent, other than to allow affirmation by persons with scruples against taking oaths.

(2) The demeanor of the witness traditionally has been believed to furnish trier and opponent with valuable clues. *Universal Camera Corp. v. N.L.R.B.*, 340 U.S. 474, 495–496, 71 S.Ct. 456, 95 L.Ed. 456 (1951); Sahm, Demeanor Evidence: Elusive and Intangible Imponderables, 47 A.B.A.J. 580 (1961), quoting numerous authorities. The witness himself will probably be impressed with the solemnity of the occasion and the possibility of public disgrace. Willingness to falsify may reasonably become more difficult in the presence of the person against whom directed. Rules 26 and 43(a) of the Federal Rules of Criminal and Civil Procedure, respectively, include the general requirement that testimony be taken orally in open court. The Sixth Amendment right of confrontation is a manifestation of these beliefs and attitudes.

(3) Emphasis on the basis of the hearsay rule today tends to center upon the condition of cross-examination. All may not agree with Wigmore that cross-examination is "beyond doubt the greatest legal engine ever invented for the discovery of truth," but all will agree with his statement that it has become a "vital feature" of the Anglo–American system. 5 Wigmore § 1367, p. 29. The belief, or perhaps hope, that cross-examination is effective in exposing imperfections of perception, memory, and narration is fundamental. Morgan, Foreword to Model Code of Evidence 37 (1942).

The logic of the preceding discussion might suggest that no testimony be received unless in full compliance with the three ideal conditions. No one advocates this position. Common sense tells that much evidence which is not given under the three conditions may be inherently superior to much that is. Moreover, when the choice is between evidence which is less than best and no evidence at all, only clear folly would dictate an across-the-board policy of doing without. The problem thus resolves itself into effecting a sensible accommodation between these considerations and the desirability of giving testimony under the ideal conditions.

The solution evolved by the common law has been a general rule excluding hearsay but subject to numerous exceptions under circumstances supposed to furnish guarantees of trustworthiness. Criticisms of this scheme are that it is bulky and complex, fails to screen good from bad hearsay realistically, and inhibits the growth of the law of evidence.

Since no one advocates excluding all hearsay, three possible solutions may be considered: (1) abolish the rule against hearsay and admit all hearsay; (2) admit hearsay possessing sufficient probative force, but with procedural safeguards; (3) revise the present system of class exceptions.

(1) Abolition of the hearsay rule would be the simplest solution. The effect would not be automatically to abolish the giving of testimony under ideal conditions. If the declarant were available, compliance with the ideal conditions would be optional with either party. Thus the proponent could call the declarant as a witness as a form of presentation more impressive than his hearsay statement. Or the opponent could call the declarant to be cross-examined upon his statement. This is the tenor of Uniform Rule 63(1), admitting the hearsay declaration of a person "who is present at the hearing and available for cross-examination." Compare the treatment of declarations of available declarants in Rule 801(d)(1) of the instant rules. If the declarant were unavailable, a rule of free admissibility would make no distinctions in terms of degrees of noncompliance with the ideal conditions and would exact no quid pro quo in the form of assurances of trustworthiness. Rule 503 of the Model Code did exactly that, providing for the admissibility of any hearsay declaration by an unavailable declarant, finding support in the Massachusetts act of 1898, enacted at the instance of Thayer, Mass.Gen.L.1932, c. 233, § 65, and in the English act of 1938, St.1938, c. 28, Evidence. Both are limited to civil cases. The draftsmen of the Uniform Rules chose a less advanced and more conventional position. Comment, Uniform Rule 63. The present Advisory Committee has been unconvinced of the wisdom of abandoning the traditional requirement of some particular assurance of credibility as a condition precedent to admitting the hearsay declaration of an unavailable declarant.

In criminal cases, the Sixth Amendment requirement of confrontation would no doubt move into a large part of the area presently occupied by the hearsay rule in the event of the abolition of the latter. The resultant split between civil and criminal evidence is regarded as an undesirable development.

(2) Abandonment of the system of class exceptions in favor of individual treatment in the setting of the particular case, accompanied by procedural safeguards, has been impressively advocated. Weinstein, The Probative Force of Hearsay, 46 Iowa L.Rev. 331 (1961). Admissibility would be determined by weighing the probative force of the evidence against the possibility of prejudice, waste of time, and the availability of more satisfactory evidence. The bases of the traditional hearsay exceptions would be helpful in assessing probative force. Ladd, The Relationship of the Principles of Exclusionary Rules of Evidence to the Problem of Proof, 18 Minn.L.Rev. 506 (1934). Procedural safeguards would consist of notice of intention to use hearsay, free comment by the judge on the weight of the evidence, and a greater measure of authority in both trial and appellate judges to deal with evidence on the basis of weight. The Advisory Committee has rejected this approach to hearsay as involving too great a measure of judicial discretion, minimizing the predictability of rulings, enhancing the difficulties of preparation for trial, adding a further element to the already over-complicated congeries of pretrial procedures, and requiring substantially different rules for civil and criminal cases. The only way in which the probative force of hearsay differs from the probative force of other testimony is in the absence of oath, demeanor, and cross-examination as aids in determining credibility. For a judge to exclude evidence because he does not believe it has been described as "altogether atypical, extraordinary. * * * *" Chadbourn, Bentham and the Hearsay Rule—A Benthamic View of Rule 63(4)(c) of the Uniform Rules of Evidence, 75 Harv. L.Rev. 932, 947 (1962).

(3) The approach to hearsay in these rules is that of the common law, i.e., a general rule excluding hearsay, with exceptions under which evidence is not required to be excluded even though hearsay. The traditional hearsay exceptions are drawn upon for the exceptions, collected under two rules, one dealing with situations where availability of the declarant is regarded as immaterial and the other with those where unavailability is made a condition to the admission of the hearsay statement. Each of the two rules concludes with a provision for hearsay statements not within one of the specified exceptions "but having comparable circumstantial guarantees of trustworthiness." Rules 803(24) and 804(b)(6). This plan is submitted as calculated to encourage growth and development in this area of the law, while conserving the values and experience of the past as a guide to the future.

Confrontation and Due Process. Until very recently, decisions invoking the confrontation clause of the Sixth Amendment were surprisingly few, a fact probably explainable by the former inapplicability of the clause to the states and by the hearsay rule's occupancy of much the same ground. The pattern which emerges from the earlier cases invoking the clause is substantially that of the hearsay rule, applied to criminal cases: an accused is entitled to have the witnesses against him testify under oath, in the presence of himself and trier, subject to cross-examination; yet considerations of public policy and necessity require the recognition of such exceptions as dying declarations and former testimony of unavailable witnesses. *Mattox v. Unit-*

ed States, 156 U.S. 237, 15 S.Ct. 337, 39 L.Ed. 409 (1895); *Motes v. United States,* 178 U.S. 458, 20 S.Ct. 993, 44 L.Ed. 1150 (1900); *Delaney v. United States,* 263 U.S. 586, 44 S.Ct. 206, 68 L.Ed. 462 (1924). Beginning with *Snyder v. Massachusetts,* 291 U.S. 97, 54 S.Ct. 330, 78 L.Ed. 674 (1934), the Court began to speak of confrontation as an aspect of procedural due process, thus extending its applicability to state cases and to federal cases other than criminal. The language of *Snyder* was that of an elastic concept of hearsay. The deportation case of *Bridges v. Wixon,* 326 U.S. 135, 65 S.Ct. 1443, 89 L.Ed. 2103 (1945), may be read broadly as imposing a strictly construed right of confrontation in all kinds of cases or narrowly as the product of a failure of the Immigration and Naturalization Service to follow its own rules. *In re Oliver,* 333 U.S. 257, 68 S.Ct. 499, 92 L.Ed. 682 (1948), ruled that cross-examination was essential to due process in a state contempt proceeding, but in *United States v. Nugent,* 346 U.S. 1, 73 S.Ct. 991, 97 L.Ed. 1417 (1953), the court held that it was not an essential aspect of a "hearing" for a conscientious objector under the Selective Service Act. *Stein v. New York,* 346 U.S. 156, 196, 73 S.Ct. 1077, 97 L.Ed. 1522 (1953), disclaimed any purpose to read the hearsay rule into the Fourteenth Amendment, but in *Greene v. McElroy,* 360 U.S. 474, 79 S.Ct. 1400, 3 L.Ed.2d 1377 (1959), revocation of security clearance without confrontation and cross-examination was held unauthorized, and a similar result was reached in *Willner v. Committee on Character,* 373 U.S. 96, 83 S.Ct. 1175, 10 L.Ed.2d 224 (1963). Ascertaining the constitutional dimensions of the confrontation-hearsay aggregate against the background of these cases is a matter of some difficulty, yet the general pattern is at least not inconsistent with that of the hearsay rule.

In 1965 the confrontation clause was held applicable to the states. *Pointer v. Texas,* 380 U.S. 400, 85 S.Ct. 1065, 13 L.Ed.2d 923 (1965). Prosecution use of former testimony given at a preliminary hearing where petitioner was not represented by counsel was a violation of the clause. The same result would have followed under conventional hearsay doctrine read in the light of a constitutional right to counsel, and nothing in the opinion suggests any difference in essential outline between the hearsay rule and the right of confrontation. In the companion case of *Douglas v. Alabama,* 380 U.S. 415, 85 S.Ct. 1074, 13 L.Ed.2d 934 (1965), however, the result reached by applying the confrontation clause is one reached less readily via the hearsay rule. A confession implicating petitioner was put before the jury by reading it to the witness in portions and asking if he made that statement. The witness refused to answer on grounds of self-incrimination. The result, said the Court, was to deny cross-examination, and hence confrontation. True, it could broadly be said that the confession was a hearsay statement which for all practical purposes was put in evidence. Yet a more easily accepted explanation of the opinion is that its real thrust was in the direction of curbing undesirable prosecutorial behavior, rather than merely applying rules of exclusion, and that the confrontation clause was the means selected to achieve this end. Comparable facts and a like result appeared in *Brookhart v. Janis,* 384 U.S. 1, 86 S.Ct. 1245, 16 L.Ed.2d 314 (1966).

The pattern suggested in *Douglas* was developed further and more distinctly in a pair of cases at the end of the 1966 term. *United States v. Wade,* 388 U.S. 218, 87 S.Ct. 1926, 18 L.Ed.2d 1149 (1967), and *Gilbert v. California,* 388 U.S. 263, 87 S.Ct. 1951, 18 L.Ed.2d 1178 (1967), hinged upon practices followed in identifying accused persons before trial. This pretrial identification was said to be so decisive an aspect of the case that accused was entitled to have counsel present; a pretrial identification made in the absence of counsel was not itself receivable in evidence and, in addition, might fatally infect a courtroom identification. The presence of counsel at the earlier identification was described as a necessary prerequisite for "a meaningful confrontation at trial." *United States v. Wade, supra,* 388 U.S. at p. 236, 87 S.Ct. at p. 1937. *Wade* involved no evidence of the fact of a prior identification and hence was not susceptible of being decided on hearsay grounds. In *Gilbert,* witnesses did testify to an earlier identification, readily classifiable as hearsay under a fairly strict view of what constitutes hearsay. The Court, however, carefully avoided basing the decision on the

hearsay ground, choosing confrontation instead. 388 U.S. 263, 272, n. 3, 87 S.Ct. 1951. See also *Parker v. Gladden,* 385 U.S. 363, 87 S.Ct. 468, 17 L.Ed.2d 420 (1966), holding that the right of confrontation was violated when the bailiff made prejudicial statements to jurors, and Note, 75 Yale L.J. 1434 (1966).

Under the earlier cases, the confrontation clause may have been little more than a constitutional embodiment of the hearsay rule, even including traditional exceptions but with some room for expanding them along similar lines. But under the recent cases the impact of the clause clearly extends beyond the confines of the hearsay rule. These considerations have led the Advisory Committee to conclude that a hearsay rule can function usefully as an adjunct to the confrontation right in constitutional areas and independently in nonconstitutional areas. In recognition of the separateness of the confrontation clause and the hearsay rule, and to avoid inviting collisions between them or between the hearsay rule and other exclusionary principles, the exceptions set forth in Rules 803 and 804 are stated in terms of exemption from the general exclusionary mandate of the hearsay rule, rather than in positive terms of admissibility. See Uniform Rule 63(1) to (31) and California Evidence Code §§ 1200–1340.

Rule 801. Definitions

The following definitions apply under this article:

(a) Statement. A "statement" is (1) an oral or written assertion or (2) nonverbal conduct of a person, if it is intended by the person as an assertion.

(b) Declarant. A "declarant" is a person who makes a statement.

(c) Hearsay. "Hearsay" is a statement, other than one made by the declarant while testifying at the trial or hearing, offered in evidence to prove the truth of the matter asserted.

(d) Statements which are not hearsay. A statement is not hearsay if—

(1) Prior statement by witness. The declarant testifies at the trial or hearing and is subject to cross-examination concerning the statement, and the statement is (A) inconsistent with the declarant's testimony, and was given under oath subject to the penalty of perjury at a trial, hearing, or other proceeding, or in a deposition, or (B) consistent with the declarant's testimony and is offered to rebut an express or implied charge against the declarant of recent fabrication or improper influence or motive, or (C) one of identification of a person made after perceiving the person; or

(2) Admission by party-opponent. The statement is offered against a party and is (A) the party's own statement, in either an individual or a representative capacity or (B) a statement of which the party has manifested an adoption or belief in its truth, or (C) a statement by a person authorized by the party to make a statement concerning the subject, or (D) a statement by the party's agent or servant concerning a matter within the scope of the agency or employment, made during the existence of the relationship, or (E) a statement by a coconspirator of a party during the course and in furtherance of the conspiracy. The contents of the statement shall be considered but are not alone sufficient to establish the declarant's authority under subdivision (C), the agency or employment relationship and scope thereof under subdivision (D), or the existence of the conspiracy and the participation therein of the declarant and the party against whom the statement is offered under subdivision (E).

ADVISORY COMMITTEE NOTES
1972 Proposed Rules

Note to Subdivision (a). The definition of "statement" assumes importance because the term is used in the definition of hearsay in subdivision (c). The effect of the definition of "statement" is to exclude from the operation of the hearsay rule all evidence of conduct, verbal or nonverbal, not intended as an assertion. The key to the definition is that nothing is an assertion unless intended to be one.

It can scarcely be doubted that an assertion made in words is intended by the declarant to be an assertion. Hence verbal assertions readily fall into the category of "statement." Whether nonverbal conduct should be regarded as a statement for purposes of defining hearsay requires further consideration. Some nonverbal conduct, such as the act of pointing to identify a suspect in a lineup, is clearly the equivalent of words, assertive in nature, and to be regarded as a statement. Other nonverbal conduct, however, may be offered as evidence that the person acted as he did because of his belief in the existence of the condition sought to be proved, from which belief the existence of the condition may be inferred. This sequence is, arguably, in effect an assertion of the existence of the condition and hence properly includable within the hearsay concept. See Morgan, Hearsay Dangers and the Application of the Hearsay Concept, 62 Harv.L.Rev. 177, 214, 217 (1948), and the elaboration in Finman, Implied Assertions as Hearsay: Some Criticisms of the Uniform Rules of Evidence, 14 Stan.L.Rev. 682 (1962). Admittedly evidence of this character is untested with respect to the perception, memory, and narration (or their equivalents) of the actor, but the Advisory Committee is of the view that these dangers are minimal in the absence of an intent to assert and do not justify the loss of the evidence on hearsay grounds. No class of evidence is free of the possibility of fabrication, but the likelihood is less with nonverbal than with assertive verbal conduct. The situations giving rise to the nonverbal conduct are such as virtually to eliminate questions of sincerity. Motivation, the nature of the conduct, and the presence or absence of reliance will bear heavily upon the weight to be given the evidence. Falknor, The "Hear–Say" Rule as a "See–Do" Rule: Evidence of Conduct, 33 Rocky Mt.L.Rev. 133 (1961). Similar considerations govern nonassertive verbal conduct and verbal conduct which is assertive but offered as a basis for inferring something other than the matter asserted, also excluded from the definition of hearsay by the language of subdivision (c).

When evidence of conduct is offered on the theory that it is not a statement, and hence not hearsay, a preliminary determination will be required to determine whether an assertion is intended. The rule is so worded as to place the burden upon the party claiming that the intention existed; ambiguous and doubtful cases will be resolved against him and in favor of admissibility. The determination involves no greater difficulty than many other preliminary questions of fact. Maguire, The Hearsay System: Around and Through the Thicket, 14 Vand.L.Rev. 741, 765–767 (1961).

For similar approaches, see Uniform Rule 62(1); California Evidence Code §§ 225, 1200; Kansas Code of Civil Procedure § 60–459(a); New Jersey Evidence Rule 62(1).

Note to Subdivision (c). The definition follows along familiar lines in including only statements offered to prove the truth of the matter asserted. McCormick § 225; 5 Wigmore § 1361, 6 *id.* § 1766. If the significance of an offered statement lies solely in the fact that it was made, no issue is raised as to the truth of anything asserted, and the statement is not hearsay. *Emich Motors Corp. v. General Motors Corp.*, 181 F.2d 70 (7th Cir. 1950), rev'd on other grounds 340 U.S. 558, 71 S.Ct. 408, 95 L.Ed. 534, letters of complaint from customers offered as a reason for cancellation of dealer's franchise, to rebut contention that franchise was revoked for refusal to finance sales through affiliated finance company. The effect is to exclude from hearsay the entire category of "verbal acts" and "verbal parts of an act," in which the statement itself affects the legal rights of the parties or is a circumstance bearing on conduct affecting their rights.

The definition of hearsay must, of course, be read with reference to the definition of statement set forth in subdivision (a).

Testimony given by a witness in the course of court proceedings is excluded since there is compliance with all the ideal conditions for testifying.

Note to Subdivision (d). Several types of statements which would otherwise literally fall within the definition are expressly excluded from it:

(1) *Prior statement by witness.* Considerable controversy has attended the question whether a prior out-of-court statement by a person now available for cross-examination concerning it, under oath and in the presence of the trier of fact, should be classed as hearsay. If the witness admits on the stand that he made the statement and that it was true, he adopts the statement and there is no hearsay problem. The hearsay problem arises when the witness on the stand denies having made the statement or admits having made it but denies its truth. The argument in favor of treating these latter statements as hearsay is based upon the ground that the conditions of oath, cross-examination, and demeanor observation did not prevail at the time the statement was made and cannot adequately be supplied by the later examination. The logic of the situation is troublesome. So far as concerns the oath, its mere presence has never been regarded as sufficient to remove a statement from the hearsay category, and it receives much less emphasis than cross-examination as a truth-compelling device. While strong expressions are found to the effect that no conviction can be had or important right taken away on the basis of statements not made under fear of prosecution for perjury, *Bridges v. Wixon,* 326 U.S. 135, 65 S.Ct. 1443, 89 L.Ed. 2103 (1945), the fact is that, of the many common law exceptions to the hearsay rule, only that for reported testimony has required the statement to have been made under oath. Nor is it satisfactorily explained why cross-examination cannot be conducted subsequently with success. The decisions contending most vigorously for its inadequacy in fact demonstrate quite thorough exploration of the weaknesses and doubts attending the earlier statement. *State v. Saporen,* 205 Minn. 358, 285 N.W. 898 (1939); *Ruhala v. Roby,* 379 Mich. 102, 150 N.W.2d 146 (1967); *People v. Johnson,* 68 Cal.2d 646, 68 Cal.Rptr. 599, 441 P.2d 111 (1968). In respect to demeanor, as Judge Learned Hand observed in *Di Carlo v. United States,* 6 F.2d 364 (2d Cir.1925), when the jury decides that the truth is not what the witness says now, but what he said before, they are still deciding from what they see and hear in court. The bulk of the case law nevertheless has been against allowing prior statements of witnesses to be used generally as substantive evidence. Most of the writers and Uniform Rule 63(1) have taken the opposite position.

The position taken by the Advisory Committee in formulating this part of the rule is funded upon an unwillingness to countenance the general use of prior prepared statements as substantive evidence, but with a recognition that particular circumstances call for a contrary result. The judgment is one more of experience than of logic. The rule requires in each instance, as a general safeguard, that the declarant actually testify as a witness, and it then enumerates three situations in which the statement is excepted from the category of hearsay. Compare Uniform Rule 63(1) which allows any out-of-court statement of a declarant who is present at the trial and available for cross-examination.

(A) Prior inconsistent statements traditionally have been admissible to impeach but not as substantive evidence. Under the rule they are substantive evidence. As has been said by the California Law Revision Commission with respect to a similar provision:

"Section 1235 admits inconsistent statements of witnesses because the dangers against which the hearsay rule is designed to protect are largely nonexistent. The declarant is in court and may be examined and cross-examined in regard to his statements and their subject matter. In many cases, the inconsistent statement is more likely to be true than the testimony of the witness at the trial because it was made nearer in time to the matter to which it relates and is less likely to be influenced by the controversy that gave rise to the litigation. The trier of fact has the declarant before it and can observe his demeanor and the nature of his testimony as he denies or tries to explain away the inconsistency. Hence, it is in as good a position to determine the truth or falsity of the prior statement as it is to determine the truth or falsity of the inconsistent testimony given in court. Moreover, Section 1235 will provide a party with desirable protection against the 'turncoat' witness who changes his story on the stand and deprives the party calling him of evidence essential to his case." Comment, California Evidence Code § 1235. See also McCormick § 39. The Advisory Committee finds these views more convincing than those expressed in *People v. Johnson*, 68 Cal.2d 646, 68 Cal.Rptr. 599, 441 P.2d 111 (1968). The constitutionality of the Advisory Committee's view was upheld in *California v. Green*, 399 U.S. 149, 90 S.Ct. 1930, 26 L.Ed.2d 489 (1970). Moreover, the requirement that the statement be inconsistent with the testimony given assures a thorough exploration of both versions while the witness is on the stand and bars any general and indiscriminate use of previously prepared statements.

(B) Prior consistent statements traditionally have been admissible to rebut charges of recent fabrication or improper influence or motive but not as substantive evidence. Under the rule they are substantive evidence. The prior statement is consistent with the testimony given on the stand, and, if the opposite party wishes to open the door for its admission in evidence, no sound reason is apparent why it should not be received generally.

(C) The admission of evidence of identification finds substantial support, although it falls beyond a doubt in the category of prior out-of-court statements. Illustrative are *People v. Gould*, 54 Cal.2d 621, 7 Cal.Rptr. 273, 354 P.2d 865 (1960); *Judy v. State*, 218 Md. 168, 146 A.2d 29 (1958); *State v. Simmons*, 63 Wash.2d 17, 385 P.2d 389 (1963); California Evidence Code § 1238; New Jersey Evidence Rule 63(1)(c); N.Y.Code of Criminal Procedure § 393–b. Further cases are found in 4 Wigmore § 1130. The basis is the generally unsatisfactory and inconclusive nature of courtroom identifications as compared with those made at an earlier time under less suggestive conditions. The Supreme Court considered the admissibility of evidence of prior identification in *Gilbert v. California*, 388 U.S. 263, 87 S.Ct. 1951, 18 L.Ed.2d 1178 (1967). Exclusion of lineup identification was held to be required because the accused did not then have the assistance of counsel. Significantly, the Court carefully refrained from placing its decision on the ground that testimony as to the making of a prior out-of-court identification ("That's the man") violated either the hearsay rule or the right of confrontation because not made under oath, subject to immediate cross-examination, in the presence of the trier. Instead the Court observed:

"There is a split among the States concerning the admissibility of prior extra-judicial identifications, as independent evidence of identity, both by the witness and third parties present at the prior identification. See 71 ALR2d 449. It has been held that the prior identification is hearsay, and, when admitted through the testimony of the identifier, is merely a prior consistent statement. The recent trend, however, is to admit the prior identification under the exception that admits as substantive evidence a prior communication by a witness who is available for cross-examination at the trial. See 5 ALR2d Later Case Service 1225–1228. * * *" 388 U.S. at 272, n. 3, 87 S.Ct. at 1956.

(2) *Admissions.* Admissions by a party-opponent are excluded from the category of hearsay on the theory that their admissibility in evidence is the result of the adversary system rather than satisfaction of the conditions of the hearsay rule. Strahorn, A Reconsideration of the Hearsay Rule and Admissions, 85 U.Pa.L.Rev. 484, 564 (1937); Morgan, Basic Problems of Evidence 265 (1962); 4 Wigmore § 1048. No guarantee of trustworthiness is required in the case of an admission. The freedom which admissions have enjoyed from technical demands of searching for an assurance of truthworthiness in some against-interest circumstance, and from the restrictive influences of the opinion rule and the rule requiring firsthand knowledge,

when taken with the apparently prevalent satisfaction with the results, calls for generous treatment of this avenue to admissibility.

The rule specifies five categories of statements for which the responsibility of a party is considered sufficient to justify reception in evidence against him:

(A) A party's own statement is the classic example of an admission. If he has a representative capacity and the statement is offered against him in that capacity, no inquiry whether he was acting in the representative capacity in making the statement is required; the statement need only be relevant to represent affairs. To the same effect in California Evidence Code § 1220. Compare Uniform Rule 63(7), requiring a statement to be made in a representative capacity to be admissible against a party in a representative capacity.

(B) Under established principles an admission may be made by adopting or acquiescing in the statement of another. While knowledge of contents would ordinarily be essential, this is not inevitably so: "X is a reliable person and knows what he is talking about." See McCormick § 246, p. 527, n. 15. Adoption or acquiescence may be manifested in any appropriate manner. When silence is relied upon, the theory is that the person would, under the circumstances, protest the statement made in his presence, if untrue. The decision in each case calls for an evaluation in terms of probable human behavior. In civil cases, the results have generally been satisfactory. In criminal cases, however, troublesome questions have been raised by decisions holding that failure to deny is an admission: the inference is a fairly weak one, to begin with; silence may be motivated by advice of counsel or realization that "anything you say may be used against you"; unusual opportunity is afforded to manufacture evidence; and encroachment upon the privilege against self-incrimination seems inescapably to be involved. However, recent decisions of the Supreme Court relating to custodial interrogation and the right to counsel appear to resolve these difficulties. Hence the rule contains no special provisions concerning failure to deny in criminal cases.

(C) No authority is required for the general proposition that a statement authorized by a party to be made should have the status of an admission by the party. However, the question arises whether only statements to third persons should be so regarded, to the exclusion of statements by the agent to the principal. The rule is phrased broadly so as to encompass both. While it may be argued that the agent authorized to make statements to his principal does not speak for him, Morgan, Basic Problems of Evidence 273 (1962), communication to an outsider has not generally been thought to be an essential characteristic of an admission. Thus a party's books or records are usable against him, without regard to any intent to disclose to third persons. 5 Wigmore § 1557. See also McCormick § 78, pp. 159–161. In accord is New Jersey Evidence Rule 63(8)(a). Cf. Uniform Rule 63(8)(a) and California Evidence Code § 1222 which limit status as an admission in this regard to statements authorized by the party to be made "for" him, which is perhaps an ambiguous limitation to statements to third persons. Falknor, Vicarious Admissions and the Uniform Rules, 14 Vand.L.Rev. 855, 860–861 (1961).

(D) The tradition has been to test the admissibility of statements by agents, as admissions, by applying the usual test of agency. Was the admission made by the agent acting in the scope of his employment? Since few principals employ agents for the purpose of making damaging statements, the usual result was exclusion of the statement. Dissatisfaction with this loss of valuable and helpful evidence has been increasing. A substantial trend favors admitting statements related to a matter within the scope of the agency or employment. *Grayson v. Williams*, 256 F.2d 61 (10th Cir.1958); *Koninklijke Luchtvaart Maatschappij N.V. KLM Royal Dutch Airlines v. Tuller*, 110 U.S.App.D.C. 282, 292 F.2d 775, 784 (1961); *Martin v. Savage Truck Lines*, Inc., 121 F.Supp. 417 (D.D.C.1954), and numerous state court decisions collected in 4 Wigmore, 1964 Supp. pp. 66–73, with comments by the editor that the statements should have been excluded as not within scope of agency. For the traditional view see *Northern Oil Co. v. Socony Mobil Oil Co.*,

347 F.2d 81, 85 (2d Cir.1965) and cases cited therein. Similar provisions are found in Uniform Rule 63(9)(a), Kansas Code of Civil Procedure § 60–460(i)(1), and New Jersey Evidence Rule 63(9)(a).

(E) The limitation upon the admissibility of statements of co-conspirators to those made "during the course and in further-ance of the conspiracy" is in the accepted pattern. While the broadened view of agency taken in item (iv) might suggest wider admissibility of statements of co-conspirators, the agency theory of conspiracy is at best a fiction and ought not to serve as a basis for admissibility beyond that already established. See Levie, Hearsay and Conspiracy, 52 Mich.L.Rev. 1159 (1954); Comment, 25 U.Chi.L.Rev. 530 (1958). The rule is consistent with the position of the Supreme Court in denying admissibility to state-ments made after the objectives of the conspiracy have either failed or been achieved. *Krulewitch v. United States*, 336 U.S. 440, 69 S.Ct. 716, 93 L.Ed. 790 (1949); *Wong Sun v. United States*, 371 U.S. 471, 490, 83 S.Ct. 407, 9 L.Ed.2d 441 (1963). For similarly limited provisions see California Evidence Code § 1223 and New Jersey Rule 63(9)(b). Cf. Uniform Rule 63(9)(b).

1974 Enactment

Note to Subdivision (d)(1). Present federal law, except in the Second Circuit, permits the use of prior inconsistent state-ments of a witness for impeachment only. Rule 801(d)(1) as proposed by the Court would have permitted all such statements to be admissible as substantive evidence, an approach followed by a small but growing number of State jurisdictions and recently held constitutional in California v. Green, 399 U.S. 149 (1970). Although there was some support expressed for the Court Rule, based largely on the need to counteract the effect of witness intimidation in criminal cases, the Committee decided to adopt a compromise version of the Rule similar to the position of the Second Circuit. The Rule as amended draws a distinction between types of prior inconsistent statements (other than state-ments of identification of a person made after perceiving him which are currently admissible, see United States v. Anderson, 406 F.2d 719, 720 (4th Cir.), cert. denied, 395 U.S. 967 (1969)) and allows only those made while the declarant was subject to cross-examination at a trial or hearing or in a deposition, to be admissible for their truth. Compare United States v. DeSisto, 329 F.2d 929 (2nd Cir.), cert. denied, 377 U.S. 979 (1964); United States v. Cunningham, 446 F.2d 194 (2nd Cir.1971) (restricting the admissibility of prior inconsistent statements as substantive evidence to those made under oath in a formal proceeding, but not requiring that there have been an opportunity for cross-examination). The rationale for the Committee's decision is that (1) unlike in most other situations involving unsworn or oral statements, there can be no dispute as to whether the prior statement was made; and (2) the context of a formal proceeding, an oath, and the opportunity for cross-examination provide firm additional assurances of the reliability of the prior statement. House Report No. 93–650.

Note to Subdivision (d)(1)(A). Rule 801 defines what is and what is not hearsay for the purpose of admitting a prior state-ment as substantive evidence. A prior statement of a witness at a trial or hearing which is inconsistent with his testimony is, of course, always admissible for the purpose of impeaching the witness' credibility.

As submitted by the Supreme Court, subdivision (d)(1)(A) made admissible as substantive evidence the prior statement of a witness inconsistent with his present testimony.

The House severely limited the admissibility of prior inconsis-tent statements by adding a requirement that the prior state-ment must have been subject to cross-examination, thus preclud-ing even the use of grand jury statements. The requirement that the prior statement must have been subject to cross-examination appears unnecessary since this rule comes into play only when the witness testifies in the present trial. At that time, he is on the stand and can explain an earlier position and be cross-examined as to both.

The requirement that the statement be under oath also ap-pears unnecessary. Notwithstanding the absence of an oath contemporaneous with the statement, the witness, when on the stand, qualifying or denying the prior statement, is under oath. In any event, of all the many recognized exceptions to the hearsay rule, only one (former testimony) requires that the out-of-court statement have been made under oath. With respect to the lack of evidence of the demeanor of the witness at the time of the prior statement, it would be difficult to improve upon Judge Learned Hand's observation that when the jury decides that the truth is not what the witness says now but what he said before, they are still deciding from what they see and hear in court. [*Di Carlo v. U.S.*, 6 F.2d 364 (2d Cir.1925)].

The rule as submitted by the Court has positive advantages. The prior statement was made nearer in time to the events, when memory was fresher and intervening influences had not been brought into play. A realistic method is provided for dealing with the turncoat witness who changes his story on the stand [see Comment, California Evidence Code § 1235; McCor-mick, Evidence, § 38 (2nd ed. 1972)].

New Jersey, California, and Utah have adopted a rule similar to this one; and Nevada, New Mexico, and Wisconsin have adopted the identical Federal rule.

For all of these reasons, we think the House amendment should be rejected and the rule as submitted by the Supreme Court reinstated. [It would appear that some of the opposition to this Rule is based on a concern that a person could be convicted solely upon evidence admissible under this Rule. The Rule, however, is not addressed to the question of the sufficiency of evidence to send a case to the jury, but merely as to its admissibility. Factual circumstances could well arise where, if this were the sole evidence, dismissal would be appropriate.]

Note to Subdivision (d)(1)(C). As submitted by the Su-preme Court and as passed by the House, subdivision (d)(1)(C) of rule 801 made admissible the prior statement identifying a person made after perceiving him. The committee decided to delete this provision because of the concern that a person could be convicted solely upon evidence admissible under this subdivi-sion.

Note to Subdivision 801(d)(2)(E). The House approved the long-accepted rule that "a statement by a coconspirator of a party during the course and in furtherance of the conspiracy" is not hearsay as it was submitted by the Supreme Court. While the rule refers to a coconspirator, it is this committee's under-standing that the rule is meant to carry forward the universally accepted doctrine that a joint venturer is considered as a coconspirator for the purposes of this rule even though no conspiracy has been charged. United States v. Rinaldi, 393 F.2d 97, 99 (2d Cir.), cert. denied 393 U.S. 913 (1968); United States v. Spencer, 415 F.2d 1301, 1304 (7th Cir., 1969). Senate Report No. 93–1277.

Rule 801 supplies some basic definitions for the rules of evidence that deal with hearsay. Rule 801(d)(1) defines certain statements as not hearsay. The Senate amendments make two changes in it.

Note to Subdivision (d)(1)(A). The House bill provides that a statement is not hearsay if the declarant testifies and is subject to cross-examination concerning the statement and if the statement is inconsistent with his testimony and was given under oath subject to cross-examination and subject to the penalty of perjury at a trial or hearing or in a deposition. The Senate amendment drops the requirement that the prior state-ment be given under oath subject to cross-examination and subject to the penalty of perjury at a trial or hearing or in a deposition.

The Conference adopts the Senate amendment with an amendment, so that the rule now requires that the prior incon-sistent statement be given under oath subject to the penalty of perjury at a trial, hearing, or other proceeding, or in a deposi-tion. The rule as adopted covers statements before a grand jury. Prior inconsistent statements may, of course, be used for impeaching the credibility of a witness. When the prior inconsistent statement is one made by a defendant in a criminal case, it is covered by Rule 801(d)(2).

Note to Subdivision (d)(1)(C). The House bill provides that a statement is not hearsay if the declarant testifies and is subject to cross-examination concerning the statement and the statement is one of identification of a person made after perceiving him. The Senate amendment eliminated this provision.

The Conference adopts the Senate amendment. House Report No. 93–1597.

1997 Amendment

Rule 801(d)(2) has been amended in order to respond to three issues raised by *Bourjaily v. United States*, 483 U.S. 171 (1987). First, the amendment codifies the holding in *Bourjaily* by stating expressly that a court shall consider the contents of a coconspirator's statement in determining "the existence of the conspiracy and the participation therein of the declarant and the party against whom the statement is offered." According to *Bourjaily*, Rule 104(a) requires these preliminary questions to be established by a preponderance of the evidence.

Second, the amendment resolves an issue on which the Court had reserved decision. It provides that the contents of the declarant's statement do not alone suffice to establish a conspiracy in which the declarant and the defendant participated. The court must consider in addition the circumstances surrounding the statement, such as the identity of the speaker, the context in which the statement was made, or evidence corroborating the contents of the statement in making its determination as to each preliminary question. This amendment is in accordance with existing practice. Every court of appeals that has resolved this issue requires some evidence in addition to the contents of the statement. *See, e.g., United States v. Beckham*, 968 F.2d 47, 51 (D.C.Cir.1992); *United States v. Sepulveda*, 15 F.3d 1161, 1181–82 (1st Cir.1993), *cert. denied*, 114 S.Ct. 2714 (1994); *United States v. Daly*, 842 F.2d 1380, 1386 (2d Cir.), *cert. denied*, 488 U.S. 821 (1988); *United States v. Clark*, 18 F.3d 1337, 1341–42 (6th Cir.), *cert. denied*, 115 S.Ct. 152 (1994); *United States v. Zambrana*, 841 F.2d 1320, 1344–45 (7th Cir.1988); *United States v. Silverman*, 861 F.2d 571, 577 (9th Cir.1988); *United States v. Gordon*, 844 F.2d 1397, 1402 (9th Cir.1988); *United States v. Hernandez*, 829 F.2d 988, 993 (10th Cir.1987), *cert. denied*, 485 U.S. 1013 (1988); *United States v. Byrom*, 910 F.2d 725, 736 (11th Cir.1990).

Third, the amendment extends the reasoning of Bourjaily to statements offered under subdivisions (C) and (D) of Rule 801(d)(2). In Bourjaily, the Court rejected treating foundational facts pursuant to the law of agency in favor of an evidentiary approach governed by Rule 104(a). The Advisory Committee believes it appropriate to treat analogously preliminary questions relating to the declarant's authority under subdivision (C), and the agency or employment relationship and scope thereof under subdivision (D).

Rule 802.   Hearsay Rule

Hearsay is not admissible except as provided by these rules or by other rules prescribed by the Supreme Court pursuant to statutory authority or by Act of Congress.

ADVISORY COMMITTEE NOTES

1972 Proposed Rules

The provision excepting from the operation of the rule hearsay which is made admissible by other rules adopted by the Supreme Court or by Act of Congress continues the admissibility thereunder of hearsay which would not qualify under these Evidence Rules. The following examples illustrate the working of the exception:

Federal Rules of Civil Procedure

Rule 4(g): proof of service by affidavit.

Rule 32: admissibility of depositions.

Rule 43(e): affidavits when motion based on facts not appearing of record.

Rule 56: affidavits in summary judgment proceedings.

Rule 65(b): showing by affidavit for temporary restraining order.

Federal Rules of Criminal Procedure

Rule 4(a): affidavits to show grounds for issuing warrants.

Rule 12(b)(4): affidavits to determine issues of fact in connection with motions.

Acts of Congress

10 U.S.C. § 7730: affidavits of unavailable witnesses in actions for damages caused by vessel in naval service, or towage or salvage of same, when taking of testimony or bringing of action delayed or stayed on security grounds.

29 U.S.C. § 161(4): affidavit as proof of service in NLRB proceedings.

38 U.S.C. § 5206: affidavit as proof of posting notice of sale of unclaimed property by Veterans Administration.

Rule 803.   Hearsay Exceptions; Availability of Declarant Immaterial

The following are not excluded by the hearsay rule, even though the declarant is available as a witness:

(1) Present sense impression. A statement describing or explaining an event or condition made while the declarant was perceiving the event or condition, or immediately thereafter.

(2) Excited utterance. A statement relating to a startling event or condition made while the declarant was under the stress of excitement caused by the event or condition.

(3) Then existing mental, emotional, or physical condition. A statement of the declarant's then existing state of mind, emotion, sensation, or physical condition (such as intent, plan, motive, design, mental feeling, pain, and bodily health), but not including a statement of memory or belief to prove the fact remembered or believed unless it relates to the execution, revocation, identification, or terms of declarant's will.

(4) Statements for purposes of medical diagnosis or treatment. Statements made for purposes of medical diagnosis or treatment and describing medical history, or past or present symptoms, pain, or sensations, or the inception or general character of the cause or external source thereof insofar as reasonably pertinent to diagnosis or treatment.

(5) Recorded recollection. A memorandum or record concerning a matter about which a witness once had knowledge but now has insufficient recollection to enable the witness to testify fully and accurately, shown to have been made or adopted by the witness when the matter was fresh in the witness' memory and to reflect that knowledge correctly. If admitted, the memorandum or record may be read into evidence but may not itself be received as an exhibit unless offered by an adverse party.

(6) Records of Regularly Conducted Activity.—A memorandum, report, record, or data compilation, in any form, of acts, events, conditions, opinions, or diagnoses, made at or near the time by, or from information transmitted by, a person with knowledge, if kept in the course of a regularly conducted business activity, and if it was the regular practice of that business activity to make the memorandum, report, record or data compilation, all as shown by the testimony of the custodian or other qualified witness, or by certification that complies with Rule 902(11), Rule 902(12), or a statute permitting certification, unless the source of information or the method or circumstances of preparation indicate lack of trustworthiness. The term "business" as used in this paragraph includes business, institution, association, profession, occupation, and calling of every kind, whether or not conducted for profit.

(7) Absence of entry in records kept in accordance with the provisions of paragraph (6). Evidence that a matter is not included in the memoranda reports, records, or data compilations, in any form, kept in accordance with the provisions of paragraph (6), to prove the nonoccurrence or nonexistence of the matter, if the matter was of a kind of which a memorandum, report, record, or data compilation was regularly made and preserved, unless the sources of information or other circumstances indicate lack of trustworthiness.

(8) Public records and reports. Records, reports, statements, or data compilations, in any form, of public offices or agencies, setting forth (A) the activities of the office or agency, or (B) matters observed pursuant to duty imposed by law as to which matters there was a duty to report, excluding, however, in criminal cases matters observed by police officers and other law enforcement personnel, or (C) in civil actions and proceedings and against the Government in criminal cases, factual findings resulting from an investigation made pursuant to authority granted by law, unless the sources of information or other circumstances indicate lack of trustworthiness.

(9) Records of vital statistics. Records or data compilations, in any form, of births, fetal deaths, deaths, or marriages, if the report thereof was made to a public office pursuant to requirements of law.

(10) Absence of public record or entry. To prove the absence of a record, report, statement, or data compilation, in any form, or the nonoccurrence or nonexistence of a matter of which a record, report, statement, or data compilation, in any form, was regularly made and preserved by a public office or agency, evidence in the form of a certification in accordance with rule 902, or testimony, that diligent search failed to disclose the record, report, statement, or data compilation, or entry.

(11) Records of religious organizations. Statements of births, marriages, divorces, deaths, legitimacy, ancestry, relationship by blood or marriage, or other similar facts of personal or family history, contained in a regularly kept record of a religious organization.

(12) Marriage, baptismal, and similar certificates. Statements of fact contained in a certificate that the maker performed a marriage or other ceremony or administered a sacrament, made by a clergyman, public official, or other person authorized by the rules or practices of a religious organization or by law to perform the act certified, and purporting to have been issued at the time of the act or within a reasonable time thereafter.

(13) Family records. Statements of fact concerning personal or family history contained in family Bibles, genealogies, charts, engravings on rings, inscriptions on family portraits, engravings on urns, crypts, or tombstones, or the like.

(14) Records of documents affecting an interest in property. The record of a document purporting to establish or affect an interest in property, as proof of the content of the original recorded document and its execution and delivery by each person by whom it purports to have been executed, if the record is a record of a public office and an applicable statute authorizes the recording of documents of that kind in that office.

(15) Statements in documents affecting an interest in property. A statement contained in a document purporting to establish or affect an interest in property if the matter stated was relevant to the purpose of the document, unless dealings with the property since the document was made have been inconsistent with the truth of the statement or the purport of the document.

(16) Statements in ancient documents. Statements in a document in existence twenty years or more the authenticity of which is established.

(17) Market reports, commercial publications. Market quotations, tabulations, lists, directories, or other published compilations, generally used and relied upon by the public or by persons in particular occupations.

(18) Learned treatises. To the extent called to the attention of an expert witness upon cross-examination or relied upon by the expert witness in direct examination, statements contained in published treatises, periodicals, or pamphlets on a subject of history, medicine, or other science or art, established as a reliable authority by the testimony or admission of the witness or by other expert testimony or by judicial notice. If admitted, the statements may be read into evidence but may not be received as exhibits.

(19) Reputation concerning personal or family history. Reputation among members of a person's family by blood, adoption, or marriage, or among a person's associates, or in the community, concerning a person's birth, adoption, marriage, divorce, death, legitimacy, relationship by blood, adoption, or marriage, ancestry, or other similar fact of personal or family history.

(20) Reputation concerning boundaries or general history. Reputation in a community, arising before the controversy, as to boundaries of or customs affecting lands in the community, and reputation as to events of general history important to the community or State or nation in which located.

(21) Reputation as to character. Reputation of a person's character among associates or in the community.

(22) Judgment of previous conviction. Evidence of a final judgment, entered after a trial or upon a plea of guilty (but not upon a plea of nolo contendere), adjudging a person guilty of a crime punishable by death or imprisonment in excess of one year, to prove any fact essential to sustain the judgment, but not including, when offered by the Government in a criminal prosecution for purposes other than impeachment, judgments against persons other than the accused. The pendency of an appeal may be shown but does not affect admissibility.

(23) Judgment as to personal, family, or general history, or boundaries. Judgments as proof of matters of personal, family or general history, or boundaries, essential to the judgment, if the same would be provable by evidence of reputation.

(24) [Transferred to Rule 807]

ADVISORY COMMITTEE NOTES

1972 Proposed Rules

The exceptions are phrased in terms of nonapplication of the hearsay rule, rather than in positive terms of admissibility, in order to repel any implication that other possible grounds for exclusion are eliminated from consideration.

The present rule proceeds upon the theory that under appropriate circumstances a hearsay statement may possess circumstantial guarantees of trustworthiness sufficient to justify nonproduction of the declarant in person at the trial even though he may be available. The theory finds vast support in the many exceptions to the hearsay rule developed by the common law in which unavailability of the declarant is not a relevant factor. The present rule is a synthesis of them, with revision where modern developments and conditions are believed to make that course appropriate.

In a hearsay situation, the declarant is, of course, a witness, and neither this rule nor Rule 804 dispenses with the requirement of firsthand knowledge. It may appear from his statement or be inferable from circumstances. See Rule 602.

Note to Paragraphs (1) and (2). In considerable measure these two examples overlap, though based on somewhat different theories. The most significant practical difference will lie in the time lapse allowable between event and statement.

The underlying theory of Exception [paragraph] (1) is that substantial contemporaneity of event and statement negate the likelihood of deliberate or conscious misrepresentation. Moreover, if the witness is the declarant, he may be examined on the statement. If the witness is not the declarant, he may be examined as to the circumstances as an aid in evaluating the statement. Morgan, Basic Problems of Evidence 340–341 (1962).

The theory of Exception [paragraph] (2) is simply that circumstances may produce a condition of excitement which temporarily stills the capacity of reflection and produces utterances free of conscious fabrication. 6 Wigmore § 1747, p. 135. Spontaneity is the key factor in each instance, though arrived at by somewhat different routes. Both are needed in order to avoid needless niggling.

While the theory of Exception [paragraph] (2) has been criticized on the ground that excitement impairs accuracy of observation as well as eliminating conscious fabrication, Hutchins and Slesinger, Some Observations on the Law of Evidence: Spontaneous Exclamations, 28 Colum.L.Rev. 432 (1928), it finds support in cases without number. See cases in 6 Wigmore § 1750; Annot. 53 A.L.R.2d 1245 (statements as to cause of or responsibility for motor vehicle accident); Annot., 4 A.L.R.3d 149 (accusatory statements by homicide victims). Since unexciting events are less likely to evoke comment, decisions involving Exception [paragraph] (1) are far less numerous. Illustrative are *Tampa Elec. Co. v. Getrost*, 151 Fla. 558, 10 So.2d 83 (1942); *Houston Oxygen Co. v. Davis*, 139 Tex. 1, 161 S.W.2d 474 (1942); and cases cited in McCormick § 273, p. 585, n. 4.

With respect to the *time element*, Exception [paragraph] (1) recognizes that in many, if not most, instances precise contemporaneity is not possible and hence a slight lapse is allowable. Under Exception [paragraph] (2) the standard of measurement is the duration of the state of excitement. "How long can excitement prevail? Obviously there are no pat answers and the character of the transaction or event will largely determine the significance of the time factor." Slough, Spontaneous Statements and State of Mind, 46 Iowa L.Rev. 224, 243 (1961); McCormick § 272, p. 580.

Participation by the declarant is not required: a non-participant may be moved to describe what he perceives, and one may be startled by an event in which he is not an actor. Slough, *supra*; McCormick, *supra*; 6 Wigmore § 1755; Annot. 78 A.L.R.2d 300.

Whether *proof of the startling event* may be made by the statement itself is largely an academic question, since in most cases there is present at least circumstantial evidence that something of a startling nature must have occurred. For cases in which the evidence consists of the condition of the declarant (injuries, state of shock), see *Insurance Co. v. Mosely*, 75 U.S. (8 Wall.) 397, 19 L.Ed. 437 (1869); *Wheeler v. United States*, 93 U.S. App.D.C. 159, 211 F.2d 19 (1953), cert. denied 347 U.S. 1019, 74 S.Ct. 876, 98 L.Ed. 1140; *Wetherbee v. Safety Casualty Co.*, 219 F.2d 274 (5th Cir.1955); *Lampe v. United States*, 97 U.S.App.D.C. 160, 229 F.2d 43 (1956). Nevertheless, on occasion the only evidence may be the content of the statement itself, and rulings that it may be sufficient are described as "increasing," Slough, *supra* at 246, and as the "prevailing practice," McCormick § 272, p. 579. Illustrative are *Armour & Co. v. Industrial Commission*, 78 Colo. 569, 243 P. 546 (1926); *Young v. Stewart*, 191 N.C. 297, 131 S.E. 735 (1926). Moreover, under Rule 104(a) the judge is not limited by the hearsay rule in passing upon preliminary questions of fact.

Proof of declarant's perception by his statement presents similar considerations when declarant is identified. *People v. Poland*, 22 Ill.2d 175, 174 N.E.2d 804 (1961). However, when declarant is an unidentified bystander, the cases indicate hesitancy in upholding the statement alone as sufficient, *Garrett v. Howden*, 73 N.M. 307, 387 P.2d 874 (1963); *Beck v. Dye*, 200 Wash. 1, 92 P.2d 1113 (1939), a result which would under appropriate circumstances be consistent with the rule.

Permissible *subject matter* of the statement is limited under Exception [paragraph] (1) to description or explanation of the event or condition, the assumption being that spontaneity, in the absence of a startling event, may extend no farther. In Exception [paragraph] (2), however, the statement need only "relate" to the startling event or condition, thus affording a broader scope of subject matter coverage. 6 Wigmore §§ 1750, 1754. See *Sanitary Grocery Co. v. Snead*, 67 App.D.C. 129, 90 F.2d 374 (1937), slip-and-fall case sustaining admissibility of clerk's statement. "That has been on the floor for a couple of hours," and *Murphy Auto Parts Co., Inc. v. Ball*, 101 U.S.App.D.C. 416, 249 F.2d 508 (1957), upholding admission, on issue of driver's agency, of his statement that he had to call on a customer and was in a hurry to get home. Quick, Hearsay, Excitement, Necessity and the Uniform Rules: A Reappraisal of Rule 63(4), 6 Wayne L.Rev. 204, 206–209 (1960).

Similar provisions are found in Uniform Rule 63(4)(a) and (b); California Evidence Code § 1240 (as to Exception (2) only); Kansas Code of Civil Procedure § 60–460(d)(1) and (2); New Jersey Evidence Rule 63(4).

Note to Paragraph (3). Exception [paragraph] (3) is essentially a specialized application of Exception [paragraph] (1), presented separately to enhance its usefulness and accessibility. See McCormick §§ 265, 268.

The exclusion of "statements of memory or belief to prove the fact remembered or believed" is necessary to avoid the virtual destruction of the hearsay rule which would otherwise result from allowing state of mind, provable by a hearsay statement, to serve as the basis for an inference of the happening of the event which produced the state of mind. *Shepard v. United States*, 290 U.S. 96, 54 S.Ct. 22, 78 L.Ed. 196 (1933); Maguire, The Hillmon Case—Thirty-three Years After, 38 Harv.L.Rev. 709, 719–731 (1925); Hinton, States of Mind and the Hearsay Rule, 1 U.Chi.L.Rev. 394, 421–423 (1934). The rule of *Mutual Life Ins. Co. v. Hillmon*, 145 U.S. 285, 12 S.Ct. 909, 36 L.Ed. 706 (1892), allowing evidence of intention as tending to prove the doing of the act intended, is, of course, left undisturbed.

The carving out, from the exclusion mentioned in the preceding paragraph, of declarations relating to the execution, revocation, identification, or terms of declarant's will represents and *ad hoc* judgment which finds ample reinforcement in the decisions, resting on practical grounds of necessity and expediency rather than logic. McCormick § 271, pp. 577–578; Annot. 34 A.L.R.2d 588, 62 A.L.R.2d 855. A similar recognition of the need for and practical value of this kind of evidence is found in California Evidence Code § 1260.

Note to Paragraph (4). Even those few jurisdictions which have shied away from generally admitting statements of present condition have allowed them if made to a physician for purposes of diagnosis and treatment in view of the patient's strong motivation to be truthful. McCormick § 266, p. 563. The same guarantee of trustworthiness extends to statements of past conditions and medical history, made for purposes of diagnosis or treatment. It also extends to statements as to causation, reasonably pertinent to the same purposes, in accord with the current trend. *Shell Oil Co. v. Industrial Commission,* 2 Ill.2d 590, 119 N.E.2d 224 (1954); McCormick § 266, p. 564; New Jersey Evidence Rule 63(12)(c). Statements as to fault would not ordinarily qualify under this latter language. Thus a patient's statement that he was struck by an automobile would qualify but not his statement that the car was driven through a red light. Under the exception the statement need not have been made to a physician. Statements to hospital attendants, ambulance drivers, or even members of the family might be included.

Conventional doctrine has excluded from the hearsay exception, as not within its guarantee of truthfulness, statements to a physician consulted only for the purpose of enabling him to testify. While these statements were not admissible as substantive evidence, the expert was allowed to state the basis of his opinion, including statements of this kind. The distinction thus called for was one most unlikely to be made by juries. The rule accordingly rejects the limitation. This position is consistent with the provision of Rule 703 that the facts on which expert testimony is based need not be admissible in evidence if of a kind ordinarily relied upon by experts in the field.

Note to Paragraph (5). A hearsay exception for recorded recollection is generally recognized and has been described as having "long been favored by the federal and practically all the state courts that have had occasion to decide the question." *United States v. Kelly,* 349 F.2d 720, 770 (2d Cir.1965), citing numerous cases and sustaining the exception against a claimed denial of the right of confrontation. Many additional cases are cited in Annot., 82 A.L.R.2d 473, 520. The guarantee of trustworthiness is found in the reliability inherent in a record made while events were still fresh in mind and accurately reflecting them. *Owens v. State,* 67 Md. 307, 316, 10 A. 210, 212 (1887).

The principal controversy attending the exception has centered, not upon the propriety of the exception itself, but upon the question whether a preliminary requirement of impaired memory on the part of the witness should be imposed. The authorities are divided. If regard be had only to the accuracy of the evidence, admittedly impairment of the memory of the witness adds nothing to it and should not be required. McCormick § 277, p. 593; 3 Wigmore § 738, p. 76; *Jordan v. People,* 151 Colo. 133, 376 P.2d 699 (1962), cert. denied 373 U.S. 944, 83 S.Ct. 1553, 10 L.Ed.2d 699; *Hall v. State,* 223 Md. 158, 162 A.2d 751 (1960); *State v. Bindhammer,* 44 N.J. 372, 209 A.2d 124 (1965). Nevertheless, the absence of the requirement, it is believed, would encourage the use of statements carefully prepared for purposes of litigation under the supervision of attorneys, investigators, or claim adjusters. Hence the example includes a requirement that the witness not have "sufficient recollection to enable him to testify fully and accurately." To the same effect are California Evidence Code § 1237 and New Jersey Rule 63(1)(b), and this has been the position of the federal courts. *Vicksburg & Meridian R.R. v. O'Brien,* 119 U.S. 99, 7 S.Ct. 118, 30 L.Ed. 299 (1886); *Ahern v. Webb,* 268 F.2d 45 (10th Cir.1959); and see *N.L.R.B. v. Hudson Pulp and Paper Corp.,* 273 F.2d 660, 665 (5th Cir.1960); *N.L.R.B. v. Federal Dairy Co.,* 297 F.2d 487 (1st Cir.1962). But cf. *United States v. Adams,* 385 F.2d 548 (2d Cir.1967).

No attempt is made in the exception to spell out the method of establishing the initial knowledge or the contemporaneity and accuracy of the record, leaving them to be dealt with as the circumstances of the particular case might indicate. Multiple person involvement in the process of observing and recording, as in *Rathbun v. Brancatella,* 93 N.J.L. 222, 107 A. 279 (1919), is entirely consistent with the exception.

Locating the exception at this place in the scheme of the rules is a matter of choice. There were two other possibilities. The first was to regard the statement as one of the group of prior statements of a testifying witness which are excluded entirely from the category of hearsay by Rule 801(d)(1). That category, however, requires that declarant be "subject to cross-examination," as to which the impaired memory aspect of the exception raises doubts. The other possibility was to include the exception among those covered by Rule 804. Since unavailability is required by that rule and lack of memory is listed as a species of unavailability by the definition of the term in Rule 804(a)(3), that treatment at first impression would seem appropriate. The fact is, however, that the unavailability requirement of the exception is of a limited and peculiar nature. Accordingly, the exception is located at this point rather than in the context of a rule where unavailability is conceived of more broadly.

Note to Paragraph (6). Exception [paragraph] (6) represents an area which has received much attention from those seeking to improve the law of evidence. The Commonwealth Fund Act was the result of a study completed in 1927 by a distinguished committee under the chairmanship of Professor Morgan. Morgan et al., The Law of Evidence: Some Proposals for its Reform 63 (1927). With changes too minor to mention, it was adopted by Congress in 1936 as the rule for federal courts. 28 U.S.C. § 1732. A number of states took similar action. The Commissioners on Uniform State Laws in 1936 promulgated the Uniform Business Records as Evidence Act, 9A U.L.A. 506, which has acquired a substantial following in the states. Model Code Rule 514 and Uniform Rule 63(13) also deal with the subject. Difference of varying degrees of importance exist among these various treatments.

These reform efforts were largely within the context of business and commercial records, as the kind usually encountered, and concentrated considerable attention upon relaxing the requirement of producing as witnesses, or accounting for the nonproduction of, all participants in the process of gathering, transmitting, and recording information which the common law had evolved as a burdensome and crippling aspect of using records of this type. In their areas of primary emphasis on witnesses to be called and the general admissibility of ordinary business and commercial records, the Commonwealth Fund Act and the Uniform Act appear to have worked well. The exception seeks to preserve their advantages.

On the subject of what witnesses must be called, the Commonwealth Fund Act eliminated the common law requirement of calling or accounting for all participants by failing to mention it. *United States v. Mortimer,* 118 F.2d 266 (2d Cir.1941); *La Porte v. United States,* 300 F.2d 878 (9th Cir.1962); McCormick § 290, p. 608. Model Code Rule 514 and Uniform Rule 63(13) did likewise. The Uniform Act, however, abolished the common law requirement in express terms, providing that the requisite foundation testimony might be furnished by "the custodian or other qualified witness." Uniform Business Records as Evidence Act, § 2; 9A U.L.A. 506. The exception follows the Uniform Act in this respect.

The element of unusual reliability of business records is said variously to be supplied by systematic checking, by regularity and continuity which produce habits of precision, by actual experience of business in relying upon them, or by a duty to make an accurate record as part of a continuing job or occupation. McCormick §§ 281, 286, 287; Laughlin, Business Entries and the Like, 46 Iowa L.Rev. 276 (1961). The model statutes and rules have sought to capture these factors and to extend their impact by employing the phrase "regular course of business," in conjunction with a definition of "business" far broader than its ordinarily accepted meaning. The result is a tendency unduly to emphasize a requirement of routineness and repetitiveness and an insistence that other types of records be squeezed into the fact patterns which give rise to traditional business records. The rule therefore adopts the phrase "the course of a regularly conducted activity" as capturing the essential basis of the hearsay exception as it has evolved and the essential element which can be abstracted from the various specifications of what is a "business."

Amplification of the kinds of activities producing admissible records has given rise to problems which conventional business records by their nature avoid. They are problems of the source of the recorded information, of entries in opinion form, of motivation, and of involvement as participant in the matters recorded.

Sources of information presented no substantial problem with ordinary business records. All participants, including the observer or participant furnishing the information to be recorded, were acting routinely, under a duty of accuracy, with employer reliance on the result, or in short "in the regular course of business." If, however, the supplier of the information does not act in the regular course, an essential link is broken; the assurance of accuracy does not extend to the information itself, and the fact that it may be recorded with scrupulous accuracy is of no avail. An illustration is the police report incorporating information obtained from a bystander: the officer qualifies as acting in the regular course but the informant does not. The leading case, *Johnson v. Lutz*, 253 N.Y. 124, 170 N.E. 517 (1930), held that a report thus prepared was inadmissible. Most of the authorities have agreed with the decision. Gencarella v. Fyfe, 171 F.2d 419 (1st Cir.1948); *Gordon v. Robinson*, 210 F.2d 192 (3d Cir.1954); *Standard Oil Co. of California v. Moore*, 251 F.2d 188, 214 (9th Cir.1957), cert. denied 356 U.S. 975, 78 S.Ct. 1139, 2 L.Ed.2d 1148; *Yates v. Bair Transport, Inc.*, 249 F.Supp. 681 (S.D.N.Y.1965); Annot., 69 A.L.R.2d 1148. Cf. *Hawkins v. Gorea Motor Express, Inc.*, 360 F.2d 933 (2d Cir.1966); *Contra*, 5 Wigmore § 1530a, n. 1, pp. 391–392. The point is not dealt with specifically in the Commonwealth Fund Act, the Uniform Act, or Uniform Rule 63(13). However, Model Code Rule 514 contains the requirement "that it was the regular course of that business for one with personal knowledge * * * to make such a memorandum or record or to transmit information thereof to be included in such a memorandum or record * * *." The rule follows this lead in requiring an informant with knowledge acting in the course of the regularly conducted activity.

Entries in the form of opinions were not encountered in traditional business records in view of the purely factual nature of the items recorded, but they are now commonly encountered with respect to medical diagnoses, prognoses, and test results, as well as occasionally in other areas. The Commonwealth Fund Act provided only for records of an "act, transaction, occurrence, or event," while the Uniform Act, Model Code Rule 514, and Uniform Rule 63(13) merely added the ambiguous term "condition." The limited phrasing of the Commonwealth Fund Act, 28 U.S.C. § 1732, may account for the reluctance of some federal decisions to admit diagnostic entries. *New York Life Ins. Co. v. Taylor*, 79 U.S.App.D.C. 66, 147 F.2d 297 (1945); *Lyles v. United States*, 103 U.S.App.D.C. 22, 254 F.2d 725 (1957), cert. denied 356 U.S. 961, 78 S.Ct. 997, 2 L.Ed.2d 1067; *England v. United States*, 174 F.2d 466 (5th Cir.1949); *Skogen v. Dow Chemical Co.*, 375 F.2d 692 (8th Cir.1967). Other federal decisions, however, experienced no difficulty in freely admitting diagnostic entries. *Reed v. Order of United Commercial Travelers*, 123 F.2d 252 (2d Cir.1941); *Buckminster's Estate v. Commissioner of Internal Revenue*, 147 F.2d 331 (2d Cir.1944); *Medina v. Erickson*, 226 F.2d 475 (9th Cir.1955); *Thomas v. Hogan*, 308 F.2d 355 (4th Cir.1962); *Glawe v. Rulon*, 284 F.2d 495 (8th Cir.1960). In the state courts, the trend favors admissibility. Borucki v. MacKenzie Bros. Co., 125 Conn. 92, 3 A.2d 224 (1938); *Allen v. St. Louis Public Service Co.*, 365 Mo. 677, 285 S.W.2d 663, 55 A.L.R.2d 1022 (1956); *People v. Kohlmeyer*, 284 N.Y. 366, 31 N.E.2d 490 (1940); *Weis v. Weis*, 147 Ohio St. 416, 72 N.E.2d 245 (1947). In order to make clear its adherence to the latter position, the rule specifically includes both diagnoses and opinions, in addition to acts, events, and conditions, as proper subjects of admissible entries.

Problems of the motivation of the informant have been a source of difficulty and disagreement. In *Palmer v. Hoffman*, 318 U.S. 109, 63 S.Ct. 477, 87 L.Ed. 645 (1943), exclusion of an accident report made by the since deceased engineer, offered by defendant railroad trustees in a grade crossing collision case, was upheld. The report was not "in the regular course of business," not a record of the systematic conduct of the business as a business, said the Court. The report was prepared for use in litigating, not railroading. While the opinion mentions the motivation of the engineer only obliquely, the emphasis on records of routine operations is significant only by virtue of impact on motivation to be accurate. Absence of routineness raises lack of motivation to be accurate. The opinion of the Court of Appeals had gone beyond mere lack of motive to be accurate: the engineer's statement was "dripping with motivations to misrepresent." *Hoffman v. Palmer*, 129 F.2d 976, 991 (2d Cir.1942). The direct introduction of motivation is a disturbing factor, since absence of motive to misrepresent has not traditionally been a requirement of the rule; that records might be self-serving has not been a ground for exclusion. Laughlin, Business Records and the Like, 46 Iowa L.Rev. 276, 285 (1961). As Judge Clark said in his dissent, "I submit that there is hardly a grocer's account book which could not be excluded on that basis." 129 F.2d at 1002. A physician's evaluation report of a personal injury litigant would appear to be in the routine of his business. If the report is offered by the party at whose instance it was made, however, it has been held inadmissible, *Yates v. Bair Transport, Inc.*, 249 F.Supp. 681 (S.D.N.Y.1965), otherwise if offered by the opposite party, *Korte v. New York, N.H. & H.R. Co.*, 191 F.2d 86 (2d Cir.1951), cert. denied 342 U.S. 868, 72 S.Ct. 108, 96 L.Ed. 652.

The decisions hinge on motivation and which party is entitled to be concerned about it. Professor McCormick believed that the doctor's report or the accident report were sufficiently routine to justify admissibility. McCormick § 287, p. 604. Yet hesitation must be experienced in admitting everything which is observed and recorded in the course of a regularly conducted activity. Efforts to set a limit are illustrated by *Hartzog v. United States*, 217 F.2d 706 (4th Cir.1954), error to admit worksheets made by since deceased deputy collector in preparation for the instant income tax evasion prosecution, and *United States v. Ware*, 247 F.2d 698 (7th Cir.1957), error to admit narcotics agents' records of purchases. See also Exception [paragraph] (8), *infra*, as to the public record aspects of records of this nature. Some decisions have been satisfied as to motivation of an accident report if made pursuant to statutory duty, United States v. New York Foreign Trade Zone Operators, 304 F.2d 792 (2d Cir.1962); Taylor v. Baltimore & O.R. Co., 344 F.2d 281 (2d Cir.1965), since the report was oriented in a direction other than the litigation which ensued. Cf. Matthews v. United States, 217 F.2d 409 (5th Cir.1954). The formulation of specific terms which would assure satisfactory results in all cases is not possible. Consequently the rule proceeds from the base that records made in the course of a regularly conducted activity will be taken as admissible but subject to authority to exclude if "the sources of information or other circumstances indicate lack of trustworthiness."

Occasional decisions have reached for enhanced accuracy by requiring involvement as a participant in matters reported. *Clainos v. United States*, 82 U.S.App.D.C. 278, 163 F.2d 593 (1947), error to admit police records of convictions; *Standard Oil Co. of California v. Moore*, 251 F.2d 188 (9th Cir.1957), cert. denied 356 U.S. 975, 78 S.Ct. 1139, 2 L.Ed.2d 1148, error to admit employees' records of observed business practices of others. The rule includes no requirement of this nature. Wholly acceptable records may involve matters merely observed, e.g. the weather.

The form which the "record" may assume under the rule is described broadly as a "memorandum, report, record, or data compilation, in any form." The expression "data compilation" is used as broadly descriptive of any means of storing information other than the conventional words and figures in written or documentary form. It includes, but is by no means limited to, electronic computer storage. The term is borrowed from revised Rule 34(a) of the Rules of Civil Procedure.

Note to Paragraph (7). Failure of a record to mention a matter which would ordinarily be mentioned is satisfactory evidence of its nonexistence. Uniform Rule 63(14), Comment. While probably not hearsay as defined in Rule 801, *supra*, decisions may be found which class the evidence not only as hearsay but also as not within any exception. In order to set the question at rest in favor of admissibility, it is specifically treated here. McCormick § 289, p. 609; Morgan, Basic Problems of Evidence 314 (1962); 5 Wigmore § 1531; Uniform Rule 63(14); California Evidence Code § 1272; Kansas Code of Civil Procedure § 60–460(n); New Jersey Evidence Rule 63(14).

Note to Paragraph (8). Public records are a recognized hearsay exception at common law and have been the subject of statutes without number. McCormick § 291. See, for example, 28 U.S.C. § 1733, the relative narrowness of which is illustrated by its nonapplicability to nonfederal public agencies, thus necessitating resort to the less appropriate business record exception to the hearsay rule. *Kay v. United States*, 255 F.2d 476 (4th Cir.1958). The rule makes no distinction between federal and nonfederal offices and agencies.

Justification for the exception is the assumption that a public official will perform his duty properly and the unlikelihood that he will remember details independently of the record. *Wong Wing Foo v. McGrath*, 196 F.2d 120 (9th Cir.1952), and see *Chesapeake & Delaware Canal Co. v. United States*, 250 U.S. 123, 39 S.Ct. 407, 63 L.Ed. 889 (1919). As to items (a) and (b), further support is found in the reliability factors underlying records of regularly conducted activities generally. See Exception [paragraph] (6), supra.

(a) Cases illustrating the admissibility of records of the office's or agency's own activities are numerous. *Chesapeake & Delaware Canal Co. v. United States*, 250 U.S. 123, 39 S.Ct. 407, 63 L.Ed. 889 (1919), Treasury records of miscellaneous receipts and disbursements; *Howard v. Perrin*, 200 U.S. 71, 26 S.Ct. 195, 50 L.Ed. 374 (1906), General Land Office records; *Ballew v. United States*, 160 U.S. 187, 16 S.Ct. 263, 40 L.Ed. 388 (1895). Pension Office records.

(b) Cases sustaining admissibility of records of matters observed are also numerous. *United States v. Van Hook*, 284 F.2d 489 (7th Cir.1960), remanded for resentencing 365 U.S. 609, 81 S.Ct. 823, 5 L.Ed.2d 821, letter from induction officer to District Attorney, pursuant to army regulations, stating fact and circumstances of refusal to be inducted; *T'Kach v. United States*, 242 F.2d 937 (5th Cir.1957), affidavit of White House personnel officer that search of records showed no employment of accused, charged with fraudulently representing himself as an envoy of the President; *Minnehaha County v. Kelley*, 150 F.2d 356 (8th Cir.1945); Weather Bureau records of rainfall; *United States v. Meyer*, 113 F.2d 387 (7th Cir.1940), cert. denied 311 U.S. 706, 61 S.Ct. 174, 85 L.Ed. 459, map prepared by government engineer from information furnished by men working under his supervision.

(c) The more controversial area of public records is that of the so-called "evaluative" report. The disagreement among the decisions has been due in part, no doubt, to the variety of situations encountered, as well as to differences in principle. Sustaining admissibility are such cases as *United States v. Dumas*, 149 U.S. 278, 13 S.Ct. 872, 37 L.Ed. 734 (1893), statement of account certified by Postmaster General in action against postmaster; *McCarty v. United States*, 185 F.2d 520 (5th Cir.1950), reh. denied 187 F.2d 234, Certificate of Settlement of General Accounting Office showing indebtedness and letter from Army official stating Government had performed, in action on contract to purchase and remove waste from Army camp; *Moran v. Pittsburgh–Des Moines Steel Co.*, 183 F.2d 467 (3d Cir.1950), report of Bureau of Mines as to cause of gas tank explosion; *Petition of W____*, 164 F.Supp. 659 (E.D.Pa. 1958), report by Immigration and Naturalization Service investigator that petitioner was known in community as wife of man to whom she was not married. To the opposite effect and denying admissibility are *Franklin v. Skelly Oil Co.*, 141 F.2d 568 (10th Cir.1944), State Fire Marshal's report of cause of gas explosion; *Lomax Transp. Co. v. United States*, 183 F.2d 331 (9th Cir. 1950), Certificate of Settlement from General Accounting Office in action for naval supplies lost in warehouse fire; *Yung Jin Teung v. Dulles*, 229 F.2d 244 (2d Cir.1956), "Status Reports"

offered to justify delay in processing passport applications. Police reports have generally been excluded except to the extent to which they incorporate firsthand observations of the officer. Annot., 69 A.L.R.2d 1148. Various kinds of evaluative reports are admissible under federal statutes: 7 U.S.C. § 78, findings of Secretary of Agriculture prima facie evidence of true grade of grain; 7 U.S.C. § 210(f), findings of Secretary of Agriculture prima facie evidence in action for damages against stockyard owner; 7 U.S.C. § 292, order by Secretary of Agriculture prima facie evidence in judicial enforcement proceedings against producers association monopoly; 7 U.S.C. § 1622(h), Department of Agriculture inspection certificates of products shipped in interstate commerce prima facie evidence; 8 U.S.C. § 1440(c), separation of alien from military service on conditions other than honorable provable by certificate from department in proceedings to revoke citizenship; 18 U.S.C. § 4245, certificate of Director of Prisons that convicted person has been examined and found probably incompetent at time of trial prima facie evidence in court hearing on competency; 42 U.S.C. § 269(b), bill of health by appropriate official prima facie evidence of vessel's sanitary history and condition and compliance with regulations; 46 U.S.C. § 679, certificate of consul presumptive evidence of refusal of master to transport destitute seamen to United States. While these statutory exceptions to the hearsay rule are left undisturbed, Rule 802, the willingness of Congress to recognize a substantial measure of admissibility for evaluative reports is a helpful guide.

Factors which may be of assistance in passing upon the admissibility of evaluative reports include: (1) the timeliness of the investigation, McCormick, Can the Courts Make Wider Use of Reports of Official Investigations? 42 Iowa L.Rev. 363 (1957); (2) the special skill or experience of the official, *id.*, (3) whether a hearing was held and the level at which conducted, *Franklin v. Skelly Oil Co.*, 141 F.2d 568 (10th Cir.1944); (4) possible motivation problems suggested by *Palmer v. Hoffman*, 318 U.S. 109, 63 S.Ct. 477, 87 L.Ed. 645 (1943). Others no doubt could be added.

The formulation of an approach which would give appropriate weight to all possible factors in every situation is an obvious impossibility. Hence the rule, as in Exception [paragraph] (6), assumes admissibility in the first instance but with ample provision for escape if sufficient negative factors are present. In one respect, however, the rule with respect to evaluative reports under item (c) is very specific: they are admissible only in civil cases and against the government in criminal cases in view of the almost certain collision with confrontation rights which would result from their use against the accused in a criminal case.

Note to Paragraph (9). Records of vital statistics are commonly the subject of particular statutes making them admissible in evidence, Uniform Vital Statistics Act, 9C U.L.A. 350 (1957). The rule is in principle narrower than Uniform Rule 63(16) which includes reports required of persons performing functions authorized by statute, yet in practical effect the two are substantially the same. Comment Uniform Rule 63(16). The exception as drafted is in the pattern of California Evidence Code § 1281.

Note to Paragraph (10). The principle of proving nonoccurrence of an event by evidence of the absence of a record which would regularly be made of its occurrence, developed in Exception [paragraph] (7) with respect to regularly conducted activities, is here extended to public records of the kind mentioned in Exceptions [paragraphs] (8) and (9). 5 Wigmore § 1633(6), p. 519. Some harmless duplication no doubt exists with Exception [paragraph] (7). For instances of federal statutes recognizing this method of proof, see 8 U.S.C. § 1284(b), proof of absence of alien crewman's name from outgoing manifest prima facie evidence of failure to detain or deport, and 42 U.S.C. § 405(c)(3), (4)(B), (4)(C), absence of HEW [Department of Health, Education, and Welfare] record prima facie evidence of no wages or self-employment income.

The rule includes situations in which absence of a record may itself be the ultimate focal point of inquiry, e.g. *People v. Love*, 310 Ill. 558, 142 N.E. 204 (1923), certificate of Secretary of State admitted to show failure to file documents required by Securities

Law, as well as cases where the absence of a record is offered as proof of the nonoccurrence of an event ordinarily recorded.

The refusal of the common law to allow proof by certificate of the lack of a record or entry has no apparent justification, 5 Wigmore § 1678(7), p. 752. The rule takes the opposite position, as to Uniform Rule 63(17); California Evidence Code § 1284; Kansas Code of Civil Procedure § 60–460(c); New Jersey Evidence Rule 63(17). Congress has recognized certification as evidence of the lack of a record. 8 U.S.C. § 1360(d), certificate of Attorney General or other designated officer that no record of Immigration and Naturalization Service of specified nature or entry therein is found, admissible in alien cases.

Note to Paragraph (11). Records of activities of religious organizations are currently recognized as admissible at least to the extent of the business records exception to the hearsay rule, 5 Wigmore § 1523, p. 371, and Exception [paragraph] (6) would be applicable. However, both the business record doctrine and Exception [paragraph] (6) require that the person furnishing the information be one in the business or activity. The result is such decisions as Daily v. Grand Lodge, 311 Ill. 184, 142 N.E. 478 (1924), holding a church record admissible to prove fact, date, and place of baptism, but not age of child except that he had at least been born at the time. In view of the unlikelihood that false information would be furnished on occasions of this kind, the rule contains no requirement that the informant be in the course of the activity. See California Evidence Code § 1315 and Comment.

Note to Paragraph (12). The principle of proof by certification is recognized as to public officials in Exceptions [paragraphs] (8) and (10), and with respect to authentication in Rule 902. The present exception is a duplication to the extent that it deals with a certificate by a public official, as in the case of a judge who performs a marriage ceremony. The area covered by the rule is, however, substantially larger and extends the certification procedure to clergymen and the like who perform marriages and other ceremonies or administer sacraments. Thus certificates of such matters as baptism or confirmation, as well as marriage, are included. In principle they are as acceptable evidence as certificates of public officers. See 5 Wigmore § 1645, as to marriage certificates. When the person executing the certificate is not a public official, the self-authenticating character of documents purporting to emanate from public officials, see Rule 902, is lacking and proof is required that the person was authorized and did make the certificate. The time element, however, may safely be taken as supplied by the certificate, once authority and authenticity are established, particularly in view of the presumption that a document was executed on the date it bears.

For similar rules, some limited to certificates of marriage, with variations in foundation requirements, see Uniform Rule 63(18); California Evidence Code § 1316; Kansas Code of Civil Procedure § 60–460(p); New Jersey Evidence Rule 63(18).

Note to Paragraph (13). Records of family history kept in family Bibles have by long tradition been received in evidence. 5 Wigmore §§ 1495, 1496, citing numerous statutes and decisions. See also Regulations, Social Security Administration, 20 C.F.R. § 404.703(c), recognizing family Bible entries as proof of age in the absence of public or church records. Opinions in the area also include inscriptions on tombstones, publicly displayed pedigrees, and engravings on rings. Wigmore, *supra*. The rule is substantially identical in coverage with California Evidence Code § 1312.

Note to Paragraph (14). The recording of title documents is a purely statutory development. Under any theory of the admissibility of public records, the records would be receivable as evidence of the contents of the recorded document, else the recording process would be reduced to a nullity. When, however, the record is offered for the further purpose of proving execution and delivery, a problem of lack of firsthand knowledge by the recorder, not present as to contents, is presented. This problem is solved, seemingly in all jurisdictions, by qualifying for recording only those documents shown by a specified procedure, either acknowledgement or a form of probate, to have been

executed and delivered. 5 Wigmore §§ 1647–1651. Thus what may appear in the rule, at first glance, as endowing the record with an effect independently of local law and inviting difficulties of an *Erie* nature under *Cities Service Oil Co. v. Dunlap*, 308 U.S. 208, 60 S.Ct. 201, 84 L.Ed. 196 (1939), is not present, since the local law in fact governs under the example.

Note to Paragraph (15). Dispositive documents often contain recitals of fact. Thus a deed purporting to have been executed by an attorney in fact may recite the existence of the power of attorney, or a deed may recite that the grantors are all the heirs of the last record owner. Under the rule, these recitals are exempted from the hearsay rule. The circumstances under which dispositive documents are executed and the requirement that the recital be germane to the purpose of the document are believed to be adequate guarantees of trustworthiness, particularly in view of the nonapplicability of the rule if dealings with the property have been inconsistent with the document. The age of the document is of no significance, though in practical application the document will most often be an ancient one. See Uniform Rule 63(29), Comment.

Similar provisions are contained in Uniform Rule 63(29); California Evidence Code § 1330; Kansas Code of Civil Procedure § 60–460(aa); New Jersey Evidence Rule 63(29).

Note to Paragraph (16). Authenticating a document as ancient, essentially in the pattern of the common law, as provided in Rule 901(b)(8), leaves open as a separate question the admissibility of assertive statements contained therein as against a hearsay objection. 7 Wigmore § 2145a. Wigmore further states that the ancient document technique of authentication is universally conceded to apply to all sorts of documents, including letters, records, contracts, maps, and certificates, in addition to title documents, citing numerous decisions. Id. § 2145. Since most of these items are significant evidentially only insofar as they are assertive, their admission in evidence must be as a hearsay exception. But see 5 id. § 1573, p. 429, referring to recitals in ancient deeds as a "limited" hearsay exception. The former position is believed to be the correct one in reason and authority. As pointed out in McCormick § 298, danger of mistake is minimized by authentication requirements, and age affords assurance that the writing antedates the present controversy. See *Dallas County v. Commercial Union Assurance Co.*, 286 F.2d 388 (5th Cir.1961), upholding admissibility of 58–year–old newspaper story. Cf. Morgan, Basic Problems of Evidence 364 (1962), but see id. 254.

For a similar provision, but with the added requirement that "the statement has since generally been acted upon as true by persons having an interest in the matter," see California Evidence Code § 1331.

Note to Paragraph (17). Ample authority at common law supported the admission in evidence of items falling in this category. While Wigmore's text is narrowly oriented to lists, etc., prepared for the use of a trade or profession, 6 Wigmore § 1702, authorities are cited which include other kinds of publications, for example, newspaper market reports, telephone directories, and city directories. Id. §§ 1702–1706. The basis of trustworthiness is general reliance by the public or by a particular segment of it, and the motivation of the compiler to foster reliance by being accurate.

For similar provisions, see Uniform Rule 63(30); California Evidence Code § 1340; Kansas Code of Civil Procedure § 60–460(bb); New Jersey Evidence Rule 63(30). Uniform Commercial Code § 2–724 provides for admissibility in evidence of "reports in official publications or trade journals or in newspapers or periodicals of general circulation published as the reports of such [established commodity] market."

Note to Paragraph (18). The writers have generally favored the admissibility of learned treatises, McCormick § 296, p. 621; Morgan, Basic Problems of Evidence 366 (1962); 6 Wigmore § 1692, with the support of occasional decisions and rules, *City of Dothan v. Hardy*, 237 Ala. 603, 188 So. 264 (1939); *Lewandowski v. Preferred Risk Mut. Ins. Co.*, 33 Wis.2d 69, 146 N.W.2d 505 (1966), 66 Mich.L.Rev. 183 (1967); Uniform Rule 63(31); Kansas Code of Civil Procedure § 60–460(cc), but the great weight of authority has been that learned treatises are not admissible as substantive evidence though usable in the cross-examination of experts. The foundation of the minority view is that the hearsay objection must be regarded as unimpressive when directed against treatises since a high standard of accuracy is engendered by various factors: the treatise is written primarily and impartially for professionals, subject to scrutiny and exposure for inaccuracy, with the reputation of the writer at stake. 6 Wigmore § 1692. Sound as this position may be with respect to trustworthiness, there is, nevertheless, an additional difficulty in the likelihood that the treatise will be misunderstood and misapplied without expert assistance and supervision. This difficulty is recognized in the cases demonstrating unwillingness to sustain findings relative to disability on the basis of judicially noticed medical texts. *Ross v. Gardner*, 365 F.2d 554 (6th Cir.1966); *Sayers v. Gardner*, 380 F.2d 940 (6th Cir.1967); *Colwell v. Gardner*, 386 F.2d 56 (6th Cir.1967); *Glendenning v. Ribicoff*, 213 F.Supp. 301 (W.D.Mo.1962); *Cook v. Celebrezze*, 217 F.Supp. 366 (W.D.Mo.1963); *Sosna v. Celebrezze*, 234 F.Supp. 289 (E.D.Pa.1964); and see *McDaniel v. Celebrezze*, 331 F.2d 426 (4th Cir.1964). The rule avoids the danger of misunderstanding and misapplication by limiting the use of treatises as substantive evidence to situations in which an expert is on the stand and available to explain and assist in the application of the treatise if desired. The limitation upon receiving the publication itself physically in evidence, contained in the last sentence, is designed, to further this policy.

The relevance of the use of treatises on cross-examination is evident. This use of treatises has been the subject of varied views. The most restrictive position is that the witness must have stated expressly on direct his reliance upon the treatise. A slightly more liberal approach still insists upon reliance but allows it to be developed on cross-examination. Further relaxation dispenses with reliance but requires recognition as an authority by the witness, developable on cross-examination. The greatest liberality is found in decisions allowing use of the treatise on cross-examination when its status as an authority is established by any means. Annot., 60 A.L.R.2d 77. The exception is hinged upon this last position, which is that of the Supreme Court, *Reilly v. Pinkus*, 338 U.S. 269, 70 S.Ct. 110, 94 L.Ed. 63 (1949), and of recent well considered state court decisions, *City of St. Petersburg v. Ferguson*, 193 So.2d 648 (Fla.App.1967), cert. denied Fla., 201 So.2d 556; *Darling v. Charleston Memorial Community Hospital*, 33 Ill.2d 326, 211 N.E.2d 253 (1965); *Dabroe v. Rhodes Co.*, 64 Wash.2d 431, 392 P.2d 317 (1964).

In Reilly v. Pinkus, *supra*, the Court pointed out that testing of professional knowledge was incomplete without exploration of the witness' knowledge of and attitude toward established treatises in the field. The process works equally well in reverse and furnishes the basis of the rule.

The rule does not require that the witness rely upon or recognize the treatise as authoritative, thus avoiding the possibility that the expert may at the outset block cross-examination by refusing to concede reliance or authoritativeness. Dabroe v. Rhodes Co., *supra*. Moreover, the rule avoids the unreality of admitting evidence for the purpose of impeachment only, with an instruction to the jury not to consider it otherwise. The parallel to the treatment of prior inconsistent statements will be apparent. See Rules 613(b) and 801(d)(1).

Note to Paragraphs (19), (20) and (21). Trustworthiness in reputation evidence is found "when the topic is such that the facts are likely to have been inquired about and that persons having personal knowledge have disclosed facts which have thus been discussed in the community; and thus the community's conclusion, if any has been formed, is likely to be a trustworthy one." 5 Wigmore § 1580, p. 444, and see also § 1583. On this common foundation, reputation as to land boundaries, customs, general history, character, and marriage have come to be regarded as admissible. The breadth of the underlying principle suggests the formulation of an equally broad exception, but tradition has in fact been much narrower and more particularized, and this is the pattern of these exceptions in the rule.

Exception [paragraph] (19) is concerned with matters of personal and family history. Marriage is universally conceded to be a proper subject of proof by evidence of reputation in the community. 5 Wigmore § 1602. As to such items as legitimacy, relationship, adoption, birth, and death, the decisions are divided. *Id.* § 1605. All seem to be susceptible to being the subject of well founded repute. The "world" in which the reputation may exist may be family, associates, or community. This world has proved capable of expanding with changing times from the single uncomplicated neighborhood, in which all activities take place, to the multiple and unrelated worlds of work, religious affiliation, and social activity, in each of which a reputation may be generated. *People v. Reeves*, 360 Ill. 55, 195 N.E. 443 (1935); *State v. Axilrod*, 248 Minn. 204, 79 N.W.2d 677 (1956); Mass. Stat.1947, c. 410, M.G.L.A. c. 233 § 21A; 5 Wigmore § 1616. The family has often served as the point of beginning for allowing community reputation. 5 Wigmore § 1488. For comparable provisions see Uniform Rule 63(26), (27)(c); California Evidence Code §§ 1313, 1314; Kansas Code of Civil Procedure § 60–460(x), (y)(3); New Jersey Evidence Rule 63(26), (27)(c).

The first portion of Exception [paragraph] (20) is based upon the general admissibility of evidence of reputation as to land boundaries and land customs, expanded in this country to include private as well as public boundaries. McCormick § 299, p. 625. The reputation is required to antedate the controversy, though not to be ancient. The second portion is likewise supported by authority, *id.*, and is designed to facilitate proof of events when judicial notice is not available. The historical character of the subject matter dispenses with any need that the reputation antedate the controversy with respect to which it is offered. For similar provisions see Uniform Rule 63(27)(a), (b); California Evidence Code §§ 1320–1322; Kansas Code of Civil Procedure § 60–460(y), (1), (2); New Jersey Evidence Rule 63(27)(a), (b).

Exception [paragraph] (21) recognizes the traditional acceptance of reputation evidence as a means of proving human character. McCormick §§ 44, 158. The exception deals only with the hearsay aspect of this kind of evidence. Limitations upon admissibility based on other grounds will be found in Rules 404, relevancy of character evidence generally, and 608, character of witness. The exception is in effect a reiteration, in the context of hearsay, of Rule 405(a). Similar provisions are contained in Uniform Rule 63(28); California Evidence Code § 1324; Kansas Code of Civil Procedure § 60–460(z); New Jersey Evidence Rule 63(28).

Note to Paragraph (22). When the status of a former judgment is under consideration in subsequent litigation, three possibilities must be noted: (1) the former judgment is conclusive under the doctrine of res judicata, either as a bar or a collateral estoppel; or (2) it is admissible in evidence for what it is worth; or (3) it may be of no effect at all. The first situation does not involve any problem of evidence except in the way that principles of substantive law generally bear upon the relevancy and materiality of evidence. The rule does not deal with the substantive effect of the judgment as a bar or collateral estoppel. When, however, the doctrine of res judicata does not apply to make the judgment either a bar or a collateral estoppel, a choice is presented between the second and third alternatives. The rule adopts the second for judgments of criminal conviction of felony grade. This is the direction of the decisions, Annot., 18 A.L.R.2d 1287, 1299, which manifest an increasing reluctance to reject *in toto* the validity of the law's factfinding processes outside the confines of res judicata and collateral estoppel. While this may leave a jury with the evidence of conviction but without means to evaluate it, as suggested by Judge Hinton, Note 27 Ill.L.Rev. 195 (1932), it seems safe to assume that the jury will give it substantial effect unless defendant offers a satisfactory explanation, a possibility not foreclosed by the provision. But see *North River Ins. Co. v. Militello*, 104 Colo. 28, 88 P.2d 567 (1939), in which the jury found for plaintiff on a fire policy despite the introduction of his conviction for arson. For supporting federal decisions see Clark, J., in *New York & Cuba Mail S.S. Co. v. Continental Cas. Co.*, 117 F.2d 404, 411 (2d

Cir.1941); *Connecticut Fire Ins. Co. v. Farrara*, 277 F.2d 388 (8th Cir.1960).

Practical considerations require exclusion of convictions of minor offenses, not because the administration of justice in its lower echelons must be inferior, but because motivation to defend at this level is often minimal or nonexistent. *Cope v. Goble*, 39 Cal.App.2d 448, 103 P.2d 598 (1940); *Jones v. Talbot*, 87 Idaho 498, 394 P.2d 316 (1964); *Warren v. Marsh*, 215 Minn. 615, 11 N.W.2d 528 (1943); Annot., 18 A.L.R.2d 1287, 1295–1297; 16 Brooklyn L.Rev. 286 (1950); 50 Colum.L.Rev. 529 (1950); 35 Cornell L.Q. 872 (1950). Hence the rule includes only convictions of felony grade, measured by federal standards.

Judgments of conviction based upon pleas of *nolo contendere* are not included. This position is consistent with the treatment of *nolo* pleas in Rule 410 and the authorities cited in the Advisory Committee's Note in support thereof.

While these rules do not in general purport to resolve constitutional issues, they have in general been drafted with a view to avoiding collision with constitutional principles. Consequently the exception does not include evidence of the conviction of a third person, offered against the accused in a criminal prosecution to prove any fact essential to sustain the judgment of conviction. A contrary position would seem clearly to violate the right of confrontation. *Kirby v. United States*, 174 U.S. 47, 19 S.Ct. 574, 43 L.Ed. 890 (1899), error to convict of possessing stolen postage stamps with the only evidence of theft being the record of conviction of the thieves. The situation is to be distinguished from cases in which conviction of another person is an element of the crime, e.g. 15 U.S.C. § 902(d), interstate shipment of firearms to a known convicted felon, and, as specifically provided, from impeachment.

For comparable provisions see Uniform Rule 63(20); California Evidence Code § 1300; Kansas Code of Civil Procedure § 60–460(r); New Jersey Evidence Rule 63(20).

Note to Paragraph (23). A hearsay exception in this area was originally justified on the ground that verdicts were evidence of reputation. As trial by jury graduated from the category of neighborhood inquests, this theory lost its validity. It was never valid as to chancery decrees. Nevertheless the rule persisted, though the judges and writers shifted ground and began saying that the judgment or decree was as good evidence as reputation. See *City of London v. Clerke*, Carth. 181, 90 Eng.Rep. 710 (K.B. 1691); *Neill v. Duke of Devonshire*, 8 App.Cas. 135 (1882). The shift appears to be correct, since the process of inquiry, sifting, and scrutiny which is relied upon to render reputation reliable is present in perhaps greater measure in the process of litigation. While this might suggest a broader area of application, the affinity to reputation is strong, and paragraph [paragraph] (23) goes no further, not even including character.

The leading case in the *United States, Patterson v. Gaines*, 47 U.S. (6 How.) 550, 599, 12 L.Ed. 553 (1847), follows in the pattern of the English decisions, mentioning as illustrative matters thus provable: manorial rights, public rights of way, immemorial custom, disputed boundary, and pedigree. More recent recognition of the principle is found in *Grant Bros. Construction Co. v. United States*, 232 U.S. 647, 34 S.Ct. 452, 58 L.Ed. 776 (1914), in action for penalties under Alien Contract Labor Law, decision of board of inquiry of Immigration Service admissible to prove alienage of laborers, as a matter of pedigree; *United States v. Mid–Continent Petroleum Corp.*, 67 F.2d 37 (10th Cir.1933), records of commission enrolling Indians admissible on pedigree; *Jung Yen Loy v. Cahill*, 81 F.2d 809 (9th Cir.1936), board decisions as to citizenship of plaintiff's father admissible in proceeding for declaration of citizenship. *Contra, In re Estate of Cunha*, 49 Haw. 273, 414 P.2d 925 (1966).

1974 Enactment

Note to Paragraph (3). Rule 803(3) was approved in the form submitted by the Court to Congress. However, the Committee intends that the Rule be construed to limit the doctrine of *Mutual Life Insurance Co. v. Hillmon*, 145 U.S. 285, 295–300 (1892), so as to render statements of intent by a declarant

admissible only to prove his future conduct, not the future conduct of another person.

Note to Paragraph (4). After giving particular attention to the question of physical examination made solely to enable a physician to testify, the Committee approved Rule 803(4) as submitted to Congress, with the understanding that it is not intended in any way to adversely affect present privilege rules or those subsequently adopted.

Note to Paragraph (5). Rule 803(5) as submitted by the Court permitted the reading into evidence of a memorandum or record concerning a matter about which a witness once had knowledge but now has insufficient recollection to enable him to testify accurately and fully, "shown to have been made when the matter was fresh in his memory and to reflect that knowledge correctly." The Committee amended this Rule to add the words "or adopted by the witness" after the phrase "shown to have been made", a treatment consistent with the definition of "statement" in the Jencks Act, 18 U.S.C. 3500. Moreover, it is the Committee's understanding that a memorandum or report, although barred under this Rule, would nonetheless be admissible if it came within another hearsay exception. This last stated principle is deemed applicable to all the hearsay rules.

Note to Paragraph (6). Rule 803(6) as submitted by the Court permitted a record made "in the course of a regularly conducted activity" to be admissible in certain circumstances. The Committee believed there were insufficient guarantees of reliability in records made in the course of activities falling outside the scope of "business" activities as that term is broadly defined in 28 U.S.C. 1732. Moreover, the Committee concluded that the additional requirement of Section 1732 that it must have been the regular practice of a business to make the record is a necessary further assurance of its trustworthiness. The Committee accordingly amended the Rule to incorporate these limitations.

Note to Paragraph (7). Rule 803(7) as submitted by the Court concerned the *absence* of entry in the records of a "regularly conducted activity." The Committee amended this Rule to conform with its action with respect to Rule 803(6).

Note to Paragraph (8). The Committee approved Rule 803(8) without substantive change from the form in which it was submitted by the Court. The Committee intends that the phrase "factual findings" be strictly construed and that evaluations or opinions contained in public reports shall not be admissible under this Rule.

Note to Paragraph (13). The Committee approved this Rule in the form submitted by the Court, intending that the phrase "Statements of fact concerning personal or family history" be read to include the specific types of such statements enumerated in Rule 803(11). House Report No. 93–650.

Note to Paragraph (4). The House approved this rule as it was submitted by the Supreme Court "with the understanding that it is not intended in any way to adversely affect present privilege rules." We also approve this rule, and we would point out with respect to the question of its relation to privileges, it must be read in conjunction with rule 35 of the Federal Rules of Civil Procedure which provides that whenever the physical or mental condition of a party (plaintiff or defendant) is in controversy, the court may require him to submit to an examination by a physician. It is these examinations which will normally be admitted under this exception.

Note to Paragraph (5). Rule 803(5) as submitted by the Court permitted the reading into evidence of a memorandum or record concerning a matter about which a witness once had knowledge but now has insufficient recollection to enable him to testify accurately and fully, "shown to have been made when the matter was fresh in his memory and to reflect that knowledge correctly." The House amended the rule to add the words "or adopted by the witness" after the phrase "shown to have been made," language parallel to the Jencks Act [18 U.S.C. § 3500].

The committee accepts the House amendment with the understanding and belief that it was not intended to narrow the scope of applicability of the rule. In fact, we understand it to clarify the rule's applicability to a memorandum adopted by the witness as well as one made by him. While the rule as submitted by the Court was silent on the question of who made the memorandum, we view the House amendment as a helpful clarification, noting, however, that the Advisory Committee's note to this rule suggests that the important thing is the accuracy of the memorandum rather than who made it.

The committee does not view the House amendment as precluding admissibility in situations in which multiple participants were involved.

When the verifying witness has not prepared the report, but merely examined it and found it accurate, he has adopted the report, and it is therefore admissible. The rule should also be interpreted to cover other situations involving multiple participants, e.g., employer dictating to secretary, secretary making memorandum at direction of employer, or information being passed along a chain of persons, as in *Curtis v. Bradley* [65 Conn. 99, 31 Atl. 591 (1894); see, also, *Rathbun v. Brancatella*, 93 N.J.L. 222, 107 Atl. 279 (1919); see, also, McCormick on Evidence, § 303 (2d ed. 1972)].

The committee also accepts the understanding of the House that a memorandum or report, although barred under this rule, would nonetheless be admissible if it came within another hearsay exception. We consider this principle to be applicable to all the hearsay rules.

Note to Paragraph (6). Rule 803(6) as submitted by the Supreme Court permitted a record made in the course of a regularly conducted activity to be admissible in certain circumstances. This rule constituted a broadening of the traditional business records hearsay exception which has been long advocated by scholars and judges active in the law of evidence.

The House felt there were insufficient guarantees of reliability of records not within a broadly defined business records exception. We disagree. Even under the House definition of "business" including profession, occupation, and "calling of every kind," the records of many regularly conducted activities will, or may be, excluded from evidence. Under the principle of ejusdem generis, the intent of "calling of every kind" would seem to be related to work-related endeavors—e.g., butcher, baker, artist, etc.

Thus, it appears that the records of many institutions or groups might not be admissible under the House amendments. For example, schools, churches, and hospitals will not normally be considered businesses within the definition. Yet, these are groups which keep financial and other records on a regular basis in a manner similar to business enterprises. We believe these records are of equivalent trustworthiness and should be admitted into evidence.

Three states, which have recently codified their evidence rules, have adopted the Supreme Court version of rule 803(6), providing for admission of memoranda of a "regularly conducted activity." None adopted the words "business activity" used in the House amendment. [See Nev.Rev.Stats. § 15.135; N.Mex.Stats. (1973 Supp.) § 20–4–803(6); West's Wis.Stats. Anno. (1973 Supp.) § 908.03(6).]

Therefore, the committee deleted the word "business" as it appears before the word "activity". The last sentence then is unnecessary and was also deleted.

It is the understanding of the committee that the use of the phrase "person with knowledge" is not intended to imply that the party seeking to introduce the memorandum, report, record, or data compilation must be able to produce, or even identify, the specific individual upon whose first-hand knowledge the memorandum, report, record or data compilation was based. A sufficient foundation for the introduction of such evidence will be laid if the party seeking to introduce the evidence is able to show that it was the regular practice of the activity to base such memorandums, reports, records, or data compilations upon a transmission from a person with knowledge, e.g., in the case of the content of a shipment of goods, upon a report from the company's receiving agent or in the case of a computer printout, upon a report from the company's computer programmer or one who has knowledge of the particular record system. In short, the scope of the phrase "person with knowledge" is meant to be coterminous with the custodian of the evidence or other qualified witness. The committee believes this represents the desired rule in light of the complex nature of modern business organizations.

Note to Paragraph (8). The House approved rule 803(8), as submitted by the Supreme Court, with one substantive change. It excluded from the hearsay exception reports containing matters observed by police officers and other law enforcement personnel in criminal cases. Ostensibly, the reason for this exclusion is that observations by police officers at the scene of the crime or the apprehension of the defendant are not as reliable as observations by public officials in other cases because of the adversarial nature of the confrontation between the police and the defendant in criminal cases.

The committee accepts the House's decision to exclude such recorded observations where the police officer is available to testify in court about his observation. However, where he is unavailable as unavailability is defined in rule 804(a)(4) and (a)(5), the report should be admitted as the best available evidence. Accordingly, the committee has amended rule 803(8) to refer to the provision of [proposed] rule 804(b)(5) [deleted], which allows the admission of such reports, records or other statements where the police officer or other law enforcement officer is unavailable because of death, then existing physical or mental illness or infirmity, or not being successfully subject to legal process.

The House Judiciary Committee report contained a statement of intent that "the phrase 'factual findings' in subdivision (c) be strictly construed and that evaluations or opinions contained in public reports shall not be admissible under this rule." The committee takes strong exception to this limiting understanding of the application of the rule. We do not think it reflects an understanding of the intended operation of the rule as explained in the Advisory Committee notes to this subsection. The Advisory Committee notes on subsection (c) of this subdivision point out that various kinds of evaluative reports are now admissible under Federal statutes. 7 U.S.C. § 78, findings of Secretary of Agriculture prima facie evidence of true grade of grain; 42 U.S.C. § 269(b), bill of health by appropriate official prima facie evidence of vessel's sanitary history and condition and compliance with regulations. These statutory exceptions to the hearsay rule are preserved. Rule 802. The willingness of Congress to recognize these and other such evaluative reports provides a helpful guide in determining the kind of reports which are intended to be admissible under this rule. We think the restrictive interpretation of the House overlooks the fact that while the Advisory Committee assumes admissibility in the first instance of evaluative reports, they are not admissible if, as the rule states, "the sources of information or other circumstances indicate lack of trustworthiness."

The Advisory Committee explains the factors to be considered:

    *   *   *   *   *   *   *

Factors which may be assistance in passing upon the admissibility of evaluative reports include: (1) the timeliness of the investigation, McCormick, Can the Courts Make Wider Use of Reports of Official Investigations? 42 Iowa L.Rev. 363 (1957); (2) the special skill or experience of the official, id.; (3) whether a hearing was held and the level at which conducted, *Franklin v. Skelly Oil Co.*, 141 F.2d 568 (19th Cir.1944); (4) possible motivation problems suggested by *Palmer v. Hoffman*, 318 U.S. 109, 63 S.Ct. 477, 87 L.Ed. 645 (1943). Others no doubt could be added.

    *   *   *   *   *   *   *

The committee concludes that the language of the rule together with the explanation provided by the Advisory Committee furnish sufficient guidance on the admissibility of evaluative reports.

Note to Paragraph (24). The proposed Rules of Evidence submitted to Congress contained identical provisions in rules 803 and 804 (which set forth the various hearsay exceptions), admitting any hearsay statement not specifically covered by any of the stated exceptions, if the hearsay statement was found to have "comparable circumstantial guarantees of trustworthiness." The House deleted these provisions (proposed rules 803(24) and 804(b)(6)[(5)]) as injecting "too much uncertainty" into the law of evidence and impairing the ability of practitioners to prepare for trial. The House felt that rule 102, which directs the courts to construe the Rules of Evidence so as to promote growth and development, would permit sufficient flexibility to admit hearsay evidence in appropriate cases under various factual situations that might arise.

We disagree with the total rejection of a residual hearsay exception. While we view rule 102 as being intended to provide for a broader construction and interpretation of these rules, we feel that, without a separate residual provision, the specifically enumerated exceptions could become tortured beyond any reasonable circumstances which they were intended to include (even if broadly construed). Moreover, these exceptions, while they reflect the most typical and well recognized exceptions to the hearsay rule, may not encompass every situation in which the reliability and appropriateness of a particular piece of hearsay evidence make clear that it should be heard and considered by the trier of fact.

The committee believes that there are certain exceptional circumstances where evidence which is found by a court to have guarantees of trustworthiness equivalent to or exceeding the guarantees reflected by the presently listed exceptions, and to have a high degree of prolativeness [sic] and necessity could properly be admissible.

The case of *Dallas County v. Commercial Union Assoc. Co., Ltd.*, 286 F.2d 388 (5th Cir.1961) illustrates the point. The issue in that case was whether the tower of the county courthouse collapsed because it was struck by lightning (covered by insurance) or because of structural weakness and deterioration of the structure (not covered). Investigation of the structure revealed the presence of charcoal and charred timbers. In order to show that lightning may not have been the cause of the charring, the insurer offered a copy of a local newspaper published over 50 years earlier containing an unsigned article describing a fire in the courthouse while it was under construction. The court found that the newspaper did not qualify for admission as a business record or an ancient document and did not fit within any other recognized hearsay exception. The court concluded, however, that the article was trustworthy because it was inconceivable that a newspaper reporter in a small town would report a fire in the courthouse if none had occurred. See also *United States v. Barbati*, 284 F.Supp. 409 (E.D.N.Y.1968).

Because exceptional cases like the *Dallas County* case may arise in the future, the committee has decided to reinstate a residual exception for rules 803 and 804(b).

The committee, however, also agrees with those supporters of the House version who felt that an overly broad residual hearsay exception could emasculate the hearsay rule and the recognized exceptions or vitiate the rationale behind codification of the rules.

Therefore, the committee has adopted a residual exception for rules 803 and 804(b) of much narrower scope and applicability than the Supreme Court version. In order to qualify for admission, a hearsay statement not falling within one of the recognized exceptions would have to satisfy at least four conditions. First, it must have "equivalent circumstantial guarantees of trustworthiness." Second, it must be offered as evidence of a material fact. Third, the court must determine that the statement "is more probative on the point for which it is offered than any other evidence which the proponent can procure through reasonable efforts." This requirement is intended to insure that only statements which have high probative value and necessity may qualify for admission under the residual exceptions. Fourth, the court must determine that "the general purposes of these rules and the interests of justice will best be served by admission of the statement into evidence."

It is intended that the residual hearsay exceptions will be used very rarely, and only in exceptional circumstances. The committee does not intend to establish a broad license for trial judges to admit hearsay statements that do not fall within one of the other exceptions contained in rules 803 and 804(b). The residual exceptions are not meant to authorize major judicial revisions of the hearsay rule, including its present exceptions. Such major revisions are best accomplished by legislative action. It is intended that in any case in which evidence is sought to be admitted under these subsections, the trial judge will exercise no less care, reflection and caution than the courts did under the common law in establishing the now-recognized exceptions to the hearsay rule.

In order to establish a well-defined jurisprudence, the special facts and circumstances which, in the court's judgment, indicates that the statement has a sufficiently high degree of trustworthiness and necessity to justify its admission should be stated on the record. It is expected that the court will give the opposing party a full and adequate opportunity to contest the admission of any statement sought to be introduced under these subsections. Senate Report No. 93–1277.

Rule 803 defines when hearsay statements are admissible in evidence even though the declarant is available as a witness. The Senate amendments make three changes in this rule.

Note to Paragraph (6). The House bill provides in subsection (6) that records of a regularly conducted "business" activity qualify for admission into evidence as an exception to the hearsay rule. "Business" is defined as including "business, profession, occupation and calling of every kind." The Senate amendment drops the requirement that the records be those of a "business" activity and eliminates the definition of "business." The Senate amendment provides that records are admissible if they are records of a regularly conducted "activity."

The Conference adopts the House provision that the records must be those of a regularly conducted "business" activity. The Conferees changed the definition of "business" contained in the House provision in order to make it clear that the records of institutions and associations like schools, churches and hospitals are admissible under this provision. The records of public schools and hospitals are also covered by Rule 803(8), which deals with public records and reports.

Note to Paragraph (8). The Senate amendment adds language, not contained in the House bill, that refers to another rule that was added by the Senate in another amendment ([proposed] Rule 804(b)(5)—Criminal law enforcement records and reports [deleted]).

In view of its action on [proposed] Rule 804(b)(5) (Criminal law enforcement records and reports) [deleted], the Conference does not adopt the Senate amendment and restores the bill to the House version.

Note to Paragraph (24). The Senate amendment adds a new subsection, (24), which makes admissible a hearsay statement not specifically covered by any of the previous twenty-three subsections, if the statement has equivalent circumstantial guarantees of trustworthiness and if the court determines that (A) the statement is offered as evidence of a material fact; (B) the statement is more probative on the point for which it is offered than any other evidence the proponent can procure through reasonable efforts; and (C) the general purposes of these rules and the interests of justice will best be served by admission of the statement into evidence.

The House bill eliminated a similar, but broader, provision because of the conviction that such a provision injected too much uncertainty into the law of evidence regarding hearsay and impaired the ability of a litigant to prepare adequately for trial.

The Conference adopts the Senate amendment with an amendment that provides that a party intending to request the court to use a statement under this provision must notify any adverse party of this intention as well as of the particulars of the statement, including the name and address of the declarant. This notice must be given sufficiently in advance of the trial or hearing to provide any adverse party with a fair opportunity to prepare to contest the use of the statement. House Report No. 93–1597.

1997 Amendment

The contents of Rule 803(24) and Rule 804(b)(5) have been combined and transferred to a new Rule 807. This was done to facilitate additions to Rules 803 and 804. No change in meaning is intended.

2000 Amendment

The amendment provides that the foundation requirements of Rule 803(6) can be satisfied under certain circumstances without the expense and inconvenience of producing time-consuming foundation witnesses. Under current law, courts have generally required foundation witnesses to testify. *See, e.g., Tongil Co., Ltd. v. Hyundai Merchant Marine Corp.*, 968 F.2d 999 (9th Cir. 1992) (reversing a judgment based on business records where a qualified person filed an affidavit but did not testify). Protections are provided by the authentication requirements of Rule 902(11) for domestic records, Rule 902(12) for foreign records in civil cases, and 18 U.S.C. § 3505 for foreign records in criminal cases.

Rule 804. Hearsay Exceptions; Declarant Unavailable

(a) Definition of unavailability. "Unavailability as a witness" includes situations in which the declarant—

(1) is exempted by ruling of the court on the ground of privilege from testifying concerning the subject matter of the declarant's statement; or

(2) persists in refusing to testify concerning the subject matter of the declarant's statement despite an order of the court to do so; or

(3) testifies to a lack of memory of the subject matter of the declarant's statement; or

(4) is unable to be present or to testify at the hearing because of death or then existing physical or mental illness or infirmity; or

(5) is absent from the hearing and the proponent of a statement has been unable to procure the declarant's attendance (or in the case of a hearsay exception under subdivision (b)(2), (3), or (4), the declarant's attendance or testimony) by process or other reasonable means.

A declarant is not unavailable as a witness if exemption, refusal, claim of lack of memory, inability, or absence is due to the procurement or wrongdoing of the proponent of a statement for the purpose of preventing the witness from attending or testifying.

(b) Hearsay exceptions. The following are not excluded by the hearsay rule if the declarant is unavailable as a witness:

(1) Former testimony. Testimony given as a witness at another hearing of the same or a different proceeding, or in a deposition taken in compliance with law in the course of the same or another proceeding, if the party against whom the testimony is now offered, or, in a civil action or proceeding, a predecessor in interest, had an opportunity and similar motive to develop the testimony by direct, cross, or redirect examination.

(2) Statement under belief of impending death. In a prosecution for homicide or in a civil action or proceeding, a statement made by a declarant while believing that the declarant's death was imminent, concerning the cause or circumstances of what the declarant believed to be impending death.

(3) Statement against interest. A statement which was at the time of its making so far contrary to the declarant's pecuniary or proprietary interest, or so far tended to subject the declarant to civil or criminal liability, or to render invalid a claim by the declarant against another, that a reasonable person in the declarant's position would not have made the statement unless believing it to be true. A statement tending to expose the declarant to criminal liability and offered to exculpate the accused is not admissible unless corroborating circumstances clearly indicate the trustworthiness of the statement.

(4) Statement of personal or family history. (A) A statement concerning the declarant's own birth, adoption, marriage, divorce, legitimacy, relationship by blood, adoption, or marriage, ancestry, or other similar fact of personal or family history, even though declarant had no means of acquiring personal knowledge of the matter stated; or (B) a statement concerning the foregoing matters, and death also, of another person, if the declarant was related to the other by blood, adoption, or marriage or was so intimately associated with the other's family as to be likely to have accurate information concerning the matter declared.

(5) [Transferred to Rule 807]

(6) Forfeiture by wrongdoing. A statement offered against a party that has engaged or acquiesced in wrongdoing that was intended to, and did, procure the unavailability of the declarant as a witness.

ADVISORY COMMITTEE NOTES
1972 Proposed Rules

As to firsthand knowledge on the part of hearsay declarants, see the introductory portion of the Advisory Committee's Note to Rule 803.

Note to Subdivision (a). The definition of unavailability implements the division of hearsay exceptions into two categories by Rules 803 and 804(b).

At common law the unavailability requirement was evolved in connection with particular hearsay exceptions rather than along general lines. For example, see the separate explications of unavailability in relation to former testimony, declarations against interest, and statements of pedigree, separately developed in McCormick §§ 234, 257, and 297. However, no reason is apparent for making distinctions as to what satisfies unavailability for the different exceptions. The treatment in the rule is therefore uniform although differences in the range of process for witnesses between civil and criminal cases will lead to a less exacting requirement under item (5). See Rule 45(e) of the Federal Rules of Civil Procedure and Rule 17(e) of the Federal Rules of Criminal Procedure.

Five instances of unavailability are specified:

(1) Substantial authority supports the position that exercise of a claim of privilege by the declarant satisfies the requirement of unavailability (usually in connection with former testimony). *Wyatt v. State*, 35 Ala.App. 147, 46 So.2d 837 (1950); *State v. Stewart*, 85 Kan. 404, 116 P. 489 (1911); Annot., 45 A.L.R.2d 1354; Uniform Rule 62(7)(a); California Evidence Code § 240(a)(1); Kansas Code of Civil Procedure § 60–459(g)(1). A ruling by the judge is required, which clearly implies that an actual claim of privilege must be made.

(2) A witness is rendered unavailable if he simply refuses to testify concerning the subject matter of his statement despite judicial pressures to do so, a position supported by similar considerations of practicality. *Johnson v. People*, 152 Colo. 586, 384 P.2d 454 (1963); *People v. Pickett*, 339 Mich. 294, 63 N.W.2d 681, 45 A.L.R.2d 1341 (1954). *Contra, Pleau v. State*, 255 Wis. 362, 38 N.W.2d 496 (1949).

(3) The position that a claimed lack of memory by the witness of the subject matter of his statement constitutes unavailability likewise finds support in the cases, though not without dissent. McCormick § 234, p. 494. If the claim is successful, the practical effect is to put the testimony beyond reach, as in the other instances. In this instance, however, it will be noted that the lack of memory must be established by the testimony of the witness himself, which clearly contemplates his production and subjection to cross-examination.

(4) Death and infirmity find general recognition as grounds. McCormick §§ 234, 257, 297; Uniform Rule 62(7)(c); California Evidence Code § 240(a)(3); Kansas Code of Civil Procedure § 60–459(g)(3); New Jersey Evidence Rule 62(6)(c). See also the provisions on use of depositions in Rule 32(a)(3) of the Federal Rules of Civil Procedure and Rule 15(e) of the Federal Rules of Criminal Procedure.

(5) Absence from the hearing coupled with inability to compel attendance by process or other reasonable means also satisfies the requirement. McCormick § 234; Uniform Rule 62(7)(d) and (e); California Evidence Code § 240(a)(4) and (5); Kansas Code of Civil Procedure § 60–459(g)(4) and (5); New Jersey Rule 62(6)(b) and (d). See the discussion of procuring attendance of witnesses who are nonresidents or in custody in *Barber v. Page*, 390 U.S. 719, 88 S.Ct. 1318, 20 L.Ed.2d 255 (1968).

If the conditions otherwise constituting unavailability result from the procurement or wrongdoing of the proponent of the statement, the requirement is not satisfied. The rule contains no requirement that an attempt be made to take the deposition of a declarant.

Note to Subdivision (b). Rule 803, *supra*, is based upon the assumption that a hearsay statement falling within one of its exceptions possesses qualities which justify the conclusion that whether the declarant is available or unavailable is not a relevant factor in determining admissibility. The instant rule proceeds upon a different theory: hearsay which admittedly is not equal in quality to testimony of the declarant on the stand may nevertheless be admitted if the declarant is unavailable and if his statement meets a specified standard. The rule expresses preferences: testimony given on the stand in person is preferred over hearsay, and hearsay, if of the specified quality, is preferred over complete loss of the evidence of the declarant. The exceptions evolved at common law with respect to declarations of unavailable declarants furnish the basis for the exceptions enumerated in the proposal. The term "unavailable" is defined in subdivision (a).

Exception (1). Former testimony does not rely upon some set of circumstances to substitute for oath and cross-examination, since both oath and opportunity to cross-examine were present in fact. The only missing one of the ideal conditions for the giving of testimony is the presence of trier and opponent ("demeanor evidence"). This is lacking with all hearsay exceptions. Hence it may be argued that former testimony is the strongest hearsay and should be included under Rule 803, supra. However, opportunity to observe demeanor is what in a large measure confers depth and meaning upon oath and cross-examination. Thus in cases under Rule 803 demeanor lacks the significance which it possesses with respect to testimony. In any event, the tradition, founded in experience, uniformly favors production of the witness if he is available. The exception indicates continuation of the policy. This preference for the presence of the witness is apparent also in rules and statutes on the use of depositions, which deal with substantially the same problem.

Under the exception, the testimony may be offered (1) against the party *against* whom it was previously offered or (2) against the party *by* whom it was previously offered. In each instance the question resolves itself into whether fairness allows imposing, upon the party against whom now offered, the handling of the witness of the earlier occasion. (1) If the party against whom now offered is the one against whom the testimony was offered previously, no unfairness is apparent in requiring him to accept his own prior conduct of cross-examination or decision not to cross-examine. Only demeanor has been lost, and that is inherent in the situation. (2) If the party against whom now offered is the one *by* whom the testimony was offered previously, a satisfactory answer becomes somewhat more difficult. One possibility is to proceed somewhat along the line of an adoptive admission, i.e. by offering the testimony proponent in effect adopts it. However, this theory savors of discarded concepts of witnesses' belonging to a party, of litigants' ability to pick and choose witnesses, and of vouching for one's own witnesses. Cf. McCormick § 246, pp. 526–527; 4 Wigmore § 1075. A more direct and acceptable approach is simply to recognize direct and redirect examination of one's own witness as the equivalent of cross-examining an opponent's witness. Falknor, Former Testimony and the Uniform Rules: A Comment, 38 N.Y.U.L.Rev. 651, n. 1 (1963); McCormick § 231, p. 483. See also 5 Wigmore § 1389. Allowable techniques for dealing with hostile, double-crossing, forgetful, and mentally deficient witnesses leave no substance to a claim that one could not adequately develop his own witness at the former hearing. An even less appealing argument is presented when failure to develop fully was the result of a deliberate choice.

The common law did not limit the admissibility of former testimony to that given in an earlier trial of the same case, although it did require identity of issues as a means of insuring that the former handling of the witness was the equivalent of what would now be done if the opportunity were presented. Modern decisions reduce the requirement to "substantial" identity. McCormick § 233. Since identity of issues is significant only in that it bears on motive and interest in developing fully the testimony of the witness, expressing the matter in the latter terms is preferable. *Id.* Testimony given at a preliminary hearing was held in *California v. Green*, 399 U.S. 149, 90 S.Ct. 1930, 26 L.Ed.2d 489 (1970), to satisfy confrontation requirements in this respect.

As a further assurance of fairness in thrusting upon a party the prior handling of the witness, the common law also insisted upon identity of parties, deviating only to the extent of allowing substitution of successors in a narrowly construed privity. Mutuality as an aspect of identity is now generally discredited, and the requirement of identity of the offering party disappears except as it might affect motive to develop the testimony. Falknor, *supra*, at 652; McCormick § 232, pp. 487–488. The question remains whether strict identity, or privity, should continue as a requirement with respect to the party against whom offered. The rule departs to the extent of allowing substitution of one with the right and opportunity to develop the testimony with similar motive and interest. This position is supported by modern decisions. McCormick § 232, pp. 489–490; 5 Wigmore § 1388.

Provisions of the same tenor will be found in Uniform Rule 63(3)(b); California Evidence Code §§ 1290–1292; Kansas Code of Civil Procedure § 60–460(c)(2); New Jersey Evidence Rule 63(3). Unlike the rule, the latter three provide either that former testimony is not admissible if the right of confrontation is denied or that it is not admissible if the accused was not a party to the prior hearing. The genesis of these limitations is a caveat in Uniform Rule 63(3) Comment that use of former testimony against an accused may violate his right of confrontation. *Mattox v. United States*, 156 U.S. 237, 15 S.Ct. 337, 39 L.Ed. 409 (1895), held that the right was not violated by the Government's use, on a retrial of the same case, of testimony given at the first trial by two witnesses since deceased. The decision leaves open the questions (1) whether direct and redirect are equivalent to cross-examination for purposes of confrontation, (2) whether testimony given in a different proceeding is acceptable, and (3) whether the accused must himself have been a party to the earlier proceeding or whether a similarly situated person will serve the purpose. Professor Falknor concluded that, if a dying declaration untested by cross-examination is constitutionally admissible, former testimony tested by the cross-examination of one similarly situated does not offend against confrontation. Falknor, *supra*, at 659–660. The constitutional acceptability of dying declarations has often been conceded. *Mattox v. United States*, 156 U.S. 237, 243, 15 S.Ct. 337, 39 L.Ed. 409 (1895); *Kirby v. United States*, 174 U.S. 47, 61, 19 S.Ct. 574, 43 L.Ed.

890 (1899); *Pointer v. Texas*, 380 U.S. 400, 407, 85 S.Ct. 1065, 13 L.Ed.2d 923 (1965).

Exception (2). The exception is the familiar dying declaration of the common law, expanded somewhat beyond its traditionally narrow limits. While the original religious justification for the exception may have lost its conviction for some persons over the years, it can scarcely be doubted that powerful psychological pressures are present. See 5 Wigmore § 1443 and the classic statement of Chief Baron Eyre in Rex v. Woodcock, 1 Leach 500, 502, 168 Eng.Rep. 352, 353 (K.B.1789).

The common law required that the statement be that of the victim, offered in a prosecution for criminal homicide. Thus declarations by victims in prosecutions for other crimes, e.g. a declaration by a rape victim who dies in childbirth, and all declarations in civil cases were outside the scope of the exception. An occasional statute has removed these restrictions, as in Colo.R.S. § 52–1–20, or has expanded the area of offenses to include abortions, 5 Wigmore § 1432, p. 224, n. 4. Kansas by decision extended the exception to civil cases. *Thurston v. Fritz*, 91 Kan. 468, 138 P. 625 (1914). While the common law exception no doubt originated as a result of the exceptional need for the evidence in homicide cases, the theory of admissibility applies equally in civil cases and in prosecutions for crimes other than homicide. The same considerations suggest abandonment of the limitation to circumstances attending the event in question, yet when the statement deals with matters other than the supposed death, its influence is believed to be sufficiently attenuated to justify the limitation. Unavailability is not limited to death. See subdivision (a) of this rule. Any problem as to declarations phrased in terms of opinion is laid at rest by Rule 701, and continuation of a requirement of firsthand knowledge is assured by Rule 602.

Comparable provisions are found in Uniform Rule 63(5); California Evidence Code § 1242; Kansas Code of Civil Procedure § 60–460(e); New Jersey Evidence Rule 63(5).

Exception (3). The circumstantial guaranty of reliability for declarations against interest is the assumption that persons do not make statements which are damaging to themselves unless satisfied for good reason that they are true. *Hileman v. Northwest Engineering Co.*, 346 F.2d 668 (6th Cir.1965). If the statement is that of a party, offered by his opponent, it comes in as an admission, Rule 803(d)(2) [sic; probably should be "Rule 801(d)(2)"], and there is no occasion to inquire whether it is against interest, this not being a condition precedent to admissibility of admissions by opponents.

The common law required that the interest declared against be pecuniary or proprietary but within this limitation demonstrated striking ingenuity in discovering an against-interest aspect. *Higham v. Ridgway*, 10 East 109, 103 Eng.Rep. 717 (K.B.1808); *Reg. v. Overseers of Birmingham*, 1 B. & S. 763, 121 Eng.Rep. 897 (Q.B.1861); McCormick, § 256, p. 551, nn. 2 and 3.

The exception discards the common law limitation and expands to the full logical limit. One result is to remove doubt as to the admissibility of declarations tending to establish a tort liability against the declarant or to extinguish one which might be asserted by him, in accordance with the trend of the decisions in this country. McCormick § 254, pp. 548–549. Another is to allow statements tending to expose declarant to hatred, ridicule, or disgrace, the motivation here being considered to be as strong as when financial interests are at stake. McCormick § 255, p. 551. And finally, exposure to criminal liability satisfies the against-interest requirement. The refusal of the common law to concede the adequacy of a penal interest was no doubt indefensible in logic, see the dissent of Mr. Justice Holmes in *Donnelly v. United States*, 228 U.S. 243, 33 S.Ct. 449, 57 L.Ed. 820 (1913), but one senses in the decisions a distrust of evidence of confessions by third persons offered to exculpate the accused arising from suspicions of fabrication either of the fact of the making of the confession or in its contents, enhanced in either instance by the required unavailability of the declarant. Nevertheless, an increasing amount of decisional law recognizes exposure to punishment for crime as a sufficient stake. *People v. Spriggs*, 60 Cal.2d 868, 36 Cal.Rptr. 841, 389 P.2d 377 (1964); *Sutter v.*

Easterly, 354 Mo. 282, 189 S.W.2d 284 (1945); *Band's Refuse Removal, Inc. v. Fairlawn Borough*, 62 N.J.Super. 522, 163 A.2d 465 (1960); *Newberry v. Commonwealth*, 191 Va. 445, 61 S.E.2d 318 (1950); Annot., 162 A.L.R. 446. The requirement of corroboration is included in the rule in order to effect an accommodation between these competing considerations. When the statement is offered by the accused by way of exculpation, the resulting situation is not adapted to control by rulings as to the weight of the evidence, and hence the provision is cast in terms of a requirement preliminary to admissibility. Cf. Rule 406(a). The requirement of corroboration should be construed in such a manner as to effectuate its purpose of circumventing fabrication.

Ordinarily the third-party confession is thought of in terms of exculpating the accused, but this is by no means always or necessarily the case: it may include statements implicating him, and under the general theory of declarations against interest they would be admissible as related statements. Douglas v. Alabama, 380 U.S. 415, 85 S.Ct. 1074, 13 L.Ed.2d 934 (1965), and Bruton v. United States, 389 U.S. 818, 88 S.Ct. 126, 19 L.Ed.2d 70 (1968), both involved confessions by codefendants which implicated the accused. While the confession was not actually offered in evidence in *Douglas*, the procedure followed effectively put it before the jury, which the Court ruled to be error. Whether the confession might have been admissible as a declaration against penal interest was not considered or discussed. *Bruton* assumed the inadmissibility, as against the accused, of the implicating confession of his codefendant, and centered upon the question of the effectiveness of a limiting instruction. These decisions, however, by no means require that all statements implicating another person be excluded from the category of declarations against interest. Whether a statement is in fact against interest must be determined from the circumstances of each case. Thus a statement admitting guilt and implicating another person, made while in custody, may well be motivated by a desire to curry favor with the authorities and hence fail to qualify as against interest. See the dissenting opinion of Mr. Justice White in *Bruton*. On the other hand, the same words spoken under different circumstances, e.g., to an acquaintance, would have no difficulty in qualifying. The rule does not purport to deal with questions of the right of confrontation.

The balancing of self-serving against dissenting aspects of a declaration is discussed in McCormick § 256.

For comparable provisions, see Uniform Rule 63(10); California Evidence Code § 1230; Kansas Code of Civil Procedure § 60–460(j); New Jersey Evidence Rule 63(10).

Exception (4). The general common law requirement that a declaration in this area must have been made *ante litem motam* has been dropped, as bearing more appropriately on weight than admissibility. See 5 Wigmore § 1483. Item (i)[(A)] specifically disclaims any need of firsthand knowledge respecting declarant's own personal history. In some instances it is self-evident (marriage) and in others impossible and traditionally not required (date of birth). Item (ii)[(B)] deals with declarations concerning the history of another person. As at common law, declarant is qualified if related by blood or marriage. 5 Wigmore § 1489. In addition, and contrary to the common law, declarant qualifies by virtue of intimate association with the family. *Id.*, § 1487. The requirement sometimes encountered that when the subject of the statement is the relationship between two other persons the declarant must qualify as to both is omitted. Relationship is reciprocal. *Id.*, § 1491.

For comparable provisions, see Uniform Rule 63(23), (24), (25); California Evidence Code §§ 1310, 1311; Kansas Code of Civil Procedure § 60–460(u), (v), (w); New Jersey Evidence Rules 63–23), 63(24), 63(25).

1974 Enactment

Note to Subdivision (a)(3). Rule 804(a)(3) was approved in the form submitted by the Court. However, the Committee intends no change in existing federal law under which the court may choose to disbelieve the declarant's testimony as to his lack of memory. See *United States v. Insana*, 423 F.2d 1165, 1169–1170 (2nd Cir.), cert. denied, 400 U.S. 841 (1970).

Note to Subdivision (a)(5). Rule 804(a)(5) as submitted to the Congress provided, as one type of situation in which a declarant would be deemed "unavailable", that he be "absent from the hearing and the proponent of his statement has been unable to procure his attendance by process or other reasonable means." The Committee amended the Rule to insert after the word "attendance" the parenthetical expression "(or, in the case of a hearsay exception under subdivision (b)(2), (3), or (4), his attendance or testimony)". The amendment is designed primarily to require that an attempt be made to depose a witness (as well as to seek his attendance) as a precondition to the witness being deemed unavailable. The Committee, however, recognized the propriety of an exception to this additional requirement when it is the declarant's former testimony that is sought to be admitted under subdivision (b)(1).

Note to Subdivision (b)(1). Rule 804(b)(1) as submitted by the Court allowed prior testimony of an unavailable witness to be admissible if the party against whom it is offered or a person "with motive and interest similar" to his had an opportunity to examine the witness. The Committee considered that it is generally unfair to impose upon the party against whom the hearsay evidence is being offered responsibility for the manner in which the witness was previously handled by another party. The sole exception to this, in the Committee's view, is when a party's predecessor in interest in a civil action or proceeding had an opportunity and similar motive to examine the witness. The Committee amended the Rule to reflect these policy determinations.

Note to Subdivision (b)(2). Rule 804(b)(3) as submitted by the Court (now Rule 804(b)(2) in the bill) proposed to expand the traditional scope of the dying declaration exception (i.e. a statement of the victim in a homicide case as to the cause or circumstances of his believed imminent death) to allow such statements in all criminal and civil cases. The Committee did not consider dying declarations as among the most reliable forms of hearsay. Consequently, it amended the provision to limit their admissibility in criminal cases to homicide prosecutions, where exceptional need for the evidence is present. This is existing law. At the same time, the Committee approved the expansion to civil actions and proceedings where the stakes do not involve possible imprisonment, although noting that this could lead to forum shopping in some instances.

Note to Subdivision (b)(3). Rule 804(b)(4) as submitted by the Court (now Rule 804(b)(3) in the bill) provided as follows:

Statement against interest.—A statement which was at the time of its making so far contrary to the declarant's pecuniary or proprietary interest or so far tended to subject him to civil or criminal liability or to render invalid a claim by him against another or to make him an object of hatred, ridicule, or disgrace, that a reasonable man in his position would not have made the statement unless he believed it to be true. A statement tending to exculpate the accused is not admissible unless corroborated.

The Committee determined to retain the traditional hearsay exception for statements against pecuniary or proprietary interest. However, it deemed the Court's additional references to statements tending to subject a declarant to civil liability or to render invalid a claim by him against another to be redundant as included within the scope of the reference to statements against pecuniary or proprietary interest. See *Gichner v. Antonio Triano Tile and Marble Co.*, 410 F.2d 238 (D.C.Cir.1968). Those additional references were accordingly deleted.

The Court's Rule also proposed to expand the hearsay limitation from its present federal limitation to include statements subjecting the declarant to criminal liability and statements tending to make him an object of hatred, ridicule, or disgrace. The Committee eliminated the latter category from the subdivision as lacking sufficient guarantees of reliability. See *United States v. Dovico*, 380 F.2d 325, 327 nn. 2, 4 (2nd Cir.), cert. denied, 389 U.S. 944 (1967). As for statements against penal interest, the Committee shared the view of the Court that some such statements do possess adequate assurances of reliability and should be admissible. It believed, however, as did the Court, that statements of this type tending to exculpate the accused are more suspect and so should have their admissibility conditioned upon some further provision insuring trustworthiness. The proposal in the Court Rule to add a requirement of simple corroboration was, however, deemed ineffective to accomplish this purpose since the accused's own testimony might suffice while not necessarily increasing the reliability of the hearsay statement. The Committee settled upon the language "unless corroborating circumstances clearly indicate the trustworthiness of the statement" as affording a proper standard and degree of discretion. It was contemplated that the result in such cases as *Donnelly v. United States*, 228 U.S. 243 (1912), where the circumstances plainly indicated reliability, would be changed. The Committee also added to the Rule the final sentence from the 1971 Advisory Committee draft, designed to codify the doctrine of *Bruton v. United States*, 391 U.S. 123 (1968). The Committee does not intend to affect the existing exception to the *Bruton* principle where the codefendant takes the stand and is subject to cross-examination, but believed there was no need to make specific provision for this situation in the Rule, since in that event the declarant would not be "unavailable". House Report No. 93–650.

Note to Subdivision (a)(5). Subdivision (a) of rule 804 as submitted by the Supreme Court defined the conditions under which a witness was considered to be unavailable. It was amended in the House.

The purpose of the amendment, according to the report of the House Committee on the Judiciary, is "primarily to require that an attempt be made to depose a witness (as well as to seek his attendance) as a precondition to the witness being unavailable."

Under the House amendment, before a witness is declared unavailable, a party must try to depose a witness (declarant) with respect to dying declarations, declarations against interest, and declarations of pedigree. None of these situations would seem to warrant this needless, impractical and highly restrictive complication. A good case can be made for eliminating the unavailability requirement entirely for declarations against interest cases. [Uniform rule 63(10); Kan.Stat.Anno. 60–460(j); 2A N.J.Stats.Anno. 84–63(10).]

In dying declaration cases, the declarant will usually, though not necessarily, be deceased at the time of trial. Pedigree statements which are admittedly and necessarily based largely on word of mouth are not greatly fortified by a deposition requirement.

Depositions are expensive and time-consuming. In any event, deposition procedures are available to those who wish to resort to them. Moreover, the deposition procedures of the Civil Rules and Criminal Rules are only imperfectly adapted to implementing the amendment. No purpose is served unless the deposition, if taken, may be used in evidence. Under Civil Rule (a)(3) the Criminal Rule 15(e), a deposition, though taken, may not be admissible, and under Criminal Rule 15(a) substantial obstacles exist in the way of even taking a deposition.

For these reasons, the committee deleted the House amendment.

The committee understands that the rule as to unavailability, as explained by the Advisory Committee "contains no requirement that an attempt be made to take the deposition of a declarant." In reflecting the committee's judgment, the statement is accurate insofar as it goes. Where, however, the proponent of the statement, with knowledge of the existence of the statement, fails to confront the declarant with the statement at the taking of the deposition, then the proponent should not, in fairness, be permitted to treat the declarant as "unavailable" simply because the declarant was not amenable to process compelling his attendance at trial. The committee does not consider it necessary to amend the rule to this effect because such a situation abuses, not conforms to, the rule. Fairness would preclude a person from introducing a hearsay statement on a particular issue if the person taking the deposition was aware of the issue at the time of the deposition but failed to depose the unavailable witness on that issue.

Note to Subdivision (b)(1). Former testimony.—Rule 804(b)(1) as submitted by the Court allowed prior testimony of an unavailable witness to be admissible if the party against whom it is offered or a person "with motive and interest similar" to his had an opportunity to examine the witness.

The House amended the rule to apply only to a party's predecessor in interest. Although the committee recognizes considerable merit to the rule submitted by the Supreme Court, a position which has been advocated by many scholars and judges, we have concluded that the difference between the two versions is not great and we accept the House amendment.

Note to Subdivision (b)(3). The rule defines those statements which are considered to be against interest and thus of sufficient trustworthiness to be admissible even though hearsay. With regard to the type of interest declared against, the version submitted by the Supreme Court included inter alia, statements tending to subject a declarant to civil liability or to invalidate a claim by him against another. The House struck these provisions as redundant. In view of the conflicting case law construing pecuniary or proprietary interests narrowly so as to exclude, e.g., tort cases, this deletion could be misconstrued.

Three States which have recently codified their rules of evidence have followed the Supreme Court's version of this rule, i.e., that a statement is against interest if it tends to subject a declarant to civil liability. [Nev.Rev.Stats. § 51.345; N.Mex.Stats. (1973 Supp.) § 20–4–804(4); West's Wis.Stats. Anno. (1973 Supp.) § 908.045(4).]

The committee believes that the reference to statements tending to subject a person to civil liability constitutes a desirable clarification of the scope of the rule. Therefore, we have reinstated the Supreme Court language on this matter.

The Court rule also proposed to expand the hearsay limitation from its present federal limitation to include statements subjecting the declarant to statements tending to make him an object of hatred, ridicule, or disgrace. The House eliminated the latter category from the subdivision as lacking sufficient guarantees of reliability. Although there is considerable support for the admissibility of such statements (all three of the State rules referred to supra, would admit such statements), we accept the deletion by the House.

The House amended this exception to add a sentence making inadmissible a statement or confession offered against the accused in a criminal case, made by a codefendant or other person implicating both himself and the accused. The sentence was added to codify the constitutional principle announced in *Bruton v. United States*, 391 U.S. 123 (1968). Bruton held that the admission of the extrajudicial hearsay statement of one codefendant inculpating a second codefendant violated the confrontation clause of the sixth amendment.

The committee decided to delete this provision because the basic approach of the rules is to avoid codifying, or attempting to codify, constitutional evidentiary principles, such as the fifth amendment's right against self-incrimination and, here, the sixth amendment's right of confrontation. Codification of a constitutional principle is unnecessary and, where the principle is under development, often unwise. Furthermore, the House provision does not appear to recognize the exceptions to the *Bruton* rule, e.g. where the codefendant takes the stand and is subject to cross examination; where the accused confessed, see *United States v. Mancusi*, 404 F.2d 296 (2d Cir.1968), cert. denied 397 U.S. 942 (1907); where the accused was placed at the scene of the crime, see *United States v. Zelker*, 452 F.2d 1009 (2d Cir.1971). For these reasons, the committee decided to delete this provision.

Note to Subdivision (b)(5). See Note to Paragraph (24), Notes of Committee on the Judiciary, Senate Report No. 93–1277, set out as a note under rule 803 of these rules. Senate Report No. 93–1277.

Rule 804 defines what hearsay statements are admissible in evidence if the declarant is unavailable as a witness. The Senate amendments make four changes in the rule.

Note to Subdivision (a)(5). Subsection (a) defines the term "unavailability as a witness". The House bill provides in subsection (a)(5) that the party who desires to use the statement must be unable to procure the declarant's attendance by process or other reasonable means. In the case of dying declarations, statements against interest and statements of personal or family history, the House bill requires that the proponent must also be unable to procure the declarant's *testimony* (such as by deposition or interrogatories) by process or other reasonable means. The Senate amendment eliminates this latter provision.

The Conference adopts the provision contained in the House bill.

Note to Subdivision (b)(3). The Senate amendment to subsection (b)(3) provides that a statement is against interest and not excluded by the hearsay rule when the declarant is unavailable as a witness, if the statement tends to subject a person to civil or criminal liability or renders invalid a claim by him against another. The House bill did not refer specifically to civil liability and to rendering invalid a claim against another. The Senate amendment also deletes from the House bill the provision that subsection (b)(3) does not apply to a statement or confession, made by a codefendant or another, which implicates the accused and the person who made the statement, when that statement or confession is offered against the accused in a criminal case.

The Conference adopts the Senate amendment. The Conferees intend to include within the purview of this rule, statements subjecting a person to civil liability and statements rendering claims invalid. The Conferees agree to delete the provision regarding statements by a codefendant, thereby reflecting the general approach in the Rules of Evidence to avoid attempting to codify constitutional evidentiary principles.

Note to Subdivision (b)(5). The Senate amendment adds a new subsection, (b)(6) [now (b)(5)], which makes admissible a hearsay statement not specifically covered by any of the five previous subsections, if the statement has equivalent circumstantial guarantees of trustworthiness and if the court determines that (A) the statement is offered as evidence of a material fact; (B) the statement is more probative on the point for which it is offered than any other evidence the proponent can procure through reasonable efforts; and (C) the general purposes of these rules and the interests of justice will best be served by admission of the statement into evidence.

The House bill eliminated a similar, but broader, provision because of the conviction that such a provision injected too much uncertainty into the law of evidence regarding hearsay and impaired the ability of a litigant to prepare adequately for trial.

The Conference adopts the Senate amendment with an amendment that renumbers this subsection and provides that a party intending to request the court to use a statement under this provision must notify any adverse party of this intention as well as of the particulars of the statement, including the name and address of the declarant. This notice must be given sufficiently in advance of the trial or hearing to provide any adverse party with a fair opportunity to prepare to contest the use of the statement. House Report No. 93–1597.

1997 Amendments

Subdivision (b)(5). The contents of Rule 803(24) and Rule 804(b)(5) have been combined and transferred to a new Rule 807. This was done to facilitate additions to Rules 803 and 804. No change in meaning is intended.

Subdivision (b)(6). Rule 804(b)(6) has been added to provide that a party forfeits the right to object on hearsay grounds to the admission of a declarant's prior statement when the party's deliberate wrongdoing or acquiescence therein procured the unavailability of the declarant as a witness. This recognizes the need for a prophylactic rule to deal with abhorrent behavior "which strikes at the heart of the system of justice itself." *United States v. Mastrangelo*, 693 F.2d 269, 273 (2d Cir.1982), *cert. denied*, 467 U.S. 1204 (1984). The wrongdoing need not consist of a criminal act. The rule applies to all parties, including the government.

Every circuit that has resolved the question has recognized the principle of forfeiture by misconduct, although the tests for determining whether there is a forfeiture have varied. *See, e.g.,* *United States v. Aguiar*, 975 F.2d 45, 47 (2d Cir.1992); *United States v. Potamitis*, 739 F.2d 784, 789 (2d Cir.), *cert. denied*, 469 U.S. 918 (1984); *Steele v. Taylor*, 684 F.2d 1193, 1199 (6th Cir.1982), *cert. denied*, 460 U.S. 1053 (1983); United States v. Balano, 618 F.2d 624, 629 (10th Cir.1979), *cert. denied*, 449 U.S. 840 (1980); *United States v. Carlson*, 547 F.2d 1346, 1358–59 (8th Cir.), *cert. denied*, 431 U.S. 914 (1977). The foregoing cases apply a preponderance of the evidence standard. *Contra United States v. Thevis*, 665 F.2d 616, 631 (5th Cir.) (clear and convincing standard), *cert. denied*, 459 U.S. 825 (1982). The usual Rule 104(a) preponderance of the evidence standard has been adopted in light of the behavior the new Rule 804(b)(6) seeks to discourage.

Rule 805. Hearsay Within Hearsay

Hearsay included within hearsay is not excluded under the hearsay rule if each part of the combined statements conforms with an exception to the hearsay rule provided in these rules.

ADVISORY COMMITTEE NOTES

1972 Proposed Rules

On principle it scarcely seems open to doubt that the hearsay rule should not call for exclusion of a hearsay statement which includes a further hearsay statement when both conform to the requirements of a hearsay exception. Thus a hospital record might contain an entry of the patient's age based on information furnished by his wife. The hospital record would qualify as a regular entry except that the person who furnished the information was not acting in the routine of the business. However, her statement independently qualifies as a statement of pedigree (if she is unavailable) or as a statement made for purposes of diagnosis or treatment, and hence each link in the chain falls under sufficient assurances. Or, further to illustrate, a dying declaration may incorporate a declaration against interest by another declarant. See McCormick § 290, p. 611.

Rule 806. Attacking and Supporting Credibility of Declarant

When a hearsay statement, or a statement defined in Rule 801(d)(2)(C), (D), or (E), has been admitted in evidence, the credibility of the declarant may be attacked, and if attacked may be supported, by any evidence which would be admissible for those purposes if declarant had testified as a witness. Evidence of a statement or conduct by the declarant at any time, inconsistent with the declarant's hearsay statement, is not subject to any requirement that the declarant may have been afforded an opportunity to deny or explain. If the party against whom a hearsay statement has been admitted calls the declarant as a witness, the party is entitled to examine the declarant on the statement as if under cross-examination.

ADVISORY COMMITTEE NOTES

1972 Proposed Rules

The declarant of a hearsay statement which is admitted in evidence is in effect a witness. His credibility should in fairness be subject to impeachment and support as though he had in fact testified. See Rules 608 and 609. There are however, some special aspects of the impeaching of a hearsay declarant which require consideration. These special aspects center upon impeachment by inconsistent statement, arise from factual differences which exist between the use of hearsay and an actual witness and also between various kinds of hearsay, and involve the question of applying to declarants the general rule disallowing evidence of an inconsistent statement to impeach a witness unless he is afforded an opportunity to deny or explain. See Rule 613(b).

The principal difference between using hearsay and an actual witness is that the inconsistent statement will in the case of the witness almost inevitably of necessity in the nature of things be a *prior* statement, which it is entirely possible and feasible to call to his attention, while in the case of hearsay the inconsistent statement may well be a *subsequent* one, which practically precludes calling it to the attention of the declarant. The result of insisting upon observation of this impossible requirement in the hearsay situation is to deny the opponent, already barred from cross-examination, any benefit of this important technique of impeachment. The writers favor allowing the subsequent statement. McCormick § 37, p. 69; 3 Wigmore § 1033. The cases, however, are divided. Cases allowing the impeachment include *People v. Collup*, 27 Cal.2d 829, 167 P.2d 714 (1946); *People v. Rosoto*, 58 Cal.2d 304, 23 Cal.Rptr. 779, 373 P.2d 867 (1962); *Carver v. United States*, 164 U.S. 694, 17 S.Ct. 228, 41 L.Ed. 602 (1897). *Contra, Mattox v. United States*, 156 U.S. 237, 15 S.Ct. 337, 39 L.Ed. 409 (1895); *People v. Hines*, 284 N.Y. 93, 29 N.E.2d 483 (1940). The force of *Mattox*, where the hearsay was the former testimony of a deceased witness and the denial of use of a subsequent inconsistent statement was upheld, is much diminished by *Carver*, where the hearsay was a dying declaration and denial of use of a subsequent inconsistent statement resulted in reversal. The difference in the particular brand of hearsay seems unimportant when the inconsistent statement is a *subsequent* one. True, the opponent is not totally deprived of cross-examination when the hearsay is former testimony or a deposition but he is deprived of cross-examining on the statement or along lines suggested by it. Mr. Justice Shiras, with two justices joining him, dissented vigorously in *Mattox*.

When the impeaching statement was made prior to the hearsay statement, differences in the kinds of hearsay appear which arguably may justify differences in treatment. If the hearsay consisted of a simple statement by the witness, e.g. a dying declaration or a declaration against interest, the feasibility of affording him an opportunity to deny or explain encounters the same practical impossibility as where the statement is a subsequent one, just discussed, although here the impossibility arises from the total absence of anything resembling a hearing at which the matter could be put to him. The courts by a large majority have ruled in favor of allowing the statement to be used under these circumstances. McCormick § 37, p. 69; 3 Wigmore § 1033. If, however, the hearsay consists of former testimony or a deposition, the possibility of calling the prior statement to the attention of the witness or deponent is not ruled out, since the opportunity to cross-examine was available. It might thus be concluded that with former testimony or depositions the conventional foundation should be insisted upon. Most of the cases involve depositions, and Wigmore describes them as divided. 3 Wigmore § 1031. Deposition procedures at best are cumbersome and expensive, and to require the laying of the foundation may impose an undue burden. Under the federal practice, there is no way of knowing with certainty at the time of taking a deposition whether it is merely for discovery or will ultimately end up in evidence. With respect to both former testimony and depositions the possibility exists that knowledge of the statement might not be acquired until after the time of the cross-examination. Moreover, the expanded admissibility of former testimony and depositions under Rule 804(b)(1) calls for a correspondingly expanded approach to impeachment. The rule dispenses with the requirement in all hearsay situations, which is readily administered and best calculated to lead to fair results.

Notice should be taken that Rule 26(f) of the Federal Rules of Civil Procedure, as originally submitted by the Advisory Committee, ended with the following:

" * * * and, without having first called them to the deponent's attention, may show statements contradictory thereto made at any time by the deponent."

This language did not appear in the rule as promulgated in December, 1937. See 4 Moore's Federal Practice ¶¶ 26.01[9], 26.35 (2d ed.1967). In 1951, Nebraska adopted a provision strongly resembling the one stricken from the federal rule:

"Any party may impeach any adverse deponent by self-contradiction without having laid foundation for such impeachment at the time such deposition was taken." R.S.Neb. § 25–1267.07.

For similar provisions, see Uniform Rule 65; California Evidence Code § 1202; Kansas Code of Civil Procedure § 60–462; New Jersey Evidence Rule 65.

The provision for cross-examination of a declarant upon his hearsay statement is a corollary of general principles of cross-examination. A similar provision is found in California Evidence Code § 1203.

1974 Enactment

Rule 906, as passed by the House and as proposed by the Supreme Court provides that whenever a hearsay statement is admitted, the credibility of the declarant of the statement may be attacked, and if attacked may be supported, by any evidence which would be admissible for those purposes if the declarant had testified as a witness. Rule 801 defines what is a hearsay statement. While statements by a person authorized by a party-opponent to make a statement concerning the subject, by the party-opponent's agent or by a coconspirator of a party—see rule 801(d)(2)(c), (d) and (e)—are traditionally defined as exceptions to the hearsay rule, rule 801 defines such admission by a party-opponent as statements which are not hearsay. Consequently, rule 806 by referring exclusively to the admission of hearsay statements, does not appear to allow the credibility of the declarant to be attacked when the declarant is a coconspirator, agent or authorized spokesman. The committee is of the view that such statements should open the declarant to attacks on his credibility. Indeed, the reason such statements are excluded from the operation of rule 806 is likely attributable to the drafting technique used to codify the hearsay rule, viz. some statements, instead of being referred to as exceptions to the hearsay rule, are defined as statements which are not hearsay. The phrase "or a statement defined in rule 801(d)(2)(c), (d) and (e)" is added to the rule in order to subject the declarant of such statements, like the declarant of hearsay statements, to attacks on his credibility. [The committee considered it unnecessary to include statements contained in rule 801(d)(2)(A) and (B)—the statement by the party-opponent himself or the statement of which he has manifested his adoption—because the credibility of the party-opponent is always subject to an attack on his credibility]. Senate Report No. 93–1277.

The Senate amendment permits an attack upon the credibility of the declarant of a statement if the statement is one by a person authorized by a party-opponent to make a statement concerning the subject, one by an agent of a party-opponent, or one by a coconspirator of the party-opponent, as these statements are defined in Rules 801(d)(2)(C), (D) and (E). The House bill has no such provision.

The Conference adopts the Senate amendment. The Senate amendment conforms the rule to present practice. House Report No. 93–1597.

Rule 807.   Residual Exception

A statement not specifically covered by Rule 803 or 804 but having equivalent circumstantial guarantees of trustworthiness, is not excluded by the hearsay rule, if the court determines that (A) the statement is offered as evidence of a material fact; (B) the statement is more probative on the point for which it is offered than any other evidence which the proponent can procure through reasonable efforts; and (C) the general purposes of these rules and the interests of justice will best be served by admission of the statement into evidence. However, a statement may not be admitted under this exception unless the proponent of it makes known to the adverse party sufficiently in advance of the trial or hearing to provide the adverse party with a fair opportunity to prepare to meet it, the proponent's intention to offer the statement and the particulars of it, including the name and address of the declarant.

ADVISORY COMMITTEE NOTES

1997 Amendments

The contents of Rule 803(24) and Rule 804(b)(5) have been combined and transferred to a new Rule 807. This was done to facilitate additions to Rules 803 and 804. No change in meaning is intended.

ARTICLE IX.   AUTHENTICATION AND IDENTIFICATION

Rule 901.   Requirement of Authentication or Identification

(a) General provision. The requirement of authentication or identification as a condition precedent to admissibility is satisfied by evidence sufficient to support a finding that the matter in question is what its proponent claims.

(b) Illustrations. By way of illustration only, and not by way of limitation, the following are examples of authentication or identification conforming with the requirements of this rule:

(1) Testimony of witness with knowledge. Testimony that a matter is what it is claimed to be.

(2) Nonexpert opinion on handwriting. Nonexpert opinion as to the genuineness of handwriting, based upon familiarity not acquired for purposes of the litigation.

(3) Comparison by trier or expert witness. Comparison by the trier of fact or by expert witnesses with specimens which have been authenticated.

(4) Distinctive characteristics and the like. Appearance, contents, substance, internal patterns, or other distinctive characteristics, taken in conjunction with circumstances.

(5) Voice identification. Identification of a voice, whether heard firsthand or through mechanical or electronic transmission or recording, by opinion based upon hearing the voice at any time under circumstances connecting it with the alleged speaker.

(6) Telephone conversations. Telephone conversations, by evidence that a call was made to the number assigned at the time by the telephone company to a particular person or business, if (A) in the case of a person, circumstances, including self-identification, show the person answering to be the one called, or (B) in the case of a business, the call was made to a place of business and the conversation related to business reasonably transacted over the telephone.

(7) Public records or reports. Evidence that a writing authorized by law to be recorded or filed and in fact recorded or filed in a public office, or a purported public record, report, statement, or data compilation, in any form, is from the public office where items of this nature are kept.

(8) Ancient documents or data compilation. Evidence that a document or data compilation, in any

---

form, (A) is in such condition as to create no suspicion concerning its authenticity, (B) was in a place where it, if authentic, would likely be, and (C) has been in existence 20 years or more at the time it is offered.

(9) Process or system. Evidence describing a process or system used to produce a result and showing that the process or system produces an accurate result.

(10) Methods provided by statute or rule. Any method of authentication or identification provided by Act of Congress or by other rules prescribed by the Supreme Court pursuant to statutory authority.

ADVISORY COMMITTEE NOTES

1972 Proposed Rules

Note to Subdivision (a). Authentication and identification represent a special aspect of relevancy. Michael and Adler, Real Proof, 5 Vand.L.Rev. 344, 362 (1952); McCormick §§ 179, 185; Morgan, Basic Problems of Evidence 378 (1962). Thus a telephone conversation may be irrelevant because on an unrelated topic or because the speaker is not identified. The latter aspect is the one here involved. Wigmore describes the need for authentication as "an inherent logical necessity." 7 Wigmore § 2129, p. 564.

This requirement of showing authenticity or identity falls in the category of relevancy dependent upon fulfillment of a condition of fact and is governed by the procedure set forth in Rule 104(b).

The common law approach to authentication of documents has been criticized as an "attitude of agnosticism," McCormick, Cases on Evidence 388, n. 4 (3rd ed. 1956), as one which "departs sharply from men's customs in ordinary affairs," and as presenting only a slight obstacle to the introduction of forgeries in comparison to the time and expense devoted to proving genuine writings which correctly show their origin on their face, McCormick § 185, pp. 395, 396. Today, such available procedures as requests to admit and pretrial conference afford the means of eliminating much of the need for authentication or identification. Also, significant inroads upon the traditional insistence on authentication and identification have been made by accepting as at least prima facie genuine items of the kind treated in Rule 902, *infra.* However, the need for suitable methods of proof still remains, since criminal cases pose their own obstacles to the use of preliminary procedures, unforeseen contingencies may arise, and cases of genuine controversy will still occur.

Note to Subdivision (b). The treatment of authentication and identification draws largely upon the experience embodied in the common law and in statutes to furnish illustrative applications of the general principle set forth in subdivision (a). The examples are not intended as an exclusive enumeration of allowable methods but are meant to guide and suggest, leaving room for growth and development in this area of the law.

The examples relate for the most part to documents, with some attention given to voice communications and computer printouts. As Wigmore noted, no special rules have been developed for authenticating chattels. Wigmore, Code of Evidence § 2086 (3rd ed. 1942).

It should be observed that compliance with requirements of authentication or identification by no means assures admission of an item into evidence, as other bars, hearsay for example, may remain.

Example (1). Example (1) contemplates a broad spectrum ranging from testimony of a witness who was present at the signing of a document to testimony establishing narcotics as taken from an accused and accounting for custody through the period until trial, including laboratory analysis. See California Evidence Code § 1413, eyewitness to signing.

Example (2). Example (2) states conventional doctrine as to lay identification of handwriting, which recognizes that a sufficient familiarity with the handwriting of another person may be acquired by seeing him write, by exchanging correspondence, or by other means, to afford a basis for identifying it on subsequent occasions. McCormick § 189. See also California Evidence Code § 1416. Testimony based upon familiarity acquired for purposes of the litigation is reserved to the expert under the example which follows.

Example (3). The history of common law restrictions upon the technique of proving or disproving the genuineness of a disputed specimen of handwriting through comparison with a genuine specimen, by either the testimony of expert witnesses or direct viewing by the triers themselves, is detailed in 7 Wigmore §§ 1991–1994. In breaking away, the English Common Law Procedure Act of 1854, 17 and 18 Vict., c. 125, § 27, cautiously allowed expert or trier to use exemplars "proved to the satisfaction of the judge to be genuine" for purposes of comparison. The language found its way into numerous statutes in this country, e.g., California Evidence Code §§ 1417, 1418. While explainable as a measure of prudence in the process of breaking with precedent in the handwriting situation, the reservation to the judge of the question of the genuineness of exemplars and the imposition of an unusually high standard of persuasion are at variance with the general treatment of relevancy which depends upon fulfillment of a condition of fact. Rule 104(b). No similar attitude is found in other comparison situations, e.g., ballistics comparison by jury, as in *Evans v. Commonwealth,* 230 Ky. 411, 19 S.W.2d 1091 (1929), or by experts, Annot., 26 A.L.R.2d 892, and no reason appears for its continued existence in handwriting cases. Consequently Example (3) sets no higher standard for handwriting specimens and treats all comparison situations alike, to be governed by Rule 104(b). This approach is consistent with 28 U.S.C. § 1731: "The admitted or proved handwriting of any person shall be admissible, for purposes of comparison, to determine genuineness of other handwriting attributed to such person."

Precedent supports the acceptance of visual comparison as sufficiently satisfying preliminary authentication requirements for admission in evidence. *Brandon v. Collins,* 267 F.2d 731 (2d Cir.1959); *Wausau Sulphate Fibre Co. v. Commissioner of Internal Revenue,* 61 F.2d 879 (7th Cir.1932); *Desimone v. United States,* 227 F.2d 864 (9th Cir.1955).

Example (4). The characteristics of the offered item itself, considered in the light of circumstances, afford authentication techniques in great variety. Thus a document or telephone conversation may be shown to have emanated from a particular person by virtue of its disclosing knowledge of facts known peculiarly to him; *Globe Automatic Sprinkler Co. v. Braniff,* 89 Okl. 105, 214 P. 127 (1923); California Evidence Code § 1421; similarly, a letter may be authenticated by content and circumstances indicating it was in reply to a duly authenticated one. McCormick § 192; California Evidence Code § 1420. Language patterns may indicate authenticity or its opposite. *Magnuson v. State,* 187 Wis. 122, 203 N.W. 749 (1925); Arens and Meadow, Psycholinguistics and the Confession Dilemma, 56 Colum L.Rev. 19 (1956).

Example (5). Since aural voice identification is not a subject of expert testimony, the requisite familiarity may be acquired either before or after the particular speaking which is the subject of the identification, in this respect resembling visual identification of a person rather than identification of handwriting. Cf. Example (2), *supra, People v. Nichols,* 378 Ill. 487, 38 N.E.2d 766 (1942); *McGuire v. State,* 200 Md. 601, 92 A.2d 582 (1952); *State v. McGee,* 336 Mo. 1082, 83 S.W.2d 98 (1935).

Example (6). The cases are in agreement that a mere assertion of his identity by a person talking on the telephone is not sufficient evidence of the authenticity of the conversation and that additional evidence of his identity is required. The additional evidence need not fall in any set pattern. Thus the content of his statements or the reply technique, under Example (4), *supra,* or voice identification under Example (5), may furnish the necessary foundation. Outgoing calls made by the witness involve additional factors bearing upon authenticity. The calling of a number assigned by the telephone company reasonably supports the assumption that the listing is correct and that the number is the one reached. If the number is that of a place of business, the mass of authority allows an ensuing conversation if it relates to business reasonably transacted over the telephone, on the theory that the maintenance of the telephone connection is an invitation to do business without further identification. *Matton v. Hoover Co.*, 350 Mo. 506, 166 S.W.2d 557 (1942); *City of Pawhuska v. Crutchfield*, 147 Okl. 4, 293 P. 1095 (1930); *Zurich General Acc. & Liability Ins. Co. v. Baum*, 159 Va. 404, 165 S.E. 518 (1932). Otherwise, some additional circumstance of identification of the speaker is required. The authorities divide on the question whether the self-identifying statement of the person answering suffices. Example (6) answers in the affirmative on the assumption that usual conduct respecting telephone calls furnish adequate assurances of regularity, bearing in mind that the entire matter is open to exploration before the trier of fact. In general, see McCormick § 193; 7 Wigmore § 2155; Annot., 71 A.L.R. 5, 105 id. 326.

Example (7). Public records are regularly authenticated by proof of custody, without more. McCormick § 191; 7 Wigmore §§ 2158, 2159. The example extends the principle to include data stored in computers and similar methods, of which increasing use in the public records area may be expected. See California Evidence Code §§ 1532, 1600.

Example (8). The familiar ancient document rule of the common law is extended to include data stored electronically or by other similar means. Since the importance of appearance diminishes in this situation, the importance of custody or place where found increases correspondingly. This expansion is necessary in view of the widespread use of methods of storing data in forms other than conventional written records.

Any time period selected is bound to be arbitrary. The common law period of 30 years is here reduced to 20 years, with some shift of emphasis from the probable unavailability of witnesses to the unlikeliness of a still viable fraud after the lapse of time. The shorter period is specified in the English Evidence Act of 1938, 1 & 2 Geo. 6, c. 28, and in Oregon R.S.1963, § 41.360(34). See also the numerous statutes prescribing periods of less than 30 years in the case of recorded documents. 7 Wigmore § 2143.

The application of Example (8) is not subject to any limitation to title documents or to any requirement that possession, in the case of a title document, has been consistent with the document. See McCormick § 190.

Example (9). Example (9) is designed for situations in which the accuracy of a result is dependent upon a process or system which produces it. X rays afford a familiar instance. Among more recent developments is the computer, as to which see *Transport Indemnity Co. v. Seib*, 178 Neb. 253, 132 N.W.2d 871 (1965); *State v. Veres*, 7 Ariz.App. 117, 436 P.2d 629 (1968); *Merrick v. United States Rubber Co.*, 7 Ariz.App. 433, 440 P.2d 314 (1968); Freed, Computer Print–Outs as Evidence, 16 Am. Jur.Proof of Facts 273; Symposium, Law and Computers in the Mid–Sixties, ALI–ABA (1966); 37 Albany L.Rev. 61 (1967). Example (9) does not, of course, foreclose taking judicial notice of the accuracy of the process or system.

Example (10). The example makes clear that methods of authentication provided by Act of Congress and by the Rules of Civil and Criminal Procedure or by Bankruptcy Rules are not intended to be superseded. Illustrative are the provisions for authentication of official records in Civil Procedure Rule 44 and Criminal Procedure Rule 27, for authentication of records of proceedings by court reporters in 28 U.S.C. § 753(b) and Civil Procedure Rule 80(c), and for authentication of depositions in Civil Procedure Rule 30(f).

Rule 902. Self-authentication

Extrinsic evidence of authenticity as a condition precedent to admissibility is not required with respect to the following:

    (1) Domestic public documents under seal. A document bearing a seal purporting to be that of the United States, or of any State, district, Commonwealth, territory, or insular possession thereof, or the Panama Canal Zone, or the Trust Territory of the Pacific Islands, or of a political subdivision, department, officer, or agency thereof, and a signature purporting to be an attestation or execution.

    (2) Domestic public documents not under seal. A document purporting to bear the signature in the official capacity of an officer or employee of any entity included in paragraph (1) hereof, having no seal, if a public officer having a seal and having official duties in the district or political subdivision of the officer or employee certifies under seal that the signer has the official capacity and that the signature is genuine.

    (3) Foreign public documents. A document purporting to be executed or attested in an official capacity by a person authorized by the laws of a foreign country to make the execution or attestation, and accompanied by a final certification as to the genuineness of the signature and official position (A) of the executing or attesting person, or (B) of any foreign official whose certificate of genuineness of signature and official position relates to the execution or attestation or is in a chain of certificates of genuineness of signature and official position relating to the execution or attestation. A final certification may be made by a secretary of an embassy or legation, consul general, consul, vice consul, or consular agent of the United States, or a diplomatic or consular official of the foreign country assigned or accredited to the United States. If reasonable opportunity has been given to all parties to investigate the authenticity and accuracy of official documents, the court may, for good cause shown, order that they be treated as presumptively authentic without final certification or permit them to be evidenced by an attested summary with or without final certification.

    (4) Certified copies of public records. A copy of an official record or report or entry therein, or of a document authorized by law to be recorded or filed and actually recorded or filed in a public office, including data compilations in any form, certified as correct by the custodian or other person authorized to make the certification, by certificate complying with paragraph (1), (2), or (3) of this rule or complying with any Act of Congress or rule prescribed by the Supreme Court pursuant to statutory authority.

    (5) Official publications. Books, pamphlets, or other publications purporting to be issued by public authority.

    (6) Newspapers and periodicals. Printed materials purporting to be newspapers or periodicals.

    (7) Trade inscriptions and the like. Inscriptions, signs, tags, or labels purporting to have been affixed in the course of business and indicating ownership, control, or origin.

    (8) Acknowledged documents. Documents accompanied by a certificate of acknowledgment executed in the manner provided by law by a notary public or other officer authorized by law to take acknowledgments.

    (9) Commercial paper and related documents. Commercial paper, signatures thereon, and documents relating thereto to the extent provided by general commercial law.

    (10) Presumptions under Acts of Congress. Any signature, document, or other matter declared by Act of Congress to be presumptively or prima facie genuine or authentic.

(11) Certified Domestic Records of Regularly Conducted Activity.—The original or a duplicate of a domestic record of regularly conducted activity that would be admissible under Rule 803(6) if accompanied by a written declaration of its custodian or other qualified person, in a manner complying with any Act of Congress or rule prescribed by the Supreme Court pursuant to statutory authority, certifying that the record—

(A) was made at or near the time of the occurrence of the matters set forth by, or from information transmitted by, a person with knowledge of those matters;

(B) was kept in the course of the regularly conducted activity; and

(C) was made by the regularly conducted activity as a regular practice.

A party intending to offer a record into evidence under this paragraph must provide written notice of that intention to all adverse parties, and must make the record and declaration available for inspection sufficiently in advance of their offer into evidence to provide an adverse party with a fair opportunity to challenge them.

(12) Certified Foreign Records of Regularly Conducted Activity.—In a civil case, the original or a duplicate of a foreign record of regularly conducted activity that would be admissible under Rule 803(6) if accompanied by a written declaration by its custodian or other qualified person certifying that the record—

(A) was made at or near the time of the occurrence of the matters set forth by, or from information transmitted by, a person with knowledge of those matters;

(B) was kept in the course of the regularly conducted activity; and

(C) was made by the regularly conducted activity as a regular practice.

The declaration must be signed in a manner that, if falsely made, would subject the maker to criminal penalty under the laws of the country where the declaration is signed. A party intending to offer a record into evidence under this paragraph must provide written notice of that intention to all adverse parties, and must make the record and declaration available for inspection sufficiently in advance of their offer into evidence to provide an adverse party with a fair opportunity to challenge them.

ADVISORY COMMITTEE NOTES
1972 Proposed Rules

Case law and statutes have, over the years, developed a substantial body of instances in which authenticity is taken as sufficiently established for purposes of admissibility without extrinsic evidence to that effect, sometimes for reasons of policy but perhaps more often because practical considerations reduce the possibility of unauthenticity to a very small dimension. The present rule collects and incorporates these situations, in some instances expanding them to occupy a larger area which their underlying considerations justify. In no instance is the opposite party foreclosed from disputing authenticity.

Note to Paragraph (1). The acceptance of documents bearing a public seal and signature, most often encountered in practice in the form of acknowledgments or certificates authenticating copies of public records, is actually of broad application.

Whether theoretically based in whole or in part upon judicial notice, the practical underlying considerations are that forgery is a crime and detection is fairly easy and certain. 7 Wigmore § 2161, p. 638; California Evidence Code § 1452. More than 50 provisions for judicial notice of official seals are contained in the United States Code.

Note to Paragraph (2). While statutes are found which raise a presumption of genuineness of purported official signatures in the absence of an official seal, 7 Wigmore § 2167; California Evidence Code § 1453, the greater ease of effecting a forgery under these circumstances is apparent. Hence this paragraph of the rule calls for authentication by an officer who has a seal. Notarial acts by members of the armed forces and other special situations are covered in paragraph (10).

Note to Paragraph (3). Paragraph (3) provides a method for extending the presumption of authenticity to foreign official documents by a procedure of certification. It is derived from Rule 44(a)(2) of the Rules of Civil Procedure but is broader in applying to public documents rather than being limited to public records.

Note to Paragraph (4). The common law and innumerable statutes have recognized the procedure of authenticating copies of public records by certificate. The certificate qualifies as a public document, receivable as authentic when in conformity with paragraph (1), (2), or (3). Rule 44(a) of the Rules of Civil Procedure and Rule 27 of the Rules of Criminal Procedure have provided authentication procedures of this nature for both domestic and foreign public records. It will be observed that the certification procedure here provided extends only to public records, reports, and recorded documents, all including data compilations, and does not apply to public documents generally. Hence documents provable when presented in original form under paragraphs (1), (2), or (3) may not be provable by certified copy under paragraph (4).

Note to Paragraph (5). Dispensing with preliminary proof of the genuineness of purportedly official publications, most commonly encountered in connection with statutes, court reports, rules, and regulations, has been greatly enlarged by statutes and decisions. 5 Wigmore § 1684. Paragraph (5), it will be noted, does not confer admissibility upon all official publications; it merely provides a means whereby their authenticity may be taken as established for purposes of admissibility. Rule 44(a) of the Rules of Civil Procedure has been to the same effect.

Note to Paragraph (6). The likelihood of forgery of newspapers or periodicals is slight indeed. Hence no danger is apparent in receiving them. Establishing the authenticity of the publication may, of course, leave still open questions of authority and responsibility for items therein contained. See 7 Wigmore § 2150. Cf. 39 U.S.C. § 4005(b), public advertisement prima facie evidence of agency of person named, in postal fraud order proceeding; Canadian Uniform Evidence Act, Draft of 1936, printed copy of newspaper prima facie evidence that notices or advertisements were authorized.

Note to Paragraph (7). Several factors justify dispensing with preliminary proof of genuineness of commercial and mercantile labels and the like. The risk of forgery is minimal. Trademark infringement involves serious penalties. Great efforts are devoted to inducing the public to buy in reliance on brand names, and substantial protection is given them. Hence the fairness of this treatment finds recognition in the cases. *Curtiss Candy Co. v. Johnson*, 163 Miss. 426, 141 So. 762 (1932), Baby Ruth candy bar; *Doyle v. Continental Baking Co.*, 262 Mass. 516, 160 N.E. 325 (1928), loaf of bread; *Weiner v. Mager & Throne, Inc.*, 167 Misc. 338, 3 N.Y.S.2d 918 (1938), same. And see W.Va.Code 1966, § 47–3–5, trademark on bottle prima facie evidence of ownership. *Contra, Keegan v. Green Giant Co.*, 150 Me. 283, 110 A.2d 599 (1954); *Murphy v. Campbell Soup Co.*, 62 F.2d 564 (1st Cir.1933). Cattle brands have received similar acceptance in the western states. Rev.Code Mont.1947, § 46–606, *State v. Wolfley*, 75 Kan. 406, 89 P. 1046 (1907); Annot., 11 L.R.A.(N.S.) 87. Inscriptions on trains and vehicles are held to be prima facie evidence of ownership or control. *Pittsburgh, Ft. W. & C. Ry. v. Callaghan*, 157 Ill. 406, 41 N.E.

909 (1895); 9 Wigmore § 2510a. See also the provision of 19 U.S.C. § 1615(2) that marks, labels, brands, or stamps indicating foreign origin are prima facie evidence of foreign origin of merchandise.

Note to Paragraph (8). In virtually every state, acknowledged title documents are receivable in evidence without further proof. Statutes are collected in 5 Wigmore § 1676. If this authentication suffices for documents of the importance of those affecting titles, logic scarcely permits denying this method when other kinds of documents are involved. Instances of broadly inclusive statutes are California Evidence Code § 1451 and N.Y.CPLR 4538, McKinney's Consol.Laws 1963.

Note to Paragraph (9). Issues of the authenticity of commercial paper in federal courts will usually arise in diversity cases, will involve an element of a cause of action or defense, and with respect to presumptions and burden of proof will be controlled by *Erie Railroad Co. v. Tompkins,* 304 U.S. 64, 58 S.Ct. 817, 82 L.Ed. 1188 (1938). Rule 302, *supra.* There may, however, be questions of authenticity involving lesser segments of a case or the case may be one governed by federal common law. *Clearfield Trust Co. v. United States,* 318 U.S. 363, 63 S.Ct. 573, 87 L.Ed. 838 (1943). Cf. *United States v. Yazell,* 382 U.S. 341, 86 S.Ct. 500, 15 L.Ed.2d 404 (1966). In these situations, resort to the useful authentication provisions of the Uniform Commercial Code is provided for. While the phrasing is in terms of "general commercial law," in order to avoid the potential complications inherent in borrowing local statutes, today one would have difficulty in determining the general commercial law without referring to the Code. See *Williams v. Walker–Thomas Furniture Co.,* 121 U.S.App.D.C. 315, 350 F.2d 445 (1965). Pertinent Code provisions are sections 1–202, 3–307, and 3–510, dealing with third-party documents, signatures on negotiable instruments, protests, and statements of dishonor.

Note to Paragraph (10). The paragraph continues in effect dispensations with preliminary proof of genuineness provided in various Acts of Congress. See, for example, 10 U.S.C. § 936, signature, without seal, together with title, prima facie evidence of authenticity of acts of certain military personnel who are given notarial powers; 15 U.S.C. § 77f(a), signature on SEC registration presumed genuine; 26 U.S.C. § 6064, signature to tax return prima facie genuine.

1974 Enactment

Note to Paragraph (8). Rule 902(8) as submitted by the Court referred to certificates of acknowledgment "under the hand and seal of" a notary public or other officer authorized by law to take acknowledgments. The Committee amended the Rule to eliminate the requirement, believed to be inconsistent with the law in some States, that a notary public must affix a seal to a document acknowledged before him. As amended the

Rule merely requires that the document be executed in the manner prescribed by State law.

Note to Paragraph (9). The Committee approved Rule 902(9) as submitted by the Court. With respect to the meaning of the phrase "general commercial law", the Committee intends that the Uniform Commercial Code, which has been adopted in virtually every State, will be followed generally, but that federal commercial law will apply where federal commercial paper is involved. See Clearfield Trust Co. v. United States, 318 U.S. 363 (1943). Further, in those instances in which the issues are governed by Erie R. Co. v. Tompkins, 304 U.S. 64 (1938), State law will apply irrespective of whether it is the Uniform Commercial Code. House Report No. 93–650.

2000 Amendments

The amendment adds two new paragraphs to the rule on self-authentication. It sets forth a procedure by which parties can authenticate certain records of regularly conducted activity, other than through the testimony of a foundation witness. See the amendment to Rule 803(6). 18 U.S.C. § 3505 currently provides a means for certifying foreign records of regularly conducted activity in criminal cases, and this amendment is intended to establish a similar procedure for domestic records, and for foreign records offered in civil cases.

A declaration that satisfies 28 U.S.C. § 1746 would satisfy the declaration requirement of Rule 902(11), as would any comparable certification under oath.

The notice requirement in Rules 902(11) and (12) is intended to give the opponent of the evidence a full opportunity to test the adequacy of the foundation set forth in the declaration.

Rule 903. Subscribing Witness' Testimony Unnecessary

The testimony of a subscribing witness is not necessary to authenticate a writing unless required by the laws of the jurisdiction whose laws govern the validity of the writing.

ADVISORY COMMITTEE NOTES
1972 Proposed Rules

The common law required that attesting witnesses be produced or accounted for. Today the requirement has generally been abolished except with respect to documents which must be attested to be valid, e.g. wills in some states. McCormick § 188. Uniform Rule 71; California Evidence Code § 1411; Kansas Code of Civil Procedure § 60–468; New Jersey Evidence Rule 71; New York CPLR Rule 4537.

ARTICLE X. CONTENTS OF WRITINGS, RECORDINGS AND PHOTOGRAPHS

Rule 1001. Definitions

For purposes of this article the following definitions are applicable:

(1) Writings and recordings. "Writings" and "recordings" consist of letters, words, or numbers, or their equivalent, set down by handwriting, typewriting, printing, photostating, photographing, magnetic impulse, mechanical or electronic recording, or other form of data compilation.

(2) Photographs. "Photographs" include still photographs, X-ray films, video tapes, and motion pictures.

(3) Original. An "original" of a writing or recording is the writing or recording itself or any counterpart intended to have the same effect by a person executing or issuing it. An "original" of a photograph includes the negative or any print therefrom. If data are

stored in a computer or similar device, any printout or other output readable by sight, shown to reflect the data accurately, is an "original".

(4) Duplicate. A "duplicate" is a counterpart produced by the same impression as the original, or from the same matrix, or by means of photography, including enlargements and miniatures, or by mechanical or electronic re-recording, or by chemical reproduction, or by other equivalent techniques which accurately reproduces the original.

ADVISORY COMMITTEE NOTES
1972 Proposed Rules

In an earlier day, when discovery and other related procedures were strictly limited, the misleading named "best evidence rule" afforded substantial guarantees against inaccuracies and fraud by its insistence upon production or original documents.

The great enlargement of the scope of discovery and related procedures in recent times has measurably reduced the need for the rule. Nevertheless important areas of usefulness persist: discovery of documents outside the jurisdiction may require substantial outlay of time and money; the unanticipated document may not practically be discoverable; criminal cases have built-in limitations on discovery. Cleary and Strong, The Best Evidence Rule: An Evaluation in Context, 51 Iowa L.Rev. 825 (1966).

Note to Paragraph (1). Traditionally the rule requiring the original centered upon accumulations of data and expressions affecting legal relations set forth in words and figures. this meant that the rule was one essentially related to writings. Present day techniques have expanded methods of storing data, yet the essential form which the information ultimately assumes for usable purposes is words and figures. Hence the considerations underlying the rule dictate its expansion to include computers, photographic systems, and other modern developments.

Note to Paragraph (3). In most instances, what is an original will be self-evident and further refinement will be unnecessary. However, in some instances particularized definition is required. A carbon copy of a contract executed in duplicate becomes an original, as does a sales ticket carbon copy given to a customer. While strictly speaking the original of a photograph might be thought to be only the negative, practicality and common usage require that any print from the negative be regarded as an original. Similarly, practicality and usage confer the status of original upon any computer printout. *Transport Indemnity Co. v. Seib,* 178 Neb. 253, 132 N.W.2d 871 (1965).

Note to Paragraph (4). The definition describes "copies" produced by methods possessing an accuracy which virtually eliminates the possibility of error. Copies thus produced are given the status of originals in large measure by Rule 1003, *infra.* Copies subsequently produced manually, whether handwritten or typed, are not within the definition. It should be noted that what is an original for some purposes may be a duplicate for others. Thus a bank's microfilm record of checks cleared is the original as a record. However, a print offered as a copy of a check whose contents are in controversy is a duplicate. This result is substantially consistent with 28 U.S.C. § 1732(b). Compare 26 U.S.C. § 7513(c), giving full status as originals to photographic reproductions of tax returns and other documents, made by authority of the Secretary of the Treasury, and 44 U.S.C. § 399(a), giving original status to photographic copies in the National Archives.

Rule 1002. Requirement of Original

To prove the content of a writing, recording, or photograph, the original writing, recording, or photograph is required, except as otherwise provided in these rules or by Act of Congress.

ADVISORY COMMITTEE NOTES

1972 Proposed Rules

The rule is the familiar one requiring production of the original of a document to prove its contents, expanded to include writings, recordings, and photographs, as defined in Rule 1001(1) and (2), *supra.*

Application of the rule requires a resolution of the question whether contents are sought to be proved. Thus an event may be proved by nondocumentary evidence, even though a written record of it was made. If, however, the event is sought to be proved by the written record, the rule applies. For example, payment may be proved without producing the written receipt which was given. Earnings may be proved without producing books of account in which they are entered. McCormick § 198; 4 Wigmore § 1245. Nor does the rule apply to testimony that books or records have been examined and found not to contain any reference to a designated matter.

The assumption should not be made that the rule will come into operation on every occasion when use is made of a photo-graph in evidence. On the contrary, the rule will seldom apply to ordinary photographs. In most instances a party *wishes* to introduce the item and the question raised is the propriety of receiving it in evidence. Cases in which an offer is made of the testimony of a witness as to what he saw in a photograph or motion picture, without producing the same, are most unusual. The usual course is for a witness on the stand to identify the photograph or motion picture as a correct representation of events which he saw or of a scene with which he is familiar. In fact he adopts the picture as his testimony, or, in common parlance, uses the picture to illustrate his testimony. Under these circumstances, no effort is made to prove the contents of the picture, and the rule is inapplicable. Paradis, The Celluloid Witness, 37 U.Colo.L.Rev. 235, 249–251 (1965).

On occasion, however, situations arise in which contents are sought to be proved. Copyright, defamation, and invasion of privacy by photograph or motion picture falls in this category. Similarly as to situations in which the picture is offered as having independent probative value, e.g. automatic photograph of bank robber. See *People v. Doggett,* 83 Cal.App.2d 405, 188 P.2d 792 (1948), photograph of defendants engaged in indecent act; Mouser and Philbin, Photographic Evidence—Is There a Recognized Basis for Admissibility? 8 Hastings L.J. 310 (1957). the most commonly encountered of this latter group is of course, the X ray, with substantial authority calling for production of the original. *Daniels v. Iowa City,* 191 Iowa 811, 183 N.W. 415 (1921); *Cellamare v. Third Acc. Transit Corp.,* 273 App.Div. 260, 77 N.Y.S.2d 91 (1948); *Patrick & Tilman v. Matkin,* 154 Okl. 232, 7 P.2d 414 (1932); *Mendoza v. Rivera,* 78 P.R.R. 569 (1955).

It should be noted, however, that Rule 703, *supra,* allows an expert to give an opinion based on matters not in evidence, and the present rule must be read as being limited accordingly in its application. Hospital records which may be admitted as business records under Rule 803(6) commonly contain reports interpreting X-rays by the staff radiologist, who qualifies as an expert, and these reports need not be excluded from the records by the instant rule.

The reference to Acts of Congress is made in view of such statutory provisions as 26 U.S.C. § 7513, photographic reproductions of tax returns and documents, made by authority of the Secretary of the Treasury, treated as originals, and 44 U.S.C. § 399(a), photographic copies in National Archives treated as originals.

Rule 1003. Admissibility of Duplicates

A duplicate is admissible to the same extent as an original unless (1) a genuine question is raised as to the authenticity of the original or (2) in the circumstances it would be unfair to admit the duplicate in lieu of the original.

ADVISORY COMMITTEE NOTES

1972 Proposed Rules

When the only concern is with getting the words or other contents before the court with accuracy and precision, then a counterpart serves equally as well as the original, if the counterpart is the product of a method which insures accuracy and genuineness. By definition in Rule 1001(4), *supra,* a "duplicate" possesses this character.

Therefore, if no genuine issue exists as to authenticity and no other reason exists for requiring the original, a duplicate is admissible under the rule. This position finds support in the decisions, *Myrick v. United States,* 332 F.2d 279 (5th Cir.1964), no error in admitting photostatic copies of checks instead of original microfilm in absence of suggestion to trial judge that photostats were incorrect; *Johns v. United States,* 323 F.2d 421 (5th Cir.1963), not error to admit concededly accurate tape recording made from original wire recording; *Sauget v. Johnston,* 315 F.2d 816 (9th Cir.1963), not error to admit copy of agreement when opponent had original and did not on appeal claim any discrepancy. Other reasons for acquiring the original may be present when only a part of the original is reproduced and the remainder is needed for cross-examination or may disclose matters qualifying the part offered or otherwise useful to the opposing party. *United States v. Alexander*, 326 F.2d 736 (4th Cir.1964). And see *Toho Bussan Kaisha, Ltd. v. American President Lines, Ltd.*, 265 F.2d 418, 76 A.L.R.2d 1344 (2d Cir.1959).

1974 Enactment

The Committee approved this Rule in the form submitted by the Court, with the expectation that the courts would be liberal in deciding that a "genuine question is raised as to the authenticity of the original." House Report No. 93–650.

Rule 1004. Admissibility of Other Evidence of Contents

The original is not required, and other evidence of the contents of a writing, recording, or photograph is admissible if—

(1) Originals lost or destroyed. All originals are lost or have been destroyed, unless the proponent lost or destroyed them in bad faith; or

(2) Original not obtainable. No original can be obtained by any available judicial process or procedure; or

(3) Original in possession of opponent. At a time when an original was under the control of the party against whom offered, that party was put on notice, by the pleadings or otherwise, that the contents would be a subject of proof at the hearing, and that party does not produce the original at the hearing; or

(4) Collateral matters. The writing, recording, or photograph is not closely related to a controlling issue.

ADVISORY COMMITTEE NOTES

1972 Proposed Rules

Basically the rule requiring the production of the original as proof of contents has developed as a rule of preference: if failure to produce the original is satisfactorily explained, secondary evidence is admissible. The instant rule specifies the circumstances under which production of the original is excused.

The rule recognizes no "degrees" of secondary evidence. While strict logic might call for extending the principle of preference beyond simply preferring the original, the formulation of a hierarchy of preferences and a procedure for making it effective is believed to involve unwarranted complexities. Most, if not all, that would be accomplished by an extended scheme of preferences will, in any event, be achieved through the normal motivation of a party to present the most convincing evidence possible and the arguments and procedures available to his opponent if he does not. Compare McCormick § 207.

Note to Paragraph (1). Loss or destruction of the original, unless due to bad faith of the proponent, is a satisfactory explanation of nonproduction. McCormick § 201.

Note to Paragraph (2). When the original is in the possession of a third person, inability to procure it from him by resort to process or other judicial procedure is a sufficient explanation of nonproduction. Judicial procedure includes subpoena duces tecum as an incident to the taking of a deposition in another jurisdiction. No further showing is required. See McCormick § 202.

Note to Paragraph (3). A party who has an original in his control has no need for the protection of the rule if put on notice that proof of contents will be made. He can ward off secondary evidence by offering the original. The notice procedure here provided is not to be confused with orders to produce or other discovery procedures, as the purpose of the procedure under this rule is to afford the opposite party an opportunity to produce the original, not to compel him to do so. McCormick § 203.

Note to Paragraph (4). While difficult to define with precision, situations arise in which no good purpose is served by production of the original. Examples are the newspaper in an action for the price of publishing defendant's advertisement, *Foster–Holcomb Investment Co. v. Little Rock Publishing Co.*, 151 Ark. 449, 236 S.W. 597 (1922), and the streetcar transfer of plaintiff claiming status as a passenger, *Chicago City Ry. Co. v. Carroll*, 206 Ill. 318, 68 N.E. 1087 (1903). Numerous cases are collected in McCormick § 200, p. 412, n. 1.

1974 Enactment

Note to Paragraph (1). The Committee approved Rule 1004(1) in the form submitted to Congress. However, the Committee intends that loss or destruction of an original by another person at the instigation of the proponent should be considered as tantamount to loss or destruction in bad faith by the proponent himself. House Report No. 93–650.

Rule 1005. Public Records

The contents of an official record, or of a document authorized to be recorded or filed and actually recorded or filed, including data compilations in any form, if otherwise admissible, may be proved by copy, certified as correct in accordance with rule 902 or testified to be correct by a witness who has compared it with the original. If a copy which complies with the foregoing cannot be obtained by the exercise of reasonable diligence, then other evidence of the contents may be given.

ADVISORY COMMITTEE NOTES

1972 Proposed Rules

Public records call for somewhat different treatment. Removing them from their usual place of keeping would be attended by serious inconvenience to the public and to the custodian. As a consequence judicial decisions and statutes commonly hold that no explanation need be given for failure to produce the original of a public record. McCormick § 204; 4 Wigmore §§ 1215–1228. This blanket dispensation from producing or accounting for the original would open the door to the introduction of every kind of secondary evidence of contents of public records were it not for the preference given certified or compared copies. Recognition of degrees of secondary evidence in this situation is an appropriate *quid pro quo* for not applying the requirement of producing the original.

The provisions of 28 U.S.C. § 1733(b) apply only to departments or agencies of the United States. The rule, however, applies to public records generally and is comparable in scope in this respect to Rule 44(a) of the Rules of Civil Procedure.

Rule 1006. Summaries

The contents of voluminous writings, recordings, or photographs which cannot conveniently be examined in court may be presented in the form of a chart, summary, or calculation. The originals, or duplicates, shall be made available for examination or copying, or both, by other parties at reasonable time and place. The court may order that they be produced in court.

ADVISORY COMMITTEE NOTES

1972 Proposed Rules

The admission of summaries of voluminous books, records, or documents offers the only practicable means of making their contents available to judge and jury. The rule recognizes this practice, with appropriate safeguards. 4 Wigmore § 1230.

Complete Annotation Materials, see Title 28 U.S.C.A.

Rule 1007.   Testimony or Written Admission of Party

Contents of writings, recordings, or photographs may be proved by the testimony or deposition of the party against whom offered or by that party's written admission, without accounting for the nonproduction of the original.

ADVISORY COMMITTEE NOTES
1972 Proposed Rules

While the parent case, *Slatterie v. Pooley*, 6 M. & W. 664, 151 Eng.Rep. 579 (Exch.1840), allows proof of contents by evidence of an oral admission by the party against whom offered, without accounting for nonproduction of the original, the risk of inaccuracy is substantial and the decision is at odds with the purpose of the rule giving preference to the original. See 4 Wigmore § 1255. The instant rule follows Professor McCormick's suggestion of limiting this use of admissions to those made in the course of giving testimony or in writing. McCormick § 208, p. 424. The limitation, of course, does not call for excluding evidence of an oral admission when nonproduction of the original has been accounted for and secondary evidence generally has become admissible. Rule 1004, supra.

A similar provision is contained in New Jersey Evidence Rule 70(1)(h).

Rule 1008.   Functions of Court and Jury

When the admissibility of other evidence of contents of writings, recordings, or photographs under these rules depends upon the fulfillment of a condition of fact, the question whether the condition has been fulfilled is ordinarily for the court to determine in accordance with the provisions of rule 104. However, when an issue is raised (a) whether the asserted writing ever existed, or (b) whether another writing, recording, or photograph produced at the trial is the original, or (c) whether other evidence of contents correctly reflects the contents, the issue is for the trier of fact to determine as in the case of other issues of fact.

ADVISORY COMMITTEE NOTES
1972 Proposed Rules

Most preliminary questions of fact in connection with applying the rule preferring the original as evidence of contents are for the judge, under the general principles announced in Rule 104, *supra*. Thus, the question whether the loss of the originals has been established, or of the fulfillment of other conditions specified in Rule 1004, supra, is for the judge. However, questions may arise which go beyond the mere administration of the rule preferring the original and into the merits of the controversy. For example, plaintiff offers secondary evidence of the contents of an alleged contract, after first introducing evidence of loss of the original, and defendant counters with evidence that no such contract was ever executed. If the judge decides that the contract was never executed and excludes the secondary evidence, the case is at an end without ever going to the jury on a central issue. Levin, Authentication and Content of Writings, 10 Rutgers L.Rev. 632, 644 (1956). The latter portion of the instant rule is designed to insure treatment of these situations as raising jury questions. The decision is not one for uncontrolled discretion of the jury but is subject to the control exercised generally by the judge over jury determinations. See Rule 104(b), *supra*.

For similar provisions, see Uniform Rule 70(2); Kansas Code of Civil Procedure § 60–467(b); New Jersey Evidence Rule 70(2), (3).

ARTICLE XI.   MISCELLANEOUS RULES

Rule 1101.   Applicability of Rules

(a) Courts and judges.   These rules apply to the United States district courts, the District Court of Guam, the District Court of the Virgin Islands, the District Court for the Northern Mariana Islands, the United States courts of appeals, the United States Claims Court, and to United States bankruptcy judges and United States magistrate judges, in the actions, cases, and proceedings and to the extent hereinafter set forth. The terms "judge" and "court" in these rules include United States bankruptcy judges and United States magistrate judges.

(b) Proceedings generally.   These rules apply generally to civil actions and proceedings, including admiralty and maritime cases, to criminal cases and proceedings, to contempt proceedings except those in which the court may act summarily, and to proceedings and cases under title 11, United States Code.

(c) Rule of privilege.   The rule with respect to privileges applies at all stages of all actions, cases, and proceedings.

(d) Rules inapplicable.   The rules (other than with respect to privileges) do not apply in the following situations:

(1) **Preliminary questions of fact.**   The determination of questions of fact preliminary to admissibility of evidence when the issue is to be determined by the court under rule 104.

(2) **Grand jury.**   Proceedings before grand juries.

(3) **Miscellaneous proceedings.**   Proceedings for extradition or rendition; preliminary examinations in criminal cases; sentencing, or granting or revoking probation; issuance of warrants for arrest, criminal summonses, and search warrants; and proceedings with respect to release on bail or otherwise.

(e) Rules applicable in part.   In the following proceedings these rules apply to the extent that matters of evidence are not provided for in the statutes which govern procedure therein or in other rules prescribed by the Supreme Court pursuant to statutory authority: the trial of misdemeanors and other petty offenses before United States magistrate judges; review of agency actions when the facts are subject to trial de novo under section 706(2)(F) of title 5, United States Code; review of orders of the Secretary of Agriculture under section 2 of the Act entitled "An Act to authorize association of producers of agricultural products" approved February 18, 1922 (7 U.S.C. 292), and under sections 6 and 7(c) of the Perishable Agricultural Commodities Act, 1930 (7 U.S.C. 499f, 499g(c)); naturalization and revocation of naturalization under sections 310–318 of the Immigration and Nationality Act (8 U.S.C. 1421–1429); prize proceedings in admiralty under sections 7651–7681 of title 10, United States Code; review of orders of the Secretary of the Interior under section 2 of the Act entitled "An Act authorizing associations of producers of aquatic products" approved June 25, 1934 (15 U.S.C. 522); review of orders of petroleum control boards under section 5 of the Act entitled "An Act to regulate interstate and foreign commerce in petroleum and its products by prohibiting the shipment in such commerce of petroleum and its products produced in violation of State law, and for other purposes", approved February 22, 1935 (15 U.S.C. 715d); actions for fines, penalties, or forfeitures under part V of title IV of the Tariff Act of 1930 (19 U.S.C. 1581–1624), or under the Anti–Smuggling Act (19 U.S.C. 1701–1711); criminal libel for condemnation, exclusion of imports, or other proceedings under the Federal Food, Drug, and Cosmetic Act (21 U.S.C. 301–392); disputes between seamen under sections 4079, 4080, and 4081 of the Revised Statutes (22 U.S.C. 256–258); habeas corpus under sections 2241–2254 of title 28, United States Code; motions to vacate, set aside or correct sentence under section 2255 of title 28, United States Code; actions for penalties for refusal to transport destitute seamen under section 4578 of the Revised Statutes (46 U.S.C. 679); actions against the United States under the Act entitled "An Act authorizing suits against the United States in admiralty for damage caused by and salvage service rendered to public vessels belonging to the United States, and for other purposes", approved March 3, 1925 (46 U.S.C. 781–790), as implemented by section 7730 of title 10, United States Code.

(Pub.L. 93–595, § 1, Jan. 2, 1975, 88 Stat. 1947; Pub.L. 94–149, § 1(14), Dec. 12, 1975, 89 Stat. 806; Pub.L. 95–598, Title II, § 251, Nov. 6, 1978, 92 Stat. 2673; Pub.L. 97–164, Title I, § 142, Apr. 2, 1982, 96 Stat. 45; Mar. 2, 1987, eff. Oct. 1, 1987; Apr. 25, 1988, eff. Nov. 1, 1988; Pub.L. 100–690, Title VII, § 7075(c), Nov. 18, 1988, 102 Stat. 4405; Apr. 22, 1993, eff. Dec. 1, 1993.)

ADVISORY COMMITTEE NOTES
1972 Proposed Rules

Note to Subdivision (a). The various enabling acts contain differences in phraseology in their descriptions of the courts over which the Supreme Court's power to make rules of practice and procedure extends. The act concerning civil actions, as amended in 1966, refers to "the district courts * * * of the United States in civil actions, including admiralty and maritime cases. * * *" 28 U.S.C. § 2072, Pub.L. 89–773, § 1, 80 Stat. 1323. The bankruptcy authorization is for rules of practice and procedure "under the Bankruptcy Act." 28 U.S.C. § 2075, Pub.L. 88–623, § 1, 78 Stat. 1001. The Bankruptcy Act in turn creates bankruptcy courts of "the United States district courts and the district courts of the Territories and possessions to which this title is or may hereafter be applicable." 11 U.S.C. §§ 1(10), 11(a). The provision as to criminal rules up to and including verdicts applies to "criminal cases and proceedings to punish for criminal contempt of court in the United States district courts, in the district courts for the districts of the Canal Zone and Virgin Islands, in the Supreme Court of Puerto Rico, and in proceedings before United States magistrates." 18 U.S.C. § 3771.

These various provisions do not in terms describe the same courts. In congressional usage the phrase "district courts of the United States," without further qualification, traditionally has included the district courts established by Congress in the states under Article III of the Constitution, which are "constitutional" courts, and has not included the territorial courts created under Article IV, Section 3, clause 2, which are "legislative" courts. *Hornbuckle v. Toombs,* 85 U.S. 648, 21 L.Ed. 966 (1873). However, any doubt as to the inclusion of the District Court for the District of Columbia in the phrase is laid at rest by the provisions of the Judicial Code constituting the judicial districts, 28 U.S.C. § 81 et seq., creating district courts therein, id. § 132, and specifically providing that the term "district court of the United States" means the court so constituted. *Id.* § 451. The District of Columbia is included. *Id.* § 88. Moreover, when these provisions were enacted, reference to the District of Columbia was deleted from the original civil rules enabling act. 28 U.S.C. § 2072. Likewise Puerto Rico is made a district, with a district court, and included in the term. *Id.* § 119. The

question is simply one of the extent of the authority conferred by Congress. With respect to civil rules it seems clearly to include the district courts in the states, the District Court for the District of Columbia, and the District Court for the District of Puerto Rico.

The bankruptcy coverage is broader. The bankruptcy courts include "the United States district courts," which includes those enumerated above. Bankruptcy courts also include "the district courts of the Territories and possessions to which this title is or may hereafter be applicable." 11 U.S.C. §§ 1(10), 11(a). These courts include the district courts of Guam and the Virgin Islands. 48 U.S.C. §§ 1424(b), 1615. Professor Moore points out that whether the District Court for the District of the Canal Zone is a court of bankruptcy "is not free from doubt in view of the fact that no other statute expressly or inferentially provides for the applicability of the Bankruptcy Act in the Zone." He further observes that while there seems to be little doubt that the Zone is a territory or possession within the meaning of the Bankruptcy Act, 11 U.S.C. § 1(10), it must be noted that the appendix to the Canal Zone Code of 1934 did not list the Act among the laws of the United States applicable to the Zone. 1 Moore's Collier on Bankruptcy ¶ 1.10, pp. 67, 72, n. 25 (14th ed. 1967). The Code of 1962 confers on the district court jurisdiction of:

"(4) actions and proceedings involving laws of the United States applicable to the Canal Zone; and

"(5) other matters and proceedings wherein jurisdiction is conferred by this Code or any other law." Canal Zone Code, 1962, Title 3, § 141.

Admiralty jurisdiction is expressly conferred. *Id.* § 142. General powers are conferred on the district court, "if the course of proceeding is not specifically prescribed by this Code, by the statute, or by applicable rule of the Supreme Court of the United States * * *" *Id.* § 279. Neither these provisions nor § 1(10) of the Bankruptcy Act ("district courts of the Territories and possessions to which this title is or may hereafter be applicable") furnishes a satisfactory answer as to the status of the District Court for the District of the Canal Zone as a court of bankruptcy. However, the fact is that this court exercises no bankruptcy jurisdiction in practice.

The criminal rules enabling act specified United States district courts, district courts for the districts of the Canal Zone and the Virgin Islands, the Supreme Court of the Commonwealth of Puerto Rico, and proceedings before United States commissioners. Aside from the addition of commissioners, now magistrates, this scheme differs from the bankruptcy pattern in that it makes no mention of the District Court of Guam but by specific mention removes the Canal Zone from the doubtful list.

The further difference in including the Supreme Court of the Commonwealth of Puerto Rico seems not to be significant for present purposes, since the Supreme Court of the Commonwealth of Puerto Rico is an appellate court. The Rules of Criminal Procedure have not been made applicable to it, as being unneeded and inappropriate, Rule 54(a) of the Federal Rules of Criminal Procedure, and the same approach is indicated with respect to rules of evidence.

If one were to stop at this point and frame a rule governing the applicability of the proposed rules of evidence in terms of the authority conferred by the three enabling acts, an irregular pattern would emerge as follows:

Civil actions, including admiralty and maritime cases—district courts in the states, District of Columbia, and Puerto Rico.

Bankruptcy—same as civil actions, plus Guam and Virgin Islands.

Criminal cases—same as civil actions, plus Canal Zone and Virgin Islands (but not Guam).

This irregular pattern need not, however, be accepted. Originally the Advisory Committee on the Rules of Civil Procedure took the position that, although the phrase "district courts of the United States" did not include territorial courts, provisions in the organic laws of Puerto Rico and Hawaii would make the rules applicable to the district courts thereof, though this would not be so as to Alaska, the Virgin Islands, or the Canal Zone, whose organic acts contained no corresponding provisions. At the suggestion of the Court, however, the Advisory Committee struck from its notes a statement to the above effect. 2 Moore's Federal Practice ¶ 1.07 (2nd ed. 1967); 1 Barron and Holtzoff, Federal Practice and Procedure § 121 (Wright ed. 1960). Congress thereafter by various enactments provided that the rules and future amendments thereto should apply to the district courts of Hawaii, 53 Stat. 841 (1939), Puerto Rico, 54 Stat. 22 (1940), Alaska, 63 Stat. 445 (1949), Guam, 64 Stat. 384–390 (1950), and the Virgin Islands, 68 Stat. 497, 507 (1954). The original enabling act for rules of criminal procedure specifically mentioned the district courts of the Canal Zone and the Virgin Islands. The Commonwealth of Puerto Rico was blanketed in by creating its court a "district court of the United States" as previously described. Although Guam is not mentioned in either the enabling act or in the expanded definition of "district court of the United States," the Supreme Court in 1956 amended Rule 54(a) to state that the Rules of Criminal Procedure are applicable in Guam. The Court took this step following the enactment of legislation by Congress in 1950 that rules theretofore or thereafter promulgated by the Court in civil cases, admiralty, criminal cases and bankruptcy should apply to the District Court of Guam, 48 U.S.C. § 1424(b), and two Ninth Circuit decisions upholding the applicability of the Rules of Criminal Procedure to Guam. *Pugh v. United States,* 212 F.2d 761 (9th Cir.1954); *Hatchett v. Guam,* 212 F.2d 767 (9th Cir.1954); Orfield, The Scope of the Federal Rules of Criminal Procedure, 38 U. of Det.L.J. 173, 187 (1960).

From this history, the reasonable conclusion is that Congressional enactment of a provision that rules and future amendments shall apply in the courts of a territory or possession is the equivalent of mention in an enabling act and that a rule on scope and applicability may properly be drafted accordingly. Therefore the pattern set by Rule 54 of the Federal Rules of Criminal Procedure is here followed.

The substitution of magistrates in lieu of commissioners is made in pursuance of the Federal Magistrates Act, P.L. 90–578, approved October 17, 1968, 82 Stat. 1107.

Note to Subdivision (b). Subdivision (b) is a combination of the language of the enabling acts, supra, with respect to the kinds of proceedings in which the making of rules is authorized. It is subject to the qualifications expressed in the subdivisions which follow.

Note to Subdivision (c). Subdivision (c) singling out the rules of privilege for special treatment, is made necessary by the limited applicability of the remaining rules.

Note to Subdivision (d). The rule is not intended as an expression as to when due process or other constitutional provisions may require an evidentiary hearing. Paragraph (1) restates, for convenience, the provisions of the second sentence of Rule 104(a), *supra.* See Advisory Committee's Note to that rule.

(2) While some states have statutory requirements that indictments be based on "legal evidence," and there is some case law to the effect that the rules of evidence apply to grand jury proceedings, 1 Wigmore § 4(5), the Supreme Court has not accepted this view. In *Costello v. United States,* 350 U.S. 359, 76 S.Ct. 406, 100 L.Ed. 397 (1965), the Court refused to allow an indictment to be attacked, for either constitutional or policy reasons, on the ground that only hearsay evidence was presented.

"It would run counter to the whole history of the grand jury institution, in which laymen conduct their inquiries unfettered by technical rules. Neither justice nor the concept of a fair trial requires such a change." *Id.* at 364. The rule as drafted does not deal with the evidence required to support an indictment.

(3) The rule exempts preliminary examinations in criminal cases. Authority as to the applicability of the rules of evidence to preliminary examinations has been meagre and conflicting. Goldstein, The State and the Accused: Balance of Advantage in Criminal Procedure, 69 Yale L.J. 1149, 1168, n. 53 (1960); Comment, Preliminary Hearings on Indictable Offenses in Phila-

delphia, 106 U. of Pa.L.Rev. 589, 592–593 (1958). Hearsay testimony is, however, customarily received in such examinations. Thus in a Dyer Act case, for example, an affidavit may properly be used in a preliminary examination to prove ownership of the stolen vehicle, thus saving the victim of the crime the hardship of having to travel twice to a distant district for the sole purpose of testifying as to ownership. It is believed that the extent of the applicability of the Rules of Evidence to preliminary examinations should be appropriately dealt with by the Federal Rules of Criminal Procedure which regulate those proceedings.

Extradition and rendition proceedings are governed in detail by statute. 18 U.S.C. §§ 3181–3195. They are essentially administrative in character. Traditionally the rules of evidence have not applied. 1 Wigmore § 4(6). Extradition proceedings are accepted from the operation of the Rules of Criminal Procedure. Rule 54(b)(5) of Federal Rules of Criminal Procedure.

The rules of evidence have not been regarded as applicable to sentencing or probation proceedings, where great reliance is placed upon the presentence investigation and report. Rule 32(c) of the Federal Rules of Criminal Procedure requires a presentence investigation and report in every case unless the court otherwise directs. In *Williams v. New York,* 337 U.S. 241, 69 S.Ct. 1079, 93 L.Ed. 1337 (1949), in which the judge overruled a jury recommendation of life imprisonment and imposed a death sentence, the Court said that due process does not require confrontation or cross-examination in sentencing or passing on probation, and that the judge has broad discretion as to the sources and types of information relied upon. Compare the recommendation that the substance of all derogatory information be disclosed to the defendant, in A.B.A. Project on Minimum Standards for Criminal Justice, Sentencing Alternatives and Procedures § 4.4, Tentative Draft (1967, Sobeloff, Chm.). Williams was adhered to in *Specht v. Patterson,* 386 U.S. 605, 87 S.Ct. 1209, 18 L.Ed.2d 326 (1967), but not extended to a proceeding under the Colorado Sex Offenders Act, which was said to be a new charge leading in effect to punishment, more like the recidivist statutes where opportunity must be given to be heard on the habitual criminal issue.

Warrants for arrest, criminal summonses, and search warrants are issued upon complaint or affidavit showing probable cause. Rules 4(a) and 41(c) of the Federal Rules of Criminal Procedure. The nature of the proceedings makes application of the formal rules of evidence inappropriate and impracticable.

Criminal contempts are punishable summarily if the judge certifies that he saw or heard the contempt and that it was committed in the presence of the court. Rule 42(a) of the Federal Rules of Criminal Procedure. The circumstances which preclude application of the rules of evidence in this situation are not present, however, in other cases of criminal contempt.

Proceedings with respect to release on bail or otherwise do not call for application of the rules of evidence. The governing statute specifically provides:

"Information stated in, or offered in connection with, any order entered pursuant to this section need not conform to the rules pertaining to the admissibility of evidence in a court of law." 18 U.S.C.A. § 3146(f). This provision is consistent with the type of inquiry contemplated in A.B.A. Project on Minimum Standards for Criminal Justice, Standards Relating to Pretrial Release, § 4.5(b), (c), p. 16 (1968). The references to the weight of the evidence against the accused, in Rule 46(a)(1), (c) of the Federal Rules of Criminal Procedure and in 18 U.S.C.A. § 3146(b), as a factor to be considered, clearly do not have in view evidence introduced at a hearing under the rules of evidence.

The rule does not exempt habeas corpus proceedings. The Supreme Court held in *Walker v. Johnston,* 312 U.S. 275, 61 S.Ct. 574, 85 L.Ed. 830 (1941), that the practice of disposing of matters of fact on affidavit, which prevailed in some circuits, did not "satisfy the command of the statute that the judge shall proceed 'to determine the facts of the case, by hearing the testimony and arguments.'" This view accords with the emphasis in *Townsend v. Sain,* 372 U.S. 293, 83 S.Ct. 745, 9 L.Ed.2d

770 (1963), upon trial-type proceedings, *id.* 311, 83 S.Ct. 745, with demeanor evidence as a significant factor, *id.* 322, 83 S.Ct. 745, in applications by state prisoners aggrieved by unconstitutional detentions. Hence subdivision (3) applies the rules to habeas corpus proceedings to the extent not inconsistent with the statute.

Note to Subdivision (e). In a substantial number of special proceedings, *ad hoc* evaluation has resulted in the promulgation of particularized evidentiary provisions, by Act of Congress or by rule adopted by the Supreme Court. Well adapted to the particular proceedings, though not apt candidates for inclusion in a set of general rules, they are left undisturbed. Otherwise, however, the rules of evidence are applicable to the proceedings enumerated in the subdivision.

1974 Enactment

Note to Subdivision (a). Subdivision (a) as submitted to the Congress, in stating the courts and judges to which the Rules of Evidence apply, omitted the Court of Claims and commissioners of that Court. At the request of the Court of Claims, the Committee amended the Rule to include the Court and its commissioners within the purview of the Rules.

Note to Subdivision (b). Subdivision (b) was amended merely to substitute positive law citations for those which were not. House Report No. 93–650.

Rule 1102.   Amendments

Amendments to the Federal Rules of Evidence may be made as provided in section 2072 of title 28 of the United States Code.

Rule 1103.   Title

These rules may be known and cited as the Federal Rules of Evidence.

Notes on the Confrontation Clause and the Hearsay Rule

Crawford v. Washington:

On March 8, 2004 the United States Supreme Court, in a 7–2 decision, announced a new approach to examining Confrontation Clause issues in criminal cases. *Crawford v. Washington*, 541 U.S. 36, 124 S.Ct. 1354, 158 L.Ed.2d 177 (2004).

The old, "*Roberts*" rule: (*Ohio v. Roberts*, 448 U.S. 56 (1980))—Hearsay offered by the prosecution against a criminal defendant at trial is inadmissible under the Confrontation Clause of the Sixth Amendment unless:

— the hearsay declarant testifies at trial; or

— the hearsay is admissible under a "firmly rooted" hearsay exception; or

— the trial judge finds that the hearsay exhibits "particularized guarantees of trustworthiness."

Crawford v. Washington did not overrule or abandon *Roberts* in its entirety. *Roberts* still applies to "non-testimonial" hearsay—at least for now.

The new, "*Crawford*" rule: If hearsay offered by the prosecution against a criminal defendant at trial is deemed "testimonial," it is inadmissible under the Confrontation Clause of the Sixth Amendment (regardless of how many hearsay exceptions it qualifies under) unless:

— the hearsay declarant testifies at trial; or

— the accused had an opportunity to cross-examine the declarant regarding the statement prior to trial *and* the declarant is now unavailable to testify at trial.

What is a "testimonial statement?"–The majority opinion declares that a comprehensive definition of "testimonial statement" must wait till a later date but the Court did give some hints.

"Testimonial statements" are those "made under circumstances which would lead an objective witness reasonably to believe that the statement would be available for use at a later trial." *Crawford* at 1364.

Examples include "ex parte in-court testimony [presumably includes grand jury testimony and plea allocutions] . . . affidavits, custodial examinations, . . . or similar pretrial statements that declarants would reasonably expect to be used prosecutorially. . . . " *Id.* at 1364, 1374.

"Statements taken by police officers in the course of interrogations are also testimonial." *Id.* at 1364.

There are two basic concerns driving confrontation clause analysis and the presence or absence of those concerns should determine whether we treat statements as testimonial or not:

1. Did the State solicit or gather the statement for purposes of criminal prosecution? (Concern: that the State actors might manipulate or coerce the witness into making a statement that will support the prosecution *or* that the State actors may purposely misrepresent what the witness said).

2. Would the declarant typically be aware that his or her statements might subject someone to prosecution? (Concern: that the declarant may be making false accusations for illegitimate personal reasons).

If an out-of-court statement is offered for a relevant nonhearsay use, it does not involve the Confrontation Clause. *Crawford* at 1369, n.9.

The Confrontation Clause does not apply to the admission of the accused's own statements. The accused cannot complain that he cannot confront himself. *United States v. Lopez*, 380 F.3d 538 (1st Cir. 2004).

There is no Confrontation Clause issue when the person who made the out-of-court statement testifies and is available for cross-examination. *Crawford* at 1369, n.9; *California v. Green*, 399 U.S. 149, 90 S.Ct. 1930, 26 L.Ed.2d 489 (1970).

Where a defendant has engaged or acquiesced in wrongdoing that was intended to, and did, procure the unavailability of the declarant as a witness, the defendant forfeits his right to confront and cross-examine that witness. *See*, Federal Rule of Evidence 804(b)(6); *Crawford*, at 1370.

Bruton v. United States

When the accused and a co-conspirator are tried together, the co-conspirator's confession generally is not admissible, even with a limiting instruction. *Bruton v. United States*, 391 U.S. 123, 88 S.Ct. 1620, 20 L.Ed.2d 476 (1968). There are exceptions in the following circumstances:

(1) if the co-conspirator testifies and is available for cross-examination; *Cruz v. New York*, 481 U.S. 186, 107 S.Ct. 1714, 95 L.Ed.2d 162 (1987);

(2) if the co-conspirator's confession does not directly incriminate the defendant; *Gray v. Maryland*, 523 U.S. 185, 118 S.Ct. 1151, 140 L.Ed.2d 294 (1998); or,

(3) if the defendant's confession is admissible and the co-conspirator's confession is no more incriminating than the defendant's own confession, then it is harmless error to admit both confessions in the same trial. *Cruz v. New York*, 481 U.S. 186, 107 S.Ct. 1714, 95 L.Ed.2d 162 (1987).

A Hearsay Flow Chart

Is it an out-of-court statement? (or nonverbal conduct that was intended at the time to communicate something?)

YES	NO
(continue)	(Stop: no hearsay issues)

Is one party offering an opposing party's out-of-court statement?

YES	NO
(Stop: it is an admission)*	(continue)

Regardless of what the proponent says are his reasons for offering the statement, would the proponent want the jury to assume that the speaker was not lying or mistaken when he made the statement and that the statement is true?

YES	NO
(continue)	(Stop: no hearsay uses)

If we assume that the person who made the statement had no idea what he was saying (or writing) at the time, would the statement still be relevant to prove motive, notice, explain conduct, etc.?

YES	NO
(Stop: has a nonhearsay use)**	(continue)

Does the party offering the statement claim that it demonstrates something relevant about the speaker's state of mind?

YES	NO
(continue)	(Stop: the statement is hearsay and inadmissible unless it falls under a hearsay exception)

If we assume that the facts asserted in the statement are independently and incontrovertibly proven, would the statement add anything of relevance or merely be cumulative?

ADDED RELEVANCE	MERELY CUMULATIVE
(Stop: has a nonhearsay use)***	(Stop: the statement is hearsay and inadmissible unless it falls under a hearsay exception)

---

* In a criminal case, the accused cannot offer statements as admissions of "The State."

** Evidence that has a relevant nonhearsay use is admissible with a limiting instruction, if requested, and is subject to the opponent's request that the court exclude the statement if the probative value of the statement for its nonhearsay use is substantially outweighed by the unfair prejudicial effect of its hearsay use.

*** If the statement is offered to prove that the speaker knew (not just believed) a certain fact to be true, there would have to be independent evidence of the underlying fact. For example, if Bob's out-of-court statement that Mary lives on Western Ave. is offered to prove that Bob knew where Mary lived, there would need to be independent evidence that Mary in fact did live on Western Ave.

Some Comments on Direct and Cross–Examination

Direct Examinations

There are three basic keys to effective direct examinations. First, thoroughly prepare the witness. This does not mean simply going over the questions you plan to ask the witness. Not all witnesses are alike and one style of direct examination does not fit all. Counsel must first evaluate the strengths and weaknesses of each particular witness and his or her testimony and then structure the direct examination and the use of any exhibits and demonstrations to maximize the clarity and persuasiveness of that witness's testimony.

Second, counsel must be prepared on all the potential evidentiary issues and try to clear away as many issues as possible with motions in limine. If there is a pre-trial hearing and order, the admission of documents and other exhibits can be determined at that time. If there is no pre-trial hearing or order, counsel in civil cases should use Requests for Admissions to establish the authenticity and/or admissibility of documents and exhibits pre-trial. Counsel's goal is to clear the evidentiary path so that the witness can testify without the interruptions and distractions of evidentiary objections.

Third, let the witness be the star of the direct examination. While some witnesses need to be kept on short reins while testifying, most are quite able to look at the jury and talk to them clearly and naturally about what they know. Do not ask a witness leading questions on direct examination unless absolutely necessary. It not only is likely to draw a sustainable objection but it also weakens both the clarity and persuasiveness of the witness's testimony. In the best direct examinations, the lawyer is like a conductor and his witness is the orchestra. The lawyer sets the tempo and cues the highs and lows but otherwise it is the witness who makes the music.

Cross-Examination

There are many "keys" to cross-examination and many books and articles on the subject. The following six keys are not exhaustive but are basic.

(1) *Preparation*. You need to know exactly what you realistically expect to establish on cross-examination and how you are going to do it. At a minimum, you should list which facts you need to get from the witness to use in setting up the examination of other witnesses or in closing argument.

(2) *Listen to the Direct Examination*. Counsel prepare for cross based on what they expect witnesses to say but opposing witnesses are often filled with surprises, some pleasant and some not so pleasant. Be prepared to adjust and supplement your cross accordingly.

(3) *Don't Ask Open Ended Questions*. Asking an opposing witness an open ended question invites the witness to, at best, repeat his direct examination or, at worst, reveal additional information damaging to your case that was not developed on direct. You cannot stop a witness from giving a detailed answer to an open ended question as long as the witness is fairly responding to the question.

(4) *Save Your Arguments for Closing*. The cross-examiner collects facts on cross; facts about the witness that reflect on his credibility, facts that might clarify or limit the witness's direct testimony, or other facts about the case. There is a great temptation to show the jury the importance of each fact on cross at the time you acquire it. This temptation leads to violations of what the late Professor Irving Younger called the "one question too many" rule. For example, in cross-examining an eyewitness to an event, you want to establish that the witness normally wears glasses but was not doing so at the time in question. Once that fact is established, do not then ask: "So you must have had a hard time seeing what was going on, isn't that true?" This merely invites the witness to defend himself. Never ask an

adverse witness to draw inferences against himself. Save them for closing argument when the opposing witness can no longer respond to your points ..

(5) **Be Afraid**. Many bad things can happen on cross-examination and when they do, the cross-examiner's misery is intensified by the fact that the wounds were self-inflicted. The longer you cross-examine the witness, the greater the likelihood that something bad will happen.

(6) **Don't Get Nasty**. Lawyers, by nature and training, have a greater pain threshold than nonlawyers when it comes to witnessing one person verbally decimate another on the witness stand. What we lawyers might appreciatively call "skillfully going for the jugular," nonlawyers (i.e., jurors) might call "unnecessary roughness."

Cross-examining a witness on a key issue is an intense experience and it is not improper for counsel to show some emotion. But there are two main ways that this can go wrong. First, you cannot raise and sustain a sympathetic emotional pitch for long. Pick your moments. Second, don't get ahead of what the jury is feeling. For example, don't show anger toward a witness's persistent evasiveness until you sense that the jury already has picked up on the evasiveness and has had enough of it themselves. You want the jury to sympathize with you, not the witness. Jurors are never convinced that a witness is lying just because the cross-examiner's face and tone of voice express disbelief.

Good Faith Basis for Questions on Cross

It is often necessary on cross-examination to ask a witness whether a particular fact is true when that fact has not yet been admitted at trial. Indeed, the main purpose of such a question is to get the witness's affirmation of the fact, based on his personal knowledge, and thereby get the fact admitted. However, the very asking of the question in its leading form, as in: "Isn't it true that you saw the accused with blood on his shirt?" suggests that the fact is true. To protect against abuse, the cross-examiner must have a good faith basis to believe that any facts asserted in his question are true *and* that the witness has personal knowledge to confirm those facts.

The cross-examiner does not have to have admissible evidence in hand to support her good faith basis. The opponent can demand a showing of the cross-examiner's good faith basis for the question. The showing should be made outside the hearing of the jury and the trial judge focuses on just two questions: (1) Why does the cross-examiner believe the facts asserted in his question are true? And (2) How can this witness confirm those facts? If the showing of good faith is inadequate because the question was based on rumor and conjecture or because the witness would have no way of confirming the fact, the opponent should move to have the question stricken and the jury instructed to disregard.

Cross-examination and the Hearsay Rule

Cross-examiners sometimes will ask a witness whether it is true that a person made a particular statement or that a document states a particular fact. This is objectionable as hearsay unless:

(1) the out-of-court statement or document already has been admitted into evidence; or

(2) the cross-examiner has a good faith basis to believe that

(a) the out-of-court statement qualifies as nonhearsay or under a hearsay exception; *and*,

(b) the witness on cross has sufficient personal knowledge regarding the statement and the circumstances of its making to lay any foundation required to qualify the statement over a hearsay objection.

A cross-examiner cannot object when his own questions induce a witness to reveal hearsay or other inadmissible evidence. This is one of the reasons why trial counsel are taught to beware of asking open ended questions on cross-examination.

Motions In Limine

Motions in limine may be used in civil or criminal cases and whether and how to handle such motions is within the discretion of the trial judge. Motions in limine are separate from and do not replace motions to suppress or other specific kinds of pre-trial motions in criminal cases.

If a court denies a motion in limine to exclude certain evidence, the objecting party does not have to object again when the evidence is offered at trial. The motion in limine preserves the objection for review on appeal. Federal Rule 103(a).

If the court grants a motion in limine to exclude certain evidence but the evidence nevertheless comes out at trial, the opposing party need not object in front of the jury but may wait until the jury is next out to request relief for the erroneous admission of the evidence.

A trial judge may defer ruling on a motion in limine until trial or issue a "conditional" ruling that stands only until a party invites further consideration of the issue at trial. Counsel must follow up and request a final ruling on the issue when the evidence is offered at trial or else any objection is waived.

Even when a trial judge is disinclined to rule on an issue until he sees the actual trial develop, a motion in limine can prepare the judge for that ruling and clarify whether any reference can be made to the evidence before the court finally rules.

Complex or legally obscure evidentiary issues always should be raised by a motion in limine in order to give counsel the time to carefully brief and argue the issues and to create an adequate record for any appeal.

Counsel often will bring motions in limine on obvious evidentiary points, such as excluding evidence of liability insurance in a civil case. The purpose of these motions is to get a court order that not only rules such evidence inadmissible but orders counsel to instruct their witnesses accordingly, thus decreasing the chances of inadvertent disclosure.

Some Sample Evidentiary Foundations

Authentication of Documents (including E-Mails)

Every document must be marked for identification before a witness is asked any questions about it. Once marked, it should be shown to opposing counsel for brief inspection. (Counsel should make courtesy copies of all exhibits for opposing counsel and the bench). Foundation questions to the witness may not reveal or solicit information about the contents of the document.

In this example, the defendant's witness is an insurance claims adjustor. The writing is a letter from the plaintiff. If the letter is authenticated, it is admissible as an admission.

[Q] Mr. Witness, handing you what has been marked as Defense Exhibit #1 for identification, do you recognize it?

[A] Yes.

[Q] Can you identify it for us?

[A] It is a letter the plaintiff sent to me about his insurance claim.

[Q] How do you know that this letter is from the plaintiff and not someone else?

[A] Well, this letter refers to things that were very specific to his claim and that only he and I discussed.

[Q] Your Honor, I now offer into evidence the document marked as Defense Exhibit #1.

[Opposing counsel may ask to voir dire the witness regarding foundation issues before deciding whether to object to the document].

In the next example, the plaintiff is offering a letter and an e-mail, both written by his deceased spouse. Assume that if they are authenticated, both would qualify for a hearsay exception as statements against interest.

[Q] Mr. Plaintiff, handing you what has been marked as Plaintiff's Exhibit #3 for identification, do you recognize it?

[A] Yes, it is a letter that my wife wrote to her sister.

[Q] Is the letter handwritten or typed?

[A] Handwritten.

[Q] Does the letter include a signature?

[A] Yes.

[Q] Did you have an opportunity during your marriage to become familiar with your wife's handwriting and signature?

[A] Yes I did.

[Q] Looking again at this letter, Plaintiff's Exhibit #3, do you recognize the handwriting and signature in that letter?

[A] Yes I do. It is my late wife's.

[Q] Handing you what has been marked for identification as Plaintiff's Exhibit #4, do you recognize it?

[A] Yes. It is a printed copy of an e-mail that my wife sent to her brother.

[Q] Where did you get this e-mail?

[A] I found it on our home computer and printed a copy.

[Q] Does your computer contain a file of e-mails that have been sent from the computer?

[A] Yes.

[Q] Did you find this e-mail, Plaintiff's Exhibit #4, in that computer file of e-mails that had been written and sent on that computer?

[A] Yes.

[Q] This e-mail is dated May of last year. Who had access to your home computer in May of last year?

[A] Only my wife and I.

[Q] Did you have to use a password to use your home computer?

[A] Yes. Only my wife and I knew it.

[Q] Did your wife ever use the home computer for e-mail?

[A] Yes.

[Q] Did you write this e-mail, Plaintiff's Exhibit #4?

[A] No I did not.

[Q] Your Honor, we offer Plaintiff's Exhibits #3 and #4 into evidence.

Sample Foundation—Authentication of Photos and Videotapes

The prosecution is examining a detective who investigated an armed robbery.

[Q] Did you examine the crime scene that night, after the robbery?

[A] I did.

[Q] Handing you what has been marked for identification as State's Exhibit #4, do you recognize it?

[A] Yes. This is a crime scene photo.

[Q] Is this photo a fair and accurate representation of the store as it appeared after the robbery?

[A] Yes it is.

[Q] Your Honor, we offer State's Exhibit #4 into evidence. . . .

The prosecution now wants to authenticate a videotape of the robbery taken by a surveillance camera in the store. If there is a witness to the robbery, such as a store clerk, that witness can authenticate the video tape in the same was the police officer authenticated the photo, above; namely, establish that the witness was present when the events recorded on the tape took place, establish that the witness has reviewed the tape, and then ask the witness whether the videotape is a fair and accurate representation of the events he witnessed.

But what if there are no witnesses to the robbery available to testify? Most states have statutes or case law supporting the "silent witness rule" which allows authentication of surveillance and other videos when there are no witnesses available to testify at trial.

[Q] Detective, handing you what has been marked for identification as State's Exhibit #5, do you recognize it?

[A] I do.

[Q] What is it?

[A] It is the videotape that I removed from the security system at the store on the night of the robbery.

[Q] Are you familiar with security cameras of the type used by this store?

[A] I am.

[Q] Was this camera automatic or did it need someone to operate it?

[A] It is automatic, points straight at the cash register.

[Q] Does the security camera in this store record the date and time along with whatever events are being taped?

[A] Yes it does. The date and time of the recording appear in the corner.

[Q] Have you reviewed this tape, State's Exhibit #5?

[A] I have.

[Q] Does this tape indicate the date and time at which it was recorded?

[A] It does.

[Q] Does the date and time indicated on this tape cover the evening of May 3, 2004, when this robbery took place?

[A] Yes it does.

174

[Q] Your Honor, we offer State's Exhibit #5 into evidence and request that it be played for the jury at this time.

This is a bare bones foundation for the videotape. The proponent should add any other facts that bolster the identify and integrity of the videotape, both to foreclose successful legal objections by the opponent and to eliminate any juror's doubts about the evidence. For example, if the witness can testify that what he saw on the videotape was consistent with his own physical examination of the scene after the robbery, this should be included in the foundation. Counsel should not race through the technical details. Although most states no longer require proof of chain of custody and the method of recording a videotape, these details can build jury confidence in the evidence and blunt expected attacks by the opposition.

Sample Foundation—Business Record Exception

[Q] Mr. Jones, what is your title at Ace Industries?

[A] I am the plant manager.

[Q] How long have you been the plant manager at Ace Industries?

[A] Eight years.

[Q] Does Ace Industries have a routine practice for recording the shipment of items out of the plant?

[A] Yes we do.

[Q] Are you personally familiar with that system and how it works?

[A] Yes I am.

[Q] Could you briefly describe that system for us?

[A] No truck leaves the warehouse until the dispatcher gives his okay. Before the dispatcher will release a truck, the driver and loader both must initial the entries on the shipping log showing which orders are loaded, the number of the truck, the time, and so forth.

[*Note*: The law requires no details of the record keeping procedure unless the opponent raises specific questions about it. However, if there is or could be any question regarding the reliability or credibility of the record, the jury should be given a full description of the system.]

[Q] Handing you now what has been marked as Plaintiff's Ex. #1 for identification, can you identify it?

[A] Yes. It is a shipment log for Ace Industries.

[Q] How do you recognize it?

[A] Well, I see these all the time at my job and I can tell that these entries relate to shipments out of our plant.

[Q] Was the shipment log, Plaintiff's Ex. #1, made and kept in the regular course of Ace's business?

[A] Yes.

[Q] Is it the routine practice at Ace to make entries in the shipping log at or near the time the shipments go out?

[A] Yes it is.

[Q] Your honor, at this time I offer Plaintiff's Ex #1 into evidence as a business record.

Sample Foundation—Character Witness (Reputation and Opinion)

[Q] Mr. Witness, do you know Sal Smith, the mailman who testified earlier in this case?

[A] Yes I do.

[Q] How do you know him?

[A] He has lived in my neighborhood for over ten years.

[Q] Are you aware of Sal Smith's general reputation in your neighborhood?

[A] Yes I am.

[Q] How have you become aware of Sal Smith's reputation in your neighborhood?

[A] I've talked with my neighbors.

[Q] What is Sal's reputation in your neighborhood?

[A] He has a reputation for being untruthful.

[Q] Mr. Witness, do you have a personal opinion of Mr. Smith's character for truthfulness?

[A] I do.

[Q] And what is your opinion of Mr. Smith's character for truthfulness?

[A] He is a very untruthful person.

[Q] Thank you.

A character witness under Rules 405(a) or 608(a) may not testify on direct examination to specific instances of the subject's conduct that support or illustrate the character trait in question unless the subject's character qualifies as a substantive issue in the case under Rule 405(b).

Sample Foundation—Past Recollection Recorded

[Q] Doctor, how long did you treat this patient?

[A] Three years.

[Q] Handing you what has been marked as Plaintiff's Exhibit #3 for identification, doctor, could you please identify it?

[A] These are my office notes regarding this patient.

[Q] Doctor, can you testify fully and accurately regarding specific treatment dates and details of the patient's progress based solely on your memory?

[A] No, I cannot.

[Q] Referring to your office notes, Plaintiff's Exhibit #3, who prepared these notes?

[A] I dictated them and my staff transcribed them.

[Q] Are these notes based on your personal knowledge?

[A] Yes.

[Q] Did you dictate these notes when your memory of the facts and events described in these notes was still fresh?

[A] Yes.

[Q] Did you review the transcription of these notes when your memory was still fresh?

[A] Yes, I did.

[Q] Are these notes true and accurate to the best of your knowledge?

[A] Yes they are.

[Q] Your Honor, I ask the court to admit Plaintiff's Exhibit #3 as a past recollection recorded.

If admitted only as a past recollection recorded, the exhibit should not be published to nor go out with the jury

Some Common Objections to the Form of the Question

- "I object. The question is **argumentative**." A question is "argumentative" when counsel states an opinion or conclusion about an issue in the case and asks the witness to agree with it. Examples: "The defendant was pretty careless, wouldn't you agree?" "When a suspect runs from the police, that's a good sign he's guilty of something, isn't that right?" Argumentative questions are basically bits of counsel's closing argument dressed up like a question.

- "I object. This question has been **asked and answered**." Once counsel receives an answer from a witness to her question, the same counsel may not ask the same question of the witness again.

- "I object. The question **assumes facts not in evidence**." Counsel may ask a witness whether certain facts are true as long as counsel has a good faith basis to believe that they are true. Thus, for example, a prosecutor may confront the accused: "You robbed that bank on May 3, didn't you?" but cannot (without a good faith basis) ask: "And you worship the devil, isn't that true?" Counsel also may not ask a question that presumes the truth of facts that the witness already has or most likely would deny. The classical examples: "Are you still beating your wife?" "How did you feel after you killed your partner?"

- "I object. The question **calls for speculation**." A layperson's testimony as to facts or opinions must be based on the witness's personal knowledge. Although an expert witness may testify to opinions based on the facts as proved by other witnesses, the expert still must have some rational basis for his opinions.

- "I object. The question is **compound**." A compound question is one that asks two or more questions at the same time. Example: "Were you standing on the corner of 10th and West St. on August 9 and did you witness a robbery?" Any time a question could be misleading or confusing to the jury, either because it is compound, or vague, or ambiguous, it is objectionable and the question should be rephrased.

- "I object. The question calls for **cumulative** (or repetitive) evidence." Evidence which merely repeats information already admitted is not only a waste of time but improperly attempts to bolster or underscore the information. But if the facts are contested, evidence from several sources pointing to the same conclusion are not cumulative but corroborative and thus admissible.

- "I object. The witness may not paraphrase what a document says—the **document must speak for itself**." When the content of a document is a matter to be proved, the best evidence of that content is the document itself and the document should be read to, not paraphrased, for the jury.

- "I object. Counsel is **harassing** (or arguing with, or badgering, or trying to embarrass) the witness." It is never a good idea to be rude to a witness.

- "I object. The question is **leading**." A leading question is one that suggests the desired answer, as in "You were driving too fast that night, weren't you?"

- "I object. The question **misstates prior testimony**." Counsel may refer to prior testimony when relevant in questioning a witness but counsel must be careful to restate that testimony accurately.

- "I object. The question calls for **narrative** testimony." Example: "Mr. Witness, just tell us what happened on the day of the accident." The problem with narrative testimony is that the witness may stray into inadmissible areas before opposing counsel has an opportunity to object. On the other hand, some judges believe narrative testimony is the most natural way for witnesses to communicate to the jury. The appellate courts generally leave the decision whether to allow narrative testimony to the sound discretion of the trial judge.

• "I object. The witness's answer is **non-responsive**." A cross-examiner may ask for the court's assistance when a witness refuses to respond to relevant questions or insists on adding comments to his answers that are not fairly responsive to the question.

• "I object. No foundation that the witness would have **personal knowledge** of these facts." When it is not obvious from the evidence that the witness would have personal knowledge of the matters to which she is testifying, foundation must be laid to establish that personal knowledge. Example: "Did the defendant own a shotgun?" (The foundation questions should be: Do you know if the defendant owns a shotgun? If so, how?)

• "I object. The witness must give a **"Yes" or "No" answer**." Counsel may insist on a "Yes" or "No" answer when the question fairly calls for one. After answering "Yes" or "No," the witness may explain the answer.

†